W9-ATQ-990

Fodor's EXPLORING
JAPAN

FODOR'S TRAVEL PUBLICATIONS
NEW YORK • TORONTO • LONDON • SYDNEY • AUCKLAND

WWW.FODORS.COM

Copyright © Automobile Association Developments
Ltd 2000
Maps copyright © Automobile Association
Developments Ltd 2000

All rights reserved under International and Pan-
American Copyright conventions. Distributed by
Random House, Inc., New York. No maps, illustrations,
or other portions of this book may be reproduced in any
form without written permission from the publishers.

Published in the United States by Fodor's Travel
Publications.
Published in the United Kingdom by AA Publishing.

Fodor's is a registered trademark of Random House, Inc.

ISBN 0-679-00684-2
ISSN 1095-4376
Third Edition

Fodor's Exploring Japan

Author: **David Scott**
Series Adviser: **Christopher Catling**
Copy Editor: **Nia Williams**
Original Photography: **Jim Holmes**
Cartography: **The Automobile Association**
Cover Design: **Tigist Getachew, Fabrizio La Rocca**
Front Cover Silhouette: **Thomas Hoepker/Magnum
Photos, Inc.**

Printed and bound in Italy by Printer Trento srl
10 9 8 7 6 5 4 3 2 1

How to use this book

ORGANIZATION

Japan Is,
Japan Was
Discusses aspects of life and culture in contemporary Japan and explores significant periods in its history.

A–Z
Breaks down the country into regional chapters, and covers places to visit, including walks and drives. Within this section fall the Focus On articles, which consider a variety of topics in greater detail.

Travel Facts
Contains the strictly practical information vital for a successful trip.

Accommodations
and Restaurants
Lists recommended establishments throughout Japan, giving a brief summary of their attractions.

ABOUT THE RATINGS
Most places described in this book have been given a separate rating. These are as follows:

▶▶▶   **Do not miss**

▶▶   **Highly recommended**

▶   **Worth seeing**

MAPS
To make the location of a particular place easier to find, every main entry in this book has a map reference to the right of its name. This includes a number, such as 176B3. The first number (176) indicates the page on which the map can be found. The letter (B) and the second number (3) pinpoint the square in which the place is located. The maps on the inside front cover and inside back cover are referred to as IFC and IBC.

Contents

A–Z

David Scott is a restaurateur and an internationally published writer specializing in Japan, food, and travel writing. He has written or co-authored a number of highly successful titles, including *Middle Eastern Vegetarian Cooking, Japanese Cooking, Elements of Zen, Samurai and Cherry Blossom,* and various travel guides to Japan.

My Japan

Three elderly couples, dressed in white, shared my carriage on the train to Takamatsu, Shikoku's main port town. They each carried a straw hat, a walking stick, and a small bundle of possessions wrapped in a square of blue cloth. They were part way into the famous 88-temple pilgrimage in commemoration of the Shingon Buddhist patriarch, Kobo Daishi. I left them at the station and found an inn. The landlady showed me into a tiny room, followed me in, sat on her heels at a low table, made a pot of green tea with hot water from a flask, and then backed out of the door, bowing. Later, she brought in the evening meal, sashimi, tempura, vegetables, and rice, plus a treat for me: hamburger and eight french fries, garnished beautifully with three perfect strawberries with their stalks!

Chitoshi Funabashi is a respectable suburb of Tokyo. It has narrow streets, small detached houses with tiny gardens, and a minature park with a signposted jogging track. I went into a local barber shop, sat down in an empty chair and showed the barber how I wanted my hair cut. He refreshed my neck and face with a hot towel, and then, with great care, cut my hair, expertly shaved me and massaged my face, neck, and shoulders. Finally, he massaged my back as I leaned forward in the chair. Before I left he cleaned my spectacles and handed them to me with a bow.

Uwajima is known for its city park and its bull ring—two bulls, like four-legged *sumo* wrestlers, try to push each other out of its bounds. At the tourist office I got an English-language map. The lady behind the counter giggled when I asked her to locate Taga Jinja. This Shinto shrine is an amusement to local people, for the priest is an avid collector of sexual memorabilia and has built, near the shrine, a museum to house his collection.

These stories illustrate why, for me, Japan is a fascinating country—a captivating mixture of the old and new coexisting side by side. The Japanese have embraced the most modern technology and ideas, and yet remain a people governed by traditional social values and etiquette. Japan is perhaps unique in being a modern, Western-style state, yet one that is relatively free of crime, litter, and drugs. As a result you are free to take in the wonders of the country, so intriguing, and sometimes so unexpected.
David Scott

The samurai *warriors of old Japan saw the cherry blossom, with its beautiful but short life, as a symbol of their own lives, which could end violently at any moment. It is in this oscillation between beauty and ugliness, tenderness and violence, delicacy and coarseness that many people find the source of their fascination of the Japanese and Japan. The natural physical expression of this union of extremes, and perhaps a potent force in forming the Japanese character, is found in the violence and gentleness of the landscape and the climate of the Japanese islands.*

10

You might think of the islands of Kyushu, Shikoku, Honshu, and Hokkaido as the peaks of a deeply submerged mountain range, the seas off the coasts plunging to great depths. These peaks are a major presence throughout Japan, and even outside mountain regions the country-side is often exceptionally hilly. The land is either flat or rises sharply, and as a result the population is largely and densely confined to the coastal plains or the occasional areas of flat land found in the mountain

Matsushima's great torii

❏ The southern peak of Sakurajima volcano, which is sited on its own broad patch of land across the bay from the city of Kagoshima, still erupts quite regularly. During eruptions, clouds of black ash from the mountain cover Kagoshima in a fine coating of dust and collect in drifts along the store fronts. ❏

ranges. Together, they cover less than one fifth of the land surface.

Many of the mountains within the various mountain chains are volcanic: there are 50 active or semi-active volcanoes scattered throughout Japan. Mount Fuji, Japan's highest peak, last erupted in the 18th century, but Mount Asama, nearby, frequently rumbles and belches smoke. Other active volcanic areas are found in southern Hokkaido, central Honshu, and Kyushu.

The Japan coastline is immensely varied in its topography, and long in relation to the country's land area. The Japan Sea coast runs smoothly from south to north in an extended line of beaches and wide banks of sand dunes. In contrast, the wind- and tide-beaten Pacific coast is rugged with jutting peninsulas, such as Izu, and deep bays, such as those of Sendai and Tokyo.

The Inland Sea coast is different again. Constant sea erosion, matched by land-forming alluvial mud deposits brought down by the rivers, has formed a flat plain that is nowadays the region of Japan's most extensive industrial zone.

Japan lies directly along a fault line marking the juxtaposition of the Pacific and Asian Plates, which grind against each other and cause earthquakes. The major cities most at risk from earthquakes are Tokyo and Osaka, and the foundations of all their newer buildings are designed to allow them to sway without cracking. Earthquakes under the sea also produce tidal waves (tsunami) that regularly pound the coasts of Japan.

Add to these perils the typhoon winds that occasionally savage the land, heavy snowfalls in the north, torrential summer rainstorms in the south, the heavy humid heat of central and western Honshu and Kyushu, and those who are nervous about visiting Japan may be forgiven their jitters.

❑ Over 20 serious earthquakes struck Japan during the last century. The most catastrophic was the Great Kanto earthquake of September 1, 1923, which hit the country's most densely populated area, including the cities of Tokyo and Yokohama. More than 100,000 people were killed, over 60,000 in Tokyo alone, mainly as a result of ensuing fires. ❑

In fact, summer heat is the most regular contender. Japanese inventiveness, foresight, and experience of natural phenomena have allowed them to adapt to and cope with the other forces.

11

The gentle beauty of Japan: Mount Fuji framed by cherry blossoms

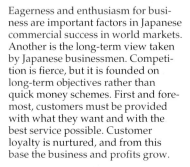

For a demonstration of the Japanese approach to business, visit a gas station. A team of attendants runs across the forecourt to meet the car. One fills the tank, another cleans the headlights, windshield, and mirrors, a third empties the ashtrays and cleans the mats, and a fourth takes the money. One of the team then stops the flow of traffic outside the garage, guides the car into the stream of vehicles, and finally waves goodbye.

Eagerness and enthusiasm for business are important factors in Japanese commercial success in world markets. Another is the long-term view taken by Japanese businessmen. Competition is fierce, but it is founded on long-term objectives rather than quick money schemes. First and foremost, customers must be provided with what they want and with the best service possible. Customer loyalty is nurtured, and from this base the business and profits grow.

POSTWAR SUCCESS After World War II, the Japanese were economically and spiritually broken by their first military defeat in history and by the horrific way in which the war was finally ended. A new start was required and a reexamination of national values was undertaken at every level. As a result, radical changes were made, such as the constitutional principle forbidding the formation of armed services other than for defense. These changes, together with certain qualities inherent in the nature of Japanese society, provided the structure for their future success.

The workforce demonstrated a sense of mutual responsibility and competitiveness, together with an unquestioned acceptance of long working hours and commitment to job and employer. Managers developed a keen understanding of the needs of specific home and overseas markets and the skills needed to fulfill them. By a combination of good marketing, an eye and an ear for what people wanted, the application of new technology, and the ability to produce high-quality goods quickly and economically, the

Bay Bridge, Yokohama

Business on the march in Tokyo

Japanese learned how to dominate world markets. At home, the Japanese government protected its markets from foreign competitors by imposing rigorous import quotas and duties. International pressure is now changing this situation, but the problem for importers is that the Japanese simply prefer to buy Japanese goods.

FUTURE PROSPECTS Having enjoyed a seemingly never-ending period of growth and prosperity, Japan is now several years into a recession which has seen the collapse of a number of financial institutions.

There have been recent demands to review the banking system, the first of many reforms that face Japan as it enters the new millennium.

Technological and social changes will mean that Japan will have to rethink many existing policies and practices.

Perhaps Japan's foremost concern, though, which affects many industrialized nations, is the aging of society. A decline in the birthrate and a rise in the number of elderly mean that within a few years one-third of the population of Japan will be over 60. This factor, taken together with the increasing automation of the workplace resulting in a rise in anticipated unemployment levels, will place a big financial burden on the country.

Assembly-line technology—the way ahead for Japan's economy

❏ Company management in Japan tries to control all aspects of their employees' lives. To help workers to escape the employer's eagle eye, a Tokyo department store has set up telephone alibi booths. Callers can select a tape with a suitable background—a hospital, railroad station, or airport, perhaps—and then phone the boss to make an excuse for being late or taking the day off. There are also "kitchen sounds" for the absent housewife who wishes to convince her husband that she is happily at home getting on with her work. ❏

On the street of any Japanese city, the man walking past in a white shirt and blue suit is probably a salaryman. A salaryman would normally expect lifelong employment with the same company, which he joins in his early 20s. The assumption on both sides is that he will remain there until he retires. Anyone voluntarily leaving a company position would be considered unreliable, and would find reemployment difficult.

LIFE STYLE Although companies do not provide as much job security as they used to due to downsizing, they do provide salaried employees and their families with health care, housing, and leisure facilities. Managers even arrange their staff's vacations. This system is accepted by most Japanese employees, who are used to the conformity it entails.

Salarymen usually work quite late. This is expected if they are to be

❑ Wages are calculated on the basis of a salaryman's expected day-to-day domestic expenses, which depend on his job status. Added to this is a twice-yearly bonus for vacations, cars, luxury items, and any other expenses concomitant with a person's position in the company, such as golf club membership for upper management. ❑

Salarymen are always on call—even when they're on the road

promoted. They may even waste time during the day to be sure of work in the evening. After work, salarymen usually go out to drink with their colleagues. The tradition is catered for by the numerous bars and restaurants in the business areas of large cities. A salaryman's wife expects her husband home late, and may even worry that he is not getting on at work if he gets home early.

IN THE OFFICE Salarymen expect their bosses to trust them and to leave the responsibility of day-to-day matters solely in their hands. A boss who makes decisions about mundane matters would lose respect. Once employees have grown to trust their managers, their loyalty is total and good relationships between management and staff are normal in Japanese business. Both parties are usually on close terms and go out drinking together. However, even outside work, company status is recognized and deferred to.

Strikes do take place but they are normally only ritualized stoppages.

14

Every year, during the second week in April, salarymen go on strike for one or two days to support their yearly wage claim; during this time they wear red armbands to signify that they are on strike. Many even stay on the company premises during the day, but they do not work, and do not go out drinking with the management.

STRESSES There is a heavy price to pay for Japan's economic prosperity. Salarymen work long hours, often under competitive and stressful conditions; Sunday is the only day they have to spend with their wives and children. This can put marriages under strain and prevent close

relationships from developing between fathers and children, as well as giving all the responsibility for their upbringing to the mother. As a group, salarymen are great cigarette consumers; the incidence of lung cancer and of stress-related illnesses is high and rising. There is a term, *karoshi*, for death from overwork.

Relaxation after the stresses of office life: a picnic in Nara (below) and (right) a drink with the boys

Japan is a self-confident country, a hothouse where the wealth created by the world's most dynamic economy is being diverted into an unprecedented consumer boom. Anything is possible—even airports in the sea—and cities such as Tokyo and Osaka have become a mecca for the world's most talented artists and designers.

TRANSPORTATION AND COMMUNICATION In a world that is rapidly adjusting to the revolution in information technology, Japan heavily emphasizes both research and development in telecommunications and transportation to meet the ever-growing need for faster methods of conveying information and people.

Japan is a world leader in the development of increasingly compact computer and digital hardware. The country that gave the world the Walkman is renowned for its expertise in producing the latest gadgets, and the Japanese are rabid consumers of all types of electronic goods.

In addition, Japan boasts the world's most efficient and reliable transportation network, a crucial factor for any country wishing to compete effectively in international affairs and commerce. The infamous bullet trains, which run regularly and

punctually, connect all Japan's major cities and they are constantly being upgraded. Testing is already under way for the new Maglev line (tentatively named) to connect Tokyo and Osaka, allowing businessmen to travel from one city to the other in about one hour (currently a two-and-a-half-hour journey)!

FUTURE CITIES You will most readily notice Japan's international commercial success and the influences of the West in urban and industrial landscapes. In the major Japanese cities, individually designed chrome, marble, and glass apartment buildings are replacing the old multistory box flats, with their balconies hung with drying clothes and airing futons. Architecturally adventurous office buildings rise in business districts, while environmentally controlled, glass-domed shopping malls shut out the noise and fumes of traffic in the city centers. Carefully sculpted and tended Zen gardens are still found in the grounds

Train of the future, landscape of the past: a bullet train races past Mount Fuji

16

of city temples, but they may now be overshadowed by the razor-sharp images of video advertising screens or the hi-tech dazzle of neon signs. Joggers in expensive designer track suits run in city parks among the falling cherry blossoms while, overhead, helicopters whirl past.

FUTURE DOUBTS Despite the technical expertise of the Japanese and their well-educated workforce, there are some doubts about the future. There are three principal problems that the Japanese are going to have to face.

Firstly, there are growing concerns that the traditional Japanese work ethic is being eroded by influences from the West. Many of Japan's youth are no longer prepared to make the same sacrifices that their parents and grandparents made to create the New Japan. Today's youth values leisure time, and they are not prepared to work the long hours of previous generations.

Secondly, Japan's success to date has been due partly to its emphasis on conformity. The Japanese have traditionally been raised to accept

Kansai International Airport, Osaka Bay, Japan's latest monumental engineering project

decisions from above rather than to question them. In a world that demands greater flexibility and where successful companies are having to flatten existing hierarchies, many worry that Japan's rigid social hierarchy and emphasis on collective responsibility, qualities that contributed so much to her economic miracle, could be the very factors that paralyze her in the coming century.

Finally, Japan is going to have to face the inevitable effect of having an increasingly automated society. Namely, that with many jobs being rendered obsolete and with increasing competition both domestically and abroad, the guarantee of lifetime employment will soon be a thing of the past. Employees are going to have to retrain constantly and adapt to new phenomena quickly, and those who cannot do this are going to have to come to terms with losing their jobs. This could have a devastating impact on Japanese society.

Shinto, a religion unique to Japan, and Zen Buddhism, practiced for over a thousand years, have exerted a significant influence on Japanese history. Known by the Japanese as Kami-no-Michi, "The Way Of The Gods," Shinto has its origins in the myths of ancient Japan. Zen Buddhism is perhaps best known in the West for the inspiration it has provided for Japanese martial arts.

SHINTO BELIEFS AND RITUALS

Followers of Shinto worship the spirit god Kami whose nature is manifested in all the things around them—rivers, mountains, trees, rocks, and animals. Each deity has a place in a hierarchy of power that culminates in the sun goddess Amaterasu, worshiped at the imperial shrines of Ise, on the Ise-Shima Peninsula of Honshu (see pages 106–107). The local *kami* are lesser deities, who look after just one village or one family's fields.

There are no fixed scriptures in Shinto. Its rituals and ceremonies, a daily part of Japanese life, are directed at receiving a blessing from the gods for a particular function or event. Shinto priests, wearing long, flowing robes and tall, lacquered silk hats, officiate at all manner of occasions: to bless babies, marriages, children starting school, new construction sites, and even new cars.

Confucianism, brought to Japan by Chinese merchants in around AD 400, had an important influence on Shinto beliefs. It emphasized loyalty to the family, with the father as patriarchal head, and demanded reverence and respect for the memory of ancestors.

Offerings are made at Shinto shrines, or *jinja*, either to ancestors or to the guardian spirits of the shrine. Before making an offering, the worshiper pours water from a trough by the inner shrine over his hands and rinses his mouth. He then attracts the gods by clapping his hands three times and pulling on a rope attached to a wooden clapper. A silent prayer is then given and an offering of fruit, money, incense, or *fuda* (strips of paper symbolizing purity, sold at the entrance) is made.

With its emphasis on the basic purity of all things, the Shinto religion was fertile ground for the assimilation of Buddhist and especially Zen Buddhist beliefs. The two schools of thought have never

*Above and opposite: many faces
of Buddhism in Japan*

exactly merged, but most Japanese follow Shinto and Buddhist practices, depending on what is customary for the occasion at hand.

ZEN BELIEFS AND RITUALS There are two main branches of Zen: the Rinzai school, founded by Eisai in 1191, and the Soto school, founded by Dogen in 1244. Both traditions developed out of the Chinese Buddhist school of Ch'an.

THE WARRIORS' ZEN The Rinzai school valued sudden enlightenment, using meditation and *koan*, questions not soluble by logical thinking such as "What is the sound of one hand clapping?" This appealed to the warrior classes of 12th-century Japan, attracted to the principles of sudden inspiration, quick intuition, and intense concentration, as opposed to learning. Eisai opened a temple in Kamakura, the site of the new warrior capital; descendants of the warrior class ruled Japan for the following six centuries and Zen became the religion espoused by the ruling classes.

Samurai warriors used Zen meditation to prepare for battle, but their interest in the spiritual essence of Zen increased during the Tokugawa era (1603–1867) and martial arts gradually became a vehicle for expressing Zen ideals.

THE PEOPLE'S ZEN Dogen believed that everyone is enlightened, but ignorant of this fact. He placed great emphasis on the detail of daily activities and saw each moment as an opportunity to express gratitude for our "Buddha nature." Now revered as one of Japan's greatest historical figures, Dogen avoided the military and aristocratic power struggles of his day, creating in Soto Zen a "people's faith." Soto Zen now has a much larger number of temples and followers than Rinzai.

Taikodani Shrine, Tsuwano

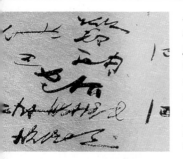

At the age of three or four, Japanese children start to attend kindergarten. The choice of a good school is crucial because, even from this early age, university entrance is the focus of a child's education, and there is intense pressure to do well. The heavy burden that is placed on the shoulders of Japanese youth, especially on young men, of whom most is expected, sometimes has disastrous consequences.

READING AND WRITING Despite having the highest literacy rate in the world, problems for the nation's children begin with the Japanese language. Schoolchildren must master four ways of writing: *Kanji, Hiragana, Katakana,* and *Romaji. Kanji* are Chinese characters adopted centuries ago and given uniquely Japanese meaning, *Hiragana* are phonetic Japanese characters used to link *Kanji* ideograms, *Katakana* is the phonetic system used to write foreign words, and *Romaji* uses the Roman alphabet to write Japanese. It is estimated that Japanese students need two years more of schooling than their Western counterparts just to grapple with the complications of their own writing system.

❑ There are over 40,000 *Kanji* Japanese characters, but today only about 3,000 are taught in schools. *Toyo-kanji* are the 2,000 most common characters chosen by the Japanese government for use in popular written books and newspapers. ❑

THE EDUCATION RACE If a child is to do well, from the time he or she starts kindergarten his or her parents need to save to pay for private tutoring and later, possibly, for private college and university. Education is the key to upward social and economic mobility.

Educational pressures start early

20

❏ *Ronin* was a term originally applied to free-roaming *samurai* warriors without a master and consequently without status. Today it refers to high-school graduates who have failed their university entrance exams. *Ronin* cram for a year or even two or three to gain entrance at their next attempt. ❏

The importance given to it in this status-conscious country is enormous. This, of course, creates intense competition for good grades, a process that itself devalues qualifications, thereby increasing the competition even more.

At the age of six a child goes to elementary school, which he or she attends from Monday to Friday, 8:40 AM to 4:30 PM, and Saturday mornings. At the age of 12, the child moves to *chugakko*, middle school, for the final three years of compulsory education. Here the pressure begins and many students attend expensive *juku* (private tutoring schools) before and after school and on Sundays.

From *chugakko*, over 90 percent of students attempt the difficult entrance examinations for *kotogakko*, senior high school. If they are unsuccessful, students aim for a less demanding, private college. Once in senior high school they sometimes work themselves close to a nervous breakdown in preparation for the forthcoming arduous university entrance examinations. Some go over the edge, and suicide is not uncommon. To fail is to fail one's family and to lose social credibility.

It used to be the case that students could treat university life as a four-year holiday, a break between the rigorous series of examinations during their school years and the long hours that awaited them in their future careers. Employment was largely assured, or at the very least university grades had no bearing on the search for work upon graduation.

This is no longer the case, however. With more and more jobs requiring graduates to enter the workplace partially trained in computer skills and the like, modern-day students

At the age of 12, schoolchildren move to middle school

are having to put as much time into their studies as their Western counterparts, and their choices of study are very important as well.

Many college students supplement their studies with computer courses

The role of women

From a Western perspective, of all the developed nations Japan is the country where the question of rights for women has been least addressed. Traditional attitudes are being modified by pressure from women and by wider changes in society as a whole. But the slow pace of change reflects the tight grip of history and traditions on contemporary Japan.

THE TRADITIONAL ROLE OF WOMEN

The traditional role of the Japanese woman has been that of the dutiful wife. Until comparatively recently women who entered the workplace did so for only a few years after university until they had met their husbands. In some cases, women entered companies with the specific intention of husband-hunting. However, working after marriage was a virtual "no-no" for women, except in clear cases of necessity. Those who attempted to continue to work after marriage invariably met with strong opposition not only from members of their own family but frequently from work colleagues.

Two faces of the Japanese woman: at a traditional wedding …

Until only a few years ago, a Japanese woman was expected to get married by her mid-twenties. Her function in life was to be a good mother, a homemaker. Indeed, the Japanese for "wife" (*oku-san*) uses Chinese characters making her role in this regard explicit. The pressure to get married was, and in rural areas still is, very strong. For the woman who found herself still single in her late twenties, arranged marriages using *o-miai-san* (go-betweens / negotiators) often resulted. These were set up by anxious parents or even at the request of the woman in question.

THE ROLE OF MARRIED WOMEN

Once married, a woman has to resign herself to domestic chores. Husband and wife live almost entirely separate

22

… and doing a sharp deal

lives as a married couple. While her husband spends increasingly longer hours at the office and socializing with his work colleagues as he climbs the corporate ladder, the wife is charged with dealing with all aspects of home life. Everything from the day-to-day running of the house to overseeing the education of her children and even planning family holidays are the responsibility of the wife. As a consequence, although newly-wed Japanese wives tend to be fairly timid, they invariably come to "rule the roost" and play a key role in decisions concerning family life.

Of particular interest to Westerners is the fact that Japanese women hold the purse strings. A husband's salary is paid into the family bank account from which often only his wife can make withdrawals. Each month the husband has a spending allowance that is determined by his wife.

THE MODERN WOMAN A number of factors have significantly changed the role of women over the last decade, however. Western pressures and influences have encouraged Japanese women to be much more

assertive, and increasingly Japanese women are marrying later. The stigma of being a single working woman at the age of 30 and beyond is fast being eradicated. Women can be seen enjoying life more and, perhaps more importantly, enjoying life as single women.

Formerly, women were paid only about 60 percent of that of a man in a similar position. This clear prejudice is fast being removed. Although the employees of many of the traditional companies are still dominated by men, women can increasingly be found in the service industries and in advertising and design companies. There are even a few companies that employ women exclusively.

As women play an increasingly important role in Japanese society, a number have risen to quite prominent positions. The current Leader of the House of Councillors (the Upper House of the National Diet), for example, is a woman, a major accomplishment in an institution that has traditionally been a strictly male concern.

Sumo *is Japan's national sport and an integral part of the country's cultural fabric. It can also lay strong claims to being the world's oldest sport: its roots lie in the realms of mythology, and it is said to have been popular with the gods. Before becoming a sport in the 6th century,* sumo *was practiced as a form of divination and as a way of invoking the good will of the spirits.*

THE RITUAL Once started, *sumo* techniques are executed with great speed, and each bout is over quickly. The *rikishi* (wrestlers) move with consummate skill and their expertise can easily be misjudged by a casual observer.

The fight is the core of *sumo*, but its attractions for the *cognoscenti* are the prefight rituals, drawn in part from the battlefield. These rituals demonstrate the Shinto origins of

Careful preparation of a sumo
star for the forthcoming show

sumo and serve to raise the psychological tension between the fighters to fever pitch.

THE RULES The *dohyo*, or wrestling area, is a circular clay ring that is surrounded by rice-straw bales. The rules of the sport are simple: the first wrestler to set a foot or any other part of his body outside the ring, or to touch the ground inside the ring with anything but the sole of his foot, loses. There is no classification by weight; lighter men try to overcome their handicap by making use of superior speed and agility.

Ranking is based on a pyramid system, with teenage beginners (*jonokuchi*) at the bottom and grand champions (*yokozuna*) at the top. Surprisingly, juniors start their training with the same build as ordinary mortals. They then steadily put on weight by eating large quantities of rice and *chanko-nabe*, a hearty stew of meat, fish, and vegetables, washed down by large quantities of beer and *sake*. Dictated by their stable master, their lifestyle is hard and strict.

THE FIGHT Once in the ring, the *rikishi* loosen up with a movement called *shiko*: they raise each leg sideways to waist height and then bring it down with a formidable stamp—this movement is said to drive out stray devils. Salt is then thrown into the air by each man to purify the ring after the last bout's loss. The wrestlers face each other in a low squat in the middle of the ring, each trying to stare the other down. Finally, at a word from the referee, they squat, lean forward, touch hands on the ground and then crash into each other at full force.

THE CHANGES *Sumo* is steeped in tradition and ritual, but it is also about professionalism and winning. Of the many hundreds of wrestlers, few become nationally known, but Western attitudes to the sport are beginning to influence the age-old traditions. Even the legendary inscrutability of the competitors has now been breached. Nowadays, winners are sometimes even known to allow themselves a smile in victory, and losers a frown in defeat.

In the past, the rigorous discipline of a *sumo* wrestler's training deterred most *gai-jin* (foreigners) from trying to join their ranks, but this situation is now changing.

The following Tokyo *sumo* stables allow overseas tourists to view morning training sessions.

❏ Top *sumo* wrestlers have the status, the media attention, and riches of Hollywood stars, and are treated with the respect and deference usually only accorded to royalty. They have private fan clubs, corporate sponsors, and, it is said, the pick of Japanese women. Despite modern influences, the Shinto origins of *sumo* are still evident, especially in pre-fight rituals. ❏

A Japanese operator will need to make an advance appointment by calling one of these:
Azumazeki, tel: (03) 3625 0033;
Tatsunami, tel: (03) 3631 2424;
Kasugano, tel: (03) 3631 1871.

Crowds enjoy the sumo *spectacle at a Tokyo arena*

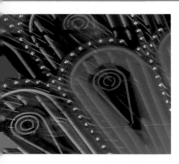

The Japanese have a rich and varied cultural history, and classical performing arts such as noh *and* kabuki *and the elegant pleasures of pastimes such as the tea ceremony continue to flourish. However, the principal source of Japanese entertainment and nightlife is the network of bars, restaurants, coffee shops, tea houses, and cocktail lounges that are an integral part of even the smallest Japanese town.*

WORK AND PLEASURE

Entertainment is a key component of the world of business deals, and corporate entertainment, which is said to drive the economy, always appears as a large (sometimes hidden) debit in the accounts of any successful Japanese company. Company employees usually meet after work for drinks and perhaps to eat, and on these occasions it is quite

Outrageous façades adorn street food and karaoke venues of Osaka

❏ The Japanese home is a wife's domain, and Japanese men entertain their friends, business colleagues, and acquaintances away from the house at a favorite restaurant or bar. If they invite you out, they expect to pick up the tab—just as though they were taking the trouble themselves. ❏

acceptable, after a fair amount of alcohol, to criticize a superior or colleague (or foreign guest) in a manner that would be inappropriate in the formal atmosphere of work. Tomorrow it will be forgotten.

STREET FOOD AND STRIPTEASE

Movie theaters, discotheques, and intimate clubs are to be found in downtown areas alongside "Soapland" districts, where striptease and massage parlors rub shoulders with street-food stands and fast-food restaurants. Historically, sex and eroticism played an important role in the nightlife of male-dominated Japan. Many of the clubs in Soapland areas are owned by the *Yakuza* (the Japanese Mafia).

Prices in restaurants and bars vary widely, and are usually high in places that do not display a price list. The cost of drinks in any bar is high; the cheapest are those frequented by young men and women, office workers, and college students. Those that employ hostesses to fill your glass and to make idle chat can be prohibitively expensive. *Geisha* bars, where expertly trained women entertain with witty conversation, traditional dancing, music and food (but not sex) are not generally open to foreigners—unless you have a respected client's introduction.

KARAOKE BARS
The Japanese invented and love karaoke. Singing songs to the sound of prerecorded music, in front of other customers or with friends, is a favorite pastime.

PLEASURES SIMPLE AND REFINED
Japanese coffee shops (*kissaten*) are one of the country's best discoveries. They pride themselves on serving exquisite coffee and on providing a first-class sound system, playing jazz, classical, rock, or other music. A cup of coffee is relatively expensive, but once you have ordered you can sit for as long as you wish reading, writing, or looking at the comics and magazines always available. (*Kissaten* frequently offer a good breakfast for the price of a coffee; ask for "morning service" in English.)

Noh theater, *bunraku* (puppet theater—see page 88) and *kabuki* (see pages 58–59) are available in major cities, and although alien in format to most Westerners, they are usually worth seeing both for the spectacle and the insight they give into Japanese culture.

Tokyo's dazzling nightlife

Traditional meals are cooked and presented with the intention of inspiring the spirit as well as the senses. The ingredients and menu are chosen to take into account the season, location, and occasion. Tableware is selected to harmonize with the texture and appearance of the food which, according to the Japanese, must be tasted with the tongue, the heart, and the eye to be truly enjoyed.

THE BUDDHIST INFLUENCE Japanese cuisine developed in a state of isolation and its style is unique. Buddhist beliefs, which forbade the eating of flesh, together with the nature of the landscape and climate, restricted the choice of food, and the main ingredients of the Japanese diet were rice, noodles, vegetables, pickles, seafood, soybean products, and fruit. To some degree, this remains the case today, but, ironically, now that such ingredients are highly recommended by nutritionists, the Japanese are adding more and more meat and dairy products to their diet.

COOKING CATEGORIES At a typical Japanese meal, individual dishes are served in smaller amounts but greater variety than in the West. They are all served at the same time, rather than in courses, and the order

A food stall in Hokkaido

28

❏ In Japan, the use of seaweed as a foodstuff is commonplace. *Kombu* seaweed is packaged in fancy boxes and given as presents by dinner guests. Unusually rich in vitamins and minerals, it has both nutritive value and seasoning properties. ❏

in which they are eaten is a matter of personal choice. Each dish is classified according to the way it is cooked, rather than by the main ingredient. For example, *yakimono* are grilled foods; fish is most widely served this way. *Agemono* are deep-fried dishes, of which *tempura* is the best known and loved. *Nimono*, such as the dish *shabu-shabu*, is food simmered in water or some other liquid such as sake. Diners pick out cooked morsels with their chopsticks and later sip the cooking liquor out of a bowl like soup.

Other categories are *sashimi*, in which pieces of very fresh raw fish are served with *wasabi*, a green Japanese mustard; *sushi*, vinegared rice patties topped with a variety of foods, particularly raw fish, and *nabe-mono*, one-pot meals such as the well-known *sukiyaki* (pronounced "ski-yaki").

BASIC FOODS Rice is eaten with every meal, including breakfast. *Han*, the Japanese word for rice, is given the honorable prefix *go*, so that rice is referred to as *go-han*, or "honorable rice" (*ho han* also means "meal"). The rice at a meal is usually eaten last, rather than as an accompani-

Minshuku-style breakfast

ment to other foods. It is the core of the meal, and the Japanese often eat two or three bowls of it at a time.

Noodles are eaten almost as often as rice. One of the great delights of being in Japan is to eat a bowl of noodles in one of the inexpensive noodle restaurants that can be found in even the smallest villages. The Japanese eat their noodles quickly, with lots of sucking and slurping noises and "aahs" of contentment.

Surprisingly few seasonings and condiments are used; the cuisine depends as much on the natural flavor of the ingredients, their aroma and visual beauty as on added flavorings. Apart from soy sauce,

miso (a fermented soybean paste), and seaweed, the most commonly used flavorings are: *goma*, a mixture of toasted and crushed sesame seeds and salt; *mirin*, a sweet fortified rice wine; gingerroot; *togarashi*, a seven-spice pepper-like condiment; and *wasabi*.

O-cha, or green tea, is the usual offering with food in Japanese homes and restaurants. In the latter, green tea is served to guests on their arrival and at the end of the meal, free of charge.

An elegant display of tempura, *the popular deep-fried dish*

*Japan is a land of festivals (**matsuri**) and cele-bratory events, and even the smallest villages have their own calendars of activities. Most have some kind of historical or religious significance, but they are generally boisterous affairs that provide an excuse for much noise, merrymaking, eating and drinking, and crowd participation.*

It is very possible, particularly in summer, that you will accidentally come across a local festival in progress, but for specific information contact the tourist information centers in Tokyo and Kyoto (see page 264), which publish monthly bulletins of events. The larger, better-known festivals mentioned here are always very popular with the Japanese; if you plan to visit one, arrange your accommodations and transportation months in advance.

SUMMER O-Bon (August 13–16):
At this time of the year, the Japanese like to return to their home towns or villages to take part in the O-Bon ceremonies that mark the return to earth of all departed ancestors. At the end of the rituals; candlelit paper lanterns are set to float down rivers and out to sea, to mark the return of the spirits to their own world. Yasukuni Shrine in Tokyo and Nachi Shrine in Katsuura, Wakayama prefecture hold large ceremonies.
Gion Matsuri (July 16–17): This is perhaps the best known of all Japanese festivals. It takes place in Kyoto, and events span a month.

Dressed up for Tokyo's White Heron Festival

The highlight is a huge procession of floats on July 17. The ceremony, over 1,000 years old, began as a purification ritual to rid the city of plague. Each of Kyoto's 29 neighborhoods builds its own elaborately decorated float for this event.

FALL Jidai Matsuri (October 22): The Imperial Palace in Kyoto is the start of a large procession to mark the founding of the city. Thousands of people dressed in the costumes of different historical eras march along in this noisy, happy event, finishing at the Heian Shrine.
Shichi-Go-San (November 15): On this day girls aged between three and seven, and five-year-old boys are dressed in their best clothes and taken to city and village shrines and temples, where prayers are offered up for their good health.

WINTER Joya-no-Kane and Ganjitsu (December 31–January 1): On New Year's Eve everybody stays up until midnight, when temple bells ring out 108 times. New Year's Day is seen as an opportunity for renewal: debts are paid and arguments settled. Festivities go on for seven days and most businesses come to a halt. On January 2, the Imperial Family appears at the Imperial Palace in Tokyo and huge crowds gather to greet them.

SPRING Cherry Blossom Viewing (March to May): At this time of the year cherry blossom (*sakura*) viewing parties take place all over Japan. The exact date depends on the flower-ing of the blossom in a particular region. Local television station weather forecasts give updates

on the state of the blossom ripeness in each area of Japan.

Kodomo-no-Hi (Children's Day, May 5): This national holiday centers around the nation's children, with a special emphasis on young boys (it is sometimes known as Boys' Day). Families fly giant paper *koi* (carp) from their homes to symbolize the strength of manhood: the larger represent the eldest sons and the increasingly smaller ones represent the younger children.

NATIONAL HOLIDAYS
January 1 New Year's Day. **January 15** Coming of Age Day. **February 11** Founding of the Nation Day. **March 21** Vernal Equinox Day (varies). **April 29** Greenery Day. **May 3** Constitution Day. **May 5** Children's Day (the period from April 29 to May 6, called "Golden Week," is essentially a national week off, and is not a good time to travel). **September 15** Respect for the Aged Day. **September 23** Autumn Equinox Day (varies). **October 10** Health–Sports Day. **November 3** Culture Day. **November 23** Labor Thanksgiving Day. **December 23** Emperor's Birthday.

Karatsu Festival, Kyushu Island

Shinto, the ancient religion of Japan, lays great emphasis on purification and cleanliness. Partly because of this, bathing and the rituals surrounding it are very much a part of the Japanese culture. No other country in the world possesses more natural hot springs, called onsen, *and the popular custom of bathing in them for physical and spiritual regeneration dates back to the distant past.*

PRIVATE BATHING At home, the Japanese find two Western habits particularly difficult to comprehend. The first is that we wear shoes in the house and the second is that we sit in the dirty water in which we wash. In Japan, the bather sits outside the tub on a small stool, scoops water over him or herself, washes, rinses off the soap, and only then, with a clean body, climbs into the tub to both soak and relax in the very hot water.

PUBLIC BATHING Communal bathing is also popular, and *sento* (public bath houses) are places to meet friends, swap gossip and jokes, and to soak away aches, pains, and worries. Consider visiting them, not just to get clean, but also to see the

The bliss of an open-air onsen

Japanese at their earthiest. *Sento* are found in cities and small towns, and come in a variety of shapes and forms varying from Gothic-style exaggeration to Zen simplicity. They have recently enjoyed a revival in popularity among young people, and many are being renovated in their original style.

ONSEN Tourist accommodations are available around most of Japan's *onsen* (hot springs). At spas such as Beppu, massive commercial resorts have developed, where the emphasis for visitors is on group togetherness (a sacred concept in Japan). At other, more isolated *onsen*, there may be only two or three thatched-roof cottages with a single *rotemburo* (outdoor bath). Here you come to seek spiritual comfort rather than material comfort.

32

The prehistoric era of Japan's history usually refers to the age before the first writing system and the Buddhist religion were introduced in the 6th century AD. Japan's earliest settlers, who arrived about 100,000 BC, are a mystery. They were probably not the ancestors of the predominantly Mongoloid modern Japanese, nor of the Ainu, the earliest known people of Japan (see pages 236–237). A similarity in language may be the only link between these original inhabitants and present-day Japanese.

A Jomon clay face mask, now in Tokyo National Museum

The near prehistoric era may be divided into three distinct periods. The Jomon age (*c.* 10,000–300 BC) was one in which pottery-making (without a wheel) and other crude technical skills emerged. During the Yayoi era (300 BC–AD 300) immigrants and invaders from mainland Asia brought agricultural and military knowledge. The third age, the Kofun period (AD 300–700), was marked by the building of *kofun* (large earthen tombs) throughout Japan and the growing influence of Chinese culture.

JOMON ERA The Jomon people were hunters and gatherers. They lived in small communities, primarily in central Honshu, and had a well-developed religion of nature worship, deifying the sun and moon. During this period, according to Japanese mythology, the sun goddess Amaterasu sent one of her descendants to the island of Kyushu to establish order and to unify the people of Japan. This aim was later partly realized by Jimmu, the great grandson of the emissary and the half-legendary first emperor of Japan.

The sun-goddess Amaterasu

❑ A Chinese traveler in southwest Japan in about AD 200 described what he saw as follows: "The people live on raw vegetables and go about barefooted. They smear their bodies with pink and scarlet. They serve food on bamboo and wooden trays, helping themselves with their fingers. Whenever they undertake an enterprise or a journey and discussion arises, they bake bones and divine in order to tell whether fortune will be good or bad…If the lowly meet important men on the road, they stop and withdraw to the roadside." ❑

YAYOI ERA During the 2nd and 1st centuries BC, craftsmen and warriors, driven from Korea and China by political turmoil, crossed the Korean Straits to Japan in large numbers. They brought with them mining and metal-working skills, pottery-making with a wheel, cloth-weaving techniques, and the cultivation of rice in flooded paddies. In their turn, they took up many of the customs and the language of the indigenous people. Japan flourished as a country of many small states, some of which were ruled by women; rule by women continued in outlying regions until almost the 9th century AD.

KOFUN ERA A later development of the Yayoi era was the formation of powerful clans and the development of a military elite skilled in horse-manship and weaponry. At the beginning of the Kofun period, clan chiefs fought to maintain or expand control of their independent king-doms. By AD 300, however, the chief-tain of the Yamato clan, based in the Yamato lowlands, south of Kyoto, had brought many of them under his command. Over the next 250 years, by intermarriage and the exercise of political and military skills, the Yamato unified Japan under a succession of single leaders. It was for the burial of such powerful men

A replica kofun *figure, in Kyushu*

❑ *Kofun* were often encircled with *haniwa*, clay figures of warriors and servants; inside the mounds were bronze mirrors, glass beads, and other objects that would be needed by the dead in their next life. You can see numerous *kofun* mounds and *haniwa* at Saitobaru, north of Miyazaki in Kyushu. ❑

that the huge *kofun* burial mounds were created. This era also saw the introduction of Buddhism into Japan and the formation of close cultural links with China, powerfully redirecting Japanese history.

35

With the introduction of Buddhism and the use of Chinese characters for writing in the 6th century, Japan entered its classical period (710–1185). During this time, the first permanent capital was established at Nara, and later at Heian-kyo (Kyoto). Early in the classical period the Japanese were influenced by Chinese cultural and scholarly ideals, but by the 10th century they had evolved a unique and sophisticated culture of their own.

36

PRINCE SHOTOKU Buddhism was already known in 6th-century Japan, but it was first fully introduced to the Japanese court by the king of a minor Korean state. In 553 he sent the emperor Buddhist images, vestments, incense, *sutras* (scriptures), and other ritual objects as part of a petition seeking Japanese military aid. Some influential members of the court found the new religion attractive, while others remained loyal to their native Shinto (see pages 18–19). Those in favor of Buddhism eventually won the struggle for power and in 604 Shotoku (574–622), prince regent to an infant empress, drafted a document, greatly influenced by Buddhist and Confucian principles, calling for political and constitutional reforms. Shotoku founded many Buddhist temples and monasteries, including the famous Horyuji Temple at Nara.

TAIKA REFORM Shotoku's vision was overtaken by political events, and in 645 Emperor Kotoku, backed by traditionalist

A clay farmer, made in the 6th century

Japanese nobles, instituted the Taika Reform. All land was declared the property of the throne and its administration was to be controlled by officials appointed by the emperor or his ministers. The reforms were not strictly enforced, but they did eventually create a hierarchical system that became the basis of the feudal system later to dominate Japanese life.

NARA PERIOD In 710, Japan's first permanent capital was established at Nara (see pages 114–115). It was built on the pattern of Ch'ang-an (Xian), the famous capital city of the Chinese Tang Dynasty. With its green-roofed, red-painted buildings, Nara became the focus of courtly and religious life, and this period saw a huge expansion of Buddhist temple construction. Much of the nation's wealth was

❑ The conflict between Buddhism and Shinto was reconciled by the Buddhist monk Gyogi. In 740, he was requested to visit Ise, location of the most important of Shinto shrines (see pages 106–107), to meditate on the propriety of the emperor's plans to erect a giant statue of the Buddha. Gyogi received a message from Amaterasu, the sun goddess, that the two religions were just different forms of the same path. This was widely accepted and, to this day, both religions are practiced side by side. ❑

spent on sculpture, painting, books, lacquerware, and other artwork to grace these sacred buildings.

As temples and monasteries continued to expand, the power of the clergy increased. In 784, Emperor Kammu decided to move the capital to avoid this influence and increase the authority of the secular government. Supported by the powerful Fujiwara clan, members of which ruled as regents for the emperor, he moved to what became an even grander capital at Heian-Kyo (Kyoto).

HEIAN PERIOD Between 794 and 1156, Japan was peaceful and prosperous and enjoyed one of the most culturally fruitful periods in its history. This was partly as a result of the imperial court's decision in 894 to end all official communication with the now failing Tang Dynasty in China. Japan once again became inward-looking, and over the next

Amitabha Buddha from the Heian period

300 years a specifically Japanese culture evolved. Toward the end of the Heian period, the influence of the Fujiwara family waned while other provincial warrior clans grew in military power. Meanwhile, the imperial family and their noble courtiers lost touch with the affairs of the country, and were finally ignored by the warrior families. The Taira and Minamoto clans engaged in a fierce civil war for control of the nation before Minamoto Yoritomo eventually led his side to victory. He subsequently established a new capital in Kamakura, leaving the imperial court in Kyoto, and formed a military government, becoming the nation's first *shogun* (see pages 38–39). This was the system of government that was destined to rule Japan for the following 700 years.

*Throughout Japanese history the emperor, although spiritually venerated, has rarely had any political power. Overall control was always held by the clan leader (*daimyo*) with the strongest army. Such leaders became known as the *shogun*; their warrior soldiers were called *samurai*.*

THE WAY OF THE WARRIOR In the late 9th century, Japan broke off all relations with the rest of the world and embarked on 300 years of isolation. It was during this time that the *samurai* developed as a distinct warrior class and the ethics of the *bushido* (the Way of the Warrior) evolved.

Samurai means "one who serves," and each soldier owed allegiance to his *daimyo* (feudal lord). *Samurai* were divided into three groups. At

A full set of samurai *warrior armor*

the top were those who served the *shogun*, second were the *samurai* of ordinary *daimyo*, and at the bottom were *ronin*, who had lost their masters through war or politics. *Ronin* roamed about, some working as mercenaries, others turning to crime. Their exploits feature in many Japanese stories, films, and plays.

CIVIL WAR From the 12th until the 16th century, Japan suffered almost continuous civil war. Battles were fought between opposing clans seeking overall power or by emperors trying to gain political control to match their spiritual rule of the land. The situation improved in the late 16th century, when General Oda Nobunaga defeated the other most powerful *daimyo* in the country, General Imagawa, to become ruler of virtually all Japan. Nobunaga was both a ruthless soldier and a devotee of the arts. Under his guidance there was a renaissance of interest in poetry, theater, dancing, and fashion, which flourished in the relative peace

❏ During the Kamakura period (1192–1333) there were women among the *samurai*. Tomoe, a member of the Minamoto, is described in records of the period as having long, black hair and a fair complexion; her face was very lovely and she was a fearless rider, whom neither the fiercest horse nor the roughest ground could dismay. So dextrously did she handle sword and bow, according to the chronicler, that she was a match for a thousand warriors and fit to meet either god or devil. ❏

of his reign. He also encouraged trade with the outside world, and European arts and Christianity became fashionable.

ISOLATION Toyotomi Hideyoshi succeeded Nobunaga in 1582. His was a different outlook: he believed that foreign influences were weakening Japan, and introduced laws forbidding the Japanese to leave the country and reducing the influx of foreign goods and people, while at the same time reinforcing the traditional feudal patterns of society.

Hideyoshi died in 1598 and was succeeded by Tokugawa Ieyasu, who moved his headquarters from Kyoto to Edo (now Tokyo). From here the Tokugawa family dominated Japanese life for the next 250 years. One after another, the Tokugawa

A samurai on horseback, armed with bow and arrows

shogun maintained hostility to all foreign religions and secular influences and carried out a determined policy of national seclusion.

SHOGUNATE OUTDATED The Tokugawa system of government finally broke down in the mid-19th century. The *samurai* had been emasculated by lack of battle opportunity, and increased interest in the arts of the tea ceremony and calligraphy as in sword-fighting, weakened their authoritarian grip on the country. Both they and the peasants had grown very poor, while a newly prosperous merchant class had emerged as a force of change. Outgunned by Western powers, the Shogunate was forced to sign treaties and Western explorers and traders were again allowed to enter Japan. In 1868, after fighting off Tokugawa loyalists, Emperor Meiji took power and ended the rule of the Shogunate.

The feudalism that is to some degree still manifest in Japanese society and the Japanese language has its origins in the laws enacted by the Tokugawa shogun. It was their intention to control every aspect of Japanese life, in every corner of the land. The place in which people lived, what they ate, the type of clothes they wore, even the posture adopted and the way they slept were all dictated by the state.

At the top of the ladder, emperors and their courts were restricted to Kyoto, their duties confined to the ceremonial. The Tokugawa family maintained the emperor in his position but only to confer the title of *shogun* (full title: "Commander-in-Chief for Quelling the Barbarians") on whomever the family nominated.

Like the emperor's, the affairs of military lords were closely monitored by the *shogun*. They were controlled by the allotment or dispossession of the territories from which they were entitled to collect taxes. Rights to land were given only in exchange for oaths of allegiance. The number of armed men they had, the types of fortifications around their castles and even their social contacts were controlled. Government inspectors ensured that they upheld their agreements, and if they broke any they were punished by loss of land or exile to a distant part of the country. As an extra safety measure, the Tokugawa *shogun* maintained control

❏ The *samurai* class enjoyed many privileges, and during the Tokugawa years (1603–1867) had little to do since there were few battles to fight. They were, however, expected to set a good example to the rest of society and to lead sober and honest lives. In two centuries of relative peace, the *samurai* brought the art of fighting to a high point of ceremonial and ritual skill, although expertise in real battle fighting and war tactics diminished. Nevertheless, it was *samurai* from the southern domains of Satsuma and Choshu who carried out the *coup d'état* of 1867 that brought along the Meiji Restoration of 1868. ❏

of the three largest cities—Edo (now Tokyo), Kyoto, and Osaka—and gave the lands around them to close relatives and loyal allies.

After the emperor and noble lords, the Buddhist and Shinto clergy were the groups most likely to make trouble for the *shogun*. They were thus split up under the Tokugawa regime into individual sects, which were themselves divided into separate independent units. No cooperation or joint decisions were allowed between sects, and rivalry for land and income was encouraged: a perfect

Two powerful feudal leaders: Ieyasu ...

example of "divide and conquer."

The rest of society was split into four groups. In descending order of status they were *samurai*, farmers, craftsmen, and merchants. Women belonged to the same class as their fathers or husbands. Membership in a particular class was hereditary and fixed. The *samurai* did not work as such and they considered the pursuit of money to be dishonorable. They were supported by taxes from the farming class, who suffered considerable hardship maintaining the top-heavy warrior class.

Farmers, the main bulk of the population, although not at the bottom of the social order, were the most exploited of the classes. Upon them depended the rice harvest and thus the *samurai's* and the *shogun's* prosperity. They had to work hard and were not allowed to leave the vicinity of their birthplace. Most lived in considerable poverty.

Craftsmen had lower status than farmers but had more mobility and freedom in the way they led their lives. Master craftsmen, particularly sword-makers, were valued for their skills and lived in the security of their lord's protection.

… and Hideyoshi. These great warriors ruled Japan in the 16th and 17th centuries

Merchants were at the bottom of the social ladder, since they produced nothing, were motivated by profit, and dealt with money. In spite of their lowly position in the social order, the merchants later became the main beneficiaries of the Tokugawa era, and as a group they were responsible for later changes in cultural and social attitudes.

Courtesans of the 18th century

During the 264-year-long Tokugawa era, the Japanese were prohibited from traveling outside the country and foreigners were not allowed in. In contrast, during the Meiji era (1868–1912), anything Japanese was despised, and many historical buildings and relics were destroyed, while American and European cultures were admired. During this period there was even a cult of marrying Westerners to "improve" the nation's bloodstock.

42

OPEN AND CLOSED There has been a cyclic character to the history of Japanese culture that follows a three-phase pattern. In the first phase, the country opens itself to outside influences, such as those from China between the 6th and 9th centuries and the West between the 16th and 17th centuries. During these periods the Japanese tend to underrate traditional Japanese values and qualities, although never completely letting them go. This phase is followed by a period of reassessment and consolidation, during which some imported notions are jettisoned and others are subtly altered, acquiring a distinctly Japanese feel. The third stage is a withdrawal from the outside world. The Japanese shut themselves off from the rest of the world and settle down to a life of regularity and security, safe from the risks created by foreign influences. This cycle has repeated itself throughout Japanese history up until the middle of the 19th century when Japan fully entered modern international affairs. Since 1868, the country has been open to the outside world.

CHINESE INFLUENCES The first major influence on Japanese thought and culture, and perhaps the most

Left and below: Commodore Perry and his U.S. Navy ships

important in its history, came from China. During the 6th and 9th centuries there was active contact with the Chinese governments of the Tang Dynasty, and tradesmen, craftsmen, artists, and scholars regularly crossed the waters between the two countries. Confucian principles were introduced into Japanese government, and Buddhism, brought from China, enjoyed a time of great popularity and prosperity.

Nara, the first permanent Japanese capital city, was modeled on Ch'ang-an (Xian), the gracious seat of the Tang Dynasty, characterized, like Nara, by green-roofed buildings with red wooden walls. During this time contact was also made with countries farther afield than China, and Shoso-in Museum, in the present grounds of the Todaiji Temple, Nara (see pages 114–115), contains beautiful artifacts of the period from Persia (now Iran), India, Greece, and Korea.

ISOLATION In the 9th century, Japan broke off all relations with the rest of the world and underwent 300 years of isolation. It was during this time that Kublai Khan made his unsuccessful attempt to invade Japan with over 100,000 Mongol soldiers. The country was saved by a typhoon wind, which swept away the enemy fleet and earned the name *kamikaze*—"the Divine Wind." Japan was not invaded again until the end of World War II.

Empress Shoken and Emperor Meiji

The Tokugawa *shoguns* also enforced a policy of national seclusion and it was not until Commodore Perry and his U.S. Navy ships arrived in 1853, demanding that Japan open to overseas trade, that relations with the West were restored.

EXPANSION During his 44-year reign (1868–1912), Emperor Meiji led Japan from being an isolated, agriculturally based, feudal society to a powerful nation with a modern navy and army, railroads, a parliament, and an industrial base.

However, by the beginning of the 1930s Japan's industrial economy needed overseas markets and new sources of raw materials. At the same time, there was a growing militarism, and a sense that Japan was the natural leader of mainland Asia and the Pacific basin. Japan withdrew from the League of Nations, and totalitarian leadership cemented its hold on the country. The movement was unlike Italian or German fascism, since the emperor remained the secular and spiritual head of the state and the focus of a consensus form of government. Japan invaded Manchuria in 1931, followed by a full-scale invasion of China in 1937. The country eventually joined forces with Hitler, and on December 7, 1941, with the bombing of Pearl Harbor, it entered World War II.

Shinto teachings that the emperor was a living kami (sacred spirit) and that the spirits of the dead were alive contributed to the development of the patriarchal, ancestor-worshiping culture of traditional Japan. The emperor, as a living god, was seen as the symbolic and literal father of the family of the Japanese people. Such beliefs lived on in World War II, when Japanese suicide squads sacrificed their lives for the emperor.

ANCIENT HISTORY Before the 4th century AD, Japan was a collection of independent states. In time, the various ruling families made alliances, one of them, the Yamato, gradually gaining precedence over the others and winning paramount control. From this background emerged the fore-bears of today's imperial family.

Contemporary knowledge of this period is vague, but all lineal ancestors of the present emperor are said to have descended from the same blood line. Whatever the truth, the Japanese imperial dynasty is generally acknowledged as the longest-reigning in world history.

In Japanese mythology, the origins of the imperial family are much more glamorous. The emperor is believed to be a direct descendant of the sun goddess Amaterasu. As such, he is a divine being who has the power to intercede with heaven on behalf of humanity.

The late Emperor Hirohito

❏ Emperor Meiji was succeeded by his son Yoshito, renamed Emperor Taisho, in 1912. Not much is known about Taisho; he suffered from mental illness and was kept out of the public eye. The illness is said to have been caused by lead poisoning; apparently his wet-nurse had used white lead to whiten her breasts, a common practice of the day. ❏

THE EMPEROR AS FIGUREHEAD In more recent times the emperor did not, despite his divine status, have real political power; this was in the hands of the *shogun*. During the Edo period (1603–1867) the emperors' upkeep and that of their courtiers was maintained by land grants from the *shogun*, from which they kept the income. This maintained them in a respectable, rather than a luxurious, lifestyle. An emperor's activities were supervised by government officials and limited to cultural pursuits. Although he was only a figurehead, his title was hereditary and the line of succession had to be maintained. This was a potential danger to the Tokugawa shogunate—and did, in fact, lead to its downfall.

POWER REGAINED By the late 18th century, the superfluousness of the *samurai* and poverty of the peasants had weakened the Tokugawa regime, and in 1867 the young Emperor Meiji was put forward as the country's leader. After fighting off Tokugawa loyalists, he attained full power in

1868 and began his revolutionary reign, the Meiji Restoration.

Emperor Meiji for the first time formally instigated Shinto as the official state religion. Since the Shinto belief is that the emperor is a living god, this gave him total power over the nation. He used it to abolish the old class system, to industrialize the country and to institute new laws and reforms intended to give more human rights to all Japanese.

MODERN TIMES Emperor Hirohito (b. 1901) died in 1989 and his son Akihito ascended to the Chrysanthemum Throne in 1990. The protracted enthronement ceremonies culminated in the Daijosai, the Great Food Offering Rite, when, in the dead of night, freshly harvested sacred rice and *sake* were offered to the gods and other ancient fertility rites were performed. The emperor was transmuted into a "living god" behind drawn curtains where, alone except for two attendant shrine virgins, he awaited the arrival of the sun goddess Amaterasu.

Emperor Meiji

In 1946, as a term of the peace, Emperor Hirohito declared that he was not a god. For some Japanese, the fact that his son has not followed his lead by diluting the Daijosai ceremony is a disappointment.

Courtesans walking to view cherry blossoms, by Kunisada Utagawa

Japan signed the Anti-Comintern Pact with Germany in 1936 and with Italy in 1937, a union which grew into the Tripartite Pact signed in 1940. By forming these alliances, Japan made obvious its hostility to Great Britain and to the United States, the only country strong enough to prevent Japanese expansion in the Pacific.

PEARL HARBOR Tension between Japan and the U.S. increased in 1940 when the U.S. banned the sale of fuel, iron, and steel to Japan, extending this to a total ban on all exports in 1941. The loss of oil was particularly severe, leading the Japanese Navy General Staff to predict that Japan's oil reserves would only last another two years.

As far as the Japanese military was concerned, the survival of their country was at stake. Prime Minister Konoe was replaced by General Tojo Hideki, and the decision was made to go to war. On December 7, 1941, the Japanese attacked the American fleet at Pearl Harbor, Hawaii. Within days they attacked the Philippine Islands and sank two British battleships.

Japanese forces seemed unstoppable, and by 1942 Japan controlled a vast empire reaching 4,000 miles southward from Sakhalin Island and 6,000 miles eastward from Burma to the Gilbert and Ellice islands (modern Tuvalu and Kiribati). However, national resentments, caused by the economic exploitation of the areas under Japanese control,

coupled with the brutal treatment of their civilian populations, meant that Japanese plans for a "New Order" in the Far East never had support.

JAPANESE LOSSES The turning point in the war came at the Battle of Midway, June 3–6, 1942. A powerful Japanese naval force attempted to destroy the U.S. Pacific Fleet, but U.S. cryptoanalysts had broken the Japanese naval codes, and the Americans were waiting. During the battle, American planes sank four Japanese aircraft carriers. The loss of its major striking force meant that the Japanese Navy was forced onto the defensive, and slowly but inexorably the Allies moved toward the main Japanese islands.

The Japanese lost almost all of their merchant fleet to Allied aircraft and submarines, which starved Japan of raw materials. The Allied policy of bombing the mainland added to the

American marines watch as shells explode on Japanese troops dug into the hills in southern Okinawa

hardships, but the tenacity and stubborn courage of civilians and troops in defense of their bases meant that the Allies, even in the face of heavy Japanese losses, could never presume they would surrender. When American forces attacked Okinawa, more than 260,000 Japanese soldiers and civilians died and more than 50,000 American troops were either

The battleship West Virginia *burning in Pearl Harbor, Hawaii, after the attack by Japanese planes*

killed or wounded before the island was taken.

THE ATOM BOMB In July, 1945 the Potsdam Declaration was issued, calling for the unconditional surrender of Japan. The Japanese refused. Rather than accept the enormous casualties they expected if forced to invade the Japanese mainland, the Allies dropped an atomic bomb on Hiroshima on August 6, 1945, destroying most of the city and killing 80,000 people. On August 9, a second bomb was dropped on Nagasaki. Faced with such devastation, the Japanese government surrendered on August 14, 1945. Foreign forces occupied the country until 1952, when, under a democratic constitution, Japan regained its independence.

❏ As pressure increased on the Japanese Imperial forces, special attack units known as *kamikaze* were formed. Named after the "divine wind" that saved Japan from invasion by the Mongols, these manned planes, boats, or flying bombs loaded with explosives crashed into enemy ships. Over 1,500 planes and flying bombs were used, sinking 34 Allied ships and damaging 288. ❏

Tokyo

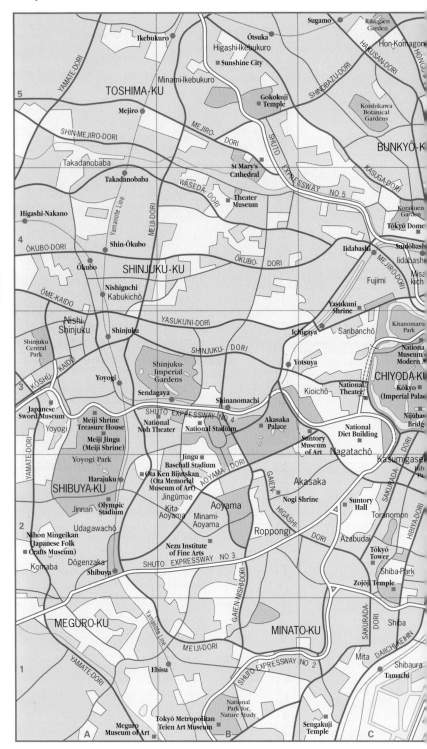

48

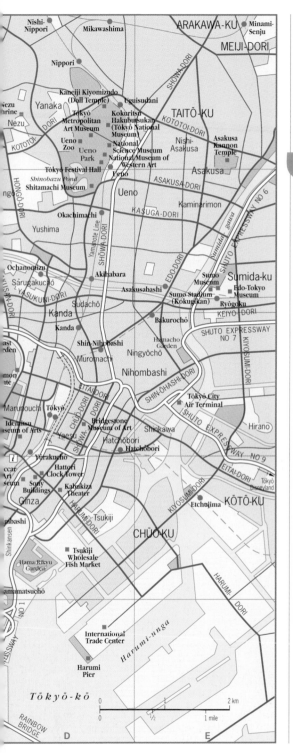

49

*Tokyo's Stark
Building*

50

TOKYO One quarter of all Japanese live within a 30-mile (50-km) radius of the Imperial Palace, Tokyo. Over 12 million live in Tokyo itself, one of the world's largest cities and the political, economic, and cultural capital of Japan. Unlike the historic cities of Kyoto and Nara, Tokyo is not a place of classic sights and traditional charms; few buildings survived both the great earthquake of 1923 and the bombing of the war, but it is a powerhouse of creative energy, global influence, and wealth.

For the first-time visitor, Tokyo may appear as a disappointing jumble of skyscrapers, concrete overpasses, and crowded sidewalks. However, any exploration on foot, away from modern thoroughfares, reveals it to be a complex metropolis of interconnected towns, each with its own neighborhoods of individual character.

For tourists with limited time, the area of Tokyo of most interest and most easily explored is that bounded by the JR (Japan Railways) Yamanote loop line. Within this circle most of the places you will wish to visit are easily reached by subway or taxi, or on foot.

In the center of Tokyo is the monumental 19th-century Imperial Palace, the seat of the emperor since the Meiji Restoration of 1868 (see pages 44–45). There are good walks near the palace, but the public is not allowed access to the actual grounds, except on January 2 and the emperor's birthday (December 23).

To the southwest of the palace is the Akasaka district, an area of government buildings that includes the Diet (Parliament), large expensive hotels and luxurious restaurants. Farther east is the Ginza, Tokyo's world-famous shopping and expense-account entertainment district.

To the south of Akasaka is Roppongi, an area served only by the Hibiya line. It has, nonetheless, become the city's most cosmopolitan and popular nightlife area, especially with young people and foreigners, who are attracted to its art movie theaters, experimental theater, and restaurants offering a variety of ethnic cuisines.

HARAJUKU AND SHINJUKU On the western edge of the area bounded by the Yamanote line are Harajuku and Shinjuku. Harajuku is the center of the teen fashion scene and the site of the historically important Meiji Shrine. Omotesando-dori, a long boulevard lined with designer shops, leads to Yoyogi Park where, until complaints by residents in the local neighborhood banned such activities, rock bands and Japanese youth would gather on Sunday afternoons to perform. The Aoyama District, nearby, is similarly fashion-conscious, but is frequented by more affluent Japanese in their late twenties and thirties. The shops of some of Japan's top designers are situated here.

Shinjuku started life as a staging post for travelers from the west coming to Edo (Tokyo) and gained a reputation for sleazy nightlife. It has, essentially, outgrown this image and outside the Shinjuku subway station are many good department stores and gift shops, and respectable restaurants and bars. However, the Kabukicho area, within Shinjuku district, is still the center of seedy massage parlors and cheap dives.

Ancient Japan survives in Asakusa

FINDING AN ADDRESS
It is extremely difficult even for local people and taxi drivers to find a place in Japan, and especially in Tokyo, just by its address. There is no logical system of house numbers, and streets do not have names, although some major roads and avenues do. Instead, addresses are by district, and within each district each building has a one- or two-digit (hyphenated) number. The best way to locate an address is to find it on a map of the vicinity. This is made easier by the practice of printing small maps on the back of business cards, restaurant matchbooks, and so on. Otherwise, travel to the general vicinity by bus or train, then for the final part of the journey, take a cab or walk and ask for help.

UENO AND ASAKUSA You can get a taste of old Japan in the Ueno and Asakusa districts, in the northeast of the city. Ueno Park is the cultural heart of Tokyo and several of the nation's major art galleries and museums are found in its grounds, as well as the zoo that houses Japan's prized giant pandas. Asakusa is a temple town and home of the famous Kannon Temple, a popular visiting place during holidays and festivals. North of Ueno is Yanaka, where flimsy wooden houses and temples have somehow escaped the bulldozer in old streets that are a favorite haunt of photographers and artists.

Traditional culture in Tokyo: Kabuki *theater in performance*

TEMPLE ORIGINS

According to legend, Asakusa Kannon Temple was established in the 7th century when two local fishermen discovered in their nets a statue of Kannon, the Buddhist Goddess of Mercy. Originally built on this site to house the statue, the temple has been rebuilt and enlarged many times over the intervening centuries. The original image of Kannon found by the fisherman is said to be buried beneath the gold-plated inner shrine found beyond the main altar in the Main Hall, but this has never been verified.

▶▶▶ Asakusa Kannon Temple (Sensoji Temple)
49E5

2-3-1 Asakusa, Taito-ku
Subway: Asakusa
Open: 24 hours

Asakusa district forms part of the old downtown, literally *shitamachi*, section of Tokyo. Settled by merchants, artisans, and craftsmen during the Edo period (1603–1867), Asakusa is still an area associated with popular Japanese culture. Asakusa Kannon Temple, in the heart of the district, is the oldest temple in Tokyo, a place of worship held in particular affection.

The Kaminarimon—the Gate of the God of Thunder—hung with a huge, red paper lantern, marks the main entrance to the temple. Nakamise-dori begins inside the gate and leads to the temple compound. Invariably crowded, the street is lined with small stands selling snack foods, traditional gifts, and souvenirs.

At the end of the street, the smaller Hozomon gateway opens on to a five-story pagoda, the temple landmark, and the Main Hall. Both buildings are postwar concrete replicas of original wooden structures. The Main Hall has little architectural merit, but the constant stream of visitors gives it life and energy. At its entrance stands a large

Asakusa Kannon Temple: detail ...

bronze incense burner. Worshipers wave the billowing incense smoke over their hands and heads, a charm to heal or prevent illness, before climbing the steps to offer prayers to Kannon, Goddess of Mercy. Inside the rather dimly lit interior is a collection of huge 18th- and 19th-century votive paintings on wood (*ema*), donated to the temple by leading artists of the Edo period.

The streets and covered passageways surrounding the temple are teeming with great little shops, restaurants, tea houses, and a variety of nightlife (see pages 68–69).

Dembo-in (Abbot's Residence)▶▶ is in the grounds of Asakusa Kannon Temple; pick up a ticket to enter from the Dembo-in temple offices, near the foot of the

... and façade

Picasso, at the Bridgestone Museum of Art

pagoda. Simply sign the visitors book to get the ticket; then walk back down Nakamise-dori, past the closed front entrance of Dembo-in. Turn right at the next corner and walk down Dembo-in-dori to the entrance gate opposite Asakusa Public Hall. Inside the peaceful temple grounds is a stroll garden, designed by the tea ceremony master Enshu Kobori (1579–1647). The garden pond contains carp and turtles, and from one angle the Asakusa Kannon pagoda is clearly reflected on its surface. The abbot's wooden residence and guest hall were built in the mid-18th century; the bronze bell at the main entrance dates from 1387.

▶▶ Bridgestone Museum of Art   49D3

1-10-1 Kyobashi, Chuo-ku
Subway: Kyobashi; JR: Tokyo
Open: 10–5:30 (last entrance 5 PM). Closed: Mon and Dec 20– Jan 6
On the third floor of the Bridgestone building, the Museum of Art displays one of Japan's best private collections of painting and sculpture, mainly of the Impressionist school and the Ecole de Paris. It includes works by Rodin, Moore, Giacometti, Picasso, Rembrandt, Utrillo, and Modigliani, as well as some fascinating post-Meiji Japanese paintings in highly derivative Western styles.

▶▶ Edo Tokyo Museum   49E4

Open daily, 10–6, Fri 9–6; closed Mon
Three minutes walk from Ryogoku station, across from Kokugikan Sumo Hall
Inside a very spacious and futuristic building, life-size dioramas re-create scenes from Tokyo's cultural and commercial past within a gallery as large as a stadium.

TEMPLE FESTIVALS
Major festivals are regularly held at the Asakusa Kannon Temple. The most popular attractions are the Setsubun ceremony on February 3; the Kinryu-no-mai (Golden Dragon Dance) on March 18 and October 18; the Sanja festival of Asakusa Shrine on May 17 and 18; the Shirasagi-no-mai (White Crane Dance) on November 3; and the year-end Hagoita-ichi market between December 17 and 18, when stalls sell *hagoita* (paddles) richly decorated with portraits of famous figures from *kabuki*. The paddle is used with a shuttlecock to play a traditional game, similar to badminton, during the New Year Festival.

▶▶▶ Ginza
49D2

Subway: Ginza (exit for the 4 chome intersection)

The most famous shopping and entertainment district in Japan, Ginza contains Tokyo's largest concentration of large department stores, expensive boutiques, galleries, coffee shops, bars, and restaurants. It is also an important commercial center, home to some of Japan's most prestigious companies, as well as the location of several hotels.

Ginza's most famous landmark is the Hattori Clock Tower, which stands at the top of the Wako department store, located at the intersection of Harumi-dori and Chuo-dori. The clock was first installed in 1894; many of the nearby shops are as old or older. The Kimuraya bakery, next door to Wako, opened in 1874 and is still very popular, especially for its bean-curd bread. Mikimoto (4-5-5 Ginza) sells cultured pearls and was, perhaps, the first shop in the world to do so, having opened in 1899.

The **Sony Building**▶▶, 5-3-1 Ginza, Chuo-ku (*open: 11–8*), contains restaurants and boutiques, in addition to three Sony showrooms (second, fourth, and fifth floors) where new products and developments are displayed to the public.

GINZA SHOPPING
Ginza is one of the most expensive shopping areas in all Japan. The area housed a mint (*gin* means silver) before Western imports and architecture were first displayed here following the opening of the country to foreign trade in the late 19th century. On Sundays and holidays Ginza-dori is closed to traffic and opened to pedestrians only.

54

Traffic in Ginza-dori (Ginza Street)

►► Idemitsu Museum of Arts 49D3

Kokusai Building, 9th Floor, 3-1-1 Maruno-uchi, Chiyoda-ku
Subway: Hibiya
Open: 10–5. Closed: Mon (and Tue if Mon is a national holiday) and Sun

Located on the tenth floor of the Kokusai Building, the Idemitsu is one of the largest and best-designed private museums in Tokyo. It also has one of the best views in Tokyo, right over the Imperial Palace. It contains an excellent collection of Zen calligraphy and ink paintings (some by the famous Zen monk Sengai), fine examples of Chinese porcelain of the Tang and Song dynasties, and Japanese ceramics. There is a Japanese-style tea room open to the public.

►► Kabukiza Theater 49D2

4-12-15 Ginza, Chuo-ku
Subway: Higashi-Ginza

Tokyo's best known *kabuki* theater sits at the intersection of two main streets in Ginza: Harumi-dori and Showa-dori. It first opened its doors in 1889, but was rebuilt in 1924 during a period of Japanese revivalism, in a baroque style inspired by castle architecture of the 16th century. The present building is a 1951 reconstruction of this structure. Kabukiza is one of the best places to see *kabuki* (see pages 58–59). English program notes and an earphone system are available, and there are daily matinée and evening performances all year, except August and December. It is possible to pay to see just one act.

►► Kokuritsu Hakubutsukan
(Tokyo National Museum) 49D5

13-9 Ueno-koen, Taito-ku
JR: Ueno (exit via Ueno-koen)
Open: Tue–Sun 9–4:30, Fri 9–8. Closed: Mon and Dec 25–Jan 3

The National Museum covers the whole history of Japan and Japanese art from the earliest periods on record. Its collection of archeology, sculpture, painting, lacquer work, ceramics, and armor make it the most complete collection of its kind anywhere in the world. Architecturally, the museum is a mishmash of buildings of opposing styles and periods, but the treasures on view are remarkable.

There are four main exhibition areas. Honkan, the main hall directly facing the front gate, is rather gloomy, but a stroll through the 25 rooms of ancient Japanese sculpture, textiles, metalwork, armor, ceramics, paintings, lacquerware, and calligraphy is well worthwhile. Hyokeikan, to the left of the main entrance, was constructed in 1909 to celebrate the marriage of the future Emperor Taisho, and houses important Japanese archeological exhibits. The third exhibition space is the Horyuji Treasure House, open only on Thursday (and not even then, if it is heavily raining or very humid). It contains rare and priceless Buddhist artifacts and works of art from the Horyuji Temple in Nara, said to be the birthplace of Japanese Buddhism. Finally, the Toyokan Gallery of Oriental Antiques specializes in archeological, historical, and cultural objects from China, southeast Asia, and India.

55

Samurai armor, Tokyo National Museum

48C3

IMPERIAL LINEAGE

Although some women held imperial power in ancient Japan, from the Nara period (710–794) until the present only males have been allowed to sit on the imperial throne. Except for the crown prince and his oldest son, who may not refuse the throne, it is possible for other descendants of the emperor to give up their imperial status and become commoners through marriage.

The Imperial Palace

▶▶▶ Kokyo (Imperial Palace)

Subway: Otemachi
Open (East Garden only): 9–4 (enter by 3 PM). Closed: Mon, Fri, and Dec 25–Jan 3

This is the residence of the reigning Emperor of Japan and his family. It is set in extensive grounds right in the heart of Tokyo's business center, on the former site of Edo Castle, the home of the Tokugawa *shogunate*. Construction of the Imperial Palace began after the Meiji Restoration of 1868, when the emperor moved from Kyoto to Tokyo.

Most of the main buildings were destroyed in World War II, but rebuilding was completed in 1968. The actual palace is closed to the public, and the private palace grounds are open only twice a year, on the emperor's birthday (December 23) and January 2. Access on these days is via the Nijubashi, a double-arched stone bridge of

German design, one of Tokyo's most familiar sights (reached from Nijubashi-mae subway station).

The Imperial Palace East Garden, formerly at the heart of Edo Castle, makes up one third of the palace grounds, and is open to the public. Popular with Japanese and foreign tourists, and with Tokyoites keen for air and a stroll in the sunlight, the garden is a welcome oasis in the noise and fumes of downtown Tokyo. The most convenient entrance is via the Otemon, once the principal gate to Edo Castle and an impressive example of a *masugata* (defensive) gate.

To the north of the palace lies Kitanomaru Park, formerly the private grounds of the Imperial Guard but now open to the public, and the home of several museums (access via Kudanshita subway station).

▶▶▶ Meiji Jingu (Meiji Shrine) 48A3

1-1 Yoyogi, Kamizono-cho, Shibuya-ku
Subway: Meiji Jingu-mae. JR: Harajuku and Yoyogi
Open: shrine and inner garden daily sunrise to sunset, except third Friday of each month. Iris garden Mar 1–Nov 3, 9–4:30, otherwise 9–4

This Shinto shrine and its large park are dedicated to the spirit of Emperor Meiji (1852–1912) and his wife, Empress Shoken (1850–1914). Emperor Meiji reigned during Japan's transformation from an isolated nation, unchanged for many hundreds of years, into a modern world power. He and Empress Shoken are buried near Kyoto, but this shrine was completed in his memory in 1920 with labor volunteered by over 100,000 Japanese people. It was destroyed in an air raid in 1945 and rebuilt to the original design in 1958. The grounds are thickly wooded (with many trees and shrubs donated by the various provinces of Japan) and contain a famous iris garden, once frequented by the emperor and his consort. It is a beautiful and cool retreat, even during Tokyo's hot, humid summer. The approach to the shrine itself is spanned by a huge *torii* gate (see panel), made of cypress wood over 1,700 years old. Behind the shrine is the Treasure House, in which articles belonging to Emperor Meiji are exhibited.

The shrine is very popular during the New Year festival, and on New Year's Eve trains run to the nearest JR station throughout the night. It is also particularly busy on Sundays, and on Thursdays young couples come here to present their newborn babies in a ceremony known as *miya mairi*; the babies and mothers are often dressed in traditional robes and kimonos.

TORII

Torii, the large gates that stand at the entrances to Shinto shrines, are made of wood, either plain or painted red. Each gate has two round, upright columns and two crossbeams. The purest and most primitive style of *torii* is made of logs with their bark intact. The red *torii* rising out of the sea at Itsukushima Shrine on Miyajima Island is one of the most famous symbols of Japan.

At the Meiji Shrine

Kabuki, *literally "song, dance, act,"* is said to have been created at the beginning of the 17th century by Okuni, a temple priestess who was also a skilled Buddhist dancer and a great beauty. She fell in love with a **ronin** (a master-less **samurai**) and fled with him, finally settling in Edo (Tokyo), where she founded a theater and began recruiting actors.

SWORD-FREE THEATER

A government edict of 1631, forbidding the wearing of swords in the theater, had the effect of excluding the *samurai*, who refused to relinquish their weapons. The nobility abandoned the theater, which became the pastime of the commercial and lower classes. By attending the theater himself in 1887, Emperor Meiji rehabilitated *kabuki* among the higher social echelons.

THE AUDIENCE

Despite the slow action, a Japanese *kabuki* theater audience takes great delight in a performance, hissing the villain and appreciating a well-delivered speech. Theatergoers may skip boring acts and return for those they enjoy. In the foyer they can meet friends, chat, drink, and buy food from a variety of restaurants and stands.

Kabuki *has villains ...*

Larger than life Two different types of plays are performed in *kabuki* theater: plays about everyday life and historical dramas. Whatever the subject, however, the sets and acting are always flamboyant and exaggerated, with the passions, lusts, and violence of life amply portrayed. Animals with human speech arrive in clouds of smoke and dance magically; rivers of blood flow from the heads of soldiers fallen to vengeful armies; victories and defeats are interlaced with the tender tragedies of failed love affairs or the triumphant reunion of lost lovers. In old Japanese society in which social and private lives were rigidly controlled, *kabuki* gave actors and their audience room to vent emotions they could not normally express.

Men as women In time, women were expelled from *kabuki* and men were required to play their roles. Since then, *onnagata*, men who specialize in female roles, have striven to present the perfect idealized version of universal woman. To play their roles well they study and practice traditional "female characteristics," even in their daily lives. Yoshisawa Ayame, an early and great *kabuki* artist, said that the ideal woman could only be expressed by an actor; he called it "the synthetic ideal." This admiration of the synthetic is frequently encountered in Japan, perhaps because the Japanese are able to judge the artificial and plastic substitute as a thing in its own right rather than as a copy of something "real." For this reason, although transvestite clubs and performers are popular all over Japan, they are taken more seriously than their Western equivalents.

Costumes, music *Kabuki* actors wear wigs, heavy make-up, and elaborate costumes. The plays unfold very slowly in a succession of tableaus; tension is maintained by the powerfully contained emotions of the actors. The orchestra, composed of traditional instruments, underlines the action and adds to the charged atmosphere. As a performance, the *kabuki* is a mix of classical theater, opera, and burlesque.

The 47 *Ronin* One of the plays that is most popular with *kabuki* theatergoers is *The Adventure of the 47 Ronin*. Its story (outlined below) contains two of the classic ingredients of a *kabuki* play: satisfaction of honor and suicide.

In 1701, in the *shogun's* palace, Lord Kira insulted Lord Asano. Asano drew his sword and sprang at Kira, who

fled. Unable to avenge his honor, Asano had no alternative but to commit *seppuku* (suicide by the sword). His
vassals thus became *ronin*. They swore to avenge their
lord, and spent two years waiting for their moment.
Eventually, one snowy night, they entered Kira's castle
and cut off his head. They carefully washed the severed
head, for an inferior must appear clean before his superior and Kira had become Asano's inferior. Then they
took the head, together with the sword that had been
used and a letter recounting what they had done, and
placed them all on Asano's grave. Finally, no longer
having any aim in life, and to avoid punishment for their
crime, all 47 *ronin* committed *seppuku* and were buried
beside their lord.

   This *kabuki* plot is based on a true story—the graves
of the 47 *ronin* are in the Sengakuji Temple in Tokyo
(see page 61).

*... and heroines—all
played by men*

TRANSVESTISM
The Tokugawa-era govern-
ment took measures
against any trend that
threatened class bound-
aries. In 1667, to prevent
over-familiarity between
male and female actors,
and the appearance in
their ranks of prostitutes,
the state banned them
from appearing on stage
together. This gave
rise to the tradition of
transvestism in Japanese
theater.

Quiet streets around Sengakuji Temple

HIROSHIGE

Hiroshige (1797–1858), now one of Japan's most famous woodblock print (*ukiyo-e*) artists, was considered eccentric in his day. Rather than portraying orthodox themes in the conventional symbolic manner, his work dealt with the lives of ordinary people, presented in a realistic manner. His prints were sold in tea houses or shops, and popular editions were published many times. By the time he was 35, Hiroshige was a well-known artist in the Tokyo area, then called Edo. In the late 19th century, Europe began to discover Japanese art and Hiroshige's work was recognized for its unusual composition, color, and freshness. His influence can be seen in paintings by Manet, Toulouse Lautrec, and Van Gogh. News of Hiroshige's reception in the West increased interest at home and, by 1900, he had become a nationally known figure.

Nizaemon VII in the role of Ki-no-Natora, *by Toshusai Sharaku, Ota Memorial Museum of Art*

▶▶ Nihon Mingeikan (Japan Folk Crafts Museum)

48A2

4-3-33 Komaba, Meguro-ku
Subway: Komabatodai-mae
Open: 10–5 (last entry 4 PM). Closed: Mon and Dec 22–Jan 3 and while changing exhibitions

At the turn of the century, Soetsu Yanagi was one of Japan's leading philosophers and critics, and wrote prolifically on Western art, literature, and philosophy. He and his circle of friends published a monthly arts magazine with the aim of introducing European culture to Japan, but gradually his interest switched from European to Asian art. He became distressed that the folk art of his own country was swiftly disappearing. Yanagi embarked on a campaign to preserve *mingei*—the term he coined to describe this "art of the people"—and to increase national awareness of the value of its "everyday beauty."

Within three decades, he had founded this museum, dedicated not to the fine arts but to the intrinsic beauty of crafts made for daily use. Items are displayed in a replica farmhouse from Tochigi prefecture, north of Tokyo, and include Soetsu Yanagi's own large collection. Exhibitions are rotated four times a year to allow all the examples of pottery, textiles, carvings, furniture, kitchen equipment, and such exhibits to be shown.

►► Ota Kinen Bijutskan (Memorial Museum of Art)   48A2

1-10-10 Jingumae, Shibuya-ku
Subway: Meiji Jingu-mae. JR: Harajuku
Open: 10:30–5:30. Closed: Mon and from the 24th to the end of every month and Dec 20–Jan 3

The late Seizo Ota, former chairman of Tokyo Mutual Life, left a formidable bequest of over 12,000 woodblock prints (*ukiyo-e*) and, in the tradition of successful Japanese entrepreneurs, the money to construct this small museum to display them. The galleries are well lit and the prints expertly displayed on a rotating basis, representing most of Japan's best-known print artists. There is a coffee shop in the basement.

Across from the museum entrance is Omotesando Avenue, busy with shoppers and, particularly on Sundays, the young and fashion-conscious. The Ota is in a small side street near Meiji-dori—a haven of peace among the trendy streets of Harajuku.

►► Sengakuji Temple   48C1

2-11-1 Takanawa, Minato-ku (turn right from the station and walk up the hill; the entrance is past the traffic lights on the left)
Subway: Sengakuji
Open: 9–4

The 47 *ronin* buried in this temple are revered by the Japanese as examples of truly loyal men (see pages 58–59). An English-language version of the story of their sacrifice for their master, Lord Asano, who had been wrongly obliged to commit *seppuku* (ritual suicide), is available at the shops near the temple entrance.

To the right of the entrance is a statue of Yoshio Oishi, leader of the *ronin* and Lord Asano's chief retainer. Beyond the main inner gate, and to the left, is the cemetery. On the way you will pass a well where the *ronin* washed the severed head of Lord Kira (Asano's betrayer) before laying it on their master's grave. The head was eventually given back to Kira's family, and in the small museum in the temple grounds a receipt issued by a temple priest for "one head" is on display in one of the dusty cabinets. The tombs of the 47 *ronin* are blackened with the smoke from sticks of incense burned in tribute.

Sengakuji Temple

SHINJUKU FRONTIER TOWN

Shinjuku was originally a small post town on the Koshu-kaido highway providing horses, brothels, inns, and tea houses for passing travelers. It became a boom town with the building of a railroad station in 1885 and earned a reputation as a brash, free and easy area. A frontier feel is still associated with eastern Shinjuku. Having been spared by the 1923 Kanto earthquake, the district expanded at a faster pace than the rest of the city. The present Shinjuku station opened in 1964.

The modern face of Japan at Shinjuku

A statue of warrior Saigo Takemori in Ueno

▶▶▶ **Shinjuku** 48A3

Subway: Shinjuku (Marunouchi line at the north end of the station, on the east side; Toei–Shinjuku line at the south end, on the west side)

Shinjuku district has the largest, busiest, and most chaotic railroad station in Japan (see pages 92–93). Railroad lines divide Shinjuku into two very different areas. The eastern side is a busy shopping district, with a warren of underground shopping malls and a lively entertainment district at night. The Kabuki-cho area, on the east side, is notorious for its sex establishments (see pages 244–245). The unplanned, vibrant quality of the east is in fine contrast to the ordered development of the west side, where highrise office buildings and modern hotels have earned the nickname "Skyscraper City." The city government recently moved there, into the Tokyo Metropolitan Government offices designed by Kenzo Tange.

Shinjuku Imperial Gardens▶▶ (*Shinjuku Gyoen*), a 32-acre (80-hectare) park at Naito-cho (*Subway: Shinjuku Gyoen-mae*), belonged to a family of feudal lords, then to Emperor Meiji. The gardens were opened to the public after World War II. The northern end of the park is given over to expanses of greenery, and in the east there is a garden in 19th-century French style. Famous for its cherry blossoms (*sakura*) in spring and chrysanthemums in the fall, the park is treasured by residents of Shinjuku (*open* 9–4:30; *closed* Mon). South of Shinjuku Gardens are the beautiful National Noh Theater and gardens, where English-language guides to *noh* theater are on sale.

▶▶ Shitamachi Museum   49D4

2-1 Ueno-Koen, Taito-ku
Subway: Ueno, Yushima
Open: Tue–Sun 9:30–4:30. Closed: Mon and Dec 29–Jan 3

Shitamachi translates as "town below" and refers to the district in a town where the merchant and artisan classes lived and worked. Asakusa and Ueno in Tokyo were such areas. These closely built, densely populated districts developed their own popular culture, customs, and social habits—such as being quick to help a neighbor or to argue, and working hard.

After World War II, the characteristic nature of these areas started to disappear and this museum was built to record their heritage. There are reconstructions of an ordinary merchant's house (look for the bamboo basket hanging from the ceiling, in which valuables were packed and carried in the event of a fire), an old schoolhouse, a tenement house with a coppersmith's workshop, and a small candy store. English-speaking guests are well cared for.

▶▶ Ueno District and Zoo   49D5

Ueno station is the gateway from Tokyo to northern Japan. Department stores, shopping centers, restaurants, and bars cluster around the station, and behind it is Ueno Park (*Ueno Koen*), Japan's first and largest public park. Within the park are several museums, including the Tokyo National Museum (see page 55) and the Shitamachi Museum (see above), and Shinobazu Pond. The **National Museum of Western Art**▶▶ (*open 9:30–5; closed Mon*), designed by Le Corbusier, houses the Matsukata Collection of 19th- and 20th-century French art; the **Tokyo Metropolitan Art Museum**▶▶ (*open 9–5; closed every third Mon*) exhibits modern Japanese arts, and the **National Science Museum**▶▶ (*open 9–4:30; closed Mon*) houses displays on science, technology, and traditional crafts. **Ueno Zoo** (*open 9:30–4:30; closed Mon*) opened in 1882; crowds flock there to see the two giant pandas given by the People's Republic of China.

DOLL TEMPLE

Kaneiji Kiyomizudo temple, in the grounds of Ueno Park, was built in imitation of the famous Kiyomizudera Temple in Kyoto (see page 129). Mothers leave dolls around the altar of the temple to protect the health of their babies. The dolls are collected throughout the year and ritually burned in a rather macabre ceremony every September 25.

63

Boating in Ueno Park, Japan's largest city park and a favorite place for springtime cherry blossom viewing

Tsukiji is Tokyo's wholesale seafood distribution center and perhaps the biggest, most colorful, and most exciting fish market in the world. The market opens before dawn, and as business is virtually over by 9:30 AM, many tourists miss the opportunity of seeing this Japanese institution.

THE OUTER MARKET
In the outer, smaller area of the market are stands and stores providing everything for the catering trade from *bonito* fish flakes to personalized toothpicks. There are also small cafés, bars, and coffee shops serving the fish-sellers, buyers, and truckers. They are the places to go for breakfast after a visit to the inner market.

64

To get to Tsukiji market, take a cab from your hotel or a train on the Hibiya subway line to Tsukiji station, two stops past Ginza station. Turn left out of the station, walk down Shin Ohashi Avenue (*Shin Ohashi-dori*) past two sets of traffic lights, turn left again and you will find yourself in the outer market. Cross the blue iron bridge that leads across a small canal to the sheds of the wholesale market. Walk past the lines of vans, piles of styrofoam boxes, and small boxwood fires, built by the truckers to keep warm while they wait to return home. Soon you will come upon the frantically bustling market, where over a thousand fish stalls and streams of buyers and sellers compete for space in a maze of alleyways, while men push and pull carts loaded with huge tuna fish, or stacks of styrofoam boxes full of ice and wriggling fish.

Tuna fish auction The market specializes in *maguro* (tuna fish), sometimes brought to the market straight from the fishing boats that tie up at the dock behind it, though most are flown in from all over Japan and from London, Boston, and Africa. The *maguro*, some of them weighing over 650 pounds (300kg), are auctioned every morning, then pushed on carts to the buyers' stalls. There they are put on marble slabs and sliced into sections with an electric saw; the sections are then cut into smaller pieces with a long and very sharp knife. Only at this stage does the buyer know if the fish has the desired high fat content

Seafood for sale well before sunrise

Marking tuna with the buyer's sign

SUSHI AND KNIVES

At lunchtime, the *sushi* bars around the market sell the freshest *sushi* you are ever likely to taste. These vinegared rice patties can be topped with a variety of food, but in Tsukiji they are prepared by the *sushi-san* with raw fish bought that morning. In winter, *sushi* is eaten with a hot *sake* for a perfect lunch. The outer market also has several stalls selling Japanese cooking knives, among the best in the world, beautifully made with plain wooden handles. Blades are marked with the maker's trademark in *kanji*.

and, thus, whether he has paid a good or bad price for it.

Late at night, trucks from village cooperatives all over Japan start to arrive with their loads of fresh fish. They reach the market and line up to be unloaded between midnight and 4 AM. Trucks carrying water tanks full of live fish go to the south end of the market, where their catch is transferred to aerated holding tanks to await the auction. At around 4 AM, the trucks leave the auctioneers, and wholesale buyers arrive to look at the produce. The buyers examine the tuna for fat content and take a good look inside the boxes of other fish to make sure they are fresh. What they buy, and the prices they pay are crucial to the profits they will make later in the day.

At 5:20 AM the auction begins. Tuna fish are auctioned on the first floor and other fish and seafood on the second floor. Meanwhile, at the market stalls, buyers' assistants are clearing up, getting boxes of fresh ice ready, sharpening knives and preparing for the arrival of the stevedores with the morning purchases. Between 6 and 9 AM, the retailers, restaurateurs, and *sushi-san* (see panel) arrive to buy fish and to catch up on the day's news. By 9:30 AM the pace in the market is slower, and it is time to leave.

At the entrance to the blue iron bridge leading to the market is the Namiyoke Temple, a Shinto shrine dedicated to the safety of seamen. A stand at its gate sells delicious, freshly baked cakes filled with red-bean jam.

TSUKIJI

Fish is a staple of the Japanese diet, and no world culture is more inventive than this in serving and eating it with relish: raw as *sashimi* or as a topping on rice, as *sushi*, grilled, smoked, pickled, and dried. Most fish caught commercially for Japanese consumption is rushed to the daily Tsukiji market auction, a remarkable spectacle.

A kamikaze flying bomb on display at Yasukuni Shrine

▶▶ Yanaka District 49D5

This neighborhood, north of the Shitamachi Museum (see page 63) was one of the few in Tokyo to escape most of the destruction of the 1923 Kanto earthquake and World War II bombing. With its narrow streets and old shops and houses, it preserves much of the flavor of a Shitamachi area, and is worth exploring on foot—if you do not mind the risk of getting lost. JR Nippori station, on the Yamanote line, is a good starting point.

▶▶ Yasukuni Shrine 48C4

3-1-1 Kudankita, Chiyoda-ku
Subway: Kudanshita
Open: shrine 24 hours, Main Hall and museum 9:30–4:30

This Shinto shrine, a national monument in Japan, was built at the request of Emperor Meiji in honor of Japanese who had died in the battle to reinstate his imperial authority in the Meiji Restoration of 1868. Since then, it has been dedicated to the spirits of all Japanese soldiers and civilians who gave their lives in the "defense" of the Japanese empire. Many of the 2.5 million souls honored at the shrine died in imperialistic wars—and as such their enshrinement is out of step with the postwar Japanese constitution, which renounces militarism and separates the state from religion. As a result of this contradiction, the shrine has been at the center of a number of political controversies.

The official visit of Japan's prime minister in 1985 created an outcry from the government of China and a torrent of protest from Japanese opposition parties, who saw the visit as sanctifying war criminals. Nevertheless, the shrine is regularly visited by many thousands of Japanese, who go simply to pay their respects to lost relatives and friends and to pray for "the repose of their souls."

Yasukuni is a complex of buildings that includes the Main Hall, the Hall of Worship, a museum called the Yushukan, a *noh* theater, and a *sumo* wrestling ring. The Main Hall and Hall of Worship are built in the primitive, unadorned *shinmei* style of the ancient shrines at Ise (see pages 106–107). The Yushukan is essentially a military museum with exhibits such as a tank, a naval gun, and the Human Torpedo (*Kaiten*), the submarine equivalent of a *kamikaze* plane. The most recent addition is a steam locomotive from the Thai–Burma "Death Railway," built by Allied prisoners of war. The museum's contents in the context of the shrine are, to say the least, disquieting.

Look for the huge steel *torii* (gate) that stands at the entrance of an avenue, lined with stone lanterns and cherry and *ginko* trees; this leads to another enormous *torii* and, finally, the main gate to the inner sanctuary.

SUMO AT YASUKUNI SHRINE
Between April 21 and 23, open-air *sumo* matches are held every afternoon at Yasukuni Shrine. The event marks the end of a Shinto spring festival and traditionally the best *sumo* men in Japan dedicate their services freely. Pre-match rituals are shortened, but otherwise the contests are conducted with the usual ceremony. Each *sumo* stable has its own open marquee, where wrestlers prepare themselves before entering the ring. You can wander freely among the enormous men. Look for top wrestlers arriving in black stretch limousines, a single man filling the whole back seat.

▶ Yoyogi Park

Subway: Omotesando. JR: Harajuku

48A2

Once a Japanese army drilling ground, this area was requisitioned by the U.S. Army after World War II and became known as Washington Heights. In 1964, the land was used for the construction of the athletes' Olympic Village, before its final conversion to public parkland. The park is a welcome open space and is of particular interest when it turns a dramatic pink in the cherry-blossom-viewing season at the beginning of April. Takeshita-dori, nearby, is a cramped alleyway where cheap boutiques and stallholders sell sunglasses, posters, pins, and cut-rate fashion clothes: a young teenager's dream.

Rock 'n' roll at Yoyogi Park

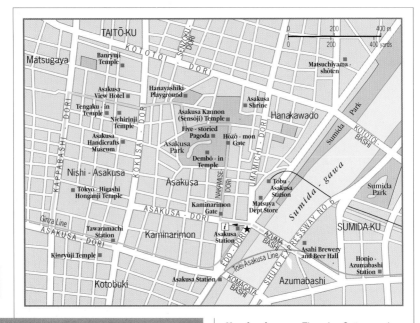

Walk

Asakusa

Distance: 1½ miles (2.5 km); time: one hour. Tokyo's "downtown" shopping and entertainment district, on the banks of the Sumida River, is the spiritual home of the *Edokko*, Tokyo's equivalent of London's cockneys. Asakusa is a great place for inexpensive souvenir shopping, or for the serious cook to look for Japanese additions to the *batterie de cuisine*.

On leaving Asakusa subway station, on the Ginza line, pause to look across the Sumida River. To the left of the bridge stand the **Asahi Brewery Company's** headquarters and the **Asahi Beer Hall▶**, both landmarks of the Tokyo 1980s style, designed by Frenchman Philippe Starck. The brewery building is said to represent a glass of beer, complete with a head of foam, while the strange golden object atop the Beer Hall represents a flame.
Turning around, walk two blocks away from the river to find the

Kaminarimon or Thunder Gate, marking the entry to the precincts of **Sensoji Temple**, also known as the **Asakusa Kannon Temple** (see page 52). The approach to the temple on Nakamise-dori is lined with stands selling all manner of traditional

souvenirs and sweetmeats, plus some more way-out articles: 55 yards (50m) along on the left-hand side, a corner stand has an intriguing line in canine formal wear. In common with even the most modest of neighborhood shopping streets in Tokyo, Nakamise-dori's decorations change with the seasons.

After visiting the temple and garden, walk around and to the west for three minutes to reach the **Hanayashiki playground▶**, a small children's amusement park. Between Hanayashiki and the Asakusa View Hotel is a group of theaters, heart of the Asakusa entertainment district, with a distinctly different, more welcoming atmosphere to fashionable Shibuya and Shinjuku. Continue walking along the street to the left of the Asakusa View Hotel, until you meet **Kappabashi-dori▶▶**, the heart of the catering trade wholesale district and the place to go for excellent knives, exotic kitchen utensils, and also the lurid plastic food replicas that grace so many restaurant and cafeteria window displays.

To end the walk, continue south down Kappabashi-dori until you reach Tawaramachi subway station, Ginza line.

Above: the Sumida River
Below: Asakusa Kannon Temple

Walk

Shinjuku

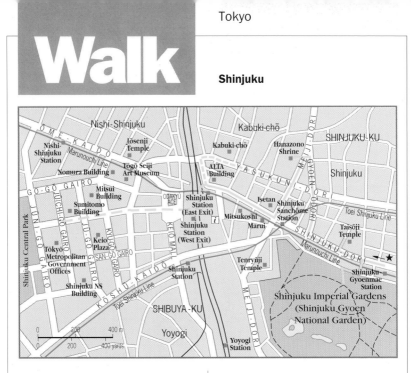

Nishi-Shinjuku • Kabuki-chō • SHINJUKU-KU

Nishi-Shinjuku Station • Jōsenji Temple • Kabuki-chō • Hanazono Shrine • Shinjuku

Nomura Building • Tōgo Seiji Art Museum • ALTA Building • YASUKUNI-DORI

Mitsui Building • ODAKYU ACE • Shinjuku Station (East Exit) • Isetan • Shinjuku-Sanchōme Station • Toei Shinjuku Line

Sumitomo Building • Shinjuku Station (West Exit) • Mitsukoshi • Marui • Taisōji Temple

Tōkyō Metropolitan Government Offices • Keio Plaza • KŌSHŪ-KAIDŌ • SAN-GO GAIRO • Shinjuku Station • Tenryūji Temple • Marunouchi Line • Shinjuku Gyoenmae Station

Shinjuku NS Building • Toei Shinjuku Line • SHIBUYA-KU • MEIJI-DORI • Shinjuku Imperial Gardens (Shinjuku Gyoen National Garden)

Yoyogi • Yoyogi Station

0 200 400 m
0 200 400 yards

Distance: 2 miles (3.5km); time: 1½ to 2 hours. Relax in the Shinjuku Gardens before taking on Tokyo's busiest shopping and entertainment district.

Start at Shinjuku Gyoen-mae subway station, Maruno-uchi line, and walk one block to the **Shinjuku Imperial Gardens**. This broad, pleasantly landscaped park allows quiet views of the cluster of skyscrapers to the northwest in Tokyo's administrative and business district. Leaving the park, walk back past the subway station and across the main street, Shinjuku-dori, to find the entrance to **Taisoji Temple**▶▶, originally built in the 17th century and housing a statue of Yama, king of the Buddhist hell.

Continue west along Shinjuku-dori, then turn right into Meiji-dori and head

Metropolitan Government offices

north, crossing the wide Yasukuni-dori, to find the entrance to the **Hanazono Shrine**▶▶▶, bright with scarlet *torii* (gates). The shrine is famous for its annual *Tori-no-Ichi*, held each November, a market for lavishly decorated bamboo rakes sold as good luck charms.

After visiting the shrine, go back across Yasukuni-dori to rejoin Shinjuku-dori and then turn right, toward Shinjuku station. Here are the department stores, **Isetan**, **Marui**, and **Mitsukoshi**. Alternatively, turn right along Yasukuni and approach Shinjuku station. The streets to the right make up **Kabuki-cho**▶, the city's largest nightlife area.

Either way leads to Shinjuku station. Opposite the east exit stands the **ALTA Building** with a giant TV screen, a popular meeting point. Follow the signs through the station to the west exit. On the lower level, the walkway leads to the right, to an underground link with the business district. Walk to street level to see the marble twin towers of the **Tokyo Metropolitan Government offices**▶, a vast and expensive show of architectural bravura. Return by underground walkway to Shinjuku station.

Walk

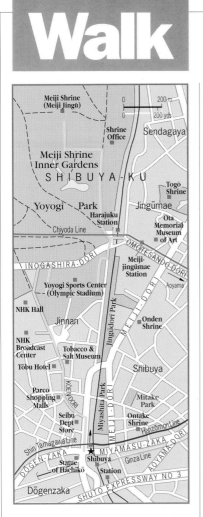

Shibuya and Harajuku

with boutiques and restaurants. Continue walking up the slope, past the **Parco shopping malls** and the **Tobu Hotel** to the **NHK (Japan Broadcasting System) Broadcast Center** and the **NHK Hall►►**, one of Tokyo's largest venues for classical music performances.

Walk northeast to the entrance to Yoyogi Park (see page 67). The **Yoyogi Sports Center►** was one of three arenas for the 1964 Olympic Games, designed by Kenzo Tange.

Skirt the Sports Center and cross the JR railroad tracks by the bridge alongside JR Harajuku station. Left is the entrance to the **Meiji Shrine** (see page 57). A gravel walk, lined with lanterns, leads to the main buildings.

Walk back to JR Harajuku station and cross into Omotesando Avenue and down the slope to the intersection with Meiji-dori. The streets around this intersection are the youth fashion center of Japan. Note the specialist condom store on the corner of Omotesando and Meiji-dori, and the tiny, enclosed basketball court on the opposite corner. Tucked in behind, off Omotesando-dori, is the **Ota Memorial Museum of Art** (see page 61). End the walk at Harajuku, or continue up Omotesando to the upscale residential district of Aoyama.

Modern buildings at Shibuya

Distance: 1½ miles (2.5km); time: at least 1½ hours. This walk leads through one of Tokyo's most fashionable districts to the somber beauty of the Meiji Shrine, then back into the mixture of tacky and high fashion in Harajuku.

Start at the north exit of JR Shibuya station, JR Yamanote line, subway Hanzomon and Ginza lines, by the statue of **Hachiko►**, a dog owned by a college professor, who met his master at Shibuya station every day and continued to wait for him for seven years after his master's death.

Walk north from Hachiko's statue, along Koen-dori (Park Street), lined

NEW CAPITAL

In the 12th century, the military leader of Japan, Minamoto Yoritomo, moved the seat of military government away from Kyoto to the isolated village of Kamakura, and established there Japan's first *shogun*-controlled military government. Over the next two centuries, a number of Japan's most important temples and shrines were built there, as the military and the clergy influenced each other to create a new breed of Zen warriors and warrior monks.

SHOPPING

Kamakura-bori, or finely chiseled wood, is the specialty of this area. Once finished, every item, such as a jewelry box, is painted, usually red and black, and then lacquered to a glossy finish.

Making offerings at the Zeniarai Benten Shrine, Kamakura

Excursions

▶▶▶ Kamakura   95D3

About 30 miles (50km) south of Tokyo

Between 1192 and 1333, Kamakura was the capital city of Japan. Today, it is one of the country's most interesting places, with 65 Buddhist temples and 19 Shinto shrines. It is also an attractive residential town. Being much smaller than Kyoto, Japan's other religious center, Kamakura is easier to navigate. The local tourist office (left of the main JR Kamakura station entrance) publishes a map of footpath routes that link the best-known temples. Paths are signposted in English, as well as Japanese.

Getting there JR's Yokosuka line connects Tokyo with Kamakura. Trains run about every 10 to 15 minutes and stop at Tokyo, Shinbashi, and Shinagawa stations on Tokyo's Yamanote loop line. A more interesting route, though longer, is to take the Odakyu line from Tokyo station to Fujisawa and change for the Enoden narrow-gauge train, which pulls three wooden cars through small villages to Kamakura station. En route, it passes Hase station, the location of the Great Buddha and Hasedera temple. Either station is a good starting point for a day's walking tour, the best way to explore Kamakura.

Among the temples and shrines worth visiting in Kamakura, the following are particularly interesting.

Engakuji Temple▶▶ was built in the 13th century by the Zen warrior Tokimune Hojo, to commemorate the deaths of Japanese and Mongolian soldiers killed during the Mongols' attempted invasion of Japan, and to mark his gratitude to Zen for the calm it had given him during the campaign. Engakuji has large gardens and numerous sub-temples, but Shari-den, the Shrine of the Sacred Tooth of the Buddha (*open 8–5, until 4 PM Nov–Mar*), is perhaps the most interesting to visit. It is in the Chinese style popular during the Kamakura era, 1192–1333.

73

Hase Kannon Temple (Hasedera)▶▶ (*open 7–5:40, until 4:40 PM Nov–Mar*), close to Hase station, is set on a hill with fine views of the open sea. The main sanctuary houses the famous 11-headed gilt statue of Kannon, over 29 feet (9m) high and carved from a single log of camphor wood. The many faces of the goddess symbolize various stages of enlightenment. The most beguiling sight in Hase temple is the thousands of tiny statues of Jizo, the guardian deity of children, dressed in tiny clothes and surrounded with children's toys as offerings. Once symbolizing parents' hopes for their children, these Jizo statues now mainly represent aborted or stillborn children.

Above and below: Buddhas at the Great Buddha Shrine

Kamakura's best-known sight is the **Great Buddha**▶▶▶, in the grounds of the Kotokuin Temple (*open 7–5:45*). This bronze figure of a seated Buddha, the Daibutsu, over 32 feet (10m) high, was cast in the 13th century and housed in a massive wooden temple building. One hundred and forty years later, the temple and Kamakura were flattened by a huge tidal wave that swept inland. The structure that housed the Buddha was washed away, but the Buddha itself remained unmoved, and for the last six centuries it has stood in the open air.

The **Zeniarai Benten Shrine**▶▶▶ (*open 8–5*), also known as the Money-Washing Shrine, is reached through a stone tunnel cut into a steep rock face. Once inside the temple grounds, you pass through a guard of honor of *torii* (gates), erected so close together that they almost form a tunnel. Off the main temple is a cave, into which flows a mountain spring, directed into a channel running around the walls. Here is where the money-washing takes place: put several coins in a wicker basket, swirl them under the water, and wish for financial success.

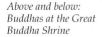

Excursions

▶▶▶ Nikko

209C2

About 88 miles (140km) north of Tokyo

Nikko town, at the center of the 543-square-mile (1,407-sq-km) Nikko National Park, has been a religious center since the 8th century. The park's numerous volcanic mountains and lakes include the sacred mountain Nantai-san, at the base of which lies the ravishing Lake Chuzenji and Kegon Waterfall, the highest in Japan. Nikko is a two-hour train ride from Tokyo or Ueno stations; Lake Chuzenji is a bus ride away from Nikko along a winding mountain road. To get to Nikko, take the Tohoku Shinkansen line from Tokyo or Ueno stations to Utsunomiya, then change for the local line. Alternatively, take the Tobu line limited express from Matsuya department store in Tokyo's Asakusa district. To reach Lake Chuzenji, take any bus from platforms 1, 2, or 3 of the bus terminal near Nikko station to Chuzenji town, at the east end of the lake.

Toshogu Shrine▶▶▶, ornately decorated in vibrant colors, was begun in 1634 by the grandson of Tokugawa Ieyasu (see panel). A mixture of Shinto and Buddhist elements and elaborate carvings give it a Chinese flavor; over 2 million sheets of gold leaf were used in the gilding that covers it. A Shinto *torii* (gate) and a Buddhist pagoda stand together in front of the black lacquer and gold-leaf adorned Niomon front gate, which bears animal and plant motifs. Nearby, on the lintel of the Sacred Stable for White Horse, is the carving of three monkeys, "Hear No Evil, See No Evil, Speak No Evil," produced by local craftsmen who regarded them as guardian spirits. Farther into the shrine's compound is Yomeimon, Gate of

Toshogu shrine: an elaborate tower ...

ONE HUNDRED TOSHOGU SHRINES
The Tokugawa shogunate encouraged the worship of Ieyasu's spirit, and eventually more than 100 Toshogu branch shrines were built throughout Japan. In 1873, Toshogu was dedicated to two other great warlords: Toyotomi Hideyoshi (1536–98) and Minamoto Yoritomo (1147–99).

... and a gate figure

Sunlight, the lavishly adorned entrance to the inner sanctum and once the limit for lower-ranked *samurai* (ordinary people were not allowed past the front gate). A succession of chambers leads to the Gokuden (Sacred Palace), which houses the gold lacquer shrine dedicated to the great warriors and leaders Toyotomi Hideyoshi, Tokugawa Ieyasu, and Minamoto Yoritomo (see panel).

The entrance to Toshogu shrine is along the broad Ote-dori, and up the Thousand Person stone steps that lead to the front gate. It is part of the **Rinnoji Temple**►► complex. The best way to see the shrine and other sites in Rinnoji is by buying a strip of tickets from the Rinnoji Temple gate-house, on the right-hand side of Ote-dori before you reach Toshogu shrine (*open* 8–5, until 4 PM Nov–Mar). The **Daiyuin Mausoleum**►►, ornate but smaller than Toshogu, is the most aesthetically pleasing of the two.

Across the street from the steps to the entrance of Rinnoji Temple, the arched red **Shinkyo (Sacred Bridge)**►► (*open* 9–4) spans the Daiya River. Built in the mid-17th century, it was originally reserved for the *shogun* and imperial envoys. You can now cross the 1907 replica for a fee. This is where the priest Shodo was said to have been carried across the river on two giant serpents in his quest to reach the summit of sacred Mount Nantai.

The bus to **Lake Chuzenji**►► climbs to 4,166 feet (1,270m) up a winding road (there is another route for the descent). Near the bus station in Chuzenji town is Kegon Waterfall, where an elevator carries visitors to the bottom of the river gorge. To the right of the lake, Futaarasan Shrine takes the old name of Mount Nantai, the volcanic cone (8,143 feet/2,482m) rising above it. Each August, pilgrims climb to the inner Futaara Shrine, on the edge of the summit crater. In Chuzenji Temple, on the left shore of the lake, is a statue of a thousand-handed Kannon, said to have been carved from a tree by priest Shodo himself.

The Kegon Waterfall, at Lake Chuzenji

NIKKO AND THE TOSHOGU SHRINE
Nikko was founded in AD 782, when a Buddhist temple was erected there by the priest Shodo (735–817). The town was known for its religious pilgrims, but it did not attract prominent national attention until after the death of Ieyasu, founder of the Tokugawa shogun-ate in 1616. He left instructions in his will that his remains were to be interred in Nikko. Toshogu was built as his mausoleum and as a memorial to his achieve-ments in unifying and governing Japan. It is thus as much a secular as a religious monument, and the shrine is a major tourist attraction, especially on May 17, the main shrine festival date, highlighted by a procession of hundreds of men in authentic *samurai* costume.

Samurai *from the ruling class were appren-ticed to masters of archery and swordmanship, and demanded equipment to match the skills they developed. As a result, there emerged a group of artist craftsmen who manufactured swords and armor combining beauty and function to the highest degree. They developed a technical mastery that far surpassed Western methods of the day, and their swords became renowned throughout the world.*

SWORD POWER

A story is told of two famous competing sword-smiths—Muramasa and Masamune—who were almost equal in skill. When a sword made by Muramasa was held upright in a running stream every dead leaf that drifted against its edge was cut in two. However, when Masamune's sword was put to the same test, the floating leaves passed either side of its edge, remaining uncut. Masamune's sword was judged the superior for its spiritual power over the leaves.

Making the sword For the main core of the blade, the swordsmith used a soft, laminated steel that was flexible and tough. The exterior was made of a combination of hard steels that were hammered together, folded over, hammered again, and so on, many times over. This technique formed a skin over the inner blade that was composed of thousands upon thousands of layers of different grades of hard steel welded together. The blade was then hardened even more by heating and cooling. Finally it was coated with clay, leaving only the cutting edge exposed. The clay-coated blade was then heated to the correct temperature and plunged into a tub of cold water. Cooling instantly, the cutting edge became so hard that, once honed, it retained its razor sharpness despite repeated use. The part of the blade covered in clay cooled at a slower rate and retained a perfect degree of softness and flexi-bility necessary to give the blade "feel" and durability.

Samurai and sword For the *samurai*, his sword was not just a weapon but the material symbol of his honor, and he invested it with a spiritual power and surrounded its use with elaborate ritual. To make a binding oath, a *samurai* swore on his sword. Swords that had been through many battles became objects of reverence and worship, passed from father to son as tokens of loyalty. If beaten in battle, a warrior would pray that his sword might regain its lost spirit. At the birth of a *samurai*, a sword was placed beside the newborn baby, and at his death a sword was laid by his corpse.

Sword and spirit Because a *samurai* sword was held to have such spiritual significance, the task of making swords was given mystical importance. The sword-maker occupied an honored place in society and was required to undergo both spiritual and technical training before being entrusted with the job. Only those with the purest hearts and the highest moral standards could become master swordsmiths. The making of each sword was analogous to a spiritual journey and the sword-maker would undergo ritual purification and fasting before he began to make a sword. While at the anvil, he wore white robes and adopted the lifestyle of a monk.

Testing the sword The actual use of the swords was more mundane and bloody. They were fitted with long hilts and wielded with both hands. A good sword could easily lop off an arm, a leg, or a head, and the best could cut through armor and could even slice a man in two at one stroke.

To test a new sword, the swordmaster or *samurai* would obtain a corpse or, in some cases, a condemned man of low rank. The body, dead or alive, would be hung up and various cutting strokes of different degrees of difficulty would be tried out. Each cut had a name and there was even a table listing cuts in ascending order of difficulty of execution. The simplest cut was "cutting the sleeve" or chopping a hand off at the wrist. The most difficult was a "pair of wheels," which required the body to be chopped in half by a stroke across the hips.

DECAPITATION
In battle, cutting off an opponent's head was the most strived-for stroke. The head was taken as a war trophy if the victim had fought with sufficient bravery and was of high enough rank. *Samurai* wore steel antidecapitation collars, and, just in case of failure in battle, would burn incense in their helmets before the fight to ensure that their heads would smell sweet for the honorable enemy.

A 19th-century print by Kuniyoshi showing swordsmen in combat

The New Otani Hotel and garden, Tokyo

Accommodations

In general, there is no shortage of accommodations in Japan. In the cities and in Tokyo, especially, there is a wide variety of options, ranging from hotels that rank with the best in the world to *minshuku*, a Japanese version of bed and breakfast.

Major hotels Tokyo itself has hotels throughout the city, but those establishments near a central location are obviously the most desirable. The best locations and the areas with most major hotels are Akasaka, Ginza, Shinbashi, Shinjuku, and around Tokyo station. Reserve in advance for luxury-class hotels, and for all hotels during major festivals and the month of February, when students arrive in Tokyo to take their university entrance exams. The service in the major hotels is invariably first class. They offer a wide range of extras, which may include a health club and massage service, an executive business center with secretarial services, a guest relations officer to help with any problems, a travel agency, a shopping mall, cocktail lounges with live music, and Japanese- and Western-style restaurants. Rooms have their own private bathrooms with a tub and shower combination, color television, clocks and usually radios, hot-water thermos flasks with tea bags, and minibars. Because they are accustomed to foreigners, all hotels in this category employ some English-speaking staff. You will find room service, laundry and dry-cleaning, and often a complimentary English-language newspaper (such as the Japan Times) delivered to your room.

HOSTEL NETWORK
The International Youth Hostel Federation (IYHF) now has an International Booking Network that includes Japan. A phone call to the YHA in your own country will get you details of how to book rooms and meals in hostels in Tokyo, Kyoto, Nara, and over 30 other cities.

Hotels with particular character or other merits are listed in the **Accommodations and Restaurants** section (pages 265–280). Whichever class of hotel you choose, standards of hygiene and service are usually excellent.

Other types of accommodations *Ryokan*, traditional Japanese inns, provide the very best of traditional Japanese taste, culture, and food. They are usually sited in beautiful areas and/or overlook elegant gardens. The service is restrained and flawless in its maintenance of correct behavior. Fully fledged *ryokan* are typically expensive, but worth at least one night's stay for the experience (see pages 220–221).

Minshuku are family homes that take guests; these give a closer insight into Japanese life. They provide a room, bed, breakfast, and evening meal (see pages 80–81).

Business hotels offer straightforward, no-frills accommodations and are clean and efficiently run. Rooms are small but well equipped, and the hotels provide facilities such as fax and photocopying machines. Food and room service are not always available. The cost is less than a major hotel, but more than a Japanese inn. Business hotels are usually located for ease of access to railroad and subway stations.

The Japanese inn is a cheap version of a *ryokan* and recommended if you are on a budget and wish to experience traditional Japanese customs and lifestyle. Tourist Information Centers (TIC's, see page 264) at Narita Airport and in Tokyo and Kyoto will make reservations with the Welcome Inn group, an association of independent inn owners.

The very cheapest places to stay are youth hostels. There are quite a number in Tokyo, and their rules and regulations are similar to those in the West. Youth hostels are convenient for one-night stays, but at busy holiday times they are popular and heavily used and need to be booked ahead. Membership and further information are available at the Japan Youth Hostel Association, Hoken Kaikan, 1-1 Ichigaya-Sadohara-cho, Shinjuku-ku, Tokyo (tel: 03 3269 5831). The National Tourist Office (see page 264) has a free pamphlet listing all youth hostels in Japan, with their locations on a map.

LOVE HOTELS
Because most Japanese live in very small houses or apartments with their families, it is very hard for young unmarried or even married couples to find somewhere to make love privately. Society's solution is short-stay hotels, called love hotels or *avec* hotels. Such establishments are quite common, and you will see their advertisements giving the details of facilities offered in most large cities. The ads are garish, but the hotels themselves are run very discreetly. They are usually surrounded by a high wall and the entrances and exits are separate, to limit the chance of embarrassing encounters. The anonymity of guests is closely guarded, and the management tries to offer all the facilities needed to allow clients to indulge in their wildest fantasies. After 10 PM room rates are often lower than those of regular hotels, so if exotic surroundings do not keep you from sleeping, they make a cheap alternative for a single night's stay.

79

The modern Prince Hotel in Tokyo

Minshuku, *family homes that take in guests, are excellent places to stay for independent visitors to Japan who are on a budget, and who want to gain an insight into Japanese life. Foreign guests are treated with real hospitality and warmth by their hosts, once they have established that their visitors respect and understand their customs.*

Enjoying a meal at a minshuku

MISO SOUP
Japanese meals of the type served at *minshuku* are usually accompanied by *miso* soup and are always served with rice. *Miso* is a very popular soup, which is also served for breakfast. Its base is a fish stock, made from the bonito, which is sold in dried flakes in every food store in Japan. This stock is then flavored with *miso* paste. Floating in the soup are small squares of *tofu* and strands of seaweed or finely chopped vegetables. In the Japanese manner, the soup is slurped with gusto from the bowl while the solid bits are held back with one's chopsticks. Rice is eaten with every meal, including breakfast.

At a *minshuku*, the most important things to remember are to leave your shoes at the door and not to soap yourself in the hot tub. You can learn other customs as you go along by being careful and observant.

Shoes In Japanese homes, *minshuku*, and other places such as temples, small hotels, and some restaurants, there are rituals attached to the wearing of shoes that need to be observed. On entering a home, leave your shoes in the hall (this is at a lower level than the house itself), then step up into the house and into a pair of slippers that has been placed out for the family and visitors. Wear these slippers unless you are invited to enter a room laid out with *tatami* (closely woven straw floor mats). At the entrance to such a room leave your slippers at the door and enter in your stockinged feet. At the entrance to the bathroom change your slippers for another pair (these are sometimes marked WC on the toe). Change back into the house slippers when you leave the bathroom. Never go into a bathroom barefoot.

Bathing For bathing you will be given a small towel and a cotton dressing gown (*yukata*). Undress in the space provided outside the bathroom. Take the small towel into the bathroom with you. Squat on the low stool placed outside the hot tub and scoop water from the tub over yourself with the small bowl provided; alternatively, use the shower that is set into the wall at knee height. Soap up the towel and use it to wash yourself, then shampoo, shave, and so on. Finally, shower or scoop water from the tub to rinse off all the soap and rinse out the towel. Now sit in the tub, soak and relax. Once out of the tub, wring out the towel and dry yourself with it, before dressing in your underclothes and the *yukata*. Use of the bath tub is generally restricted to particular times in the evening.

Other customs In a *minshuku* you are expected to set out your own futon and bedding, which will be found in a cupboard in your room. Both breakfast and supper are provided, and are served either in your room or in a communal dining area. It is normal for a mixed party of young people to share a room together: this is quite innocent and you will almost certainly be invited to join them for a beer and a chat. The house door is usually locked fairly early (around 11 PM).

Finding a *minshuku* Addresses and reservations for *minshuku* can be obtained from the information counters at most reasonably sized railroad stations. It is notoriously easy to get lost in Japanese cities, so ask the information clerk to write the address in Japanese on a piece of paper, take a cab and give this to the driver. Also ask the clerk to mark the location on a city map. A list of addresses and *minshuku* customs can be obtained from the Japan Minshuku Association, 1-19-5 Takadanobaba, Shinjuku-ku, Tokyo (tel: 03 3232-6561) or from JNTO.

JAPANESE TOILETS
Minshuku sometimes have only Japanese toilets, rather than the Western variety. They are squat, with a hood at one end (face this end). The cistern for flushing is filled through a faucet which issues water into a sink set over the cistern; wash your hands under this faucet. This ingenious flushing method saves both water and space.

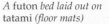

A futon *bed laid out on* tatami *(floor mats)*

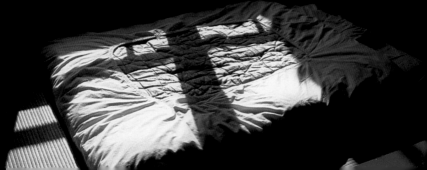

Ready to dig in to a bowl of noodles

ECONOMY
If you are traveling on a budget the following tips may help. Western-style foods such as bread, cake, and cheese are more expensive than traditional Japanese foods. Never order a meal before knowing the cost—only the most expensive restaurants do not display prices. Alcohol is expensive, sometimes exorbitantly so, in Japanese bars and clubs. To drink inexpensively, it is best to buy alcohol from a supermarket or slot machine and drink it in your hotel room. For snacking or self-catering, buy the made-up *bento* boxes of rice, pickles, fishcake, and so on sold in grocery stores. Finally, one of the many chains of hamburger places in Japan is always involved in a trade war with a competitor, so look for special, cheap offers.

Fast food in Shibuya

Food and drink

For Tokyoites, dining out is an integral part of everyday life, and many people eat more often in restaurants than they do at home. As a result, there is an enormous variety of eateries in Tokyo, with something to suit every taste and pocket.

This high density of restaurants, coupled with the size of the city, usually means that the most convenient way to eat out is to explore the area in the vicinity of your accommodations. Two notes of caution: first, avoid the places that provide only Western-style food, which tend to be expensive; secondly, the Japanese love to eat out and appreciate good food, but they are also happy to pay high prices for ambience and location. Before ordering a meal, always make sure that the price range of a restaurant suits you.

The menu Restaurants in tourist areas have menus written in both English and Japanese. Many restaurants also display plastic models of the dishes they serve that you can point to when ordering. One point worth noting is that the bowls in these displays indicate the country of origin of the food: a large bowl with a design around the rim holds a Chinese dish; smaller, plainer bowls contain Japanese cuisine; and a flat plate holds Western food.

Customs Once seated in the restaurant, you will be given *oshibori, o-hashi,* and *o-cha. Oshibori* are small, napkin-sized damp cloths, heated in cold weather and cold in hot weather. Use them to wipe your hands and face, and then as napkins during the meal. *O-hashi* are chopsticks. *O-cha,* or green tea, is an integral part of Japanese life. It is the common offering in restaurants, given out free when you arrive and at the end of the meal.

Places to eat The following are brief descriptions of the various types of Japanese eating establishments.

Sushi-ya, moderately priced *sushi* bars, are the most atmospheric and distinctive of all small Japanese restaurants. They sell rice delicately seasoned with vinegar, sugar, and salt, shaped into rolls, patties, balls, and so on, and topped and filled with slices of raw, boiled, or marinated fish, omelette, vegetables, and seaweed. They also sell *sashimi*, raw fish served without rice.

Soba-ya are noodle shops, one of the most common types of restaurant in Japan and one of the cheapest (see pages 84–85).

Nomi-ya are small, basic, local bars, recognizable by the large red lantern hanging outside. Mainly for drinking *sake* and beer, they also serve snacks and are relaxing places in which to sit and take time over a drink.

Koryori-ya serve a small menu of popular Japanese dishes such as seasonal fresh fish and vegetables. *Koryori-ya* are usually small, and each one has a couple of semi-private rooms with *tatami* (straw floor mats), perfect for an intimate, inexpensive dinner.

Chuka Ryori-ya are simple Chinese restaurants, often visited by Japanese families for a cheap meal. They sell Japanese versions of regular Chinese dishes.

Shokudo are small and inexpensive, and sell a selection of the most popular Japanese, Western, and Chinese dishes. They always display a complete menu of wax models outside. Their relaxed and friendly atmosphere makes them suitable for people traveling alone—and particularly popular with students.

At the counter in a noodle shop, one of Japan's original and enduringly popular fast-food outlets

SUSHI CHEFS

Sushi preparation is a performing art, and watching chefs assemble *sushi* on the other side of the bar is good entertainment. Chefs are incredibly deft and quick, and must remember the cost of each person's assortment of orders while preparing and serving the food. The comparative skills of neighboring *sushi* chefs is a popular topic of debate among connoisseurs.

Noodles—very cheap, fast, and tasty—are the original Japanese fast food. Quick-service noodle shops are found even in the smallest Japanese town. Many are just stands or small cafés, while others are more sophisticated establishments with jealously guarded reputations for the quality of their fresh noodles.

SPECIALIST NOODLES

Somen, a very fine wheat noodle used mostly in cold soups, is the only noodle included in traditional Shojin cookery, the vegetarian cuisine of Zen monasteries. In her book *Good Food from a Japanese Temple*, Soei Yoneda mentions that *somen*, in particular, is suited to "the cooking of nunneries having an Imperial Princess as abbess." Yellow *somen*, enriched with egg yolk, is called *tamago-somen*; green *somen*, flavored with green tea and called *cha-somen*, is also available in specialist noodle restaurants.

Above: soba *noodles on sale*
Below: a tempting noodle display

The basic noodle shop menu offers four or five different kinds of noodle, each served in a steaming hot soup with various garnishes on top. This is also the way noodles are cooked and served at home. The garnishes could be thin slices of pork, finely chopped leek, *tofu*, *nori* seaweed, *kamaboko* (fishcake), *tempura* (vegetables or fish in batter), or other traditional toppings, but connoisseurs tend to prefer good-quality fresh noodles served in a broth, with a little finely chopped scallion sprinkled over the top—or on their own, with a dipping sauce.

Noodle types Noodles are not differentiated by their shape, as is pasta, but by their ingredients. There are, in fact, only two distinct types: those made with buckwheat flour and those made with wheat flour. The former, called *soba* noodles, are most popular in Tokyo and northern Japan, where the colder climate suits the cultivation of the hardy buckwheat; they are light to dark gray in color, firm and thin in shape. The most common wheat flour noodle is *udon*, which is soft in texture, flat and round. Other types are the very fine *somen*, the slightly thicker *hiyamugi*, and the wide, long, and flat *kishimen*. Wheat noodles are white in color and are favored in Japan's wheat-growing areas, which stretch south from Osaka. One other popular type, though not traditional, is *ramen*, a Chinese egg noodle. (The Japanese roll their "r," even bounce it. If you can't do this, ask for "*damen*" when ordering.)

A big helping of noodles for a small mouth

Soba noodles *Soba* is the earliest known variety of Japanese noodle, popular with noodle lovers. Buckwheat was originally made into a gruel, but in 17th-century Edo (Tokyo) a monk called Ganchin discovered that if he mixed wheat and buckwheat flours he was able to make a dough that could be cut into noodles that held their shape. Soba noodles became the fashion and there are many references to them in the literature of the time. The best *soba* was (and still is) *ni-hachi* or "two-eight," meaning two parts wheat flour to eight parts buckwheat. Nowadays, *soba* is served hot or cold, in a broth or with a dipping sauce on the side. Cold *zaru-soba* is served on bamboo lattice baskets, set in a square wooden frame. *Cha-soba*, or green tea *soba*, is made by mixing powdered tea with the buckwheat dough; recognizable by its distinctive green color, it is often served cold. *Udon*, wheat-flour noodles, are often served hot with tempura. *Udon* and *soba* are interchangeable in practically all dishes.

The art of slurping Eating noodles in the Japanese fashion requires that you abandon what you usually think of as good table manners. This involves sucking them fast into your mouth, hot and straight out of the broth, while simultaneously drawing in a cooling intake of breath. The result, if done properly, is a loud slurping noise. Once the noodles are finished, the remaining soup is sucked straight from the bowl with equal noise and gusto. For a Westerner, trained to eat quietly, this requires shedding a lifetime's conditioning. For practice without embarrassment, go to any noodle shop in Japan at lunchtime, where you can consume a bowl of steaming noodles among the crowd of customers, with accompanying slurping noises, and not be noticed.

POPULAR NOODLE ORDERS
Kake-soba: noodles in broth with chopped leek garnishing, basic and cheap.
Zaru-soba: plain noodles served as cha-soba.
Kitsune-soba or *udon:* noodles in broth with fried *tofu* and leek garnish.
Tempura-soba or *udon:* noodles in broth with *tempura* and leek garnish.
Nabe-yake udon: vegetables, *tempura*, egg, and noodles cooked in an earthenware pot.
Ramen: Chinese noodles in pork broth with sliced pork topping and leek or spinach garnish.

A temple tourist shop

GIFTS
Choosing from the immense range of options is the biggest problem when buying gifts. Popular items include kitchen knives, paper goods, Japanese pottery, chinaware, chopsticks, fabrics, lacquerware, dolls, or cloisonné (fine wire patterned onto a metal base, with a fired glass finish filling the spaces). The following stores sell traditional folk arts and crafts: **Bingoya**, 10-6 Wakamatsu-cho, open Tuesday–Sunday 10–7 (the nearest subway station is Akebonobashi, a 15-minute walk away); and **Oriental Bazaar**, 5-9-13 Jingu-mae, open Friday–Wednesday 9:30–6:30 (the nearest subway stations are Harajuku or Meiji Jingu-mae, each a few minutes' walk away).

Shopping

Tokyo stores are wonderful, not only for the amazing range of goods available but also for the quality of the service. White-gloved, kimono-clad ladies welcome you into the better shops and department stores. Inside, the assistants are polite and helpful, and will wrap even the smallest purchase, as though it were a precious stone.

Department stores For presents or souvenirs, it is best to go to a department store (*depato*). This will save you a lot of walking, and the vast range of merchandise offers plenty of ideas. Each store is a self-contained world, in which all human needs, from baby clothes to funeral arrangements, are politely and enthusiastically looked after. Each store has a particular style and price range. But even the medium to cheap stores have service and goods of an excellent standard.

Some of the best-known department stores include: **Mitsukoshi**, 1-7-4 Nihonbashi Muromachi, Chuo-ku, which has its own subway station; **Seibu**, 21-1 Udagawa-cho, Shibuya-ku, one of the most innovative and modern (visit the separate hardware section called Loft and the basement food hall); **Wako**, 4-5-11 Ginza, Chuo-ku, an exclusive and expensive shop with an amazing range of watches, known for its prewar clock tower, a favorite meeting place for couples; and **Takashimaya**, 2-4-1 Nihonbashi, Chuo-ku, the flagship of Tokyo's department stores, with opulent décor to match the vast array of famous designer goods. Most are in the Ginza district.

Fashion and electronics Fashion buildings provide several floors of fashion boutiques, restaurants, bars, and other facilities. The best known are **Axis** 5-17-1 Roppongi, Minato-ku; **Parco**, 15-1 Udagawa-cho, Shibuya-ku; and **La Foret** (for everything a teenager may wish to buy), 1-11-6 Jingu-mae, Shibuya-ku. **Tokyo Hands**, 12-18 Udagawa-cho, Shibuya-ku, is an astonishing hardware store, said to have over 3 million different items for sale. **Wave**, 6-2-21 Roppongi, Minato-ku, is a "concept retailing outlet," with several floors of audio and visual software, such as video tapes and disks, compact disks, sheet music and books (also see Sony Building, page 54).

Teapots for sale

Japan is a world leader in electronic goods, but they are often more expensive in Tokyo than elsewhere. There is, however, an incredible variety of goods available, and the latest models and innovative equipment are often for sale in the showrooms several months earlier than anywhere else in the world. Go to Akihabara subway station and simply choose one of the nearby stores (as in North America, Japanese voltage is 100V., so you might not need an export model).

Tax-free As a visitor to Japan, you can buy tax-free goods in any store that displays a "Tax-free" sign—most major department stores, hotel malls, and specialist shops in tourist areas offer this facility. Savings range between 5 and 40 percent. Take your passport with you to the shop; export forms detailing the goods you have bought will be attached to it. Customs officers may want to see the goods when you leave Japan. Precious stones, electrical goods, cameras and watches are the types of items usually available. In large cities like Tokyo, you'll find similar goods in discount stores at reduced or even lower prices.

OPENING HOURS AND SALES

Department stores, and most other retailers, open at 10 AM, and usually close at 7 PM (family-run shops vary widely). Department stores are closed one day a week, and for the New Year (January 1–2). Discounts of 30–50 percent are common during the summer (mid-July to end August) and New Year (January 3 to mid-February) main sales.

87

A trendy shopping mall in Shibuya

Japan's long traditions of artisanry have come to define its culture, not only within the nation itself but worldwide. Among the better known of the fine arts are ukiyo-e *(woodblock prints of the Edo period), calligraphy, and* ikebana, *the highly skilled art of flower-arranging. The performing arts are defined by* noh *theater,* kabuki, *and* bunraku, *while pottery, ceramics, sword-making, and lacquerware are the best known of the Japanese crafts.*

THE ZEN OF CRAFT
In Japanese arts and crafts, the artist or crafts-man struggles to extract the essence, or true personality, of the form or material used. The motive is not to dominate the medium, but to work with its nature. Realism, rather than romanticism, is usually the byword.

Traditional tea house with tatami *(straw floor mats),* matcha *(powdered green tea), and a contemplative atmosphere*

Under the banner of *mingeihan*, crafts of the people, many less well-known Japanese craft skills are practiced. In dance and music traditional forms are still maintained and performed, while in the arts of *chanoyu* (the tea ceremony), bonsai, and garden design the Japanese exemplify their love of artifice, nature, and ritual. The source of this rich heritage is that idiosyncratic Japanese mix of Zen simplicity and Shinto nature worship, together with a class system that ensured the continuity of the master-and-apprentice relationship through many generations.

Woodblock printing *Ukiyo-e* ("images of a floating, transient world") was a school of painters in the 18th and 19th centuries who gave new life to the art of woodblock printing. Renowned for their realism, bold designs, and striking colors, they were led by four great masters: Utamaro, Sharaku, Hokusai, and Hiroshige, "discovered" by Europeans in the late 19th century (see panel, page 60).

Theater *Noh* is a stylized dance drama performed to the accompaniment of music and singing. On a stark stage, actors wear masks and gorgeous, elaborate costumes. Movement is slow and the storyline conveyed by a symbolism sometimes difficult for foreigners to understand. However, *noh* does provide an insight into the contemplative nature of Japanese arts.

Kabuki (see pages 58–59) allows only male actors, who play both male and female roles. They wear traditional costume, and the plays depict either the lives of ordinary people or those of the noble classes in a Japan of earlier times. The dialogue and gestures used to convey the stories are formalized, but there is an energy, color, and accessibility in *kabuki* missing from *noh* theater.

In *bunraku* (puppet theater), the main characters are life-like puppets, manipulated by as many as three puppeteers. The stories told are similar to *kabuki* tales: the scripts are traditional and usually well known by the audience. Osaka is considered the birthplace and capital of *bunraku* theater (see page 119), although first-class performances are also given in theaters in Tokyo and Kyoto.

The tea ceremony In the authentic setting of a tea garden, the tea ceremony (*sado*), combines the spirit of a religious service with the style of a performing art, and

**THE RITUAL OF
TEA-MAKING**
Before the arrival of
guests to a tea ceremony,
a room or tea house over-
looking a garden is set
aside and thoroughly
cleaned. Utensils are
polished, flowers are
arranged, and the garden
is swept. When the guests
arrive, conversation is
quiet and contemplative.
With deft, practiced movements, the host spoons
the green powdered tea
and hot water into each
guest's cup and whisks it
into a foam. As each
guest sips tea, comment
may be passed on the
beauty of the tea cups
and other utensils as they
are handed around for
appreciation. Guests may
also express their grati-
tude to the host and
mention the delights of
the garden or other natu-
ral phenomena such as
the sky or moon (see also
pages 126–127).

perhaps it best encapsulates all the elements of the
Japanese artistic sensibility. At its deepest level, "the
way of tea" aspires to create such an atmosphere of
harmony and tranquility that the participants will experience the same qualities in their own hearts and minds.
Tea ceremonies are held in Tokyo and Kyoto for *gai-jin*
(foreigners). In this context they are usually rather
perfunctory affairs, but nevertheless interesting, and
the green tea provides an unexpected buzz!

Kabuki *theater*

DISCOS

Entry fees are high for discos, but the price often includes drinks and simple food. Dress is usually formal and the better discos do not welcome unaccompanied males. Roppongi district has many discos, as well as live music dance clubs.

THE REAL THING

Although selling sex is illegal in Japan, what constitutes sex is narrowly defined. Only if male and female sex organs actually connect is it deemed "honban"—the real thing. This law, together with the fact that condoms are the most popular form of contraception, has helped to seriously reduce the incidence of AIDS in Japan.

90

A Tokyo nightclub

Nightlife

Tokyo's nightlife is lively, and many members of the working population go straight from the office to a bar or club for a drink and a chat before either going home or continuing an evening's carousing. The night starts early, at about 6 PM, and, for most, ends before midnight.

After midnight, night owls and young people about town head for Roppongi, where the clubs and discos stay open until the early hours of the morning. The Ginza, Asakusa, and Akasaka districts provide everything from neon-lit dazzle to the traditional singing, dancing, and *samisen*- (lute-) playing of kimono-clad *geisha*. Massage parlors, sleazy bars, and strip joints cluster in Shinjuku, especially its Kabuki-cho area, and the smaller Dogenzaka in Shibuya. These places are expensive and not aesthetically pleasing, but even here you do not need to worry unduly about physical safety or theft.

For cinema, theater, and other cultural events, the monthly *Tokyo Journal*, available in hotels, at the city Tourist Information Center (TIC) offices, or English-language bookshops, gives comprehensive details of performances, as well as restaurant reviews and up-to-the-minute information on events of interest to English-speaking foreigners.

Music Jazz, introduced into Japan during the 1930s and reintroduced after the war by G.I.s, remains very popular. A number of Tokyo jazz clubs feature live jazz, ranging from Dixieland to avant-garde. Japanese jazz fans are knowing and dedicated. Japanese and Western pop and rock is found widely in clubs and at concert venues. Classical concerts are available most nights, with performances by visiting orchestras or one of the many based in Tokyo. Details are given in the *Tokyo Journal*.

Practical

Before going to Japan, contact the nearest Japanese National Tourist Organization office (see page 264) and ask for tourist maps of Japan and Tokyo. If you do not book a hotel in Tokyo in advance, arrive in the city before 5 PM in time to visit a Travel Information Center (TIC) office—there is one at Narita Airport and one in the city center—where you can get help in finding a place to stay.

Information As soon as you arrive in Tokyo obtain, either from the TIC office or from any large railroad station, an English-language subway map. This is essential. Before deciding what to do in the city, get a free copy of *Tour Companion*, a weekly English-language newspaper for tourists, and buy a copy of the monthly *Tokyo Journal*. Both these publications contain details of current events, and both are available at TIC offices and large hotels. For taped information (in English) on current events, phone 3503-2911. The Tokyo English Life Line, on 5721-4347, helps with problems. For advice and information on hotels, restaurants, etc., contact the TIC office.

Getting about Driving a car in Tokyo is no fun. Driving is on the left, and traffic is dense and parking expensive and difficult. Buses are slow because of the heavy traffic, and destination signs are shown only in Japanese. Train and subway networks are fast, efficient, clean, and comprehensive, in terms of the places you may wish to visit. Services operate from the very early morning to around midnight. After this time, you can rely on a good taxi service (11 PM–5 AM a 20 percent surcharge is payable so make sure the driver is clear about your destination). See pages 92–93 and 252–254 for more tips on public transportation.

Even taxi rides can be slow in Tokyo

Subway signs

Shinjuku, Ueno, and Tokyo stations are the three busiest stations in Tokyo, handling over 3 million passengers a day commuting within the city and traveling to places all over Japan.

THE TOKAIDO SANYO LINE

The Tokaido Sanyo Shinkansen train service opened in 1964, just before the Tokyo Olympics. At that time, it linked Tokyo and Osaka, a distance of 345 miles (552km), and followed for most of its length the route of the old Tokaido post road between Edo (old Tokyo) and Kyoto. Nowadays, the line reaches Fukuoka (Hakata station), on the southern island of Kyushu. Trains leave Tokyo station three or four times an hour for the 668-mile (1,069-km), six-hour journey.

Shinkansen (bullet trains) grinding to a halt …

Shinjuku station This is said to be the world's biggest and busiest station. It serves nine railroad and subway lines, as well as accommodating huge complexes of shops and restaurants, both above and under the ground. There are few signs in English. Shinjuku station is the equivalent of a small city; any visitor who masters it will be able to use the city's other stations with ease.

Shinjuku has two wings, divided by two long parallel passageways, off which runs a maze of underground shopping parades. Subway and surface lines run into the station for both private lines and Japanese Railways (JR itself is no longer owned by the state, but private). If it is necessary to change from a private line to a JR line, you must go out through a ticket barrier, find your next train's line, and purchase a new ticket (this is not needed if you change lines within the same company's network). To buy a ticket, find the correct train or subway line, then use the ticket machine nearest that line's entrance. If you make a mistake (and it is easy to do so, as the signs and instructions are sometimes only in *kanji*), there is a refund office—but it is not easy to find. If you do not know how much your ticket will be, buy the cheapest and pay the excess at your destination.

If you get lost, take your time to wander around until you find a signpost in English to help get your bearings. The ticket collectors at the barrier gates are also very helpful

92

and used to dealing with bewildered travelers. Avoid Shinjuku if you have a busy timetable. Otherwise, you can happily enjoy it as a place of interest in its own right. On a rainy day, Shinjuku is a good place for experiencing the lively hustle and bustle of Japanese urban life.

Tokyo station Housed in an old red-brick building, Tokyo station was designed by Kingo Tatsuno, one of Japan's first modern architects. It was completed in 1914, damaged by wartime bombing, and restored in 1954. A new east extension containing the Daimaru department store was added two years later, and there are current plans to renovate and remodel the original building. The bus stop for the Tokyo City Air Terminal (TCAT), where you can check in luggage for some international flights before taking a coach to Narita Airport, is located outside the south exit of the station. Buses leave here for Narita Airport.

Maruno-uchi, the district to the west side of Tokyo station, is a major business center. Its name means roughly "within the castle compound"; this area was once within the walls of the Shogun's castle. From Maruno-uchi central exit an avenue leads to the Imperial Palace grounds.

JR Ueno station The JR station at Ueno in northern Tokyo was the gateway to Japan's first public park, museum, and zoo, and remains the exit and arrival point for travelers to and from Japan's northern provinces. It was completed in 1883 and became a focal point for people migrating to Tokyo from villages in Tohoku to the north. Ueno-Hirokoji, the main thoroughfare of Ueno, runs from the Shinobazu exit (south side) of JR Ueno station. It is lined with restaurants, stores, and discount shops, and the back alleys are teeming with small places to eat and drink.

… and speeding off

TRAVEL BY SHINKANSEN
Shinkansen (bullet-train) platforms at Tokyo and JR Ueno stations are divided into car-length spaces, and above the exact place that each car's door will be there hangs a numbered plate. This relates to the passenger's ticket, and you should wait in the appropriate place, as the Shinkansen pulls into and out of the station within the space of five minutes.

LEAVING TOKYO
JR trains to the Japan Alps (Matsumoto) use Shinjuku station, while the JR Shinkansen and JR express trains on the Tokaido line (to Nagoya, Kyoto, Kobe, Osaka, Hiroshima, and the island of Kyushu) use Tokyo station. The JR Shinkansen and express trains on the Tohoku line use Ueno station, as do the JR Shinkansen and express trains on the Joetsu line and the direct Shinkansen line to Nagano.

Central Honshu

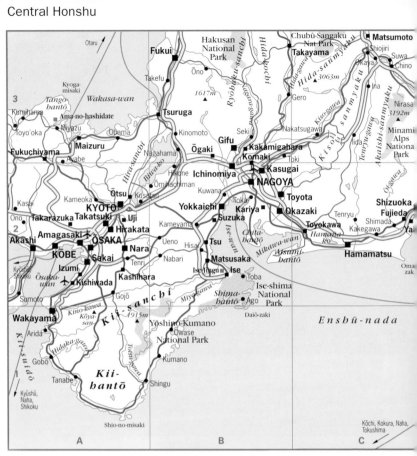

Grandeur reflected: Mount Fuji

94

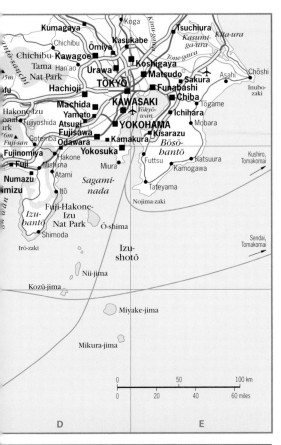

Koga
Kumagaya
Chichibu
Tsuchiura
Kasumi-
ga-ura
Kita-ura
Ōmiya
Kasukabe
Chichibu-Kawagoe
Tama
Nat Park
Han'ao
Koshigaya
Tone-gawa
Urawa
Matsudo
Sakura
Asahi
Chōshi
TŌKYŌ
Funabashi
Inubo-
zaki
Hachioji
Machida
Chiba
Yamato
KAWASAKI
Tōgame
Atsugi
Ichihara
Fujisawa
YOKOHAMA
Mobara
Odawara
Kisarazu
Kamakura
Bōsō-
bantō
Yokosuka
Fujinomiya
Hakone
Miura
Futtsu
Katsuura
Kushiro,
Tomakomai
Fuji
Mishima
Kamogawa
Numazu
Atami
Sagami-
nada
mizu
Itō
Tateyama
Nojima-zaki
Fuji-Hakone-
Izu
Izu-
bantō
Nat Park
Ō-shima
Shimoda
Irō-zaki
Izu-
shotō
Sendai,
Tomakomai
Nii-jima
Kozū-jima
Miyake-jima
Mikura-jima

Fujiyoshida
Gotemba
Fuji-san

Kinu-gawa
Tōkyō-
wan

| 0 | | 50 | | 100 km |
| 0 | 20 | | 40 | 60 miles |

D   E

A deity guards the entrance (above) of Horyuji Temple in Nara (detail, below)

CENTRAL HONSHU With its heavy concentration of business, educational, and cultural activities, Central Honshu is second only to Tokyo in economic importance and density of population. Historically, it constitutes the geographical, cultural, and spiritual heart of Japan, containing within its boundaries the two ancient capital cities of Kyoto and Nara and the sacred mountain of Fuji-san. This chapter concentrates on the Fuji-Hakone-Izu and the Ise Shima National Parks and the cities of Osaka, Kobe, Nara, and Nagoya; for convenience of use and clarity, a separate chapter is devoted to Kyoto.

FUJI-HAKONE-IZU NATIONAL PARK Located 60 miles (96km) southwest of Tokyo, this is possibly the most popular excursion destination for residents of the capital, and it is flooded with visitors spring and summer. The park includes several distinct areas: Mount Fuji, the Fuji Five Lakes, the Izu Peninsula, and Hakone, a hot-spring resort area that lies within a 25-mile-(40-km-) diameter volcanic crater at the base of Mount Fuji.

OSAKA Japan's major port and center of commerce once had a reputation for being grimy, chaotic, and cramped. Some of that description still holds true, but Osaka is a city of immense energy, and the city fathers, with an eye to the economic and sociological importance of ecological issues, are spending considerable sums of money in an attempt to improve the city environment. Osaka is not a tourist town, nor are there many places of scenic or historic interest to visit, but for a keyhole view of real Japanese city life, and the closest there is to a working-class Japan, it should not be missed.

KOBE Osaka's main port, built on a hillside overlooking Osaka Bay, Kobe is a major industrial city, rivaling Yokohama as Japan's busiest port. Kobe has a long history as a harbor city, but real growth began in the late 19th century, when the port's docks were opened to foreign shipping. Western-style merchants' houses still stand in the Kitano district, and Kobe continues to be occupied by a substantial number of foreign residents. Despite the 1995 earthquake (see page 112), Kobe remains a modern, cosmopolitan, and sophisticated city, good for shopping, nightlife, and international cuisine.

NARA From AD 710 to 794, Nara was the first political and cultural center of a united Japan. The capital moved to Kyoto toward the end of the 8th century, and Nara slowly lapsed into relative obscurity. This was a blessing in disguise, as the city escaped much of the damage suffered by other cities in Japan's long civil wars. As a result, Nara and the monastery estates around it contain some of the best examples of traditional Japanese art and architecture. The sights may be roughly divided into two areas: those in and around Nara Park, a large but not particularly attractive park, well known for its sacred tame and sometimes pushy deer; and the southwest district of the city, where several major temples are situated. Contemporary Nara is a large city with a population of 300,000.

ISE-SHIMA NATIONAL PARK Located on the Shima Peninsula, which juts out into the Pacific Ocean, this park is the site of the Ise Shrine, the most venerated Shinto shrine in the whole of Japan. This is the symbolic home of Amaterasu, the sun goddess and ancestral divine spirit of the Japanese imperial line. The park itself stretches to the east from Ise to Toba, center of the pearl industry, then to the south to Kashikojima, famous for its coastline and pine-clad islands.

NAGOYA Japan's third largest city was flattened during World War II by Allied bombs, and rebuilt according to the best city planning theories of the time. As a result, Nagoya is architecturally sterile and uninteresting—an agreeable place to live, but not necessarily to visit. It is, however, a central location for excursions to other towns and areas, especially Gifu for its cormorant fishing.

KANSAI AND KANTO

For practical purposes, Central Honshu is a sensible description of the area covered in this chapter. However, in terms of the way the Japanese divide their country, it straddles two regions: Kansai and Kanto. Kansai, or "west of the barrier," refers to the region containing the cities of Osaka, Kobe, Nara, and Kyoto. Kanto, "east of the barrier," refers to the region around Tokyo. The "barrier" is an arbitrary division between Kansai and Kanto, made by the government in the 10th century and marked by three barrier stations along its length.

GETTING TO OSAKA

Osaka is connected to Tokyo by more than 100 express trains a day, and international flight connections between the cities are usually free. Prices are a little lower and hotel accommodations are easier to get here than in Kyoto or Tokyo, so it can be a convenient base for exploring Kyoto, Nara, and Kobe, all within half an hour of Osaka.

GETTING TO NARA

Nara tends to be a day-trips city, but a two-day visit is ideal. The JR Nara line connects Kyoto to Nara (68 minutes); trains run twice an hour. The JR Kansai line connects Osaka to Nara (30 minutes); trains run three times an hour. A city map and walk route is available from the tourist office in Kintetsu-Nara station (second floor). Kintetsu (a private railroad) services are quicker and more frequent than those of JR.

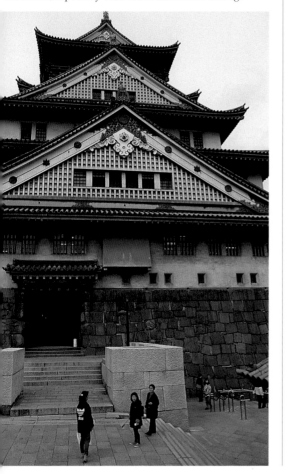

Osaka Castle

*Mount Fuji and
Lake Ashi*

BACK TO TOKYO
As an alternative to returning to Tokyo all the way by
bus, you can take a bus
from Kawaguchi-ko to
Mishima. The scenic bus
circles Mount Fuji in two
hours. From Mishima it is
just over one hour by bullet
train to Tokyo.

Fuji-Hakone-Izu National Park

This area of crater lakes, volcanic mountain ranges, hot
springs, and beaches, 63 miles (100km) southwest of
Tokyo, is the most heavily visited national park in Japan.
The original wildness of the habitat has been sacrificed to
some extent to the needs of tourists, but it is still a beautiful area. Indeed, the Japanese believe that the symmetrical
reflection of Mount Fuji (*Fuji-san*) in the calm surface of
Lake Ashi is *the* most beautiful sight in the world. The
park can be divided into four distinct areas. Although a
grand tour of all of them at once is possible, many visitors
prefer to make separate excursions from Tokyo. On pages
101, 102–103, and 108–109 three of the areas—Mount Fuji,
Hakone, and the Izu Peninsula (*Izu-hanto*)—are described
individually; the fourth, the Fuji Five lakes, is described
below. Throughout spring and summer, the whole park is
crowded with visitors, but at other times, partly as a
result of the colder weather, it is relatively quiet. See map
on page 100.

▶▶ Fuji Five Lakes (Fuji-Go-ko)   *100A6*

Kawaguchi-ko▶▶, on the southeastern shore of Lake
Kawaguchi, is the area's transportation center, served by
train and bus from Tokyo and from other regions of the
national park. Buses also go from Kawaguchi-ko station
to the other four lakes. The town itself is a busy resort
with a mix of *ryokan*, hotels, restaurants, bars, and
souvenir shops. A 10-minute walk from the station leads

to the shore of Lake Kawaguchi, and fine views of the lake and Mount Fuji there are from the observation tower at the top of Mount Tenjo, reached by a ropeway (cable-car) operating from the lakeside near the station. From the nearby pier, boats offer 30-minute tours of the lake. Other attractions are the Fuji Museum on the north shore (*open 8:30–4*), an odd mix of geology and history exhibits and a display of erotica, and the Fuji-kyu Highland Amusement Park, one train stop from Kawaguchi-ko station. Lake Kawaguchi is the most developed and visited of the five lakes.

Lake Shoji (Shoji-ko)▶▶▶ opens on its southeast side toward a glorious view of Mount Fuji, while the other three sides are secluded and enclosed by wooded mountains. The smallest of the lakes, and considered by many to be the prettiest, this is the starting point for the Shoji Trail, which leads through *Jukai*, "the Sea of Trees" (see panel), all the way to the summit of Mount Fuji. Lake Shoji is 50 minutes by bus from Kawaguchi-ko station. Ice-skating on the lake and fishing (through holes made in the ice) are very popular winter activities for visitors to the area.

Asahigaoka, a commercial district on the southern shore of **Lake Yamanaka (Yamanaka-ko)▶**, the largest of the lakes, is 35 minutes by bus from Kawaguchi-ko. Favored by affluent young Tokyoites, the lake shore is heavily developed with fashionable restaurants, expensive hotels, college and company clubhouses, and villas. Cruise boats from Asahigaoka offer short tours of the lake.

Lake Sai (Sai-ko)▶, the third largest lake, lies to the west of Kawaguchi-ko, 25 minutes away by bus. The lakeside is only moderately developed and, apart from hiking, there is little to do.

The westernmost and deepest of the five lakes is **Lake Motosu (Motosu-ko)▶**. It never freezes over, and is renowned for its beautiful blue waters and fine trout. The bus stop on the eastern shore is 50 minutes from Kawaguchi-ko. Aside from the souvenir shops in the immediate vicinity of the bus stop, the lake shore and surroundings are quiet.

SEA OF TREES
Called the *Jukai* in Japanese, this area is a part of the Aokigahara Forest, between lakes Sai and Shoji. The trees survive on a thin layer of volcanic soil covering a field of lava, which is magnetic and distorts compasses. This makes it easy to get lost and difficult to find if you are. Fortunately, you can pick up a marked nature trail at the Fugaku Fuketsu (lava caves) near the Fuketsu bus stop, 40 minutes from Kawaguchi-ko bus station (platform 6).

GETTING TO HAKONE OR IZU PENINSULA
To go to Hakone from Kawaguchi-ko, take the bus to Gotemba. Change at Sengoku for Hakone-Yumoto or Togendai in the Hakone region. The Izu Peninsula is reached by bus from Mishima (see **Back to Tokyo** panel, opposite page).

Lake Yamanaka

Central Honshu

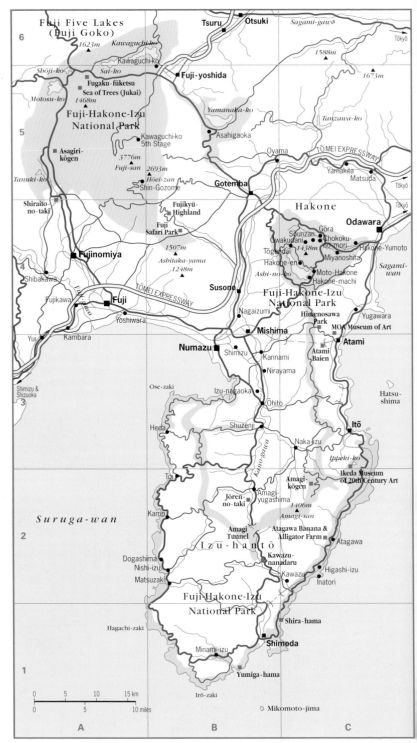

Fuji Five Lakes
(Fuji Goko)

1623m
Kawaguchi-ko
Shōji-ko
Fugaku-fūketsu
Sea of Trees (Jukai)
1468m
Motosu-ko
Fuji-Hakone-Izu
National Park
Tanuki-ko
Asagiri-
kōgen
3776m
Fuji-san
2693m
Hōei-zan
Shin-Gozome
Shiraito-
no-taki
Fujikyū-
Highland
Fuji
Safari Park
Fujinomiya
1507m
Ashitaka-yama
1248m
Shibakawa
Fujikawa
TŌMEI EXPRESSWAY
Fuji
Yoshiwara
Yui
Kambara
Shimizu &
Shizuoka
Ose-zaki
Heda
Toi
Kamo
Dogashima
Nishi-izu
Matsuzaki
Suruga-wan
Hagachi-zaki
Minami-izu

Tsuru
Otsuki
Sagami-gawa
Tōkyō
Kawaguchi-ko
1588m
Fuji-yoshida
1673m
Yamanaka-ko
Tanzawa-ko
Asahigaoka
Oyama
TŌMEI EXPRESSWAY
Kawaguchi-ko
5th Stage
Yamakita
Matsuda
Gotemba
Tōkyō
Hakone
Odawara
Sounzan
Gōra
Ōwakudani
Chokoku-
no-mori
Hakone-Yumoto
Tōgendai
1438m
Miyanoshita
Hakone-en
Moto-Hakone
Ashi-no-ko
Hakone-machi
Sagami-
wan
Susono
Fuji-Hakone-Izu
National Park
Nagaizumi
Himenosawa
Park
MOA Museum of Art
Yugawara
Mishima
Atami
Numazu
Shimizu
Kannami
Atami
Baien
Nirayama
Izu-nagaoka
Ōhito
Hatsu-
shima
Shuzenji
Itō
Naka-izu
Ippeki-ko
Ikeda Museum
of 20th Century Art
Amagi-
kōgen
Jōren-
no-taki
Amagi-
yugashima
1406m
Amagi-san
Amagi
Tunnel
Atagawa Banana &
Alligator Farm
Atagawa
Izū-hantō
Kawazu-
nanadaru
Higashi-izu
Kawazu
Inatori
Fuji-Hakone-Izu
National Park
Shira-hama
Shimoda
Yumiga-hama
Irō-zaki
Mikomoto-jima

0   5   10   15 km
0   5   10 miles

Mount Fuji (Fuji-san) is a perfectly shaped volcanic cone, that rises to a 12,388-foot (3,776-m) peak. It is the highest and most popular mountain in Japan, praised by poets throughout the ages and portrayed in numerous paintings and prints. The summit is often covered with clouds, but on a clear day you can see it from 100 miles (160km) away.

Hokusai (1760–1849), the famous *ukiyo-e* painter, immortalized the mountain in two series of woodblock prints featuring Fuji-san in all its moods: *Thirty-Six Views of Mount Fuji* and *One Hundred Views of Mount Fuji.*

The ascent Most people climb Mount Fuji in the hope of witnessing a sunrise from the top. This means either climbing overnight or climbing during the day and staying on the summit overnight in a mountain hut. It is an arduous climb and, once past the tree line, the mountain at close quarters is not beautiful. The rock is black and volcanic and there is no vegetation. Only the view (if there is no cloud) lifts the spirits. The Japanese say that to climb *Fuji-san* once is wise, but to climb it twice is foolish.

Mount Fuji is open to the public for climbing from July 1 to August 31, and every year up to 400,000 people make the ascent along one of the five trails marked off at 10 stations or stages (levels). Kawaguchi-ko 5th Stage, which is halfway up, is the most popular starting level, and can be reached by bus. From Kawaguchi-ko the climb to the summit at a moderate pace is about seven hours; the descent takes half this time.

During the winter, Fuji is snow-covered from base to peak, and even in summer the summit is never clear of snow.

SACRED MOUNTAIN
A Shinto shrine to Konohana Sakuya Hime, a divine princess who is the spirit of the cherry blossom, is maintained on the summit of Mount Fuji. The mountain itself is considered sacred by Shintoists, and especially revered by a religious sect known as Fujiko. Pilgrims making the ascent dressed in traditional white tunics and gaiters are a regular sight. Women were not allowed on Mount Fuji or other sacred mountains until the Meiji Restoration (1868).

101

GETTING THERE
The easiest way to reach Kawaguchi-ko 5th Stage is by direct bus from either Hamamatsu-cho or Shinjuku bus terminal, in operation several times a day from July 9 to August 31. Less frequent bus services are also available from about the end of April to July and again during the months of September and October. Journey times are two and a half hours from Shinjuku and three hours from Hamamatsu-cho.

Opposite: map showing Fuji-Hakone-Izu National Park

Hakone Komagatake Ropeway, with Mount Fuji in the distance

Contemplating the view at Lake Ashino

HAKONE SHRINE

The Hakone Shrine was founded in 757 in Moto-Hakone, one of the busiest tourist towns in the Hakone area. A red *torii* (gate) out in the lake provides an obvious landmark and a huge Japanese cedar tree (*Cryptomeria*), encircled by a sacred rope, sits in the forecourt. Known as *Yatate no sugi* ("standing arrow cedar"), the tree marks the spot where generals fighting battles in the area offered arrows to the gods. The shrine is also famous as the site of an act of filial piety by the two Soga brothers, medieval warriors who earned fame for their military exploits. In the past, *samurai* would come here to venerate the spirits of these men of honor.

▶▶▶ Hakone   100C4

Lying between Mount Fuji and the ocean in Fuji-Hakone-Izu National Park, Hakone is an area of high mountains (most over 4,000 feet/1,220m), with Lake Ashi nestling in the center and Mount Fuji nearly always in view to the northwest. This is a popular day-trip from Tokyo, and in summer trains, cable cars, buses, and accommodations, in the region are heavily used. However, Hakone's beautiful scenery, its closeness to Tokyo, and its network of public transportation make it a very convenient place to explore.

Traveling to Hakone There is an "Odakyu Sightseeing Service Centre" offering travel advice to individual foreign tourists traveling to the Hakone area at the Odakyu Shinjuku station (tel: 03 5321 7887). The cheapest way to get to and around Hakone is to buy the Hakone Free Pass, or the Q tour package, available from the Odakyu ticket office in Shinjuku station. From Shinjuku station in Tokyo, take the Odakyu private railroad to Odawara (one hour, 25 minutes). If you travel in the more expensive "Romance Car," with its comfortable seating and viewing windows, go one stop farther to Hakone-Yumoto. This is the oldest of Hakone's spa towns, with a famous *senninburo* ("thousand-people baths") in the center. From here or Odawara, take the Hakone Tozan Tetsudo line for Gora. The train travels up steep mountainsides; with each switchback the views increase in grandeur. One of the

Shrine detail, Hakone

earlier stops is **Miyanoshita▶**, a more sophisticated, smaller resort than Hakone-Yumoto. Farther along the line is **Chokoku-no-mori▶▶** and the Hakone Open-Air Museum (*open* daily 9–4:30), with Western and Japanese sculpture in an open, cliffside setting. The train terminus is at **Gora▶**, a town popular with hikers and climbers. Transfer to the cable-car up to Sounzan. Here transfer to the Hakone Ropeway, the longest gondola ride in Japan (33 minutes). Some way out of Sounzan the ropeway crests a ridge and suddenly you are suspended over the **Owakudani Gorge (Great Boiling Valley)▶▶▶**, hundreds of feet below. From the gorge floor sulfurous steam spurts out of cracks in the earth and clouds of reeking fumes hover in the air. If you ask the conductor, you can get off at **Owakudani▶▶**, the next stop and the ropeway's highest point. Here you can take a hike along a nature trail and visit the Natural Science Museum (*open* daily 9–5).

The ropeway finally descends to Togendai on the shores of **Lake Ashi▶▶▶**. From here, cruise boats travel to Hakone-machi. Look for reflections of the surrounding mountains, particularly Mount Fuji, in the lake surface. The mountains bloom with cherry blossoms in April, azaleas in May and June, and red maple leaves in the fall.

Historical route The old Tokaido Road between Kyoto and Edo (old Tokyo) ran through Hakone, and one of the most important barrier gates was in **Hakone-machi▶▶** (see pages 104–105). The Barrier Guardhouse (Hakone Sekisho) has been reconstructed, and some of the narrow, cobbled Tokaido is preserved. A short walk from where the boat docks, the guardhouse and exhibition hall display mannequins of guards and travelers, samurai armor and weapons, and macabre early photographs of crucified and beheaded criminals. For a feeling of old Japan, walk down the nearby tree-lined stretch of the old Tokaido. A bus service runs from Hakone-machi to Hakone-Yumoto (50 minutes) and on to Odawara (one hour). From here, take the Odakyu line back to Tokyo.

VOLCANOES
The Japanese islands lie in the volcanic zone that surrounds the Pacific Rim, and cataclysmic eruptions have always affected the lives of Japanese people. Physically, many volcanoes here are shaped like a cone with a wide base (*Fuji-san* is the best-known example). They are formed by a build-up of layers of lava issuing from an erupting crater. The death and life brought by volcanoes and their imposing presence on the landscape have always given them an elevated place in the Shinto pantheon of divine spirits (*kami*). Many traditions and festivals designed to appease them are still maintained.

103

Mount Fuji provides a dramatic backdrop to Lake Ashi

ROAD SIGNS
As the remaining short stretch of the original Tokaido Road shows, the Tokaido was not very wide and, because no carts used it, was unpaved. Distances were carefully marked, as this quote from a 17th-century Portuguese traveler illustrates: "There is no need to enquire about distances because all the leagues are measured out, with a mound and two trees to mark the end of each one. Should it happen that a league ends in the middle of a street, they will do no man a favor by making the measurement either longer or shorter, but pull down the houses there in order to set up the sign."

Sankin kotai required each of the feudal lords, or *daimyo*, of Japan's noble families to build a substantial home in Edo (old Tokyo) and to spend alternate years in residence there while in attendance at the *shogun's* court. The year in between was to be spent on the noble's own estates. Close family members of the *daimyo* were restricted at all times to their homes in Edo and the surrounding district. At one stroke, the *shogun* ensured that at any one time half his feudal lords were under his eye at court and for the rest of the time he could, if need be, hold their families hostage. He also required that on his journey from his estate to Edo each *daimyo* should have a stipulated entourage of soldiers, ladies-in-waiting, servants, and craftsmen. The size of the entourage was directly proportional to the size of the *daimyo's* estate, and the outlay required to pay for it was designed to ensure the *daimyo* never had enough money to finance a rebellion.

The Tokaido Road This law also meant that *daimyo* had to travel between their estates and Edo once a year. There were five main routes radiating from Edo, and the Tokaido, which followed the eastern seaboard to Kyoto, was the most traveled. It was used not only by nobles from the western provinces but also by normal traffic journeying between the seat of government and Kyoto, the home of the emperor and the religious capital of the land.

The Tokaido followed the coast from Edo to Yokkaichi before striking inland to Kyoto via Kameyama, Otsu, and the southern end of Lake Biwa. The scenery along the way was both picturesque and rugged: open sea, landlocked bays, distant mountains (including Mount Fuji), high cliffs, paddy fields, and many towns and villages all came in and out of view along the route. These changing

Hiroshige's changing seasons on the Tokaido

landscapes and colors and the human traffic on the road were the inspiration for Hiroshige, the great *ukiyo-e* painter, in his work *Views from the Fifty-Three Stations of the Tokaido*.

Noble progress The journey of a great lord along the Tokaido was an impressive sight. Nobles were carried in beautifully lacquered palanquins. Attendants bore aloft colorful banners, and the marching men and *samurai* on horseback wore full uniform. The whole effect was designed to illustrate the power and authority of the lord.

A noble procession was heralded well in advance so that post stations and inns could prepare beforehand for the extra provisions, horses, and accommodations that would be required. Other travelers who knew of it would also stay clear of the road, both for their own safety and in order not to hinder the progress of the lordly person-age. The procession was preceded by horsemen, who would shout "Down! down!" and people of inferior rank were required to prostrate themselves on the ground as the *daimyo* passed. Anyone foolish enough to show disrespect and refuse to pay homage in this way was literally chopped down by one of the *samurai* escorting the lord.

Barrier gates Barriers such as the Hakone barrier gate ensured that none of the *daimyo* could move any of their families out of Edo without permission. This applied especially to womenfolk, and any woman traveling with a procession was subjected to the closest scrutiny. As well as discouraging travel, the system also gave rise to many Japanese stories of intrigue, adventure, and thwarted love.

ARISTOCRATIC TRAFFIC
Carriages drawn by oxen were the sole privilege of the imperial court and would usually only be seen in and around Kyoto. If a *daimyo's* procession leaving the Tokaido crossed the path of the carriage of an aristocrat from the Imperial Palace, the *daimyo* himself would have to get out of his palanquin and prostrate himself on the ground. To avoid this embarrassing situation, the *daimyo* would send a guard ahead to offer gifts of money to traveling aristocrats with the suggestion that it was a good time to stop for refreshments.

FUTAMIGAURA

Futamigaura, connected to Ise and Toba by bus or train, is the site of the "wedded rocks," which represent man and wife. Large straw ropes, used in the Shinto religion to mark sacred spaces and to symbolize marriage, connect the two rocks. On the larger, "husband" rock is a *torii*, which is also used to denote a sacred space. The Japanese tend to visit at dawn, to see the sun rising between the two rocks.

106

THE THREE SACRED TREASURES

Ise Shrine houses the sacred mirror (*Kagami*), one of the three imperial regalia symbolizing imperial power. According to legend, the sun goddess sent her grandson to Japan so that he and his descendants could rule over the country. Before he left she gave him three insignia: a mirror, a sword, and a set of jewels. As she handed him the mirror, she is said to have remarked, "When you look upon this mirror, let it be as if you look upon me." The sword is kept in Atsuta Shrine in Nagoya, and the jewels are in the Imperial Palace in Tokyo.

▶▶▶ Ise-shima National Park   94B2

Set on Shima Peninsula, which juts out into the Pacific Ocean south of Nagoya, Ise-shima National Park covers a total area of over 210 square miles (550sq km). Its fame derives from the Ise Jingu, also called the Grand Shrines of Ise, which enshrine the Sun Goddess Amaterasu o Mikami, the ancestral divine spirit of the Japanese imperial line. Apart from its beautiful coastline and mountainous interior, Ise-shima's other attractions are the cultured pearl farms at Toba, the "wedded rocks" of Futamigaura, and Ago Bay, at the southern tip of Shima Peninsula, with its host of tiny islands and abundant marine life. The simplest way to tour Ise-shima is to start in the small town of Ise, the northern gateway to the park and location of the Grand Shrines. Then move south down the peninsula to Toba and on to Kashikojima town (on Ago Bay's largest island, connected by bridge to the mainland) for a boat trip around Ago Bay.

Ise is an hour and 25 minutes from Nagoya on the private Kintetsu Ise-shima line, two hours from Kyoto or Osaka on the Kintetsu Yamada line. Trains and buses connect Ise to Toba and Kashikojima. Tour buses travel from the Inner Shrine to Toba along the Ise-shima Skyline Highway, crossing over Mount Asama, the roof of the peninsula.

The **Ise Jingu▶▶** are the most important of Shinto shrines, consisting of the Outer Shrine, the Inner Shrine, and over 100 minor shrines. The Outer Shrine (Geku), first erected in the 5th century AD, is dedicated to the goddess of food, clothing, and housing, and is surrounded by a tranquil forest of old Japanese cedars. Each morning offerings of food, attended by a white stallion from the emperor's stables, are made at the shrine. The main building, like that of the Inner Shrine, is made of unpainted cypress wood joined without nails. Both shrines stand on wooden piles and are roofed with thatch in the style of ancient Japanese houses. Only members of the imperial family and high-ranking priests are allowed into these buildings, which are surrounded by wooden palisades and are mostly out of sight for ordinary visitors. This does not deter the thousands of Japanese who visit the shrines every year. For them, Ise Shrine and its serene grounds are magical, embodying the very heart of old Japan. The Outer Shrine, 10 minutes' walk from Ujiyamada, Ise

Shopping in traditional dress at Ise

Crossing the bridge to the Inner Shrine

town's main station, is approached through a large wooden *torii* and down a long avenue lined with various pavilions. You can go no farther than the third of the four gates that lead to the shrine.

The Inner Shrine (Naiku), founded in AD 260, is about 4 miles (6km) from the Outer Shrine; the two are connected by a regular bus service. By far the most important of the two, it closely resembles Geku Shrine in its structure, general layout, and practical arrangements. Enshrined in the deepest recesses of Naiku is the Sacred Mirror, one of the Three Sacred Treasures of the Shinto religion (see panel). Through the first *torii* and after the second small bridge approaching the shrine, pilgrims and visitors wash and purify their hands and mouths with water from the Isuzu River, whose source lies within the Inner Shrine.

Toba▶ is a prosperous port town, whose main point of interest is Mikimoto Pearl Island, a five-minute walk from Toba station, connected to the mainland by Pearl Bridge. The Pearl Museum and Mikimoto Memorial Hall (*open* 8:30–5; Nov 20–Feb 28 9–4:30), on the island, trace the fascinating story of the cultivation of pearls. *Ama* (women divers) in traditional white outfits demonstrate how the women of Shima Peninsula used to dive for oyster pearls as well as abalone, seaweed, and other sea foods. Toba Aquarium, five minutes from Toba station, has an impressive collection of sea creatures, including otters and the dugong, a small sea mammal.

RECONSTRUCTED SHRINES
The Inner and Outer Shrines are torn down and rebuilt every 20 years, using the same plans and new wood, in a ritual known as *shikinen sengu*. The present buildings are the 61st in succession. The most recent shrine rebuilding ceremonies were completed in 1993. The most ancient sacred shrines in Japan are thus less than ten years old! For each shrine there are two sites, one occupied and one vacant. The old wood from a demolished shrine is cut into pieces and given to the pilgrims at the ceremony.

Loose tea ready for sale at the Grand Shrines of Ise

Erotic art at Ryosenji Temple, Shimoda

▶▶ Izu Peninsula (*Izu-hanto*)   *100C3*

The Izu Peninsula, plunges down from the mainland into the Pacific Ocean in Fuji-Hakone-Izu National Park. It has a mountainous interior, a dramatic coastline, fine beaches, and many hot springs. Only about an hour from Tokyo station by bullet train to Atami, at the northern end of the peninsula, Izu is a popular resort with Tokyo residents. During mid-July to the end of August, the region is very crowded and to be avoided (at the very least, make sure your accommodations are reserved in advance). Regular train and bus services operate along the scenic east coast from Atami to Ito, a spa resort, and Shimoda, location of the first American consulate. From Shimoda, there are bus services around the southern tip of the coast to Dogashima, a small fishing village on the less developed west side of the peninsula, or through the mountainous interior to Shuzenji, a traditional and rather prestigious spa town. From Shuzenji, there are trains back to Atami or Mishima and on to Tokyo. Alternatively, for a complete peninsula round trip, there is a bus service from Dogashima to Shuzenji. The Izu Peninsula has numerous hotels, *ryokan*, and *onsen minshuku*, a sort of hot-spring bed and breakfast where your room is in a large family-style house, fitted with a public bath, and fed by underground hot springs.

   Atami▶, one of the largest and best-known hot spring resorts in Japan, is a collection of hotels, souvenir shops, red-light districts, bars, and restaurants. Many of the

WILL ADAMS

William Adams was born in England in 1564. At the age of 12 he was apprenticed to a shipyard, where he studied astronomy and navigation as well as shipbuilding. In 1598, he set out from Holland as chief pilot of a fleet heading for the Orient. After a long voyage his ship was caught in a gale and washed ashore off the coast of Kyushu. He was taken to Osaka castle and interrogated by Tokugawa Ieyasu himself. The *shogun* was so impressed by Adams and his knowledge of ships that he appointed him adviser on foreign affairs. In 1604, on the *shogun's* orders, Adams built an 80-ton Western-style sailing ship on the estuary of the Matsa-kawa (river) in Ito. Pleased with the result, Ieyasu ordered Adams to build an ocean-going vessel, which the *shogun* lent to a Spanish diplomat, who sailed the ship to Acapulco and never returned it to Japan. Adams was rewarded for his services with a large estate and the status of a *samurai*, and adopted the Japanese name Miura Anjin. He died in Japan of natural causes, aged 56.

town's visitors are businessmen or workers on company-sponsored vacations, and they can get pretty rowdy in the evenings. Unless you wish to visit the MoA (Museum of Art), it is best just to pass through Atami. The museum (*open* 9:30–4:30; closed Thu), located on a hill above the station, was opened in 1982 by a religious organization founded by Mokichi Okada (1882–1955). It has an excellent collection of Japanese, Chinese, and European art, as well as a garden, tea-ceremony room, and theater for *noh* drama.

In 1604, Will Adams, the English ship's pilot who inspired the novel *Shogun*, built a ship at the old established spa town of **Ito**▶ for Tokugawa Ieyasu (see panel). Near the harbormaster's office a shabby memorial stone records his exploits in Japanese and English. Thirty minutes by bus from Ito station is the Ikeda Art Museum (*open* 10–4:30; Jul–Aug 10–5:30), which houses a collection of 20th-century Japanese and Western art in an impressive stainless steel building.

Shimoda▶▶ holds an important place in Japanese history, as it was here, in 1854, that the first important trade treaty between America and Japan was signed. All the major sites in Shimoda are linked in one way or another with its American associations (see panel). Shimoda Tourist Office, in front of the station, has an easy itinerary in English.

About one hour by bus from Shimoda, **Dogashima**▶▶ is a quiet fishing village in an area of unusual rock formations jutting out from the coast into the sea. A sightseeing boat leaves from the village pier. Dogashima is a place for gentle exploration and relaxation, where you can swim and sunbathe in season.

Shuzenji▶ is a rather expensive inland spa town. The trip there through the mountainous interior from Shimoda is of rather more interest than the town itself (see panel). From Shuzenji, you can travel back to Atami or catch the private railroad line to Mishima and change for the bullet train to Tokyo.

THE ROAD TO SHUZENJI
From Shimoda, the road to Shuzenji zigzags up Mount Amagi to Nonadani Bridge near the summit, where the mountain is too steep to continue the road. Four massive steel legs standing on a ledge halfway down the mountain support a double spiral structure that carries the road and juts out over the valley thousands of feet below.

TOJIN OKICHI
In 1857, the first U.S. consul to Japan, Townsend Harris, moved to a village near Shimoda with his Japanese consort, Tojin Okichi. According to the Japanese, she was forced to leave her lover for Harris and, as soon as he left, committed suicide. She has since become a folk heroine. Harris's version was very different: he claimed that he was offered the girl but refused her, and that after his departure she attempted a reconciliation with her lover, which failed. She then opened a restaurant, which was not a success, and finally took to drink.

109

Fishing boats on the Izu Peninsula

Earthquakes (jishin) are a common phenomenon in Japan. The country sits over the junctions of four tectonic plates, huge sections of the earth's crust that slip against each other, sometimes gently, occasionally violently. Within the plates are fault lines where slippage is rarer but can be catastrophic. Scarcely a day passes without a tremor in some part of the archipelago. Fortunately, almost all are mild, hardly noticed by the inhabitants.

Top: the Great Kanto Earthquake of 1923. Above: an earthquake cartoon

BEING PREPARED

Every year on September 1, the anniversary of the 1923 Tokyo earthquake, which left a death toll of over 140,000, Japan observes Disaster Prevention Day. During the day evacuation procedures are tested and children run through smoke-filled corridors with wet handkerchiefs over their noses and mouths. The Self Defense Force practices helicopter rescues, and fire departments rehearse their routines. Simulators the size of a small house put people through the experience of a violent tremor while they try to remember the survival drill.

Unpredictably, every 10 or 20 years, a more powerful shock hits a populated area and causes fatalities. At even longer intervals, disaster strikes on the scale of the Great Kanto Earthquake of 1923, which is estimated to have reached 8.2 on the Richter Scale. Its midday timing meant that countless *hibachi* (charcoal grills), ready for cooking lunch, ignited the wooden houses of Tokyo and Yokohama as they collapsed. Far more people died in the resulting firestorms than in the quake itself.

Kobe At 5:46 AM, on January 17, 1995, the Great Hanshin Earthquake shook a wide area of southern Honshu with a force measuring 7.2 on the Richter Scale. Its epicenter was somewhere under Awaji Island offshore from Kobe, Japan's second-largest port with a population of 1,500,000. Worst hit were the residential areas of the city, built in the 1950s and '60s. Thousands of wooden houses collapsed, their heavy tile roofs falling on their inhabitants as they slept, causing many of the 5,000 fatalities. Domestic gas heaters running during the cold winter night ignited fatal fires when main gas pipes fractured during the earthquake.

The attitude of the survivors was remarkable—a resigned acceptance of their misfortune. In the world's most technologically advanced country, 310,000 people were left with nothing. Their legendary grit was displayed as many walked to work that same morning. If the Japanese reputation for stoicism was reinforced, that for efficiency was undermined. Fire and rescue services were woefully slow to react, and local authorities had to make a written request for help from the Self Defense Force.

Lessons The media savaged the government and bureaucracy for their inadequate response. There was great alarm, too, that buildings, expressways, and the tracks of the fabled *Shinkansen* had not stood up to the shock as well as predicted. What was wrong with the calculations? When cooler assessments were made, it turned out that post-1980 structures, including high-rise buildings, had survived well. More worrying is the evidence that reclaimed land can shake like a jelly, or even behave like a liquid, causing severe damage to Kobe's port installations.

Tokyo In the capital, 20 years of complacency vanished overnight in a shudder of fear. The idea that structures could be "earthquake proof" had been disproved convincingly. "Earthquake resistance" is all that can be aspired to now, and levels of that are going to have to be stepped up. Some of the elevated highways date from the 1960s. Strengthening programs are under way, and there has been talk of relocating the capital somewhere safer, but where? Until 1995, Kobe had been considered safe. Seismology is an inexact science, and Japan cannot change its geology. For the moment, though, Tokyo watches and waits for the next inevitable, but unpredictable, earthquake.

Damage caused by the Kobe Earthquake

Painted screen, Kobe City Museum

CORMORANT (*UKAI*) FISHING

Trained cormorants on leashes are used to fish for *ayu* (small trout). To prevent them swallowing the fish they catch, the birds are fitted with small rings around their necks. The boats that carry the birds work at night and a bright wood brazier is suspended from the bow to attract the fish.

▶ ▶ Kobe

Japan's sixth-largest city prospered as a gateway for trade with China in the 15th and 16th centuries. When Japan's isolation ended in 1868, Kobe was among the first ports to open to Western ships. Many foreign traders settled here and it became a cosmopolitan center, with one of the world's busiest harbors. The narrow strip of land between the mountains and the sea was soon outgrown: residential quarters climbed the slopes, and the port facilities occupied reclaimed land and artificial islands.

As mentioned on page 110, before dawn on January 17, 1995, a devastating earthquake shook the city. Thousands of older houses and small apartment buildings collapsed. More than 5,000 people died. Part of the elevated Hanshin Expressway fell over and train links, including *Shinkansen* lines, were severed (fortunately the early hour meant that the bullet trains themselves were not running). Buildings put up since 1980, to higher standards of earthquake resistance, survived with little or no damage. Communication networks and damaged buildings in the city proper have now been restored and life is back to normal.

Many restaurants and stores and most hotels are within walking distance of the two central stations, Sannomiya and Motomachi. The lively entertainment quarter, Ikuta, lies west of Sannomiya, and Japan's biggest "Chinatown" is just south of Motomachi. Main street names are given in English, as well as Japanese.

Bullet trains connecting Kobe and Osaka (15 minutes), Kyoto (33 minutes), and Tokyo (3 hours, 30 minutes) use Shin-Kobe station, a short subway ride from Sannomiya station. Both have good information desks.

Kobe City Museum▶▶ (*open* 10–5; closed Mon), 24 Kyomachi, Chuo-ku, is a 10-minute walk south of Sannomiya station. It specializes in the history of Kobe, the influence of Western taste and techniques on Japanese design, and the way the Japanese viewed Westerners, shown in amusing scrolls and screens. The building and some exhibits suffered damage in the 1995 earthquake and the museum closed for repair, but it is now fully open.

Kitano▶▶ is a hilly district of narrow streets, a 15-minute walk north of Sannomiya, where Western traders and other foreign residents have lived since the 19th century. Some of the houses are open to the public.

▶ Nagoya · · · · · · · · · · · · · · · · · · · 94B2

Razed to the ground by Allied bombing during World War II, Nagoya has since been rebuilt and is now the fourth-largest city in Japan. There are few historical attractions beyond its two national treasures: Nagoya Castle and the Atsuta Jingu shrine. This is, however, a very convenient base for the Grand Shrines of Ise (see pages 106–107), Nara (see pages 114–115), and Gifu (see below). *Shinkansen* service connects Nagoya with Kyoto (43 minutes), Osaka (1 hour), and Tokyo (2 hours, 30 minutes).

Nagoya Castle▶▶▶ was built in 1612 as a residence and military base for the Tokugawa clan. The five-storied castle was destroyed in World War II, and a copy, built in 1959, houses treasures such as screen paintings and sliding doors. Two bronze dolphins covered with gold scales, reconstructed atop the castle roof, are believed to protect it from fire. Ninomaru garden and Ninomaru Tea House (*open* 9:30–4:30) are next door.

Atsuta Jingu Shrine▶▶▶, 1-1-1 Jingu, Atsuta-ku (*open* sunrise to sunset; subway: Jingunishi), houses the sacred sword that is one of Japan's most treasured objects (see panel above right).

Gifu▶▶ is 30 minutes by JR train north of Nagoya. The main reason to visit is to view the cormorant fishing on the Nagara-gawa (see panel). This traditional event takes place every evening between May 11 and October 15. Before and after the fishing, the Japanese gather on the banks of the river to drink, eat, and make merry. The tourist office at the station will give you details of how to get to the river and reserve accommodations.

THE ATSUTA SWORD
Prince Yamatotakeru was a legendary war hero of the 3rd century. The sword that saved his life during a military campaign is that held (but not displayed) in Atsuta Shrine, Nagoya. It is called Grass-Cutting Sword, because the prince used it to cut the grass down around him when it was set alight by attacking bandits. The Yamato originated the rule of the Japanese emperors, and the shrine housing the sword was later given the highest rank of a Shinto shrine.

113

Atsuta Jingu Shrine

Horyuji Temple

THE GREAT BRONZE BUDDHA
Daibutsu, the bronze Buddha of Todaiji Temple, is 53 feet (16.15m) tall, weighs 330,000 pounds 149,688kg and took five years to cast. Its completion in AD 749 was marked by a spectacular ceremony of consecration in 752, attended by the imperial family. The cost of building Todaiji itself crippled the economy and led to a peasants' revolt.

▶ ▶ ▶ **Nara**   94A2

In order to preserve Shinto ritual purity, the imperial court of ancient Japan moved to a different location on the succession of each new emperor. By the 8th century, the size of the state and the administrative arrangements needed to run it finally made this tradition too impractical to maintain. In AD 710, Nara was chosen as the first permanent political and cultural center of a newly united Japan. There followed a great flowering of every field from art to religion, influenced by the imported culture of the Tang Dynasty in China and Buddhism, which was promoted by the Japanese imperial court as a way of unifying the country. During this period, many remarkable temples and monuments were built, some of which have survived in Nara and are described below. (For details on how to get to Nara, see panel on page 97.)

To the southwest of Nara, **Horyuji Temple▶ ▶ ▶** is a little off the beaten track, but well worth a visit. It is the oldest intact temple complex in Japan and houses the world's oldest wooden buildings. Horyuji was founded in 607 by Prince Shotoku, a great patron of Buddhist religion and culture, who made his court into a renowned center of learning. The complex is divided into the West Temple, containing the Kondo main hall and pagoda, and the East Temple, mainly comprising the Yumedono pavilion and Chuguji Nunnery. Horyuji owns a magnificent collection of Buddhist art (*open* 8–5; until 4:20 PM Nov 20–Mar 10; bus from Kintetsu-Nara station, 40 minutes).

Kofukuji Temple▶ ▶ is famous for its five-storied pagoda (built in 1426 as an exact replica of the 8th-century original). It is Nara's best-known landmark, and its name, meaning "Happiness-Producing Temple," dates back to AD 710, when it was constructed as a teaching temple for children of the Fujiwara family. Nanendo Hall, which contains a fine gilded statue of Kannon carved in 1188, is a sacred pilgrimage site and is often very crowded. The Kokuhokan Treasure House contains the best of the temple's works of Buddhist art (*open* 9–5; access from Sanjo Street, running east from Nara JR station). Founded in 745, **Todaiji Temple▶ ▶ ▶**, in Nara Park (*open* Oct–Feb, Mar 8–5, Apr–Sep 7:30–5:30; walk or take number 2 bus from JR or Kintetsu stations, get off at the Daibutsuden stop), was built to be the headquarters of all temples in Japan. For the Japanese, it remains the most important sight in Nara. Todaiji's main hall, the Daibutsuden, is claimed to be the largest

Detail, Horyuji Temple

Todaiji's Daibutsuden

wooden building in the world. It houses the Great Buddha of Nara, the largest bronze Buddha ever cast, completed in 752 after many years of failed attempts (see panel). Entrance to the temple is through the massive Nandaimon gate; look for the giant wooden statues on either side. Todaiji took several thousand carpenters, metal-workers, and laborers five years to complete. Its cost crippled the economy and led to a peasants' revolt. Nearly all the original buildings were destroyed in 1180 by the Taira clan, to punish the armed monks of Todaiji for their support of the rival Minamoto clan.

Toshodaiji Temple▶▶ (*open* 8:30–5), near Nishinokyo station on the Kintetsu Kashiwara line, is one of the loveliest of Nara's temples. It was founded in 759 by the Chinese priest Ganjin, who had been invited to Japan by the emperor to spread Buddhism and faced many trials on his journey to Japan, including the loss of his sight. At the age of 66, he supervised the construction of this fine temple. The main hall and lecture hall are national treasures. The eight pillars at the front of Kondo Hall show the influence of Greek architecture, which reached Japan via the "Silk Road."

PRIESTLY POWER
The great Buddhist temples of Nara owned large, tax-free estates, and with growing prosperity they became increasingly powerful and avaricious. The priest Dokyo, an 8th-century Rasputin figure, became mentor and love of the empress Koken (718–70). Alarmed by the power of the very temples they had helped to foster, the Fujiwara ruling clan moved the court to Heian-Kyo (Kyoto), and severed the government's strong Buddhist connections.

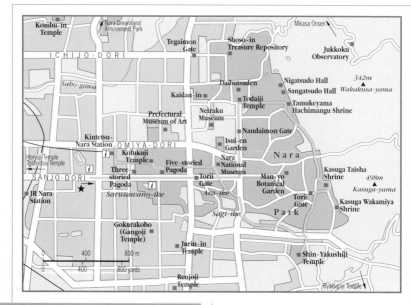

Walk

Nara

Distance: 2 miles (3km); time: 2½ to 3 hours. The major historical sites of

Nara are laid out in a huge deer park, with Wakakusa Hill as a backdrop. Despite the sightseers, Nara is imbued with a sense of peace, a comfort for jangled nerves.

Start from the **Nara City Tourist Center**, between JR Nara and Kintetsu-Nara stations. Walk two

Main hall, Shin-Yakushiji Temple

Wooden Buddhist deity at Kofukuji

blocks east to discover the three-storied pagoda of **Kofukuji Temple▶**, founded in 710 and once comprising over 1,300 buildings. Of the remaining structures, the three-storied pagoda dates from the 12th century, the five-storied pagoda and eastern main hall from the 14th century. The view of the five-storied pagoda from across the neighboring Sarusawa Pond is one of the most famous in Nara. From Kofukuji, continue east, passing through the *torii* into the park area, then turn left for the approach to **Todaiji Temple▶▶▶**. The temple's main building, the world's largest wooden structure, houses a 53-foot (16.2-m) bronze Buddha.

Over 1,000 tame deer roam the park in Nara. From Todaiji, walk southeast through the park to the **Kasuga Taisha▶▶**, one of the most famous Shinto shrines, its vermilion lacquered buildings set against the green woodlands. Thousands of stone lanterns line the approach to the shrine, and hundreds of bronze lanterns hang from the eaves of the shrine buildings. The grassy slopes of the 1,122-foot- (342-m-) high Wakakusa-yama, north of the shrine, are ritually burned each year on January 15. South of Kasuga Taisha, outside the park, is **Shin-Yakushiji Temple▶**, another 8th-century monument. Picturesque old houses line the street that leads west from Shin-Yakushiji along the edge of the park. Return to the park, and go back toward the *torii*, passing three ponds to the left. This leads to the **Nara National Museum▶▶**, housing a collection of works of ancient art, including masterpieces of early Buddhist art. The museum's West Wing specializes in objects of archeological interest.

From the National Museum, walk back past Kofukuji to either station.

BUNRAKU

One of the three classical forms of theater in Japan, *bunraku*, or puppetry, has been popular since the 17th century. A typical play could deal with a story of tragic love, a well-known historical event, or a comic story of urban life. The puppets, usually dressed in elaborate period costume, are about two-thirds human size, each one made up of interchangeable parts. Each of the major characters is handled by three puppeteers dressed in black. The chief puppeteer (it takes 30 years to become an expert) manipulates the puppet's head, eyes, mouth, and right arm and hand.

▶ ▶ ▶ Osaka 94A2

For centuries a mecca for merchants, Osaka is Japan's third-largest city. Like Tokyo, it is an important industrial, financial, and commercial center, but it has an energy and pride of its own, and its styles and fashions are very different from those of the capital. Osakans describe themselves as *shominteki*, people with no time for pretensions, and consider Tokyoites to be wimps. It is a crowded, busy city with no obvious town planning, where cherry orchards, Buddhist temples, choked traffic, grimy commercial buildings, and chrome and glass high-technology skyscrapers all exist side by side.

Osaka is famous for its food, and its citizens are known to the rest of Japan as *kuidaore*, or those who will eat to physical and financial ruin. There are restaurants of every type and price throughout the city and choice is limitless. Compared with Tokyo, prices are low.

Osaka is a place to wander, shop, and eat. Of the tourist sights, the two priorities are Osaka Castle and the National *Bunraku* Theater. To find out what is going on in Osaka, pick up a copy of *Kansai Time Out*, a monthly magazine with information on sightseeing, festivals, restaurants, and other items of interest, available at bookshops, restaurants, and other places frequented by English-speaking tourists.

Getting there and around Osaka is connected to Tokyo by frequent domestic flights and *Shinkansen* train service (2½ to 3 hours). All trains arrive at Shin-Osaka station. Change here and travel a few stops south on the loop line to Osaka station in the center of town. Osaka also has a futuristic new airport, the Kansai International Airport (see pages 16–17). The Osaka tourist information office is

NIGHTLIFE

The busiest nightlife area is around the narrow Dotonburi Street, near Namba station. Here there is a hive of bars, coffee lounges, discos, and nightclubs, lit up after dark by gaudy neon signs and a huge, open-air video screen. Singles and *avecs* (couples) throng the streets. For low life, the seamy but fascinating place to go is Shin-Sekai, west of Tennoji Park. This is an area of massage parlors, cheap restaurants, and strip joints. The Yakuza (Japanese Mafia) control most of the business and occasionally you can see members cruising by in their extravagantly large, chrome-laden Cadillacs.

Osaka façades

Downtown restaurant

at the east exit of Osaka station; staff speak English and the office is open 8–7. Osaka City Air Terminal (OCAT) operates check in and transfer services to Kansei International Airport. It is housed in a new building adjacent to Namba station, central Osaka.

Shopping The Umeda area, around Umeda and Osaka stations, is the hub of department stores and high fashion shops. It extends beneath the ground, where there is a maze of streets and malls. Three of the local department stores have underground basements that descend into this subterranean complex. If you get lost, take an elevator to the first floor of one of the stores and head for an open-air exit.

Sightseeing Osaka is considered the capital of *bunraku* (see panel), and if you are in the city you should take the opportunity to see a play in the **National Bunraku Theater▶▶**, 1-12-10 Nipponbashi, Chuo-ku. Performances are scheduled for six periods each year, with each production running for two to three weeks. Information is available at the Osaka tourist information office. The theater is two minutes' walk from Nipponbashi station on the Kintetsu line (exit 7).

Toyotomi Hideyoshi, the warlord who unified Japan, built **Osaka Castle▶▶** (Osaka-jo) in 1583 on a strategic hilltop in the city's northern district and used it as his headquarters. After he died, armies of the Tokugawa shogunate (1603–1867) took Osaka Castle in 1615. The castle was also damaged in the fighting that led to the Meiji Restoration of 1868. Its main gate and several towers have survived, however, and the eight-story *donjon*, the main stronghold, was rebuilt in 1931 and extensively renovated again in 1997. Inside the castle is a museum with displays and exhibits relating to old Osaka and the Toyotomi family, but the main reasons to visit are the view from the top of the *donjon* and the castle's majestic exterior. The park that surrounds the castle is also one of the best places in the city for people-watching (*open* 9–5). To get to Osaka Castle, take the JR loop line from Osaka station to Osaka-jo Koen-mae station and walk up the hill from there.

FOOD
Favorite local specialties are the street food, *tako yaki*, a wheatflour dumpling stuffed with octopus meat and baked over charcoal; *udon*, a fat, white wheat noodle; and Osaka *sushi*, squares of sticky sweet rice and raw fish. *Chanko-nabe* restaurants, also very popular, are named after the unpretentious stew that is the mainstay of a *sumo* wrestler's diet. The stew is not fattening—the huge amount of rice wrestlers eat performs that function—but it is tasty and nutritious. Retired *sumo* wrestlers often open their own *chanko-nabe* restaurants and jealously guard their favorite recipes.

Detail, Osaka Castle

Kyoto

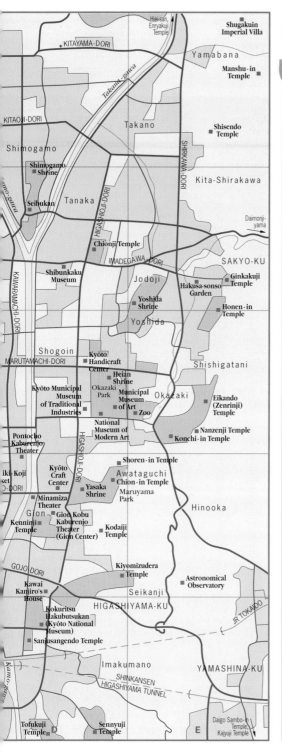

Kyoto

Kyoto

Kyoto sakura *(cherry blossoms)*

GEISHA
In the Gion quarter of Kyoto, you'll see young girls called *maiko*. These apprentice *geisha*, aged between 17 and 25, will graduate to full *geisha* status, when they will probably acquire a rich patron. *Geisha* are hired, often in pairs, to entertain parties of men after dinner, at a restaurant or tea house.

MOUNT HIEI
In the 8th century, Emperor Kammu decided to build a new capital city, to be called Heian-Kyo (present-day Kyoto). He ordered a Buddhist monk, Saicho, of the Tendai sect, to establish a temple on Mount Hiei to protect the city from evil spirits. The temple became the center of a monastery complex that grew in size and importance as rapidly as Heian-Kyo below. By the 11th century Enryakuji contained over 3,000 temple buildings. The monks had their own army and they warred with any political or religious faction that opposed their control of the city. In 1571 General Nobunaga invaded the mountain, burned every temple to the ground, and executed every monk. Although the monastery was reestablished in the 17th century, it never regained its former power.

KYOTO Established in AD 794, Kyoto remained the center of civilization in Japan for over a thousand years. Even today, although the capital has now moved to Tokyo, Kyoto retains its unique position as the country's historical and cultural center, birthplace of much of the spirit and technology of traditional Japan. The Japanese describe the city as *Nihon no Furusato*—"The Heart of Japan."

The Allies spared Kyoto from bombing during World War II, and it remains a living museum of Japan's great artistic heritage, the setting for historical and religious sites and a vast wealth of traditional art, crafts, architecture, dance, and drama.

The original layout of the city was modeled on Ch'ang-an (modern Xian), the ancient capital of Tang Dynasty China. Its grid plan makes it easy to get around, and the mountains that ring Kyoto on three sides help you keep your bearings. On the approaches to these mountains, modern Kyoto gently reverts to its older self, with Buddhist temples and Shinto shrines, villas, gardens, craft shops, Japanese inns, and narrow streets of old houses that lead back into the countryside. The most famous mountain, Mount Hiei, rising above the city to the northeast, is the site of the Enryakuji Temple complex, at one time the most influential Buddhist monastery in Japan.

SIGHTSEEING More than 30 million tourists a year visit Kyoto, but there is so much to do (nearly 2,000 temples and shrines alone) that crowds tend to form only at the most popular places. Avoid the city on public holidays and the best-known sites on weekends if you dislike crowds.

The major attractions are the Kyoto Imperial Palace, Nijo Castle and gardens, Daitokuji Temple, with its many sub-temples, Ginkakuji (Temple of the Silver Pavilion), Kinkakuji (Temple of the Golden Pavilion), the sand and rock Zen garden at Ryoanji Temple, the Heian Shrine, and Kiyomizudera Temple, built on a steep hillside with wonderful views over the city. Kyoto also has several museums and a botanical and zoological garden.

FESTIVALS AND CRAFTS There are also many popular annual festivals (*matsuri*) held in Kyoto, normally associated with the changing of the seasons or with religious occasions. For the three best known, the Gion (July 16–17), Jidai (October 22), and Aoi (May 15) *matsuri*, make hotel reservations well in advance.

Kyoto is renowned for traditional Japanese crafts, especially pottery, lacquerware, woodblock prints, fans, Yuzen silk-dyeing, and Nishijin silk-weaving. Major schools of the tea ceremony, flower arranging, classical dance, and *noh* drama have their headquarters in Kyoto.

CONTRASTS Apart from its temples, shrines, and gardens, Kyoto is also a city of fashionable stores and restaurants, and a number of modern buildings such as Kyoto Tower, which provides breathtaking views, and spectacular Kyoto Station, which is a marvel of futuristic architecture. The atmosphere of the city is perhaps best captured in the Gion district. Here, a famous center where the classical Japanese arts are performed is next door to a very busy betting shop, itself adjacent to the entrance of a temple. In the spring, cherry blossoms might be blowing down streets busy with traffic, *geisha*, monks, and tourists, while peace and tranquility are found inside the grounds of the temple.

FESTIVALS

May 15: Aoi Matsuri. The *aoi*, or hollyhock, is thought to prevent both hurricanes and earthquakes. This festival is said to date back to the 6th century. People in traditional court costume walk from the old imperial palace to two Shinto shrines.

August 16: Daimonji Gozan Okuribi. Huge bonfires form Chinese characters on five of the mountains that surround Kyoto.

October 22: Kurama-No-Hi-Matsuri. The Fire Festival of Kurama takes place in Sakyo-ku in Kyoto. The main event is a procession of people carrying lighted torches to the gate of Yuki Shrine, passing between rows of bonfires.

See also pages 30–31.

Kyoto worshippers burning incense

IKKYU SOJUN

Ikkyu Sojun (1394–1481) entered Daitokuji at the age of 20 to study Zen and, according to tradition, achieved enlightenment when he heard crows cawing, while seated in a boat meditating. He constantly criticized the Zen priesthood as corrupt, and scandalized the Buddhist establishment by frequenting the pleasure quarters of Kyoto. When he was an old man he became involved with a young blind singer named Mori and dedicated poems to her in his *Kyounshu* (Crazy Cloud Collection). Ikkyu described himself as:
"Hating incense,
Distrusting Satori,
Disbelieving talk of Zen,
Thoroughly despising priestly piety,
Wrinkling my nose with disgust here in the dimness of the Buddha Hall."

THE ZEN LIFE

The Kyoto International Zen Center offers interested visitors a taste of the Zen life. For information, telephone the Jotokuji Temple on (0771) 24 0152.

The Zen Garden at Daitokuji Temple

▶▶▶ Daitokuji Temple   120B5

Daitokuji-cho, Murasakino, Kita-ku
Bus: 1, 12, 61, 204, 205, 206 to Daitokuji-mae

The Daitokuji (Temple of Great Virtue) is composed of the main temple plus 23 sub-temples (*tatchu*) belonging to the Rinzai sect of Zen Buddhism (only eight of the sub-temples are usually open to the public). Founded in 1319 by Daito Kokushi (1282–1337), the original buildings were damaged by fire in 1453 and 1468, during the Onin Wars. In 1474, the Zen monk Ikkyu Sojun (1394–1481) became head priest of Daitokuji. Although he once said that "brothels are more suitable settings for meditation than temples," he solicited funds from rich merchants and rebuilt the temple. The great warlord Toyotomi Hideyoshi (1537–98) also contributed to the restoration of the complex; one of the sub-temples, Soken-in, was built by Hideyoshi in memory of his predecessor, Oda Nobunaga (1534–82). Both Nobunaga and Hideyoshi were devotees of the tea ceremony (*chanoyu*), and its greatest master, Sen no Rikyu (1521–91), built tea houses and gardens in the grounds of Daitokuji (see panel, opposite page).

From north to south the temple buildings are: the Chokushi-mon, San-mon Gate, Butsuden (Buddha Hall), Hatto (Lecture Hall), and the Hojo (Abbot's Quarters), which are entered through the Kara-mon (Chinese Gate). The Hojo is open to the public only on October 10, when its famous collection of paintings is put on display. The Chokushi-mon (Gate of the Imperial Messengers) was originally the south gate of the Imperial Palace in Kyoto. Built in 1590 with curved gables, typical of the style of the Momoyama period, it was given to the Daitokuji by the empress Meisho in 1640.

Daisen-in▶▶ (*open 9–4:30*) is a sub-temple of Daitokuji, famous for its eastern Zen garden, created by the founder Kogaku Zenshi with some help from his friend, the artist Soami. The arrangement of rocks (representing mountains), sand (representing a stream of water, the flow of life), and sparse vegetation is symbolic of an individual's journey through life. A rock symbolizing Mount Horai, the home of immortal sages in the Eastern Sea, stands in the northeastern corner. A stream of imaginary water

Stone Buddhist deities …

TEA MASTER
Sen no Rikyu (1521–91)
was the greatest master
of the tea ceremony. The
son of a rich merchant,
he became one of
Hideyoshi's most trusted
advisers, until he was
forced to commit suicide
by Hideyoshi in 1591. Why
this happened is unclear,
but it is said that Hideyoshi
objected very strongly to
walking under a statue of
Rikyu that the artist had
placed on the upper floor
of the outer gate (*san-mon*)
of the Daitokuji, thus
placing himself "above"
the warlord.

*… and a monk at
Daitokuji Temple*

flows rapidly from the rock, representing youth. Then various obstacles present themselves, with the "tigerhead stone" representing tragedy. The flow of water is checked and slowed by the stones and a rocky wall, representing doubt and contradiction, and the water eddies and swirls, as if lost and confused. Once the stream moves past this point, it becomes faster and wider, having learned from hard experience. In the middle of this section of the stream, a turtle is observed trying to swim against the flow, demonstrating the pointlessness of trying to return to the past. The southern end of the garden is apparently empty, composed only of white sand, which symbolizes the mind freed from thoughts and emotions.

▶▶▶ Ginkakuji Temple   121E4

Ginkakuji-machi, Sakyo-ku
Bus: 5, 17, 203
Open 8:30–5 (last entry 4:30 PM)
Ginkakuji (The Temple of the Silver Pavilion) is one of Kyoto's most popular sights. Built originally as a retirement villa for the *shogun* Ashikaga Yoshimasa (1453–90), it was originally to be covered in silver foil in imitation of his grandfather Yoshimitsu's building, the Kinkakuji or Gold Pavilion. The silver was never applied, but the name survived. Yoshimasa surrounded himself with a circle of artists and aesthetes and devoted his time to the appreciation of women, the tea ceremony, moon-gazing, incense-sniffing, and other refinements. The arts that flourished under Yoshimasa's patronage are known as the *Higashiyama Bunka* (Culture of the Eastern Mountains), taking their name from the Higashi mountains that the villa faces.

In 1485, Yoshimasa became a Zen Buddhist monk, and after his death the villa became a Buddhist temple, known as the Joshoji. The gardens are attributed to the artist Soami, and are famous for two piles of white sand that sparkle in the moonlight.

125

One of the most beautiful Zen gardens in Kyoto, and possibly one of the least visited, is that of the Zen temple, Koto-in, a small sub-temple of Daitokuji with only three buildings. The garden is a masterpiece of elegant simplicity, renowned for the beauty of its maple trees in the fall.

CEREMONIAL EXCESSES
During the 14th century, the *chanoyu* or tea ceremony became a social ceremony, a luxurious court ritual. In their splendid apartments, richly decorated and adorned with precious objects, amid odors of incense, great lords reclining on couches would receive their guests and offer them exotic dishes, and tea, whose origin they were supposed to guess to be rewarded with a prize.

Above: Zen garden, Ginkakuji Temple
Below: Daitokuji graves

Early morning reverie The best time to arrive at Koto-in is at around 9 AM, just as the doors are being opened. Only the doorkeeper is likely to be there. The altar room in the main temple is dark, and you will only just be able to distinguish the Buddhas and other images surrounding the altar itself. The temple rooms are divided by *shoji* (paper screens), which can be opened or closed to make rooms of different sizes, or taken away altogether to make one large room. There is a tangible atmosphere of peace and calm as you pass over the *tatami* floors onto the veranda overlooking the gardens. Outside, the light strikes the bamboo fences, *shoji*, roof eaves, and unpolished wooden beams of the monks' quarters. At this time of the day, if you listen carefully, you may also catch the sound of Zen clappers somewhere in the grounds of Daitokuji, calling the monks to meditation, prayer, or morning tea.

Lord Hosokawa Koto-in was established in 1601 at the behest of a famous military leader, Hosokawa Tadaoki. Hosokawa was a great warrior of his time and one of the

Koto-in gardens

VIEWS OF THE TEA CEREMONY

Toyotomi Hideyoshi and other warriors were great lovers of the tea ceremony. Hideyoshi's interpreter, the Portuguese Jesuit Juan Rodriguez, observed that in all aspects the tea ceremony "is as rustic, rough, completely unrefined and simple as nature made it, after the style of a solitary and rustic hermitage." It is intended to "produce courtesy, politeness, modesty, exterior moderation, calmness, peace of body and soul without any pride or arrogance, fleeing from all ostentation, pomp, external grandeur and magnificence."

The stone lantern grave of Lord Hosokawa and Lady Gracia, Koto-in Zen Garden, Daitokuji

few to survive the bloody civil war that culminated in the establishment of the Tokugawa shogunate. In addition to his martial skills, he was a man of considerable intellectual achievement and an accomplished diplomat. His wife, Lady Gracia, was a devout believer in the then-outlawed Catholic faith, and her father was the disgraced leader of an unsuccessful revolt against the reigning *shogun*. Hosokawa overcame this potentially fatal association and became a prominent figure in the early Tokugawa regime. He was rewarded with vast domains of land, but later in life devoted himself to the study of Zen under the famous Daitokuji abbot Seigan (1588–1661). He was also noted as one of the most distinguished disciples of the great tea master, Sen no Rikyu. Lord Hosokawa and Lady Gracia are buried in the garden of Koto-in; their grave is marked by a stone lantern.

The tea pavilion Shoko-ken (*open* 9–4:30), one of the main buildings in Koto-in, is a tea house built by Hosokawa but inspired by the teachings of Sen no Rikyu. During the 15th and 16th centuries, the rituals surrounding the tea ceremony became ever more elaborate and luxurious, finally provoking a return to simplicity and austerity. The reaction was initiated and led by Sen no Rikyu, who devised a set of rules governing the *chanoyu* (tea ceremony) that still applies today. Shoko-ken is reached by a stone flagged path across a small landscaped garden. It has a tiny kitchen for washing the vessels used in the ceremony, a *tokonoma* (alcove) decorated with an elegant *kakemono* (hanging scroll) and a simple vase with simple flowers, complying perfectly with Sen no Rikyu's rules for the tea pavilion.

TEA CEREMONY

The tea ceremony is a formal ritual for preparing and drinking the bitter-tasting powdered green tea called *matcha*. The ceremony originated in Buddhist monasteries in China, where the monks, on special occasions, shared tea in front of an ink painting of Bodhidharma, founder of the Zen tradition. Sen no Rikyu (1522–1591) formalized the Japanese-style tea ceremony as still practiced today.

Heian Shrine

121D3

HEIAN SHRINE FESTIVALS
Emperor Komei is honored at a festival on January 30 and Emperor Kammu on April 3. Perhaps the most interesting festival is the Jidai Matsuri (Festival of the Ages), on October 22, when men and women wear costumes dating from the end of the Tokugawa period to the Heian period, when Kyoto was founded. Their procession starts at the Imperial Palace at 10 AM and ends at the Heian Shrine at 3:30 PM.

KINKAKUJI ARCHITECTURE
One unusual feature of the Kinkakuji is its architecture. The second floor is built in the Shinden style of the Heian palaces, while the third floor resembles a temple hall and enshrines a statue of Kannon Bosatsu. The fourth floor is as sparse as a Zen hall, yet contains a statue of a Jodo-style Amida, the Buddha of the Western Paradise, or Pure Land.

▶▶▶ Heian Shrine 121D3
Okazaki Park
Bus: 2, 3, 5
Open (garden): Mar 15–Aug 31 8:30–5:30,
Sep–Oct and Mar 1–14 8:30–5, Nov–Feb 8:30–4:30

The Shrine of Peace and Tranquility is a Shinto shrine, built in 1895 to celebrate the 1,100th anniversary of the founding of Kyoto and dedicated to the spirits of Emperor Kammu (781–806), who established Kyoto, and Emperor Komei (1831–66), the father of Emperor Meiji.

Erected as a two-thirds scale replica of the original Imperial Palace (dating from 794 and destroyed by fire in 1227), the Heian Shrine is decorated with vermilion paint and roofed with glazed green tiles, and has an enormous ferro-concrete *torii* (gate). Behind the main buildings, a modern version of Heian period gardens can be found, which center on a large pond spanned by a Chinese-style bridge. Unlike many of the Zen gardens in the Kyoto area, the gardens of the Heian Shrine make extensive use of flowers, and are famous for their display of *sakura* (cherry blossoms) in spring, lotus flowers in summer, and maple trees in the fall.

▶▶▶ Kinkakuji Temple 120B5
Kinkakuji-cho, Kita-ku
Bus: 59 to Kinkakuji-mae, 204 or 205 to Kinkakuji-michi.
Open: Oct–Mar 9–5, Apr–Sep 9–4:30

The Temple of the Golden Pavilion was built by the shogun Ashikaga Yoshimitsu (1358–1409) for his retirement in 1394. Three stories tall and topped with a bronze statue of a phoenix, the pavilion is covered in gold leaf and extends over a pond that reflects the building. The Golden Pavilion was built according to descriptions of the Western Paradise of the Buddha Amida and is intended to illustrate the harmony between Heaven and Earth.

Like other buildings erected by powerful warriors and politicians, the Kinkakuji symbolizes the mandate to rule granted by Heaven to the Ashikaga shogunate.

On Yoshimitsu's death, his son, obeying his father's wishes, turned the building into a temple known as the Rokuonji. In 1950, one of the temple priests set fire to the building, but an exact replica was built in 1955. Novelist Yukio Mishima based his *Temple of the Golden Pavilion* (1956) on the destruction of the Kinkakuji. The temple was further restored in 1990 and houses many treasures of Buddhist art. The grounds include a beautiful landscaped garden and a large pond.

▶▶▶ Kiyomizudera Temple   121D2

Kiyomizu 1-Chome, Higashiyama-ku
Bus: 16, 202, 206, 207 to Kiyomizu-michi or Gojo-zaka
(10-minute walk up Kiyomizu-michi or Gojo-zaka)
Open: 6 AM–sunset

The Clear Water Temple was established in 780 by a Buddhist priest from Nara named Enchin, who was commanded in a vision to seek the pure source of the Kizu River. In 798, the main hall was rebuilt by General Sakanoue no Tamuramaro, using materials taken from the abandoned Imperial Palace at Nagaoka. Damaged in the power struggles between the monks of Mount Hiei and Nara, most of the present buildings were erected in 1633 by Tokugawa Iemitsu.

Originally the Kiyomizudera was affiliated to the Kofukuji temple in Nara, but it now belongs to the Shingon-Hosso sect, dedicated to the worship of Kannon, the personification of divine mercy. The main attraction for visitors is the *butai* (dancing stage), a large platform in front of the *hondo* (main hall). Wooden scaffolding 40-feet- (12-m-) high supports the *butai* above a gorge, giving a panoramic view of Kyoto.

Stone steps lead down from the main hall to the Otowa-no-taki (Sound of Feathers Waterfall), the source of the pure water found by Enchin. Here pilgrims often drink the water, said to be efficacious for all illnesses.

The streets around Kiyomizudera Temple

129

KIYOMIZUDERA PROVERB
Kiyomizudera is the source of a Japanese saying—"to leap from Kiyomizu's *butai*"—which means to make an important decision, or do something that demands great courage.

Kiyomizudera Temple

Kyoto National Museum

NANZENJI "CATHEDRAL"
Following the Chinese tradition, Zen temples are grouped into fives. Nanzenji Temple was the head of the Gozan (Five Monasteries) of Kyoto and when Ashikaga Yoshimitsu wanted to include the Shokokuji among the group, the Nanzenji was promoted above all others. In effect, Nanzenji acted as a kind of Zen "cathedral;" whoever was the abbot held the highest Buddhist office in Japan.

BOILED ALIVE
The Sanmon Gate was the hiding place of Ishikawa Goemon, a kind of Japanese Robin Hood. When he and his young son were captured in 1632 they were sentenced to be boiled alive in a big iron tub, but Goemon held the boy above the boiling water until he himself died. His courage is remembered in the *kabuki* play *Sanmon Gosan no Kiri*, and Goemon was the subject of a wood-block print by the artist Kunisada. Goemon's name was also used for the old-fashioned iron baths known as *Goemon-furo*.

►► Kokuritsu Hakubutsukan (Kyoto National Museum)   *121D1*

Yamato-oji-dori, Higashiyama-ku
Bus: 206
Open: Tue–Sun 9–4:30 (last entry 4 PM)

Established in the second half of the last century, the National Museum is housed in two buildings, and its extensive collection is shown in continuously changing displays. Neolithic relics from the Jomon and Yayoi periods can be found in the archeology section, along with clay figurines (*haniwa*) associated with the burial mounds (*misasagi*) of the early rulers of Japan. The museum is noted for its collection of Japanese pictorial art. The sculpture section is dominated by Heian period statues. There are also examples of metalwork, ceramics, calligraphy, and lacquerware from many periods of Japanese history.

►►► Kyoto Gosho (Kyoto Imperial Palace)   *120C4*

Imperial Park
Subway: Marutamachi, Imadegawa
Open: 30-minute tours of the grounds start at 10 AM; arrive by 9:40 AM (except Sun and the second and fourth Sat of every month). An English-language tour is available Mon–Fri at 2 PM, arrive by 1:40

The Imperial Palace was originally built in 794, but has been destroyed by fire on many occasions. The present building was built in 1855. The imperial household moved to Tokyo after the Meiji Restoration, but the Kyoto Gosho is still used for the ceremonies that must be performed when a new emperor ascends the throne.

Foreign visitors are given preferential treatment for access; they must complete an application form and show their passport. Contact the Imperial Household Agency (Kunaicho), located in Kyoto Imperial Park near the Imadegawa subway station (tel: 075 211 1215).

►► Kyoto Municipal Museum of Traditional Industries   *121D3*

Located in the Kyoto International Exhibition Hall near the gate of Heian shrine
Open: 10–6; closed Mon

This new museum displays traditional crafts such as ceramics, Kimono dyeing, bamboo, and laquerware, and many others. The entrance gallery re-creates a street scene from old Kyoto. Audiovisual sites and free computer databanks allow more detailed investigation.

►►► Nanzenji Temple   *121E3*

Fukuchi-cho, Sakyo-ku
Bus: 5 to Eikando-mae, then a five-minute walk
Open: Mar 6–Nov 15 8:30–4:30, Nov 16–Mar 5 8:30–5

Nanzenji (Southern Zen) Temple was built as a retirement villa for Emperor Kameyama (1249–1305) at the base of the hills in the east of Kyoto. The building was given to the Rinzai sect of Zen Buddhism in 1291 at the emperor's command, and is now the headquarters of Rinzai Zen. During the Onin Wars the temple was badly damaged but was restored in the late 16th and early 17th centuries; the Sanmon (Triple Gate) was built in 1628 and offers a famous view of Kyoto and the Higashiyama mountains.

Kyoto Gosho

SQUEAKING FLOORS
While Nijo Castle may not have been built primarily as a fortress, it does contain surprises for any potential spy or assassin. Every building contains hidden rooms, where the *shogun's samurai* could observe visitors for signs of treachery, and many of the corridors were constructed with "nightingale floors" (*uguisu-bari*) that squeak when walked upon to warn of anyone approaching.

▶▶▶ Nijo Castle and Gardens   *120C3*

Horikawa Nijo, Nijojo-cho, Nakagyo-ku
Subway: Oike, then a 10-minute walk;
bus: 9, 12, 50, 52, 61, 67
Open: Tue–Sun 8:45–4; closed Dec 26–Jan 4

Built in 1603 by Tokugawa Ieyasu, Nijo Castle has thick outer walls and a moat to defend it. Within the walls, the main buildings are beautifully decorated with paintings by Kano Tanyu (1602–74) and his pupils. The gardens to the southwest of the Great Hall were laid out by Enshu Kobori shortly before Emperor Gomizuno-o's visit in 1626; no trees were used, as falling leaves are suggestive of the transience of life, and the *Shogun* wanted to impress the emperor with his power. The central island in the lake is flanked by two smaller islands in the shape of a crane and a tortoise, symbols of strength and longevity.

Entrance is through the East gate, then via the Kara-mon (Chinese Gate) to a diagonal row of five buildings. The Ohiroma Hall contains a reconstruction of the occasion when Tokugawa Keiki returned power to the imperial line.

PATH OF PHILOSOPHY
Nanzenji and Ginkakuji Temples are linked by a canalside path about 1½ miles (2km) long, known as Philosopher's Walk (see page 136). It was named after Nishida Kitaro (1870–1945), a noted philosopher whose specialty was the comparison of Western and Zen philosophies, and who enjoyed walking along this route. The walk is now lined with cherry trees, interesting shops, and coffee bars, and is busy with tourists as well as academics.

Nanzenji Temple

▶▶ Nishiki-Koji Market 121D2

Open: daily, early morning–7 PM. Some stalls close on Sun, others on Wed

Situated in the heart of town on Nishiki-Koji-dori, this fresh produce and fish market is the main food-buying center for the city's restaurants and hotels, as well as for the general public. Open stalls, selling everything from seaweed to beans, line the market lanes.

Nishiki-Koji Market

▶▶▶ Ryoanji Temple and Garden 120A4

13 Goryoshita-machi, Ryoanji, Ukkyu-ku
Bus: 59 to Ryoanji-mae
Open: 8–5, Dec–Feb 8:30–4:30

The Temple of the Peaceful Dragon was founded in 1473. Originally the estate of Katsumoto Hosokawa (1430–73), it became a Zen temple of the Rinzai sect on his death. The main attraction is the famous rock garden. Attributed to the artist Soami, it was created in the 16th century in a space of 100 feet by 33 feet (30m by 10m). Following the *karesansui* (waterless stream) style, the garden is composed of 15 rocks set into raked white gravel. Simply sit and enjoy the view, but arrive early to avoid the crowds and try to ignore the intrusive "explanations" that are broadcast over the loudspeakers, destroying the mood (see also pages 134–135).

RYOANJI TEA HOUSE
In the small garden behind Ryoanji there is a tea house, the Zoroku, whose stone wash basin (the *tsukubai*) has a unique inscription arranged as a rebus around the rim, which can be translated as "I learn only to be content." In Zen, he who achieves contentment is considered to be spiritually rich. The *tsukubai* is said to have been given to the temple by the *daimyo* Tokugawa Mitsukuni (1628–1700), remembered as the compiler of the great history of Japan, the *Dai Nippon Shi*. Copies of the inscription can be purchased as souvenirs.

▶▶▶ Sanjusangendo 121D1

657 Sanjusangendo, Mawari-cho, Higashiyama-ku
Bus: 206, 208 to Sanjusangendo-mae, or 15 minutes' walk east of Kyoto station
Open: Mar 16–Oct 31, 8–5; Nov 1–Mar 15, 9–4

Sanjusangendo, the Hall of the 33 Bays, is also known as the Rengeo-in Temple; its popular name derives from the 33 spaces between the 35 pillars found in the hall, which is 387 feet (118m) long by 59 feet (18m) wide. Thirty-three is also the number of the manifestations of Kannon, the Buddhist goddess of mercy to whom this Tendai sect temple is dedicated. A gilded statue of the 1,000-armed Kannon, carved by Tankei (1173–1256) in 1254, is enshrined in the middle of the hall surrounded by 1,000 smaller gilded statues of Kannon, the work of 70 sculptors supervised by Tankai and his father Unkei. A tradition has developed among visitors to the Sanjusangendo of trying to find the features of a relative or friend among the faces portrayed on the statues.

The Sanjusangendo was originally built by the emperor Goshirakawa (1126–91) in 1164. It was burned down and rebuilt in 1266, when the statues of Kannon were installed in the middle of the hall and the statues of the 28 guardians of Buddhism were erected in the corridor behind the main hall. Many of the guardians are derived from the Hindu pantheon, such as the bird-man playing the flute, Karurao (Garuda), and the emaciated holy man, Basusennin.

▶▶ Zenrinji Temple   121E3

Shishigatani-dori, Higashiyama (north of Nanzenji Temple)
Bus: 5 to Eikando mae, then a 15-minute walk
Open: 9–4:30

Located at the end of the Philosopher's Walk (see panel, page 131), Zenrinji Temple is also known as Eikando. Established in 836 by the priest Shinsho, the buildings were destroyed during the Onin Wars (1467–77) and rebuilt during the 16th century. The temple enshrines a statue of the Amida Buddha with his face turned to the side as if he is looking over his shoulder. According to legend, this came about when the statue came to life and joined a group of worshipers who were dancing to honor the Amida Buddha. The dancers were led by the priest Eikan, who stood still in surprise. The statue looked backward to encourage Eikan to keep dancing, and when he climbed back onto his pedestal he retained the twist in his neck.

If you have the energy to climb the stairs to the top of the pagoda, you'll get a superb view of Kyoto. The excellent gardens include many maple trees that burst with color when the leaves begin to turn in the fall.

ARCHERY CONTEST
Sanjusangendo is the site of an archery contest first held in 1606. On January 15 and May 2, archers gather at the temple to see who can fire the greatest number of arrows at a target placed at the end of the hall's outer veranda. The record of 8,133 bull's eyes established in 1686 has yet to be beaten, but the upright wooden posts bear the scars of many misdirected shots.

TEMPLE FOOD
Two restaurants that serve vegetarian and *tofu* dishes typical of the meals served in Buddhist temples can be found on the road leading to Eikando Temple, to the north of Nanzenji Temple. The Okutan Restaurant is the most famous and most expensive. Cheaper and nearby is the Koan restaurant, which also serves good vegetarian meals and *tofu*.

133

Sanjusangendo

There are three basic types of Japanese garden: the tea garden, usually designed by tea masters as a site for the tea ceremony; the hill garden, designed for private estates as a small park with miniature artificial hills; and the flat garden. The Zen garden at Ryoanji is a famous version of the flat garden.

Above: taking tea in Daitokuji Temple's Zen garden
Below: Ryoanji Garden

Ryoanji Garden In the flat garden style few shrubs are used and the most common elements are stones, sand, and gravel. They are designed, like a painting, for contemplation. Several of the best Zen gardeners were also well-known painters in ink, and in this medium they intended, with just a few strokes of black ink on white paper, to evoke an atmospheric natural scene. Their gardens were three-dimensional evocations of the same idea, using sand or gravel instead of silk, and shrubs, trees, or stones instead of brush strokes. The stones they chose were also charged with different meanings according to their shapes, their textures, and the angles at which they were placed.

The garden at Ryoanji was said to have been created by Soami (although this is by no means certain), a famous ink-line artist. It consists of raked gravel and 15 stones in five groupings, and certainly obeys the injunction of an anonymous 16th-century painter and gardener: "Caution should be taken not to be too anxious to overcrowd the scenery to make it more interesting. Such an effect often results in a loss of dignity and a feeling of vulgarity." The temple authorities publish a small pamphlet describing the garden as symbolizing "a group of mountainous

TOUR ITINERARIES
F: Kyoto station–
Tenryuji Temple–
Ryoanji Temple–
Daitokuji Temple–
Daisen-in Temple–
Myoshinji-Taizoin Temple–
Kyoto station (9:30 AM;
five hours, 30 minutes,
including a Japanese-style
lunch).
J: Kyoto station–
Hakusasonso–
Konchi-in Temple–
Nanzenji Temple–
Shoren-in Temple–
Daigo Sambo-in Temple–
Kajyuji Temple–
Kyoto station (10 AM; six
hours, including a
Japanese-style lunch).
R: Kyoto station–
Tenryuji Temple–
Ryoanji Temple–
Zuihoin Temple–
Kyoto station (2 PM; three
hours, 30 minutes).

islands in a great ocean, or mountain tops rising above a
sea of clouds. We can see it as a picture framed by the
ancient mid wall, now in itself regarded as a national
treasure, or we can forget the frame as we sense the
truth of this sea [the grave] stretching out boundlessly."

Daisen-in Zen Garden Soami was an official painter in the
court of Yoshimasa, the eighth Ashikaga *shogun*. In 1480
he designed and built one of the earliest and, to this day,
most famous Zen flat gardens for the abbot's residence
at Daisen-in, a sub-temple of Daitokuji Temple (see pages
124–125). At the time, Soami was influenced by Chinese
Song period paintings which, by their portrayals of
dramatic and awe-inspiring mountain landscapes, highlight
human vulnerability. His garden at Daisen-in, designed to
be viewed from the veranda of the abbot's quarters, rather
than to be walked around, is constructed of rocks and
sand. Unlike the abstract garden of Ryoanji Temple, it is a
three-dimensional representation of a Song-style painting
featuring a mountain (Mount Horai, the mythical home of
enlightened beings), a river, and a boat with a cargo of
treasure. It has been suggested that the garden may be
seen as a representation of the bridge between being and
non-being. As such, it rewards quiet contemplation, and it
is a good idea to visit Daisen-in early in the day and to
avoid weekends and public holidays.

Like other Zen gardens, Ryoanji and Daisen-in *kare
sansui* ("waterless stream gardens") were designed to
promote the meditative practice of Zen monks. Rock and
sand gardens, unaffected by the changes of the seasons,
gave the monks a sense of the calm of eternity.

*The perfect precision of
Ryoanji Garden*

Walk

with the occasional trendy coffee shop along the way. After it passes the **Kano Shoju-an** Japanese patisserie, with its elegant tearoom, the canal goes underground by the entrance to the **Nyakuoji Shrine**. Turn right, then turn left, to pass the gate to **Zenrinji Temple** (see page 133). To the right is the **Nomura Art Museum▶▶**, which has a collection of tea-ceremony artifacts. The lane bends to the right and then left before reaching the entrance to **Nanzenji Temple** (see page 130), where the massive **Sanmon gate**, **Konchi-in Temple**, and the Abbot's quarters are well worth a visit: the latter two have exquisite Zen gardens. The restaurants at the entrance to the temple specialize in *yu-dofu*, a Buddhist vegetarian dish.

From Nanzenji, walk away from the entrance, past Yachiyo *ryokan's* elegant forecourt on the left, then turn right and walk for three minutes to the Eikando-mae bus stop to catch City Bus 5 back to Kyoto station.

As evening descends, paper lanterns (chochin) are lit to decorate a canal-side restaurant

Along the old canal

Distance: 1 mile (1.6km); time (excluding temple visits): 50 minutes. This pleasant canal-side stroll follows the Path of Philosophy, from Ginkakuji, the Silver Pavilion, to Nanzenji Temple.

Begin at bus stop A-1, Ginkakuji-michi (City Bus 5), and walk toward the entrance of **Ginkakuji Temple**. On the right-hand side, before the bus parking lot, is the pleasant and modest **Hakusa-Sonso Garden▶**, once the home of the early 20th-century painter, Hashimoto Kansetsu. Ahead are the immaculate hedges that form the entrance to the **Ginkakuji Temple** (see page 125). From Ginkakuji, walk back to join the path that runs south along the little canal. This is the start of the **Path of Philosophy** (see panel, page 131), linking **Ginkakuji Temple** and **Nanzenji Temple** . The canal passes through a quiet, residential district

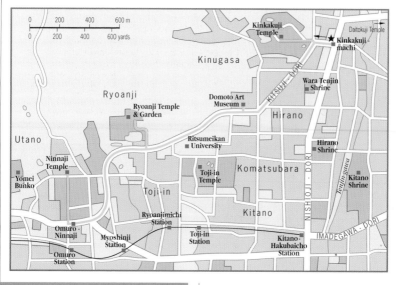

137

Walk

Kinkakuji Temple and Ryoanji Garden

Distance: 1 mile (1.6km); time: about one hour, including visits to both the temples. This walk in the western foothills links two of Kyoto's most celebrated monuments: the dazzling Golden Pavilion and the Ryoanji rock garden at the Ryoanji Temple.

Start from Kinkakuji-michi bus stop, B-3 (City Bus 59 or 205). A driveway lined with low, clipped pine trees and hedges leads to the entrance, to the left of an enormous tour bus parking lot. Bamboo groves and tile-capped walls striped in ocher and white line the approach path to **Kinkakuji** (see pages 128–129), built as a villa retreat at the end of the 14th century by the third Ashikaga *shogun*. Once through the gate, the path turns sharply right. A high bamboo fence obscures the view until suddenly the Golden Pavilion appears, floating above its reflection in the lake. Covered in thick gold leaf, the pavilion glows even under rainy skies. The path skirts around the lake, with the main temple buildings to the right, past the pavilion, then winds up and around the garden, past a lotus pond and a tiny thatched tea house, before leading to a flight of steps back to the entrance. In the gardens of the temple, visible from the path, is a large pine tree in the shape of a boat. The gift shop by the parking lot has a surprisingly good selection of high-quality souvenirs.

Leaving the temple, walk back to the main road and turn right. Follow the road, which curves along the hillside, past the **Domoto Art Museum▶** and on to **Ryoanji Temple and Garden** (see pages 132 and 134). From Ryoanji, the walk can be extended, turning right along the main road to **Ninnaji Temple▶ ▶**, first built in the 9th century and famous for its late-blooming cherry trees. From Ninnaji, take City Bus 26 back to the city center.

Kinkakuji Temple

SELF-DISCIPLINE

The monks of Mount Hiei still discipline themselves by undergoing austere practices involving fasting, meditation, and chanting. One of the most severe disciplines is conducted by the famous "Marathon Monks" who, for 1,000 days, complete a daily 19-mile (30-km) marathon. During a specially intensive period of 100 days they are expected to cover 53 miles (85km) a day. Jodo-in is the temple for the practice of Sweeping Hell. Here the monks rise very early and spend half the day brushing the temple grounds and the other half in prayer. At the Mudo-Ji-Dani (the Valley of the Still Temple), in the eastern precinct, the monks rise at 2 AM and set out to walk to each temple in the monastery complex, praying at each one on the way—no easy task, with 125 temples in the complex.

The view of Kyoto from the Mount Hiei cable car

BUDDHA OF HEALING

The Kompon-chodo of the Enryakuji temple enshrines an image of the *Yakushi Nyorai* (Buddha of Healing), carved by Saicho from the trunk of a sandalwood tree. It is faced by three lanterns glowing with the "eternal light of the Dharma," said to have been lit by Saicho himself. They have been kept burning through the centuries.

►►► Mount Hiei (*Hei-san*)

Sakamoto Honmachi, Otsu, Shiga Prefecture
Bus: 16, 17, 18 to Yase-Yuenchi stop. Entrance to Keifuku cable car on the left; departs every 30 minutes. Transfer at Hiei to the Hiei-zan Ropeway to the observatory on the summit; from there follow the path down to Enryakuji
Open: Mar–Nov 8:30–4:30, Dec–Feb 9–4

Standing to the northeast of Kyoto, Mount Hiei is, at 2,790 feet (850m) the second-highest mountain in the vicinity of the city. Its location is significant: the northeast was feared as the "Devil's Gate" (*Ki-mon*), through which all malevolent forces entered the city. Even today, buildings in Kyoto can be seen that have the northeast corners cut off to ward off evil.

The emperor Kammu (737–806), concerned for the city's safety, ordered the priest Saicho (767–822) to build a temple on Mount Hiei to protect the city from malign influences. Saicho built a small meditation hut on Mount Hiei in 785, which he enlarged three years later into a small temple. When the temple was inaugurated in 794, the emperor climbed Mount Hiei to attend the inauguration ceremony.

In 797, Saicho was appointed one of a group of 10 "imperial monks" and Kammu ordered that his temple be supported by funds gathered from Saicho's home province of Omi. The temple was renamed Enryakuji in 823 after Saicho's death, and Saicho was given the posthumous title of *Dengyo Daishi* or "Great Teaching Master."

Saicho was the founder of a new sect of Japanese Buddhism known as Tendai. He believed that the world was coming to an end and was convinced that the only way to avert this catastrophe was to unify all the sects of

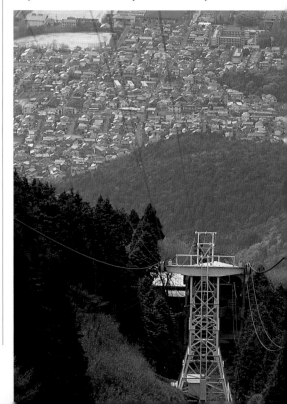

Buddhism. He went to China in 804 and studied Buddhism at Mount T'ien-t'ai. In the summer of 805 he returned to Japan with over 460 works on Buddhism, Taoism, and various schools of Chinese philosophy. Within a very short time, Tendai was acknowledged as an independent sect by the court, and the temple on Mount Hiei became the recipient of a great deal of patronage by the court and aristocracy.

Within two centuries or so, the complex of temples on Mount Hiei had become very wealthy. To protect their wealth, the monks established their own army of *sohei*, fierce warrior-monks willing and able to fight and destroy anyone who offered any kind of threat to their power and authority. Emperor Shirakawa (1053–1129) once said that there were three things he could not control: the fall of dice when gambling, the floodwaters of the Kamo River, and the monks of Mount Hiei.

Eventually the arrogance of the monks proved their undoing. They challenged the might of Oda Nobunaga (1534–82), who ordered his forces to destroy the monastic complex of over 3,000 buildings and slaughter the monks. In response to protests from some of his advisers, he said "I am not the destroyer of this monastery. The destroyer of the monastery is the monastery itself."

Set among towering cedar trees, Enryakuji was later rebuilt on a smaller scale. Most of the buildings seen today date from the 17th century. From the train station the path leads to the Daidoko (Great Lecture Hall), rebuilt after a fire in 1956. Climb the hill to the Kaiden-in, built in 1604 as the ordination hall for Tendai priests. Following the path through the trees, turn left at the Sanno-in (the Temple of the Mountain King) and down the stairs to the Jodo-in (Pure Land Temple), founded by Saicho and rebuilt in the 17th century. His tomb can be found behind the main hall. Go down the steps to the Kompon-chudo (Fundamental Central Hall), erected in 1642, which contains paintings of flowers on the ceiling "donated" by all the *daimyo* (great landowners) at the command of the Tokugawa shogunate.

Enryakuji Temple

MISCREANT MONKS
The monks of Mount Hiei influenced Japanese political and religious life until the 16th century and the arrival of General Oda Nobunaga. He is quoted as saying: "If I do not take them away now, this great trouble will be everlasting. Moreover, these priests violate their vows: they eat fish and stinking vegetables, keep concubines, and never unroll the sacred books. How can they be vigilant against evil, or maintain the right? Surround their dens and burn them, and suffer none within them to live." Nobunaga invaded the mountain, burned every temple to the ground, and executed every monk.

Sandals at Enryakuji

Kyoto

Pavilion in Katsura Imperial Villa garden

THREE CONDITIONS
It is said that when Kobori Enshu was commissioned by Hideyoshi to build the Katsura Villa he imposed three conditions on his employer: no limit on expense, no limit on time, and no interference until the building was completed. Hideyoshi died before the work was complete and he never saw the building that he paid for.

BORROWED SCENERY
In contrast to Katsura Imperial Villa, Shugakuin is reputed more for its gardens than for its architecture. They make particularly good use of the style of landscaping known as *shak kei*, or borrowed scenery, in which views of distant hills and, in this case, of Kyoto itself, are incorporated into the design.

►►► Katsura Imperial Villa *120A1*

Katsura Shimizu-cho, Ikyo-ku
Train: Katsura station on the Hankyu Arashiyama line (10-minute walk from station), Kyoto station (3-mile (5km) cab ride); bus: 33 from Kyoto station to Katsura Rikyu-mae
Open: tours on weekdays at 10 AM and 2 PM, Sat at 10 AM.
Closed: Sat afternoon, Sun, national holidays, and Dec 25– Jan 25; see below

Katsura Imperial Villa, in western Kyoto, was originally built at the beginning of the 17th century by Prince Toshihito, the brother of Emperor Goyozei. Set on the banks of the Katsuragawa, it is constructed from carefully selected materials so that the buildings and gardens harmonize elegantly with their natural surroundings, within sight of the Arashiyama and Kameyama hills.

The Katsura garden is judged to be the masterpiece of Kobori Enshu, Japan's greatest landscape gardener. Each turn of the path that meanders through the garden brings a new view. Stone lanterns, carefully cultivated trees, bridges gracefully arching over water, and a number of rustic tea houses are all cleverly arranged to provide viewers with an aesthetic experience reminiscent of the tea ceremony. The garden is built around a central pond with tea houses designed to reflect each of the four seasons. Katsura has been described as the epitome of Japanese culture and aestheticism, and many contemporary Western architects have been drawn to it and influenced by its elegant simplicity, its use of natural materials, and the harmony of interior and exterior design. For example, the ground running away from the building is laid in strips of bare earth, pebbles, stepping stones, and then moss with the intention of gradually leading one away from the human order of the house, to the naturalness of the garden, or vice versa.

Special permission is needed to visit the villa and details can be obtained at the Kyoto Tourist Information Center on the ground floor of Kyoto Tower opposite JR Kyoto station. Visitors must be aged at least 20 and must take their passports when collecting permits. Tours are in Japanese, but information is available on an English-language video tape that is played in the waiting room before the tour begins. Apply for a permit in advance.

▶▶▶ Shugakuin Imperial Villa   *121E5*

Shugakuin Muromachi, Sakyo-ku
Train: Eizan Railway from Yase Yuen station to Shugakuin-mae station, then a 30-minute walk; bus: 5 from Kyoto station to Shugakuin Rikyu Michi bus stop, then a 15-minute walk from there
Open: tours in Japanese at 9, 10 and 11. On Sat extra tours are held at 1 and 3. Closed: Sun, national holidays, Dec 25–Jan 5. Permission must be obtained from the Imperial House-hold Agency (see Katsura Imperial Villa)

This villa in northeast Kyoto was built in 1659, on a foothill of Mount Hiei by the Tokugawa shogunate, as a retirement home for Emperor Go Mizuno-o. The grounds are divided into three large gardens, each with its own tea house. The upper garden, which is the largest, is centered around a lake with islands, bridges, waterfalls, and a long winding path through the gardens that gives fine views over Kyoto to the surrounding hills.

The Rakushiken pavilion, in the middle garden, was built for the emperor's daughter, Princess Ake. When she became a nun, the building was converted into a temple for her use. Jugetsukan pavilion in the lower garden contains only four rooms. The rooms are laid out in an "L" shape and surrounded by a veranda. The three raised and framed mats in the 15-*tatami* (closely woven straw floor mats) room were the emperor's sitting place. From the back gate of the lower garden you step onto a patio area that gives unimpeded views of far-off mountain ranges.

IMPERIAL PATRONS OF THE ARTS
Emperor Go Mizuno-o and his empress Tofukuman-in designed Shugakuin them-selves and continued to visit their "rustic" retreat after their retirement from office and into old age. Both were avid patrons of the arts, especially the tea ceremony and flower-arranging, and were also the driving force behind the 17th-century rebuilding of Kyoto after the ravages of many centuries of war.

The view across the lake from Shugakuin Imperial Villa

Kyoto

Ana Hotel, Kyoto

TEMPLE LODGING

Temple accommodation is a specialty of Kyoto. Rooms are small, in the traditional *tatami* style, and the lodgings are usually located in temple grounds, often in a quiet garden setting. Facilities may or may not include a bath or shower, but one or the other will be available nearby. Breakfast is provided if required and in some places an evening meal may be ordered. Prices for lodging and food are usually very reasonable (see **Accommodations and Restaurants**, pages 269 and 278).

Gion Hotel, Kyoto

Accommodations

The hotels and *ryokan* of Kyoto are renowned for their impeccable service and hospitality. However, Kyoto is essentially a tourist town, and space is at a premium. Rooms are not large, and during the peaks of the spring and autumn seasons and over public holidays the best places need to be reserved in advance.

Fortunately, Kyoto is also rich in a variety of accommodations. If you travel on a flexible timetable you will find, except at exceptionally busy festival times, somewhere to rest your head, even if it is only a dormitory-style lodging (see pages 80–81). *Ryokan*, traditional Japanese inns, are found in an unusually wide range of price categories in Kyoto; if you particularly wish to stay in one, Kyoto is the ideal city (see pages 220–221).

Budget accommodations The Japanese Inn Group has a number of member inns in the Kyoto area, providing cheap and simple *tatami* (floor-mat) rooms and communal dining areas in hostel-like environments. These are a good choice if you are on a budget, and want to meet fellow travelers. Other tips to help keep down your costs: reserve a room without a bathroom; in more expensive hotels ask for a small or inconveniently placed room, so that you can enjoy the facilities without paying the full price; do not use the hotel telephones, bars, or restaurants. Many *ryokan* and hotel accommodations are focused around the Kyoto station area, but as Kyoto is not a large city, and is served by an excellent bus network, it is not essential to stay in the heart of the city, and accommodations are sometimes cheaper farther out.

The best First-class hotels in Kyoto are excellent, and the services they provide are of a high international standard. English-language television, English-speaking staff, well-stocked information desks, computer equipment for businesspeople, rapid room service, and guest relations officers are all standard, even in the less than top-notch establishments. Tea bags, instant coffee packets, and thermoses of hot water are provided in the rooms of every category of hotel. A 3 percent government tax is added to all Japanese hotel bills and, for hotels in Kyoto, a further 3 percent city tax is added to bills over a certain amount. The highest-class establishments also add a 10 to 15 percent service charge. Tipping is not expected.

Where to stay The Kyoto bus network operates on a grid pattern and is easy to follow (maps of the bus routes are available from the Tourist Information Center). If, however, you have only a few days in Kyoto and wish to explore on foot, it would be best to choose one area and to stay in that vicinity. For most visitors the eastern district, Higashiyama, provides the best cross section of attractions, including Gion, an area with many traditional shops and a *geisha* entertainment quarter, plus some of the most famous sights in Kyoto, such as Ginkakuji Temple (Temple of the Silver Pavilion) and the Heian Shrine. Central Kyoto has a similar mix of shopping, evening entertainment, and major sights, while western and northern Kyoto are the places to stay if you want a quieter experience of Kyoto.

HOTEL-CHECKING
If you are visiting Japan as part of an arranged trip or for business reasons, your travel agent will book you into an approved hotel. Some offer Japanese as well as Western-type rooms; if you want a room with a *tatami*-covered floor and sunken bath tub, request a reservation in a Japanese-style room.

Kyoto Tower

O-BENTO AND EKI-BEN
O-bento are everyday box
lunches prepared at home
or bought in local shops.
Eki-ben are box lunches
specially for train trips.
They are sold on train
platforms, in and around
stations and on express
trains. The boxes
themselves are made from
thin, unpainted wood or,
for the deluxe version,
lacquered wood. Inside
they divide into neat
compartments and contain
such foods as sushi rice,
grilled chicken,
mushrooms, smoked fish,
pickled plums, fresh and
cooked vegetables. They
are sold neatly wrapped in
decorative paper and tied
with string. Each region of
Japan has its own version
of o-bento and eki-ben,
containing a particular
selection of food and one
or two local specialties.

Food and drink

Kyoto's cuisine is derived from that of the imperial court
and the vegetarian food of Buddhist temples. *Kyo-ryori* or
Kyoto cooking is the most refined of all styles of Japanese
cooking, the *haute cuisine* of culinary traditions.

Kyoto's specialties can be divided into two categories:
shojin-ryori, Zen-style vegetarian dishes developed to serve
the needs of monks and pilgrims; and *kaiseki-ryori*, food
originally prepared for the tea ceremony, but eventually
evolving into an elegant full-course meal, popular with the
nobility. A restaurant advertising *kyo-ryori* will usually
offer a selection of each of these styles of cooking. Many of
Kyoto's traditional Japanese restaurants are located in the
heart of the city. *Yusoku-ryori*, cooking inspired by the
dishes of the imperial court, is not now generally available
and only one restaurant, the Mankamero (see **Accommodations and Restaurants**, from page 266), specializes in this
style of cuisine. The Kyoto Tourist Information Center
publishes a *Kyoto Gourmet Guide* that is worth picking up.

Zen food The *shojin* cook emphasizes the importance of
simple meals prepared from locally available foods. These
include rice, fresh vegetables, pickled vegetables, sea
vegetables (seaweed), and soybean products such as *miso*,
tofu (beancurd), and *shoyu* (soy sauce). The cook strives to
create a harmonious balance of five *flavors*—*shoyu*, sugar,
vinegar, salt, and spices (gingerroot, sesame seeds, and
wasabi, a Japanese mustard)—with the other ingredients to
make a vegetarian meal that is appropriate to the season as
well as delicious, good to look at, and nutritious. Local
shojin-ryori specialties are *yu-dofu*, a pot of *tofu* simmered
at your table, and other *tofu* dishes (see pages 146–147); *fu*,
a glutinous wheat cake, and *yuba*, dried soybean milk skin.

*Kyoto noodle
restaurant*

Noodle soup: preparation …

Tea ceremony food *Kaiseki-ryori* is often very expensive, but it is an essential experience for visitors to Kyoto. The meal consists of a procession of tiny courses, each presented in carefully selected porcelain dishes or lacquered bowls, chosen to match in shape and size their portions of vegetable, fish, or other foods. The ingredients of the dishes are valued for their scent, texture, flavor, and seasonal freshness. Ideally, a *kaiseki-ryori* should be presented in a traditional *tatami* room decorated with a hanging scroll and flower arrangement, within earshot of running water.

If you are on a budget, try a *kyo-bento*, or box lunch, a commonly available version of *kaiseki-ryori* (see panel). These are very popular in Kyoto and are available in the basement food halls of most of the city's department stores. Exquisite versions are also offered by many *ryotei*, the top restaurants that serve *kaiseki-ryori*.

Tradition and convenience Many of the restaurants in Kyoto have been in business for generations, and old practices die hard. Several still do not accept credit cards, so check ahead if you plan to use one. The better places expect you to dress somewhat formally and tend to serve dinner early (7 PM–8 PM). If you wish to try a variety of Japanese cooking styles, visit the inexpensive restaurant complexes in the Hankyu department store (see page 149) or the Kintetsu Mall, under the tracks on the west side of Kyoto station. In eastern Kyoto there is a variety of informal restaurants selling temple-style *shojin-ryori* food in and around the Kiyomizudera temple.

There are also outlets of many American fast-food chains.

Daily special The *teishoku* is a daily, fixed-price menu that many Japanese restaurants present at lunchtime. The menus of expensive restaurants offering *kaiseki-ryori* meals are also often much better value at lunchtime than in the evening.

HEALTHY COOKING
Shojin cookery is also sometimes referred to as *yukuseki* or "medicine." Food selection and its preparation are seen to be inseparable from the treatment of disease and the cultivation of good health. The traditional Chinese medical view is the same: "If one falls ill one should first examine one's diet, then choose well, chew carefully and give thanks. In this way the curative powers of nature, with which mankind is blessed, are given full rein to act and nearly all diseases are conquered."

145

… and presentation

Tofu *(beancurd) is rich in vitamins and minerals, and is fat-free. This wonderfully versatile food can be used fresh or deep fried, grilled (broiled), baked or simmered, and is one of the world's best sources of vegetable protein. Once all Japanese towns and villages had their own* tofu-maker. *This is less common now, but in Kyoto, where the* tofu *has the reputation of being the finest in Japan, the tradition is still alive and thriving.*

146

TOFU-MAKING CONTESTS

In the past, each year throughout Japan, *tofu*-making contests were held among master craftsmen. First on the city, then on the provincial, and finally on the national level, master craftsmen met for a period of several days and were judged by retired masters on the speed and accuracy of their cutting, and, above all, on their ability to make *tofu* with fine flavor, texture, bouquet, and appearance.

TYPES OF *TOFU* AND DISHES

Momengoshi-dofu: regular cotton-strained *tofu*.
Kinugoshi-dofu: delicate silky *tofu*.
Aburage: thin sheets of deep-fried *tofu*.
Nameage: thick blocks of deep-fried *tofu* with soft centers.
Ganmodoki: deep-fried balls of *tofu* and vegetables.
Goma-dofu: sesame-flavored *tofu*.
Yu-dofu: tofu heated in seaweed-flavored water and served with soy sauce, grated gingerroot, *bonito* (dried fish) shavings, and chopped spring onions.
Hiyayakko: chilled *tofu*, served as *yu-dofu*.
Agedashi-dofu: tofu dipped in potato flour and deep fried, served with soy sauce and grated *daikon* (a type of white radish).

The raw materials: soybeans

Tofu is made by soaking and grinding soybeans, then extracting the milky liquid from the resulting mixture, and curdling it. The set product is pressed into slabs to produce soft-textured, delicately flavored, pale cream *tofu*, which is sold the day it is prepared.

The *tofu* shop At the Morika *tofu* shop on the outskirts of Kyoto, the family tradition of *tofu*-makers has been maintained and the shop is owned and run by brothers whose father was a *tofu* master. Work starts at 5 AM, and by 6:30 the shop is a hive of controlled activity. The stone floor of the work area is awash with water from the rinsing of beans, buckets, and wooden storage boxes. Deep tanks of water hold huge slabs of *tofu*, ready to be cut into standard 17.5-ounce (400-g) blocks. Large drums hold soaking soybeans that will later be crushed between stone rollers and boiled, before filtering through a cotton cloth into a steel mold. The hot soy milk collected in the mold will be set with *nigari* (magnesium chloride), an almost tasteless salt that serves the same function as rennet in cheese-making, before being pressed under weighted wooden boards.

Fresh *tofu* made in this way and seasoned with a little good-quality soy sauce is delicious and creamy and as

Making tofu, *the traditional way*

different from day-old *tofu* as newly baked French bread is from a stale baguette.

The *tofu*-maker's wife Traditionally, the *tofu* craftsman's wife has complete responsibility for all deep-frying work, and at Morika the mother of the family is still in charge of this task. Apart from their reputation for the highest standards of cleanliness, *tofu* shops are known for their lack of waste; the mother at Morika is also responsible for collecting *tofu* left from the previous day and that day's offcuts. She crumbles and mixes it with slivers of vegetables, forms the mixture into small balls and deep fries them golden brown to make *ganmodoki*, a popular *tofu* snack and box lunch food.

***Tofu* seasons** For the *tofu*-maker, the year has a rhythm. January and February, when the air and water are cold, are the best months for making regular *tofu* (*momengoshi tofu*), and keeping it fresh. With the arrival of spring, the demand starts for *kinugoshi*, a silky smooth, more watery *tofu* supplied throughout the summer. During the hot months the *tofu*-maker begins work even earlier to take advantage of the cool, predawn air. The fall finds *kinugoshi* replaced with grilled *tofu* (*yaki-dofu*), a firmer ingredient for winter vegetable stews. In November, the new crop of soybeans arrives and then the *tofu* has an added sweetness and aroma. Toward the last day of the year, demand for *yaki-dofu* peaks, as it is a traditional New Year food. From New Year's Eve, the *tofu* shops all over Japan are closed and the *tofu*-maker and his family take a vacation.

ORIGINS OF *TOFU*
Tofu is said to have been discovered in about 200 BC in China by Lord Liu of Huai-nan, a Chinese scholar, philosopher, and ruler. He was a Taoist and undertook experiments to make *tofu* in order to introduce variety and nutrition into a meatless diet. In the craft tradition of old Japan, the daily work of the craftsman was regarded as part of a spiritual path that had as its goal self-realization and liberation. The paths of the swordsmith, the potter, the calligrapher, and the *tofu*-maker were united by this same underlying principle.

Gift shop sign, Kyoto

SHUENSU
The *shuensu* is a brocade-covered booklet of blank, heavy paper sheets, available at any stationery store and many temples. Used as a passport to collect ink stamps from places visited, the *shuensu* is very popular with the Japanese; most sights and places of interest provide stamps and ink stamp pads.

148

Antiques on sale in Kyoto

Shopping

For over 1,000 years, while Kyoto was the nation's capital, a collection of the best craftsmen of each generation lived in the city and catered to the demands of the imperial court. Even today, Kyoto is a center of artistry and refinement, and the place to shop for all traditional goods, as well as contemporary craftware.

Specialty shops The largest concentration of small specialty shops is in the Gion district, along both sides of Shijo-dori, which runs east–west, and Kawaramachi-dori running north–south. In the square formed by these two avenues and Sanjo-dori and Teramachi-dori are shops selling everything from lacquerware to combs to swords. The square also encloses Shin-Kyogoku, a mall with many souvenir shops. For the latest in modern shopping malls, try the huge underground one, named Porta, at Kyoto station.

The shopping avenues radiate, like subterranean catacombs, outward from the Karasuma (north) side of the station. There are over 200 boutiques and restaurants. For pottery shops, food shops, and tea houses the establishments that line the steep roads leading up to Kiyomizudera Temple in Higashiyama-ku district are the places to explore.

Art and antiques Head toward Shinmonzen-dori, also in the Gion district, for art and antiques. This unprepossessing street of two-story wooden houses runs parallel and to the north of Shijo-dori. The shopkeepers here have an excellent reputation for selling authentic goods at the correct price. Together they publish a free booklet called *Shinmonzen Street Shopping Guide*. Copies are available at the TIC and from some hotel reception desks. *Netsuke*, woodblock prints, scrolls, paintings, and antiques are some of the specialties of the Shinmonzen traders.

Nishijin Textile Center

NETSUKE

Netsuke are carved, ornamental ivory toggles by means of which purses, pouches, or medicine boxes were suspended from waist bands. During the Tokugawa regime they were popular with merchants, who wore them to vie with the ornamental sword guards of the *samurai*. Later, *netsuke* carving developed into a specialized art form. The international trade ban on ivory has reduced the number of contemporary practitioners of *netsuke* carving.

Department stores Kyoto department stores are not as large or glamorous as their Tokyo counterparts, but they are the places to visit for modern goods, clothing, and accessories. The basement floors are always given over to a cornucopia of food counters. Many offer free samples of their particular foodstuffs, and are good places to wander, to taste, and to put names to the strange and wonderful array of foods that are often uniquely Japanese. **Takashimaya** department store (closed Wednesday), right in the center of Kyoto, is one of the oldest such stores in Japan, and has a good selection of traditional and modern goods, a money-exchange facility, and an information counter with English-speaking staff. **Hankyu** department store, right across from Takashimaya, has two floors devoted to a variety of restaurants, each with window displays showing the types of dishes available and their prices, which are usually very reasonable.

Silk Kyoto is celebrated for its silk, and in the Nishijin silk-weaving district, to the west of Horikawa-dori and north of Ichijo-dori, the sound of looms fills the air. The **Nishijin Textile Center**, in central Kyoto on Horikawa-dori, Imadegawa-minamiiru, and Kamigyo-ku (*open 9–5, admission* free), is a museum established in 1915, where a large display of Nishijin products is exhibited and kimonos are on sale. Note that new silk kimonos are *very* expensive; used kimonos are much less so. **Aizan Kobo** (Omiya Nishi-iru, Nakasuji-dori, Kamigyo-ku; *open 9–5*) is the home of a traditional weaving family, who show and sell a variety of hand-woven and dyed silk goods and garments.

FLEA MARKETS

On the 21st day of each month a famous flea market is held at the Toji Temple, 15 minutes' walk southwest of Kyoto station. Renowned throughout Japan, it is said to be part of a tradition going back several hundred years. The market opens from dawn to dusk and is the place to buy old kimonos at a fraction of the cost of new ones (the Japanese are not fans of secondhand goods and old bric-à-brac is very cheap). There is another good flea market held on the 25th day of each month at the Kitano Temmangu Shrine.

Gifts are an important part of Japanese life and ritual. Meeting for dinner at a friend's house, saying goodbye, meeting someone important for the first time, thanking someone for their help or a service provided are all occasions marked by giving or receiving a gift, and as a place to buy appropriate Japanese presents, Kyoto is second to none.

GIFT-WRAPPING

In Japan, the wrapping of a present is an art form in itself. Whether you buy from an expensive department store or a street vendor, your goods will be deftly, swiftly, and beautifully wrapped. When receiving a gift, unwrap it with care and respect.

SOUVENIR SHOPS

One of the regular features of Japanese life is the many small souvenir and gift shops found near temples and train stations and in vacation resorts. They provide for the tiny numerous presents (*miyage*) bought to take home to relatives and friends after a day out or a weekend away from home. For the Japanese, one of the joys of traveling is the purchase of such gifts.

The art of giving Before leaving home, it is useful to buy a number of small, lightweight gifts with some characteristic of your home country. Always wrap your gift and do not press the recipient to open it while you are there. As with much else in Japanese life, there are many subtleties to present-giving that you will not understand, but the one golden rule to remember in this situation, and others, is that neither party should be embarrassed or lose face.

Kyoto craftware The boundary between art and craft is not clearly defined within the tradition of Japanese craftwork, and nowhere is this more evident than in Kyoto, where craftsmen serving the imperial court left a legacy of artistry and refinement maintained to this day. Locally made specialist craftwork is prefixed with *kyo*—for example, *kyo-yaki* are ceramics made in local kilns. Such items are relatively expensive but renowned throughout Japan for their craftsmanship.

Traditional gifts Dolls are generally regarded as works of art to be appreciated for their beauty, rather than played with. Expensive dolls are often encased in glass cases and displayed in Japanese homes. *Kyo-ningyo* are display dolls, produced in Kyoto since the 9th century, made of wood coated with a white paste and dressed in traditional costumes of the finest materials.

Lacquer, the sap of the lacquer tree (*urushi-no-ki*), has been used in Japan since the 6th century to coat both precious and well-used objects to give them a beautiful appearance and to protect them from the elements. Lacquerwork is commonly decorated with designs created by sprinkling gold and silver powders onto damp lacquer; mother of pearl, ivory, and metals are also used. While decorative and often precious, lacquerware is intended for daily use. *Kyo-shikki*, Kyoto lacquerware products, include cabinets, writing boxes, bowls, serving trays, and spoons.

The two most common types of Japanese fan are the folding fan and the flat fan. The former, called *sensu*, are used on ceremonial occasions by men and women alike. They are given as presents on auspicious

Souvenir ideas: ceram objects ...

occasions and used as accessories in the *noh* play and classical Japanese dance and as props in storytelling. *Kyo-sensu* are decorated folding fans made by Kyoto craftsmen.

The craft and art of making pottery and ceramic objects has attained an exceptional degree of refinement in Japan. Skills flourished particularly in the 16th century with the popularity of the tea ceremony. In the Kyoto region especially, numerous kilns produced tea bowls, serving dishes, tea storage jars, and so on. Feudal lords competed with one another to have the finest wares, and their demands inspired technical and artistic enterprise. The most popular *kyo-yaki* products are perhaps the hand-painted red, green, and blue on white tableware, made in the Kiyomizu district. The area around Kiyomizudera temple is also a good place to look for shops specializing in *kyo-yaki*.

Kimonos Nowadays, most Japanese wear Western clothing and only put on their kimonos for special occasions such as the New Year Festival or a wedding. New kimonos are extremely expensive, but secondhand kimonos can be a tenth of the price and are frequently in perfect condition.

... or wind chimes

151

MONEY AND TIPPING

If you receive a present and plan to give one back, it should be of approximately the same value. If you plan to give money to someone Japanese, be it to a child or for exceptional services rendered, always present it enclosed in an envelope. Remember, however, that tipping is not a custom in Japan and tips will not be expected or, in some cases, accepted.

GOOD-LUCK DOLL

The *papier-mâché daruma* (*dharma*) doll is a popular good-luck figure and present, named after the legendary monk Bodidharma. A *daruma* doll is always painted red, with a fierce, bearded face. It is weighted at the base and if pushed over will right itself.

... or Japanese parasols

Kyoto

GEISHA
Gei means culture and *sha* person; a *geisha* is therefore a person practiced in the arts. The profession of *geisha* is traditionally respected in Japan and the young ladies who follow it are highly esteemed. Most *geisha* never marry, although some may form a liaison with a regular client and prominent Japanese men may sometimes maintain a *geisha* as a sort of social secretary. Nowadays, it is said that a few *geisha* do in fact accept sexual assignations outside their professional activities—yet a *geisha* is never obliged by the terms of her contract, and *makura* (*geisha* cushions) can be summoned as stand-ins, if necessary, after dinner. Seasonal dances (Miyako Odori and Kamogawa Odori) performed by *geisha* and their apprentices to celebrate spring and autumn are held in Kyoto in April, May, and October. These ravishing spectacles are held at the Gion Kaburenjo Theater, Gion Hanamikoji, Higashiyama-ku and the Pontocho Kaburenjo Theater, Pontocho Sanjo-sagaru, Nakagyo-ku.

A maiko *in Gion*

Nightlife

Kyoto is not noted for its nightlife, nor does it aspire to be, but, for those who wish it, there are enough bars, restaurants, *geisha* houses, and hostess bars. For a more cultural experience, the Gion quarter after dark gives a real taste of old Japan, as well as the opportunity to see performances of traditional theatrical arts. Strolling the streets of Kyoto or the banks of the Kamo River on a lively evening is an excellent way of finding free entertainment. For a whole range of Kyoto nighttime entertainment, from pool to disco to karaoke, you can go to the eight-story entertainment building **Imagium**, Shijo-dori, Kobashi-nishi-iru.

Culture Gion, a small district of Kyoto, is the geisha entertainment quarter of the city. Here, especially in the evening, you can see *geisha* and their *maiko* (young apprentices), dressed in gorgeous kimonos with beautiful hair and make-up, on their way to work. Gion Corner, a theater in the heart of Gion, presents one-hour shows that give a brief taste of a variety of Kyoto's performing arts. Dancing, puppet theater, court music, demonstrations of the tea ceremony, flower arrangement, and comic routines are all included. The show is very good value. Tickets are available at most hotels, travel agents, and Gion Corner. Two performances are given nightly, at 7:40 PM and 8:40 PM, March 1–November 29 (no performances are offered on August 16 or from December to February).

Bars and clubs Kawaramachi-dori and the area around it, including Kiyamachi-dori to the east, is a district of small, inexpensive drinking clubs, bars, and restaurants. Those with red lanterns outside are the most reasonable. If you are unsure of the cost, order a drink and then ask for the check. In hostess bars, you will quickly be offered tiny tidbits to eat. Avoid these places unless you have plenty of yen to spend.

Practical

Avoid Kyoto on public holidays and avoid the best-known temples at weekends. Otherwise, it is very easy to get around on foot, by bus, subway, or rented bike or, if you are in a hurry, by taxi. There are probably more guidebooks on Kyoto than on any other city in the world.

What's on The once dowdy Kyoto station was rebuilt in 1997, and is now a suitable entranceway to this important city. Almost opposite the main entrance of the station, across a busy road, is the Tourist Information Center (TIC) office, at the base of Kyoto Tower (visible from most places in town). At the TIC you can obtain free brochures, street and subway/railroad maps of Kyoto, and you can reserve accommodations. They have the latest information on what is going on and also stock *Kyoto Visitors Guide*, a monthly publication in English. Kyoto also has two English-language telephone information services: call 361 2911 for a recording of the week's events, including sports, arts, and festivals (24 hours); or 371 5649 for general information and an English-speaking guide (9–5).

Walking and cycling It is best to see the city in sections and to catch its flavor at a meditative pace, rather than rushing from place to place. A fun way to get around is to go by bicycle. Several places rent bikes by the day, including **Nippon Rent a Car** (tel: 672 3045), across from the Hachijo exit of Kyoto station; **Rent a Cycle Heian** (tel: 431 4522), on the west side of the Imperial Palace, **Cycle Yasumoto** (tel: 751 0595), near Keihan Sanjo station, and **Rent Pia Cycle**, Kyoto station (tel: 672 0662).

GETTING TO KYOTO

Journeys to Kyoto take about two hours, 40 minutes (319 miles/514km) from Tokyo station, 45 minutes (92 miles/148km) from Nagoya, and three hours, 20 minutes (412 miles/663km) from Fukuoka (Hakata), by the "Hikari" on the JR Shinkansen. The new Haruka Express train now also links Kyoto with Kansai International Airport in just over one hour. A long-distance night bus leaves from Tokyo station, arriving in eight hours, and a bus from Nagoya takes two hours, 40 minutes.

TAXIS

Taxis in Kyoto come in three different sizes, increasing in price from the smallest to the largest category. Taxis are readily available from taxi stands and hotels, or they can be flagged down.

City traffic

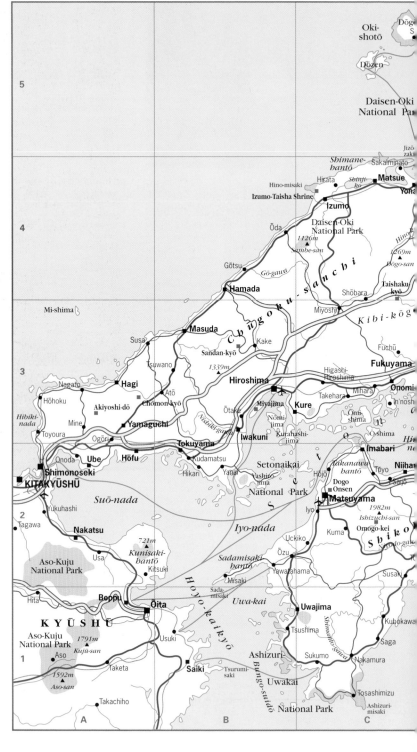

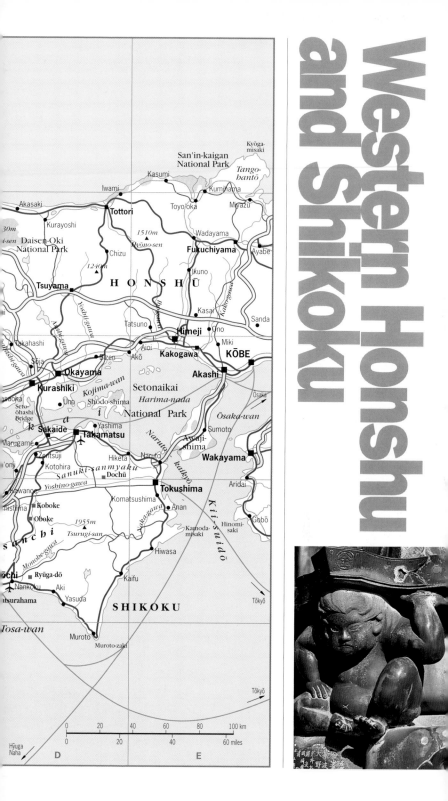

Kyōga-misaki

San'in-kaigan National Park

Tango-hantō

Kasumi

Kumihama

Iwami

Toyo'oka

Miyazu

Akasaki

Tottori

Toyo/oka

Kurayoshi

1510m
Hyōno-sen

Wadayama

Ayabe

30m
i-sen

Daisen-Oki National Park

Chizu

Fukuchiyama

1240m

Ikuno

Tsuyama

H O N S H Ū

Kasai

Sanda

Yoshii-gawa

Tatsuno

Uno

Himeji

Miki

Takahashi

Aioi

Kakogawa

KŌBE

Sōja

Bizen

Akō

Osaka

Okayama

Akashi

Kurashiki

Kojima-wan

Setonaikai

Harima-nada

Ōsaka-wan

Uno

Shōdo-shima

saoka

Seto-ōhashi Bridge

î

National Park

Sumoto

k

a

Sakaide

Yashima

Awaji-shima

Marugame

Takamatsu

Hiketa

Wakayama

'onji

Zentsūji

Naruto

Kotohira

Sanuki-sanmyaku

Dochū

Aridai

kawano

Yoshino-gawa

Komatsushima

Tokushima

Gobō

ishima

Koboke

Anan

Oboke

1955m
Tsurugi-san

Kamoda-misaki

Hinomi-saki

Monobe-gawa

Hiwasa

s u n c h i

Ki-suidō

ōchi

Ryūga-dō

Kaifu

Nankoku

Aki

atsurahama

Yasuda

S H I K O K U

Tōkyō

Tosa-wan

Muroto

Muroto-zaki

Tōkyō

0   20   40   60   80   100 km

0   20   40   60 miles

Hyūga
Naha

D

E

Western Honshu and Shikoku

Miyajima

WESTERN HONSHU This region is divided down the middle by a chain of mountains running from east to west. The San-yo region on the southern coast, facing the Seto Inland Sea, is a corridor of heavy residential development and industry. The San-in region, which stretches along the northern coast and faces the Sea of Japan, is, by contrast, a less developed area where tourists are few and agriculture and fishing remain the major economic activities.

SAN-YO COAST The JR Shinkansen express Tokaido train line, from Tokyo to Kyushu, runs along the San-yo coast. Three of the main stops, Hiroshima, Okayama, and Himeji, are also the cities of most interest to foreigners.

For the Japanese, Hiroshima has been an important town since the early 16th century; to the rest of the world it is known and visited as the target of the first nuclear weapon attack in history. Apart from a trip of homage to the dead, one of the reasons to visit Hiroshima is to take an excursion from there to Miyajima, a picturesque small island in the Inland Sea. Miyajima is traditionally regarded as one of the top scenic attractions in Japan.

Okayama is of interest chiefly for its Korakuen Gardens, which were laid out on the banks of the Ashigawa 300 years ago, and are one of the three most famous gardens in Japan (Kenrokeun in Kanazawa and Kairakuen in

One section of the vast Seto-Ohashi bridge

Mito, being the other two). After a visit to Korakuen Gardens in Okayama, Kurashiki is a good place to spend the rest of the day and the following morning. Fifteen minutes from Okayama JR station, it is an oasis of traditional Japan amid the industrial development of the San-yo coastal plain.

Himeji is the site of perhaps the finest surviving castle in Japan, the second largest after Osaka Castle. Set on a hill overlooking the city, the castle goes by the name of Shirasagi, the White Egret (or Heron). Train service to Himeji is excellent, and you can arrive, visit the castle, and leave within a morning or afternoon.

SAN-IN COAST There is much to see of ordinary Japanese rural life along the San-in coast: the main reason to go there is to enjoy a quiet part of Japan that *gai-jin* (foreigners) don't often see. There are three towns and a famous shrine worth special visits: Matsue, a pleasant, busy town best known for being the home of Lafcadio Hearn, the 19th-century writer-expatriate, and for its hot springs; Tsuwano, a small, well-preserved castle town; Hagi, a castle town and port, and Izumo-Taisha Shrine near Matsue, a famous Shinto shrine to which many Japanese travel to pray for good fortune in marriage.

THE INLAND SEA Separating western Honshu from Shikoku island (see pages 168–177), the *Setonaikai* (Inland Sea) is about 315 miles (500km) long and ranges in width from 40 miles (64km) to just 4 miles (6km). Mountainous coastlines and over a thousand small, pine-covered islands, scattered throughout its length, add to the beauty of this area, which has been designated a national park. Nevertheless, the once abundant marine life has been decimated by pollution and over-fishing. Increased environmental awareness and the growth of fish-farming make the sea's future look brighter. In the past, the Inland Sea was the major route for the distribution of goods and the spread of culture between Kyushu and the old capitals of Nara and Kyoto in Honshu. Sightseeing cruises are available from Hiroshima and Takamatsu, on Shikoku.

THE SETO-OHASHI BRIDGE
Seto-Ohashi, the longest bridge in the world, is actually composed of six bridges that connect a series of small islands in the Seto Inland Sea, using them as stepping stones from western Honshu to Shikoku. Claimed to be virtually earthquake-proof, the bridge was built using cables that could wrap around the earth several times. The authorities proudly advertise that construction costs measured in Y10,000 notes would create a stack three times as high as Mount Fuji. Train and bus service from Okayama to Takamatsu, on Shikoku, cross the bridge.

San-in Region

▶▶▶ Hagi   154A3

In 1604, the Mori family built their castle at Hagi. Suspicious of the Tokugawa shogunate, they selected a defensive site bounded by the Hashimoto-gawa and Matsumoto-gawa (rivers) on two sides and the Sea of Japan on the third. For tourist information, contact the Hagi Ryokan Association (tel: 0838 22 7599). Their office is to the left of the Higashi-Hagi station, near the entrance of the Rainbow Plaza shopping mall. Hagi downtown area

Tokoji Temple

158

is a 30-minute walk from the station or a short cab ride. Tamachi Mall is the busiest shopping street, with shops offering everything from French ball gowns to local crafts products, particularly pottery (Hagi is best known for a pinkish-beige tea ceremony stoneware).

Westernmost Hagi is equally accessible by bus and train. Express buses run from Ogori (one hour, 15 minutes), from Tsuwano (one hour, 50 minutes), and from Akiyoshi-do (one hour, 10 minutes). By train there is a JR San-in line express from Masuda (one hour, 10 minutes) and from Shimonoseki (two hours).

Hagi Castle▶▶ was built in 1604 and dismantled in 1874; only the massive outer walls and moat now remain, and the grounds have been turned into the Shizuki Park. From the castle walls there are wonderful views of Hagi, the Sea of Japan, and the mountains that surround the city on three sides.

Horiuchi▶▶▶ is an old *samurai* quarter southeast of the castle ruins, between the castle moat and the town center. Once the domain of high-ranking *samurai* of the Mori Lords, this area is a maze of the earthen walls that surround each residence. There are three imposing *samurai* mansion gates still standing.

Tokoji Temple▶▶▶ is a simple but impressive Zen temple of the Obaku sect. The austere but grand tombs of five of the Mori Lords stand at the end of a pathway lined with 500 stone lanterns donated by the Lords' retainers. Each year, on August 15, all the lanterns are lit in a guard of honor. Toko-ji is east of the *Matsumoto-gawa* (Matsumoto River) along the road that crosses *Matsumoto-bashi* (Matsumoto bridge).

LAFCADIO HEARN
The son of an Irish father and a Greek mother, the writer Lafcadio Hearn (1850–1904) spent his childhood years in Greece and later traveled to Britain and the United States. Having arrived in Japan in 1890 and taken a teaching post in Matsue, he met and married a Japanese woman who had nursed him during a bout of illness. Hearn took Japanese citizenship and the name Koizumi Yakumo, and started to write about Japan. His accounts, including *Glimpses of an Unfamiliar Japan* (1894) and *A Japanese Miscellany* (1901), enthralled Westerners and the Japanese, who were fascinated to see themselves through the eyes of a foreigner. Hearn's books are still in print in Japan and the U.S.

▶▶ Matsue

154C4

Situated on the Ohashi River in the middle of the Sen-in coast, Matsue is best known as the home of Lafcadio Hearn, a European-born writer who took Japanese nationality in the 1890s (see panel). Somewhat off the beaten track for Westerners, this relatively small town is a popular resort for many Japanese who spend their summer vacations here.

The simplest way to visit Matsue is by train. From Tsuwano, southwest of Matsue, it takes three hours, 30 minutes. From Okayama the trip takes three hours, and the single daily express from Hiroshima takes one hour. On arrival, visit the tourist information office in the station (*open* 9:30–5:30), where English-language brochures and maps of the city are available. Most of the sights are within walking distance of each other and the station, and there is a good bus network.

Lafcadio Hearn's residence, **Koizumi Yakumo Kyukyo▶▶** (*open* 9–12:30, 1:30–4:30; closed Wed), is a former *samurai* dwelling, across from the northern moat of the castle. The house has been preserved as Hearn left it in 1891, and next door is a memorial hall where items of memorabilia concerned with his life and work are collected.

Matsue Castle▶▶ was built in 1611 and partially restored in 1642. Never taken or damaged, the castle's five-storied façade actually contains six levels. There is a collection of *samurai* arms and armor on the lower floors, and the view from the top floor makes the climb worthwhile. Take the bus to Kencho-mae from stop 1 or 2 outside the JR station, then walk to the castle in Jozen Park. The Western-style building within the grounds is a fascinating museum of local history. There are displays of items from everyday life and photographs covering the period 1808 to the present day (castle and museum *open* 8:30–5, 8:30–6 Apr–Sep).

Boats at Matsue

CASTLE AUCTION
Matsue Castle is one of the few original Japanese castles to have survived without major reconstruction or rebuilding. In 1875, it was sold at auction for $90 to an individual who planned to demolish it. Fortunately, it was saved for posterity by a group of interested local people, who pooled their money to buy it from the successful bidder.

159

Matsue Castle tea house

Izumo Taisha is the oldest and largest Shinto shrine in Japan and the second most important, after the imperial shrines at Ise. The original buildings collapsed in 1031 and were later rebuilt on a smaller scale, the main shrine being built in 1744, and other important buildings dating from 1874.

DAIKOKU

To the northwest, behind the main shrine buildings, the former Treasure House (Shokokan) houses a large collection of images of Okuninushi-no-mikoto in the form of Daikoku. This happy, chubby character stands on a number of rice bales, holding a sack over his shoulder with one hand and a mallet in the other. He is normally accompanied by his son Ebisu, who stands beside him with a fish under his arm.

GETTING THERE

Izumo Taisha is several miles northwest of Izumo, and is served by two train stations—the Ichihata Izumo Taisha station and the JR Izumo Taisha station—and a bus terminal. A more or less straight road leads up to the shrine, and you can find a range of accommodations and restaurants in the shrine area. A tourist information office can be found on the main street close to the shrine entrance.

Happy marriage Set in pleasantly wooded grounds against a backdrop of the Yakumo Hill, Izumo Taisha is dedicated to the worship of Okuninushi-no-mikoto (Master of the Great Land), the *kami* (spirit god) of fishing, silk production, and marriage. According to legend, Okuninushi-no-mikoto was a descendant of Susa-no-o, a *kami* of the Yamato line who married an Izumo princess. In time, Okuninushi-no-mikoto married a Yamato princess and agreed to serve the Yamato line, as long as he was worshiped at a great shrine. Scholars believe that this tale reflects the struggle for dominance between rival clans during the earliest period of Japanese history, and that Okuninushi-no-mikoto's acceptance of Yamato authority reflected the emerging political and military dominance of the Yamato clan. The legend has led to the belief that a visit to the shrine is extremely beneficial to those who are contemplating marriage or to promoting harmony for any union. Visitors to the shrine clap four times instead of the normal two to attract the deity's attention; twice for themselves and twice for their intended partner or partners.

Taisha architecture The shrine buildings are constructed according to the Taisha style, an ancient form of architecture thought to be purely Japanese. The Haiden (Hall of Worship), with extremely heavy, tapering *shimenawa* (sacred twisted straw ropes) hanging over the entrance, is the first building you will see inside the entrance *torii* (gate). The Honden (Main Hall) is not open to the public. Along the sides of the shrine compound are *juku-sha*, special buildings or shelters erected to house the 8 million *kami* that are said to assemble at Izumo every year. To the southeast is the Shinko-den, or Treasure House (*open* 8–4:30), which contains a collection of shrine artifacts.

Hanging good luck notes at the shrine

▶▶▶ Tsuwano

154B3

This small town in a narrow valley, high in the mountains, is nicknamed "Little Kyoto" and preserves many features of the past, including large numbers of carp, originally bred as food in case of siege. They live in the water channels flowing through the old *samurai* quarter, Tonomachi. There are good mountain walks, well maintained temples, and castle ruins above the town. The tourist office has maps and details of bike rental shops.

Tsuwano is just over one hour by train by JR from Ogori, which is on the Shinkansen line, 40 minutes west of Hiroshima. From April 29 to May 5, and July 20 to August 31, and on Sundays and national holidays in May, September, October, and November, you can make the trip from Ogori, on the last steam locomotive in Japan.

Maria Sei-do▶▶ is a tiny chapel on a hill east of the station, built in 1948 by a German Catholic priest in memory of Japanese Catholics who were exiled to Tsuwano.

High on a hillside above Tsuwano, the vermilion red **Taikodani-Inari Shrine▶▶▶** is reached by stone steps and through a long tunnel of over a thousand small, red *torii*. The steps, which are quite steep, start behind the Yasaka Shrine, on the river bank.

Tsuwano Castle▶▶ was originally built over a period of 30 years and completed in 1325, but was dismantled during the Meiji Restoration. The grounds, high above the town, offer spectacular views, and are reached by a steep walk or by chair lift, followed by a 10-minute walk.

Detail of the tunnel of torii *(gates) at Taikodani-Inari Shrine*

161

THE OGAI MORI CONNECTION

Yomeiji Temple, a Soto Zen temple to the east of Tsuwano station, has a charming garden and a handsome thatched-roof main hall, but is best known as the tomb of Ogai Mori (1862–1922). One of the leading literary figures of the Meiji Restoration, Ogai Mori spent his childhood in Tsuwano. On Tonomachi Street, lined with the whitewashed walls that used to surround *samurai* residences, the Yorokan Museum was once Ogai Mori's house and the local *samurai* school. It now houses exhibitions of folk craft in what was once the fencing *dojo* or training hall (*Open* 8:30–5:30).

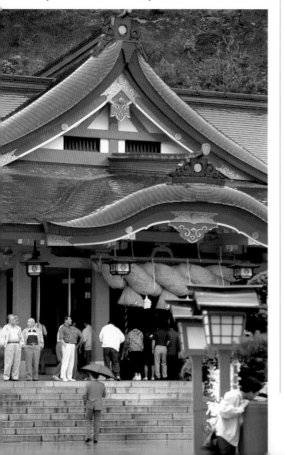

Taikodani-Inari Shrine

WELL WHISPERS

Himeji Castle is rich in myths and stories. One of them concerns a well known as Okiku no Iso, found within the castle precincts. According to legend a maid, Okiku, was found guilty of breaking a valuable plate and thrown down the well as punishment. Her voice can still be heard at night as she mournfully counts her lord's remaining crockery.

LESSONS IN CULTURE

Himeji Shinmen Kaikan, at 112 Sosha Nonmachi, Himeji (tel: 84 2800), offers free lessons in the arts of flower-arranging, tea ceremony, and the correct way to wear a kimono, on an alternating basis from Monday to Friday. A free English-language leaflet giving more details is available at the tourist information office at the station.

Himeji Castle

San-yo Region

▶▶ Himeji
155E3

Himeji was severely bombed during World War II and has little of interest except its magnificent castle, which has survived almost intact. Bullet trains run here from the following major cities: Tokyo (four hours), Kyoto (one hour), Okayama (30 minutes), and Shin-Osaka (40 minutes). The private Hankyu line also operates a service between Kobe and Himeji. A tourist information office is located to the right of the north exit of Himeji station.

Himeji Castle▶▶▶ (*open* 9–5; closed Mon) is also known as Shirasagi Castle, or "The Castle of the White Crane," because of its white plastered walls and silhouette from a distance. One of the few original medieval castles remaining in Japan, and one of the most beautiful, its first fortifications were erected in the 14th century and extended by Hideyoshi in 1581. The main tower is supported by three smaller towers and three rings of defensive compounds, which feature loopholes for firing guns or arrows at the enemy as well as *ishiotoshi*, openings through which rocks or boiling oil could be dropped onto attackers. Altogether, the castle presented the best defensive system of its day in Japan. From the central, north exit of Himeji station, the castle is a 15-minute walk.

Housed in a fine building in the northeast corner of the Himeji Castle grounds, the **Hyogo-kenritsu Rekishi Hakubutsukan (Hyogo Prefectural Museum of History)**▶ (*open* 10–5; closed Mon) contains material from prehistoric times to the present, including displays of Himeji Castle and other castles from around the world. There is also a splendid exhibition of puppet heads, used in *ningyo joruri* (puppet drama), from Awajishima, an island in the Inland Sea, where the art originated.

Hiroshima's peace bell

KOREAN VICTIMS
As well as the Japanese killed by the A-bomb, there were 20,000 Koreans who had been brought to Japan as slave labor during World War II. Koreans and their descendants still suffer discrimination in Japan, and their fate was ignored by the authorities until 1970, when a cenotaph for Korean victims was erected outside the park.

A-BOMB CHILDREN
The statue of the A-Bomb Children in the Peace Memorial Park was inspired by Sadako, a girl dying from radiation poisoning who believed that if she folded 1,000 paper cranes she would recover. She died after folding 664 cranes. Children now fold paper cranes in her memory and the statue is surrounded by millions of paper cranes.

Paper cranes in the Peace Memorial Park

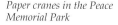

Founded in the 12th century, the large complex of temples making up the **Shoshazan Enkyoji▶▶** includes the oldest surviving Kamakura-period (14th-century) structure, the Yakushido, and the Kongo Satta Buddha, carved in 1395. To get there take a number 6 or 8 bus from the front of Himeji station to the Shosha bus stop. Walk to the temple grounds or transfer to the ropeway, by the bus stop, which takes you to the temple. Alternatively, take one of the horse-drawn carriages usually waiting at the stop. They are as cheap as the ropeway.

▶▶▶ Hiroshima   *154B3*

The city of Hiroshima is known worldwide as the target of the first atomic bomb ever used in a war. The bomb was dropped by the Allies during World War II on August 6, 1945 at 8:15 AM, killing half the population of 400,000 people (about 80,000 people died immediately) and almost totally destroying the heart of the city. Hiroshima has been rebuilt, but the charred and twisted skeleton of the Industrial Promotion Hall, renamed the A-Bomb Dome, has been allowed to remain as a reminder of the destruction.

A new airport was opened in Hiroshima in 1993, connected by flights to Tokyo (Haneda Airport), Kagoshima (Kyushu), and Sapporo (Hokkaido). Bullet trains run from the following major cities: Tokyo (four hours, 30 minutes), Kyoto (two hours), Fukuoka/Hakata (one hour, 20 minutes). Two tourist information offices in Hiroshima station provide maps and English brochures. They also offer goodwill, free city tours.

A visit to the **Peace Memorial Park▶▶▶** is solemn and sobering. Set in the center of the city, it contains a number of monuments, including the Peace Memorial Museum and the Peace Memorial Hall, all concerned with recording and describing the story of the A-bomb that devastated the city. A Peace Flame burns in front of the Memorial Cenotaph, never to be extinguished until all nuclear weapons are abolished.

Kurashiki Toy Museum

*Feeding deer on
Miyajima Island*

▶▶▶ Kurashiki 155D3

"Warehouse Village" was originally an important center
of the rice trade. Surprisingly, it escaped war damage and
many of the large rice granaries still exist in the old part of
the town, known as the Bikan Historical Area. They and
many other Edo-period buildings have been turned into
museums, shops, *ryokan*, and restaurants. Kurashiki is
famous for its museums and art collections; it is also a
picturesque and charming town, and its tourist appeal
now sustains the Kurashiki town coffers.

Bullet trains run from Kyoto (two hours) or Tokyo (four
hours, 30 minutes) to Shin-Kurashiki station. Here you
change for the local train to Kurashiki station (departure
every 15 minutes). There is also a frequent commuter
train service from Okayama JR station to Kurashiki
station, journey time about 15 minutes. The tourist information office, on the third floor of Kurashiki station, has
maps and information available in English.

Kurashiki Folkcraft Museum▶▶▶ (*open* Dec–Feb 9–4:30,
Mar–Nov 9–5; closed Mon) is well worth a visit. It houses
a collection of Japanese and foreign items to
tie in with its slogan, "Usability Equals Beauty."

The **Nihon Kyudo Gangukan (Japan Rural Toy
Museum)**▶▶▶ (*open* 8–5) contains a fine collection of over
2,000 toys from all over Japan and other countries, and
sells Japanese rural toys.

▶▶▶ Miyajima 154B3

"Shrine Island" is considered to be one of the three most
beautiful scenic attractions in Japan. The entire island has
been consecrated as a shrine, and is also the site of the
famous Itsukushima Shinto Shrine, noted for its huge *torii*
set in the sea.

The easiest way to visit the island is to take the JR Sanyo
line from Hiroshima station to Miyajima-guchi station (25
minutes); from there, it is a short walk to the pier and the
ferry to the island (22 minutes). A tourist information

office is located in the JR ferry terminal, which can be visited on arrival in Miyajima.

The island is 20 miles (30km) in circumference, with Mount Misen at its center, rising to 1,740 feet (530m). Although its beauty has been tainted by tourist attractions, this is still a lovely place and worth a day's visit or an overnight stay.

To the west of the ferry pier, **Itsuku Shrine**▶▶▶ is approached through Miyajima Village (a tourist trap) and then a park where many tame deer roam. Originally built in AD 593 and last rebuilt in the 16th century, the shrine is dedicated to the three daughters of Susano-o-no-Mikoto, the Shinto god of the moon and oceans. Most of the shrine is private, but the five-storied pagoda and Senjokaku Hall, on a hill above the shrine, are open to the public.

▶▶ Okayama   155D3

This major city lies on the Inland Sea and is famous for Korakuen Gardens. *Shinkansen* run to Okayama: four hours from Tokyo and just under one hour from Hiroshima. The tourist information office is located near the central exit of the east side of Okayama station.

Okayama is a busy commercial city, not a tourist destination, but it is worth visiting **Korakuen Gardens**▶▶▶ (*open* Apr–Sep 7:30–6, Oct–Mar 8–5), constructed between 1687 and 1700 and considered to be one of the three most beautiful landscape gardens in Japan. The 27 acres are composed of streams, a pond, bamboo groves, pine, plum, and cherry trees, as well as "borrowed views" of the surrounding hills and Okayama Castle. The park gets crowded on weekends and bank holidays.

Okayama Castle▶▶ (*open* 9–5), or "Crow Castle," was destroyed in World War II and rebuilt in 1966. Painted black to contrast with Himeji's famous castle, Okayama-jo houses a collection of *samurai* arms and armor, palanquins, and so on. There is also an elevator to the top of the *donjon*.

ITSUKUSHIMA *TORII* (GATE)

The Itsukushima gate is the subject of countless photographs and many paintings, always taken or painted when the tide is in and the *torii* shimmers above the water. In fact, it stands most of the time in mud flats. From inside the Itsukushima Shrine grounds there is a good view of the brilliant vermilion gate. Offerings are made by individuals or companies to keep the lanterns in the shrine galleries lit at night, producing a spectacular sight if viewed on a dark night at high tide.

165

The striking torii (gate) *at Itsuku Shrine on Miyajima*

The Japanese approach to landscape gardening has traditionally veered away from military precision and geometric perfection. Forcing mechanical order on nature is unattractive to the Japanese spirit, and it is also felt to be wasteful in terms of time and energy. Japanese landscape gardeners thus aspire to work with nature, extending and enhancing natural beauty.

GARDEN POEMS

Japanese poets have always been inspired by a love of nature. The garden, reflecting nature, has served as inspiration for a number of poets. The following poem from a Zen master catches the immediacy of the Zen experience:
"The spring flowers, the autumn moon
Summer breeze, winter snow
If useless things do not clutter your mind
You have the best days of your life."

A gardener maintains a water feature

Artificially natural Japanese landscape gardeners design their work as microcosms of the real world, aiming to show nature on a small scale. For example, when Muso Soseki laid out the gardens of the Saihoji Temple (the "Moss Temple" of Kyoto), he did not first level the ground to form a flat surface. Instead he allowed the moss to follow the natural undulations of the ground, and to display a wide range of different shades of green, complementing and contrasting with one another. Trees and stones were then placed subtly among the moss, so that they would seem quite natural; the hand of the landscape gardener is unseen.

As well as moss, Japanese gardens extensively use trees such as pine and maple, and bamboo groves, small streams and ponds, rocks, stones, and sand. The materials are arranged so as to represent mountains, rivers, lakes, and waterfalls, and are planted with a variety of flowering trees such as cherry, peach, and plum. Other features are flowering shrubs such as azaleas, wisteria, camellias, and rhododendron, and evergreen plants and ferns, usually planted alongside streams and ponds. From these components three basic types of garden evolved: the *tsuki-yama* (hill style), *kare sansui* ("waterless stream gardens," see pages 134–135), and *cha-niwa* (tea garden).

Hill gardens The *tsuki-yama* style of garden typically features streams with stepping stones and a bridge leading to a small island set in a pond. A twisting path leads the visitor from one feature to another past ever-changing scenes. Some gardens imitate in miniature places of beauty famous in Japanese art or literature. One variation of the *tsukiyama* style of garden is known as the *kaiyu* or "many pleasure" style. Popular with the *daimyo* (feudal lords) of the Tokugawa shogunate, the *kaiyu* style features several gardens built around a central pond. Often one or more of them incorporates views that lie outside the garden itself, a technique known as *shakkei* (borrowed views), or *ikedori* (capturing alive). This feature is often seen in gardens in the Kyoto area, where the spectacular mountains that surround the city are seen framed by gateposts and trees.

Tea gardens The *cha-niwa* is designed to enhance the peaceful, spiritual nature of the tea ceremony, hence its description as the "fourth wall" of the tea house. The traditional *cha-niwa* is always planted with ferns, moss,

*Rikugien Garden
in Tokyo*

A WESTERN VIEW
In his book *Around the World Through Japan*, written at the turn of the century, Walter Del Mar described the requirements of a Japanese landscape garden as: "a cart-load of rocks, a pail of water, a modicum of ingenuity, and unlimited imagination—all concentrated on a space the size of a mat." A more elaborate garden would need a dwarf pine, tortured out of its natural shape with permanent bandages and bits of wood and string, or some that "the patient gardeners have bent, interlaced, tied, weighed down, and propped up the limbs and twigs." Multiplied by 10, these would provide "a leafy, lake-centered paradise, and a marvel of artistic arrangement."

167

evergreen trees, and shrubs set against bamboo fences and stone lanterns. You move through the *cha-niwa* and toward the tea house along stepping stones placed asymmetrically on the ground. You then encounter a *machiai* (waiting room), separated from the inner garden around the tea house by a *chumon* (small gate). Within the inner garden there is a stone water basin, used to wash hands and rinse the mouth before entering the tea house. The tea gardens of the Kinkakuji Temple and the Katsura Imperial Villa, both in Kyoto, are among the most famous in Japan (see pages 128–129 and 140).

*Kenrokuen Garden,
Kanazawa*

Shikoku

CLIMATE
Shikoku has two climatic regions, separated by the mountain ranges that run east to west across the island. The Pacific Coast area, to the south, is subtropical, with hot summers and mild, wet winters. The Inland Sea region, to the north, is less rainy, and most days are bright and sunny.

SHIKOKU The smallest of the four main islands of Japan hunkers under the San-yo coast, across the Inland Sea from Western Honshu. It is a mountainous, wooded island, lacking in natural resources, limited in industrial development, and restricted in inter-island communications. Except for its major sights, Shikoku is still relatively unexplored by foreign and Japanese tourists. However, in 1988, after 10 years of construction, the Seto-Ohashi Bridge connecting Shikoku with Honshu by road and railroad line was opened, and tourism has vastly increased in that area.

GEOGRAPHY The northern coast has attracted most of the island's industry and is the location of its two largest cities, Takamatsu and Matsuyama. Here also, rice, wheat, mandarin oranges, and tobacco are farmed on terraced mountain slopes and any flat land not taken by housing or industry. The interior of the island, to which access is difficult, is a place of clean rivers, Buddhist temples, small villages, and remote hiking trails. The southern half of the island, except for the Kochi plain, is steeply mountainous and, outside of the few towns, sustains a small population of rice farmers and fishermen.

PAPER CRAFTS
Shikoku, and especially the Kochi area, is famous for its paper products. The raw material is pulp from Japanese mulberry trees, cultivated on the mountain slopes of Shikoku's interior. High-quality paper is used to make many goods, including *shoji* (screens), lanterns, paper wallets, *daruma* dolls, and masks. Small, flat paper items make excellent, lightweight presents to take home.

168

KOBO DAISHI To the Japanese, Shikoku is best known as the center of Shingon Buddhism. Every year thousands of followers make a pilgrimage by walking tour (or, more recently, bus tour) of the island's 88 temples in memory of Kobo Daishi, founder of the sect (see pages 184–185 and 178). Many temples offer overnight accommodation. Devout pilgrims believe that by visiting all 88 temples they will be released from the cycle of birth and death.

MAIN TOWNS Takamatsu is a medium-sized town and a pleasant, convenient center for exploring the rest of Shikoku. Ritsurin Park is the town's main tourist destination. After dark, Takamatsu has a busy nightlife and the "entertainment area" is a maze of neon-lit, pedestrian-only arcades lined with bars, restaurants, and late-night shops. **Matsuyama** is Shikoku's largest city, but with more of a country town atmosphere than Takamatsu, and is famous for its Dogo Onsen, one of the best-known hot-

Aspects of Shikoku: a floating restaurant ...

Shikoku

… dramatic mountain scenery …

HAIKU POETRY

Haiku is a highly stylized and refined form of Japanese poetry, in which the poet aspires to express deep and spontaneous insights about nature and human life. The *haiku* always consists of 17 syllables, arranged in three lines, the first of 5 syllables, the second of 7, and the last of 5. It is traditional to use the name of a flower, animal, custom, or event that invokes the feeling of a particular season. Matsuo Basho (1644–94) is considered the father and greatest exponent of *haiku* in its present form. Here are two examples of his poetry:

The sea dark
The call of the teal
Dimly white

Soon it will die
Yet no trace of this
In the cicada's screech.

spring resorts in Japan. A unique cultural aspect of Matsuyama is the local love of *haiku* poetry.

Kotohira, also in the north of the island, is a small town nestling beneath the nationally revered Kotohiragu Shrine, to Omononushi-no-mikoto, the Shinto protector of travelers and sailors, whose popular name is Kompira-san. For tired pilgrims, there is a *kago* service (a chair suspended from poles and carried by porters) up the hundreds of stairs to the shrine summit. Kotohira also has one of the oldest *kabuki* theaters in Japan.

Uwajima is the last stop on the railroad line west from Takamatsu—a five and a half-hour journey. Trains leave Takamatsu about five times daily for this small country town, well known locally for its bullring (two bulls, like four-legged *sumo* wrestlers, try to push each other out of a small ring). Outside Uwajima train station is a small tourist office. Taga Jinja is the local Shinto shrine.

Kochi, in the south of the island, is a friendly market town. The major attraction is Kochi Castle.

GETTING THERE A direct train to Takamatsu leaves Tokyo station every night at 9:05, arriving at 7:35 the following morning. There are regular services to Takamatsu from Okayama station (one hour). JR ferry and hovercraft services connect Uno on Honshu to Takamatsu. Uno is connected to Okayama by a frequent train service, and Takamatsu is connected by an air service to Osaka and Tokyo. Shikoku's three main railroad lines begin at Takamatsu: the JR Yosan line to Matsuyama; the JR Dosan line to Kochi; and the JR Kotoku line to Tokushima.

… and hay stacks in the rural center

169

*Bargaining at Kochi's
Sunday market*

DOG-FIGHTING
Dog fights are popular in
particular areas of Japan.
Among *aficionados*, top
dogs and their owners
achieve the same status
as star *sumo* wrestlers. A
sumo ranking system is
used and winning dogs are
even paraded around the
ring in miniature *sumo*-
style aprons. Fights take
place on a caged circular
stage, surrounded by tiers
of seats. The dogs, which
unexpectedly do not bark,
weigh in at around 330
pounds (150kg); they
jockey for a grip on one
another's shoulders and
then try to throw the other
dog down. The fight is over
when one dog stays down.
A judge sits in a high chair
within the caged stage,
punishing illegal moves
such as nose- or testicle-
biting by spraying the nose
of the offender with a
stinging liquid or, in severe
cases, placing a lit piece
of paper under the penis
of the attacker!

▶▶ Kochi   155D2

This castle town is located on the central southern coast of
Shikoku, two and a half hours by train from Kotohira. The
local microclimate is subtropical, and farming and agriculture are the main industries in the lush and fertile
surrounding countryside.

Almost every day of the week there is a street market in
Kochi; the biggest is on Sunday morning, on palm-lined
Otesuji-dori, near the center of town. *Onagadori* show
birds (see panel on opposite page) may also be on display.
Kochi Castle▶▶ (*Open* 9–4:30), in the middle of Kochi
Park in the west of the city, dates from 1603. The top of the
intact five-storied keep (*donjon*) provides a panoramic
view of the city. There is a museum in the grounds with
much information about Lord Sakamoto Ryoma
(1835–67), a local swashbuckling hero who helped topple
the shogunate. The Lord's Residence, Kaitokukan, is open
on the second floor of the *donjon;* kept in its original condition, it acts as a window onto the life of the *daimyo*.

Katsura-hama▶▶, a white, coarse-grained, sandy beach,
35 minutes by bus from Kochi station, is popular with
locals in the summer, particularly for swimming, and in
the fall for gazing at the moon. Kochi is famous for breeding the Tosa fighting dog.

▶▶▶ Kotohira   155D3

Kotohira, 45 minutes by JR Dosan line express from
Takamatsu, is best known for its Kotohiragu, one of the
oldest, grandest, and most popular Shinto shrines
in Japan, and for the Kyu Kompira Oshibai, the only
complete Edo-period *kabuki* playhouse left in Japan.

Known as Kompira-san, **Kotohiragu Shrine▶▶▶** was
originally founded in the 11th century. It is dedicated to
Omononushi-no-mikoto (nicknamed Kompira), the
guardian of seafarers, who would visit the shrine
to pray for safe journeys at sea. Part of the shrine complex
houses models and photographs of boats left there by
fishermen soliciting protection. Nowadays, Kompira's
aid is sought by all travelers, and by those seeking
good fortunes.

The shrine is built on the slopes of Mount Zozu, and the main complex is at the top of 785 stone steps. Turn left out of Kotohira station, under a *torii*, and then turn right down a narrow shopping street and you will quickly come to the steps. The climb will take 30–40 minutes and is quite daunting if you are not in shape. Litter-bearers will carry you up in a *kago* for a reasonable sum, given the arduousness of the task. The steps are lined with souvenir shops, inns, and refreshment stands, but once through the main gate the atmosphere becomes more refined. At the top, there are wonderful panoramic views of the surrounding Sanuki Plain, the Inland Sea to the north, and the Shikoku mountain ranges to the south.

Near the first flight of steps leading to Kotohiragu Shrine is the **kabuki playhouse**►►► (*Open* 9–5; closed Tue), built in 1835 in traditional style, with paper lanterns, *tatami*, and sliding *shoji* to adjust the light. The revolving stage, which has two trap doors, is turned by eight men in the basement. The entrance to the building is small, to keep out gate-crashers. Plays are staged once a year in April, but the theater is open daily for viewing.

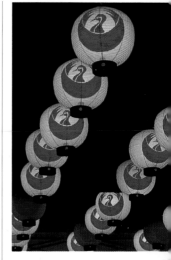

Kotohira's kabuki *play-house lit by lanterns*

171

LONG-TAILED ROOSTERS
An unusual feature of Kochi is the rearing of *onagadori* (long-tailed roosters). The tradition began with the wish to provide decorative features for the local *daimyo*. Three centuries later, selective breeding has produced roosters with tails as long as 33 feet (10m). You'll find *onagadori* at the Nagaodori Center (*open* 9–5; closed Mon).

KOTOHIRAGU
The inner shrine complex includes the Treasure House, which contains scrolls, sculpture and Noh masks; Shoin, the original reception hall, housing paintings by Maruyama Okyo, an 18th-century artist; Asahi-no Yashiro, a carved hall, dedicated to Amaterasu, the sun goddess; and Ema-do, a pavilion containing ship models and old photographs, offered by pilgrims.

Pilgrims at Kotohiragu Shrine

SWORDS AND ARMOR

Omishima Island is one hour by hydrofoil boat from Imabari Port, 40 minutes on the JR Yosan line from Matsuyama. The boat docks at Miyaura and from here it is a short cab ride to Oyamazumi Shrine. There, most unexpectedly, housed in the shrine treasure hall, is the best collection of swords and armor in Japan. For many centuries Oyamazumi was a popular place of worship for emperors and *shogun* and it became a tradition for them to donate swords and armor to the shrine. Today 80 percent of the nation's most treasured items of this type are to be found here, including armor worn by Minamoto Yoritomo, first *shogun* of the Kamakura period (1192–1333).

Looking out over Matsuyama from the castle

▶▶▶ Matsuyama   *154C2*

Matsuyama, on the northwest coast of Shikoku, is the island's largest city, renowned in the past as a center of art and literature. The most convenient way to get there is by train from Okayama, Honshu (two hours, 40 minutes) or Takamatsu, Shikoku (two hours, 50 minutes). The city tourist information office is located just inside the JR station. The main sights in town are Matsuyama Castle, one of the finest surviving feudal castles in Japan, and Dogo Onsen, a celebrated hot springs. Matsuyama has an excellent network of cable cars and finding one's way around is quite easy. (World War II bombing devastated Matsuyama and postwar city planners favored practicality, hence the characterless network of straight avenues and boulevards, given color only by the cable cars.)

Matsuyama's local crafts include *iyo-kasuri*, an indigo-dyed cotton once used to make working clothes for farming women; *tobe-yaki*, a thick porcelain decorated with brushed cobalt-blue designs on a white ground; and oval-shaped dolls designed in honor of Empress Jingu, who visited Dogo Onsen when she was pregnant. For these and other items from the Ehime Prefecture, visit the Ehime no Bussan store, Ichiban-cho 4-chome (Kencho-mae cable car stop; *open* Mon–Fri 8:30–5).

Matsuyama Castle▶▶▶ (*open* 9–5) was constructed in 1603 by the head of the Matsudaira clan, and later destroyed by fire. The stone walls, turret, and keep, all in good condition, dominate a hill in the center of the city and command fine views of the Inland Sea and the central mountain ranges of Shikoku. A castle museum exhibits the armor and swords of the Matsudaira family, and the surrounding park is worth exploring. Cable car 5, from the square in front of the station, takes you to the entrance to the castle grounds; from here you can take the steep walk or a streetcar to the castle summit.

Dogo Onsen▶▶▶ is one of the best-known hot spring resorts in Japan. (A cable car line runs here from the train station.) Part of the spa, still preserved and open for

Ishiteji Temple, near Dogo Onsen, is the 51st on the Shikoku pilgrimage route

HAIKU MASTERS

Matsuyama was the birthplace of many famous *haiku* poets, including Masaoka Shiki (1867–1902) and Takahama Kyoshi (1874–1959), and the people of Matsuyama have special affection for *haiku* poetry (see panel, page 169). Throughout the city one can see stone monuments inscribed with the finest poems of the great *haiku* masters. The city even organizes *haiku* contests with special "*haiku* mailboxes" for residents to submit their entries.

viewing, was originally set aside for the exclusive use of visiting royalty from Kyoto. This area is ornate, but the section open for public bathing is simply designed in the best tradition of functional Japanese architecture. At the entrance, you pay a small fee, and collect soap and a miniature towel. This is used for washing, then wrung out for drying, and also as a cover-up while in the spa. In the pools, the natural mineral water is just cool enough to sit in, and the salts it contains soften and vitalize the skin. For an extra fee, you can gain access to a communal *tatami* (mat) room on the third floor; a more expensive private room, with tea and access to the imperial pool, is also available.

Slippers from the weary feet of worshipers

Ishiteji Temple►►, a short walk east of Dogo Onsen station, is the most interesting of eight temples in Matsuyama that are part of the Shikoku pilgrimage. Built in 1318, it is a fine example of Kamakura architecture, with a three-story pagoda, main gate, hall, and bell tower. The deity has a reputation for relieving aching legs, and the straw sandals of many elderly Japanese hoping for a cure for their failing legs hang from the main gate.

Japan sits on a geological region of intense volcanic activity, which gives rise to many hot springs (onsen). Spas, fed by these natural sources of mineral-rich hot water, are popular with the Japanese for their curative, health-giving, and relaxing properties. Public washing baths, sento, were invented as a public service when most houses had no bathrooms. They provide hot running water for washing and a large bath full of very hot water for soaking in. Many also have mineral baths, whirlpools, electric baths, and cold plunges.

174

ROTEMBURO ETIQUETTE

Young women do not generally swim in outdoor pools during the day, but in the evening mixed groups gather in the pools. After dinner *sake*, floated from person to person in tiny wooden tubs, is drunk, inhibitions drop away, singing may start up, and formal conversation gives way to gossipy chatter and heart-to-heart revelations.

Dogo Onsen, where the emperor had his own spa built

Onsen Built near or directly above a hot-spring source, *onsen* are Japanese inns where guests hope to benefit from the water's health-promoting qualities, as well as enjoying the regional food that is often a specialty. Some of the larger *onsen* are built like modern hotels, attracting large family groups and parties of company workers; others are set deep in the mountains, in beautiful, isolated areas. The latter are usually composed of three or four thatched wooden buildings around a series of *rotemburo* (outdoor pools).

For the cognoscenti, exploring such places in search of the ultimate spa can be akin to a spiritual journey. Most *onsen* are open all year round, and in the smaller country establishments you may sit in the winter in a steaming outdoor pool, surrounded by snow-covered rocks and trees.

Onsen cities The Japanese love to do things together, not only as a way of socializing but, particularly with company and sports-team parties, to engender solidarity. For this reason, many of the best-known *onsen* have become resort areas with hotels, busy nightlife districts, and huge swimming halls with an exotic variety of pools. The Arita Kanko Hotel in Kinki district, Honshu, offers hot tubs

inside a cable car that rises high above a very dramatic coastline. Famous resorts such as Beppu in Kyushu, Noboribetsu in Hokkaido, and Atami in Honshu are often vulgar, gaudy, and kitsch, but they have their own charm, and offer the chance to join in with ordinary Japanese letting their communal hair down.

Sento For independent tourists traveling on a budget, *sento* are excellent places to relax and to experience something quintessentially Japanese. *Sento* can be identified by their tall, narrow, metal chimneys and the distinctive flame logo painted over the entrance. In the last few years they have become fashionable with young people, and, like old movie houses, are being renovated in their original style.

Nowadays, *sento* are not mixed, and the men's and women's pools are usually looked after by an *obasan* (old woman), who sits on a platform inside the entrance astride the wall that divides the two sides. Men enter on the right, and women on the left. The *obasan* takes entrance fees and sells shampoo, soap, and razors. You can rent towels, but most Japanese make do with a small piece of cotton toweling called a *tenugui*, used initially as a washcloth and then as a towel.

Bathers put their clothes in a locker and lock it with a numbered wooden key, which is kept on the wrist. Inside the bathing area, plumbed into the walls, is a series of pairs of hot and cold faucets. Sit at one of these on a low plastic stool and pour water over yourself with one of the small bowls scattered around the floor, before rubbing soap into the *tenugui* and soaping yourself all over. Then rinse the soap off thoroughly and sit in the hot tub, adding cold water if the heat is unbearable. Use the same facilities and washing procedure at *onsen* before and after entering one of the communal hot-spring pools.

Thermal baths outdoors …

MASSAGE CHAIRS
Many *sento* provide a massage armchair in the changing rooms to relieve backs stiff from too much walking. To use one, put the correct coins into the slot in the arm of the chair and adjust yourself against the moving rollers. They can be moved up and down by using the control lever near your right hand.

… and indoors

▶▶ Takamatsu

The second-largest town in Shikoku, Takamatsu is the most convenient arrival point and center for exploring Shikoku. It was bombed flat in World War II but rebuilt, exceptionally, on a human scale. And fortunately Ritsurin Park, in the north of the city, famous even outside Shikoku, escaped damage. The main train station, the ferry port, the downtown and nightlife area, and the park are all within walking distance. For travel directions to Takamatsu from the main island of Honshu, see page 169.

Crossing the bridge at Takamatsu

Ritsurin Park▶▶▶ is part of the former estate of the Matsudaira clan, originally designed as a summer retreat. An unusually wide variety of tree and flower species grows in the park, including Neagari Kashi oak trees, with exposed, leg-like roots, and Hako Matsu pine trees, characterized by their surreal branch configurations. Plum trees bloom in February, followed by camellias and yulan in March, cherry blossoms in April, wisteria and azalea in May, irises and water lilies in June, and lotus flowers in August. Work was begun on the park in the early 17th century, and was not completed on the formal gardens until over 100 years later. Two distinct areas make up the park: the south garden is of classical design featuring the landscaping, rock arrangements, ponds, and artificial hills of the kind popular in the early and middle part of the Edo period. Winding paths and bridges lead past striking, stark trees with sculpted branches, over ponds stocked with carp and through flower beds of seasonal flowers. Be sure to stop at the Scoop The Moon Tea House (*Kikugetsu-tei*) for some whisked green tea and some bean-jam cake. The north garden is landscaped in a more

open, European style. It was originally designed for wild duck hunting parties led by the *daimyo* of Takamatsu. Nowadays, the open spaces are used for picnics, park games and, in season, for Cherry Blossom Viewing festivities. The park is open daily from sunrise to sunset.

Very near the entrance to Ritsurin Park is **Sanuki Mingeikan**►► (*Open* 8:45–4), a folk art museum that exhibits handicraft products from Sanuki (the old name for the Kagawa Prefecture, of which Takamatsu is the capital) and sells a range of locally made pottery.

Zentsuji Temple►►, one-sixth of a mile west of Zentsuji station, 40 minutes south of Takamatsu on the JR Dosan line, is the birthplace of Kobo Daishi, who founded the temple in AD 813, and the 75th station of the 88 temples (see pages 184–185). An imposing statue of the saint holding a cane guards the entrance to the main temple. Within the complex is a five-storied pagoda and a treasure house exhibiting various "Important Cultural Properties," including Buddhist artifacts brought back from China by Kobo Daishi. The two large camphor trees growing in the grounds are said to have been planted at the time of the temple's foundation.

Near the main entrance are two wooden cut-outs of traditionally dressed pilgrims with holes where their faces should be, offering a photo opportunity for visitors. If offered a little money, one of the temple monks may agree to lead you through a "secret" tunnel that runs beneath the main temple. A pitch-black passage, its walls worn smooth by countless searching hands, the tunnel leads to the back of the main altar. The tunnel darkness is said to inspire reflection on the human condition, while the tunnel itself represents life before and after the light of spiritual enlightenment.

Ritsurin Park

RITSURIN PARK AND MOUNT SHIUN
The original design of the park incorporated the green backdrop provided by the adjacent Mount Shiun and took into account the way it would influence views from particular vantage points in the garden. To appreciate this aspect of the design, walk counterclockwise around the garden.

The imperial emblem at Zentsuji Temple

Kobo Daishi is the posthumous name of a Buddhist monk known as Kukai (AD 774–835), born in Zentsuji in Shikoku and famous as the founder of the Shingon (True Word) sect of Buddhism. Kobo Daishi, or Dharma-Spreading Great Master, is the name by which he is best known. It was given to him in AD 921, nearly a century after his death.

MOUNT KOYA (*KOYA-SAN*) MONASTERY

Kobo Daishi petitioned Emperor Saga to give him Mount Koya, claiming that: "According to the meditation sutras, meditation should be practiced preferably on a flat area, deep in the mountains. When young, I ... often walked though mountainous areas and crossed many rivers. There is a quiet, open place called Koya, located two days' walk to the west from a point that is one day's walk south from Yoshino. High peaks surround Koya in all four directions; no human tracks, still less trails are to be seen there. I should like to clear the wilderness in order to build a monastery there for the practice of meditation, for the benefit of the nation and of those who desire to discipline themselves..."

A statue of Kobo Daishi at Takamatsu Temple

At 19 Kukai abandoned his study of Confucianism and Taoism and a potential career in the government bureaucracy to become a pupil of the Buddhist priest Gonso. In 795, he was ordained as a monk at Nara's Todaiji (Great Eastern) Temple, taking the name Kukai ("Sea of Void").

In 804, Kukai joined the retinue of the Japanese imperial ambassador to the Tang Court and traveled with him to China, where he studied esoteric Buddhism under Hui-kuo, the seventh patriarch of a line of teachers that had originated in India. Kukai was an exceptional student. He collected many scrolls of esoteric lore and ritual and studied tantric Buddhist traditions from Central Asia. When Hui-kuo died in 804, Kukai was chosen to be the eighth patriarch of the sect and entrusted with the task of introducing its teachings into Japan.

Return home Kukai returned to Japan in August 806. He settled in Kanzeonji Temple in Kyushu and sent a list of the Buddhist sutras and other works to the Japanese court. As a result, Kukai's esoteric teaching earned the support of the court, and in 823 Emperor Saga gave Kukai a new temple: Toji (Eastern Temple), in Kyoto, which became the headquarters of the Shingon sect.

Death and reincarnation Kukai died on April 20, 835, at the age of 61. His followers claim that he did not actually die, but went into the meditative state known as the Diamond Meditation, from which he will return as the Buddha Maitreya. His remains were entombed on Mount Koya, where his grave is now a shrine for the faithful.

▶▶ Uwajima 154C1

This small, charming country town is the last stop on the JR Yosan line west of Takamatsu (five hours) and Matsuyama (two hours). It is worth visiting for its castle, bullfights, and the outrageously explicit sex museum at Taga Jinja, a local Shinto shrine.

Although it is one of the few surviving feudal strongholds in Japan, **Uwajima Castle**▶ was never a great castle. For defense, it depended on its excellent position on a promontory once surrounded by interlocking sea moats. The castle is a short walk from the center of town.

Uwajima is famous for **Togyu bullfights**▶▶▶, in which two bulls test their strength by locking horns and trying to push one another out of the ring. Tournaments are held six times a year, usually on January 2, the first Sunday in March, April, and November, the third Sunday in May, and August 14. The bull ring, or Togyu-ju, is at the base of Mount Tenman, a cab ride or a 30-minute walk from the middle of town. Dozens of bouts take place, and the atmosphere is usually less than sober.

Taga Jinja▶▶ (*Open* 8–5), a Shinto shrine 10 minutes' walk from the station (directions from the tourist office), is said to be something of an embarrassment to local people, for the priest in charge is an avid collector of sexual paraphernalia. Next to the shrine he has built a three-story museum to house his collection, which includes perhaps the only catalogued display of pubic hair in the world. At the entrance, a statue of a masturbating Buddha sets the tone for what follows. Cabinets display sexual gadgets, sexually explicit statues, and representations of male and female genitalia of all sizes and shapes, and the walls and ceilings are covered with pornography. Taga has become a fertility shrine and nowadays infertile couples and newlyweds make up the shrine's and the museum's usual customers.

Togyu bullfights at Uwajima

DUTCH BULLS
Bullfighting started here in the 19th century with a gift of bulls from a Dutch sea captain, saved from a typhoon by Uwajima fishermen. Bulls were new to the Japanese, and were set to fight each other because they were so fierce.

FESTIVAL
Uwajima's biggest festival, Warei Jinja Matsuri, is held on July 23–24 at Warei Jinja Shrine. The main features include bullfights, and an appearance by *ushi-oni*, or ox demons.

In Japan, sex is not something to be shy about, nor is it separated from the spiritual life. The traditional belief is that we have two souls: one that is timeless and sublime and another that is earthbound and pleasure-seeking. Both parts of our being need nourishment. Within this context, romantic love and male and female sexuality have been equally celebrated in Japanese cultural and religious life.

EROTIC ART

Remains of erotic pictures of sexual activity have been preserved in Japan from as early as the 8th century. Of the two earliest complete *shunga (a* general term for erotic art painted or printed onto scrolls to be viewed horizontally), one, *The Phallic Contest,* depicts a test of male sexual powers by ladies of the imperial court, while the other, *The Catamites,* portrays the homosexual activities of Buddhist monks.

Sex comic

In the past in Japan, the sexual emphasis has always been on male gratification; the woman's role was to fulfill a man's needs. Until recently, this was the view generally accepted and approved by society. Lack of inhibition and a confidence in his role gave the Japanese male a reputation for coarseness in his bold approach to sex, while the female became known for her demureness and her willingness to please. There is still some belief in these notions, but the reality of sexual relations in Japan can be as paradoxical as it is everywhere else.

Sex comics and prudery One of the shocks to a Westerner visiting Japan is to flick through the popular sex comic books sold at all newspaper outlets and available to read in many coffee shops. Glossy nude female pinups are followed by cartoons and a center-page picture story, in which the woman heroine undergoes all sorts of sexual humiliations at the hands of an evil monster or pervert.

Neither Japanese men nor women (nor children, who do read them) seem embarrassed or surprised at these comics; neither do they take them seriously. A more recent development is the arrival of the sadistic heroine. The suitably attired dominatrix, usually a successful sports or business woman in her ordinary life, ritually humiliates a male slave. He normally turns out to be a corrupt politician or ruthless financier.

In real-life, sexual violence toward women is rare in Japan. Assaults are virtually unknown, and women are generally safe to move around at any time of the day or night, without fear of violence or theft.

Another paradox, given Japanese ribald history and the explicit nature of their comics (and some Shinto shrines), is the prudery of the authorities toward the genitals. As a result of this, cartoonists and film-makers are experts at being titillating without being explicit.

The neon signs of soapland

THE FLOATING WORLD
Ukiyo, "The Floating World," was a description of the areas licensed by the Tokugawa shogunate (1603–1868) for sex and entertainment. The name carried the sentiment that life is short and that one might as well enjoy its pleasures while one can. Tea houses, theaters, and bath houses were the venues, and money and sex the catchwords. Woodblock print (*ukiyo-e*) artists of the era are well known for their portraits of the women and *kabuki* actors of the pleasure quarters. "Water trade" was the phrase used to describe the nighttime world of bars, adult entertainment, and sex found in "soapland" districts of Japanese cities.

Personal relations It is more common for Western men to date Japanese women than vice versa, but either practice is generally considered socially acceptable. However, public displays of affection are usually embarrassing for the Japanese. Kissing and hugging is frowned on: holding hands is about as far as you should go.

Gay sex Homosexuality is neither discouraged nor flaunted in Japanese society. In the past, some Buddhist sects taught that homosexuality was natural and even virtuous compared with sex with women. These teachings were mainly from Buddhist sects forbidding sexual relations with women, but they did for a time influence the upper-class *samurai* of the period, who developed a school of thought that homosexual love was purer than the heterosexual variety.

Taga-jinja Shrine, Uwajima

A fisherman's house, Shodo-shima

TOURING SHODO-SHIMA
If you have the time, Shodo-shima is great to explore on foot or bicycle. All details can be obtained from the island tourist office, in the Town Hall at Tonosho, or from the Kagawa Prefecture tourist information office, 1-10-4-chome, Bancho, Takamatsu.

YASHIMA PLATEAU
The highest point of the Yashima plateau is reached by a short cable-car ride, which operates from a terminal close to Yashima station, or by a 30-minute walk north along a tree-lined path. From the top—980 feet (300m)—there is a magnificent view that takes in the Inland Sea, Shodo Island, Takamatsu, and Mount Goken.

Excursions

►► Shodo-shima   55D3

Twelve miles off the coast to the northeast of Takamatsu, Shodo-shima is the second-largest island in the Inland Sea (there are almost 1,000 in all). There is a frequent ferry service from Takamatsu Pier to Tonosho port, on the western side of the island, which takes approximately one hour (or 35 minutes on the high-speed ferry). The island has a warm, dry, almost Mediterranean climate and it was here that olives were first cultivated in Japan. Shodo-shima is best known for its scenic beauty.

The main attraction is **Kankakei Gorge►►►** ("Cold and Misty Valley"), found in the central mountainous region of the island. Imprisoned by mountainous rock faces, eroded into surreal shapes by the weather, the gorge is brightened by wild cherry and azaleas in the spring and pine and maple trees in the fall. A one-hour bus journey from Tonosho takes you to a nerve-racking aerial ropeway ride up and over the gorge to the summit of a precipice. There is a bus back to Tonoshu from the summit via Kusakabe.

A shorter bus ride from Tonosho (25 minutes), en route to Kankakei, takes you to **Choshikei Gorge►►**, which lies on the upper reaches of Denpo River and is known for its spectacular waterfall and profusion of spring and fall colors. Nearby is the Monkey Park (*Osaru-no-Kuni*), a reserve where wild Japanese monkeys roam freely and show off for the visiting humans.

An extensive public network of buses operates from Tonosho for all the island sights and along the coast to the east. Buses on the coastal route depart for Sakate every 30 minutes, passing Futagoura Beach, just outside Tonosho.

▶▶ Yashima and Shikoku Mura 155D3

Yashima station is 20 minutes by train on the JR line east of Takamatsu station. On the hill outside the station is **Shikoku Mura▶▶▶** (*open* Apr–Oct 8:30–5, Nov–Mar 8:30–4:30), an exceptionally good open-air museum, exhibiting a collection of reconstructed Shikoku architecture brought from all over the island. Included in the display are thatched-roof farms and fishermen's houses dating from the Edo period, an open-air *kabuki* theater, a sugar mill, a tea house, a paper-maker's hut, and a suspension bridge made of vines, a feature once common across the many rivers, valleys, and gorges of Shikoku. Near the entrance to the "village" are two restaurants, one of which is designed as a traditional farmhouse and sells good *udon* noodle dishes.

Yashima was formerly an island, but is now a headland connected to the Shikoku mainland. Its summit plateau is the site of the 12th-century battle in which the rival Taira and Minamoto clans fought for the supremacy of all Japan. The Minamoto family won and went on to establish the country's first shogunate in Kamakura. **Yashimaji Temple▶▶**, the 84th of Shikoku's 88 temples, located on the southern ridge of the plateau, close to the cable car, houses a collection of relics of the land and naval battles fought by the two opposing clans. It was originally constructed in 754. Views from the top of the hill are expansive.

YASHIMA AND MINAMOTO

In 1182 Taira Munemori, third son of the then head of the Taira clan, was pursued out of Kyoto by warriors of the Minamoto clan. Among his party was Emperor Antoku, son of Munemori's sister. They fled to Yashima and there enlisted the aid of clan chiefs from Shikoku. With new forces they transferred their headquarters back to Kobe on the Honshu mainland, but were defeated again by Minamoto forces and fled back to Yashima. It was here, in 1185, that the Taira clan was finally destroyed by its old foes, easing the way for Minamoto Yoritomo to unite Japan under his command and become the country's first *shogun*.

Cleaning the nets, Shodo-shima

The pilgrimage around the 88 temples of Shikoku is the most famous of the Japanese Buddhist temple pilgrimages. It is part of a tradition of religious discipline that has a long history in Japanese Buddhism. The journey is undertaken on foot, and pilgrims dress in white breeches and jackets, straw sandals, and straw hats. They carry no money and depend on charity for all their needs.

NAKED FESTIVAL
Every year, on the Saturday closest to January 20, the *Hadaka Matsuri*, or "Naked Festival," is held at Zentsuji Temple, the 75th temple on the route and the site of Kobo Daishi's birthplace. In the bitter cold, hundreds of young men dressed only in white loin cloths (nakedness symbolizing innocence and white cloth purity), fight over two "good luck sticks" blessed and tossed into the crowd by the abbot of the temple. The winners, known as the "fortunate men," carry good luck with them throughout the following year. Zentsuji is 20 minutes' walk from JR Zentsuji station, which is 40 minutes from Takamatsu on the JR Dosan line.

184

Most pilgrimages are connected with Kannon, the Goddess of Mercy, who is regarded as the deity of the common people, but the Shikoku route is inspired by the Shingon patriarch, Kobo Daishi (see page 178). The journey does, however, attract Buddhists of all sects.

The pilgrims' route The 88 temples are visited along a 906-mile (1,450-km) route, taking between 40 and 60 days on foot. Nowadays most people travel by bus or taxi and wear everyday clothes, with perhaps just a white scarf to indicate their purpose. This is not surprising, since the walk is long and arduous and Shikoku is an island of high mountains, deep valleys, and a rugged coastline. If you wish to follow some or all of the route, problems increase, since maps and instructions are essential and all those available are published only in Japanese. Traditionally, there are two pilgrim seasons: spring and fall. At the respective equinoxes, pilgrims are presented with gifts and goods by people living near the temple where they are spending the night. Generally, accommodations are available in and around all the temples.

Best foot forward on the pilgrims' route

*Zentsuji Temple, the
75th temple on the
pilgrims' route*

ORIGIN OF THE PILGRIMAGE

In the spring of 835, Kobo Daishi (*Daishi*, or "Great Master," is a title given by the imperial court to the most accomplished Buddhist priests) announced that he would die on April 22 of that year. He bade farewell to the ruling emperor and the two retired emperors, appointed successors to maintain his spiritual legacy, made a will, and then retired to a monastery on Mount Koya, south of Osaka, where his tomb had been prepared. He died on the predicted day, and soon after his death many disciples began the pilgrimage to places on Shikoku associated with his name, as a mark of their commitment to the spiritual path that he had established.

A four-temple alternative To give some idea of the variety of style and location of the 88 temples, it is possible to reach four temples by bus from Kochi. The same bus connects all four—or you may walk between them.

Hotsumisakiji Temple (24), Murotomisaki-cho, Muroto City, takes two hours by bus from Kochi City and 40 minutes on foot from the bus stop. Located at the cliff top, Cape Muroto, it is often called the Mecca of the pilgrims. The temple's local name is Higashi-dera, or "East Temple."

Shinshoji Temple (25), Murozusakai, Muroto City, is one hour and 50 minutes by bus from Kochi City and then 10 minutes on foot. Called Tsuji by locals, Shinshoji Temple is known for its image of Jizo, guardian deity of children. It is also popular with those making a living from the sea.

Kongochoji Temple (26), Moto, Muroto City, takes one hour and 40 minutes by bus from Kochi City. Found at the top of Cape Gyodo, its local name is Nishi-dera ("West Temple"). The treasure house contains important Shingon artifacts, and there is a whale museum in the temple grounds.

Konomineji Temple (27), Tonohama, Yasuda-cho, is one hour and 20 minutes by bus from the JR Gomen station, 15 minutes from Kochi station on the JR Dosan line. Considered to be one of the five temples most difficult to reach, it is now accessible by road. The temple's principal deity is the 11-faced image of Kanzeon.

For more information, visit Kochi tourist information office, just outside Kochi station exit. All buses for these temples travel in the Muroto direction.

*Feeding the birds at
Zentsuji Temple*

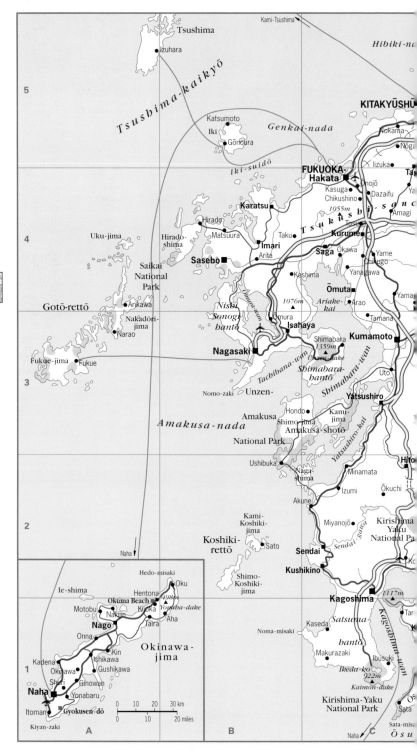

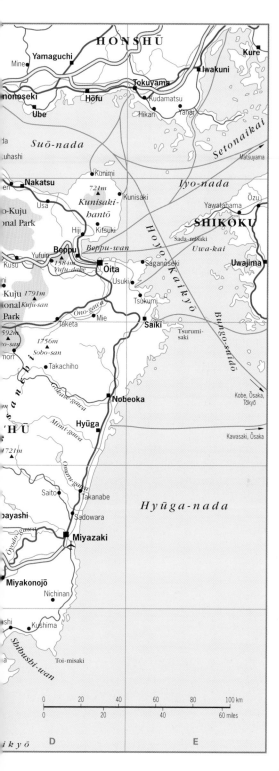

HONSHŪ

Yamaguchi
Mine
Kure
Iwakuni
Tokuyama
nonoseki
Hōfu
Kudamatsu
Ube
Hikari
Yanai

Suō-nada
uhashi
Setonaikai
Matsuyama
Kunimi
Nakatsu
Iyo-nada
721m
Usa
Kunisaki
Ōzu
Kunisaki-
hantō
Yawatahama
o-Kuju
nal Park
Hiji
Kitsuki
SHIKOKU
Beppu-wan
Sada-misaki
Beppu
Uwa-kai
Kusu
Yufuin
1584m
Uwajima
Yufu-dake
Ōita
Saganoseki
Kuju 1791m
Usuki
onal Kuju-san
Tsukumi
Park
Ono-gawa
592m
Taketa
Mie
Saiki
o-san
Tsurumi-
saki
mori
1756m
Sobo-san
Takachiho
a
n
s
h
i
Gokase-gawa
Nobeoka
Kobe, Ōsaka,
Tōkyō
721m
Hyūga
Mimi-gawa
Kawasaki, Ōsaka
Omaru-gawa
Saito
Takanabe
Hyūga-nada
bayashi
Sadowara
gawa
Miyazaki
Oyodo-
Miyakonojō
Nichinan
shi
Kushima
Shibushi-wan
Toi-misaki

0   20   40   60   80   100 km
0   20   40   60 miles

ikyō   D   E

Kyushu and Okinawa

THE BOMB
Kumamoto is said to
have been the original
target of the atomic bomb
later dropped by the U.S.
Airforce on Hiroshima.
On the day of the flight,
Kumamoto was covered
in cloud and the bombers
passed it by. A peace
pagoda, donated by the
Indian government, has
been erected in memory
of the event on a hill overlooking the city.

*Kagoshima port, on
Kyushu Island*

KYUSHU AND OKINAWA The most southerly and third
largest of the four main islands of Japan, Kyushu is
separated from the main island, Honshu, by the 1¼-mile
(2-km) wide Kammon Strait. Railroad and car tunnels
connect the two islands. Four great volcanic ranges cross
the island from north to south.

Okinawa is the largest and most developed island of the
Ryukyu archipelago, a group of subtropical islands
stretching south from Kyushu through the Pacific and
East China Sea, almost to the tip of Taiwan.

FOREIGN INFLUENCES Because of its geographical position, Kyushu became a stage post for the transmission to
Japan of Korean and Chinese cultural ideas, influences
that significantly shaped the development of early
Japanese civilization. The first European explorers,
traders, and missionaries to Japan also arrived via this
island, and its people are traditionally less xenophobic
and easier to get to know than their northern cousins.

Kyushu is mountainous and volcanic. The mountain
ranges contain many peaks over 5,000 feet, (1,525m) and
the caldera in Aso-Kuju National Park, with the active
volcano, Mount Nakadake, at its center, is the largest in the
world. There are hot-spring resorts on the island, and the
spas of Kyushu are popular with Japanese tourists.

FUKUOKA A modern, commercial city, Fukuoka is the
gateway to Kyushu and a good base from which to
explore the island. The rewards of the economic success
of Japan have been put to unusually good use in this city.
Stylish modern architectural developments and a state-
of-the-art subway system have been happily married to
older dockland, residential, and parkland areas. There is
also a thriving nightlife and street life.

KUMAMOTO Kyushu's third-largest city is at the heart of
the island geographically and administratively, and it

188

Dragons and lions adorn the ancient city in Naha, Okinawa

was once the southwestern headquarters of the Tokugawa shogunate. You can use it as an alternative to Fukuoka as a base, lying at one end of the scenic Yamanami Highway, which splits Kyushu in two. Kumamoto is between the two volcanic areas of Aso-Kuju National Park, to the east, and the Amakusa and Unzen National Parks, to the west.

NAGASAKI This lovely cosmopolitan, harbor town was the first Japanese port to establish trading contacts with foreign countries, and during the 220 years of Japanese seclusion from the rest of the world, one tiny island in Nagasaki Bay was allowed to continue as a trading post. Ironically, given its history of communication with the West, Nagasaki was the second target, after Hiroshima, for atomic bombing.

OKINAWA The climate of the Ryukyu archipelago group of Japanese islands is subtropical, and luxurious plants and fruits thrive all year round. Many of the islands are surrounded by coral reefs and fringed by sandy beaches. Okinawa, in Okinawa prefecture, is the largest and by far the most heavily developed island of the group and the one most popular with mainland Japanese tourists, who go not only for the sun, sea, and nightlife, but for Okinawan arts, crafts, and customs, all of which are markedly different from their own. Okinawa is also the focal point for a network of inter-island ferries that make even remote and barely inhabited islands accessible. U.S. forces occupied the island until 1972, when it was handed back to the Japanese. It is still the site of several U.S. military bases.

OKINAWAN TRADITIONS
Okinawan culture has survived the influence of mainland Japan, especially on the more remote of the surrounding islands and in small towns and villages. Festivals of folk dancing and music, contests such as tug-of-war and boat races, and various craft exhibitions are popular forms of local entertainment. Often based on ancient Shinto ceremonies, they provide a happy mix of noisy religious ritual and other, more earthy pursuits.

The Eight Hells

THE EIGHT HELLS
Beppu's most popular
attractions are eight hot
springs known as Jigoku
(Hell Pools), in which the
waters reach boiling point.
Each pool has a particular
characteristic: for exam-
ple, Chino-ike Jigoku
(Blood Pond Hell) runs
blood red as a result of
dissolved clay. The Eight
Hells are a year-round
attraction and are almost
always crowded. Regular
sightseeing bus tours
taking in the pools and
other major sights run
from Kitahama bus
station, just east of
Beppu JR station. The
Beppu city information
office, in Beppu JR
station, has maps and
leaflets in English.

**OLD AND FANTASTICAL
SPAS**
One of the oldest spas in
Beppu is the Takegawa
bath house, built in
1879, with an interior
reminiscent of an old,
well-used boxing gym.
Takegawa is best known
for its sand baths, where
attendants bury you in hot,
black sand up to the neck
and leave you to sweat for
10 minutes. Afterward
there is plenty of hot water
to wash it all off. The most
fantastical baths are in
Suginoi Palace, adjoining
the Suginoi Hotel. Two
aircraft-hangar-sized baths
provide every variety of
hot-spring and other
bathing experience (including a coffee bath for
improving the complexion).
One bath is for men, the
other for women, and as
each one is different, the
facilities are alternated
each day.

▶▶▶ Aso-Kuju National Park   187D4

Aso-Kuju National Park lies in the center of Kyushu
between Beppu and Kumamoto, and it is best to plan a
trip there in conjunction with a visit to one or both of these
towns. Mount Aso (*Aso-san*) is, in fact, a joint name for
five volcanic peaks, all sitting in the world's largest crater
basin (technically a caldera). The most central peak,
Nakadake, is a very active volcano. There is a cable-car
service to the rim of its crater, where you can catch
glimpses, through the rising vapor, of the green lake at its
bottom, smell the lake's sulfurous fumes, and sometimes
even hear the mountain's portentous volcanic rumblings.
On a clear day, the outer rim of the Aso caldera, 80 miles
(128km) in circumference, is also visible. The floor of the
caldera, 410 feet (125m) deep at its lowest point, is undu-
lating grassy meadowland, a rare landscape feature in
Japan. Grazing cows and horses bear *kanji* (ideogram)
brand marks—an unusual sight to Westerners.

From Kumamoto there is a regular service on the JR
Hohi line to Aso town (one hour). Aso itself is not a place
of great interest, but from just outside the JR station
there is a frequent bus service to the Aso-san Nishi
ropeway (cable-car) station (40 minutes). From
Kumamoto there is also a direct bus service to the Nishi
ropeway station (1½ hours). If the volcano is too active, the
cable car does not operate, and the road and railroad links
may even be closed. This is unusual, but you may wish to
check with your hotel or local tourist office before leaving
for Aso.

The journey to Mount Aso from Kumamoto is itself
interesting, passing through areas of traditional farmland
neatly planted with crops of rice, tobacco, wheat, and
bamboo. Within the park, the designated sights have not
been sensitively developed (the power of Nakadake
overwhelms most human interference) and are usually
crowded, but outside these areas, particularly in the
southwest around Takamori, there are delightful old-
fashioned, rustic hot-spring *minshuku*, inns, and hotels.
Takamori is 30 minutes by train, or 40 minutes by bus
from Tateno (which is between Aso and Kumamoto).
Takamori is connected to Takachiko, another small *onsen*
(hot-spring town), by a very scenic bus route along back
roads (1½ hours).

►► Beppu 187D4

Set on the east coast of Kyushu, Beppu is Japan's most popular hot-spring resort. With more than 3,000 hot springs, Beppu can accommodate the 12 million or so tourists who visit the resort each year to relax in the waters of the public bath houses, or in the private baths of their hotel, inn, or *ryokan*. Baths in mineral-rich waters, mud, and sand as well as steam rooms, outdoor pools, saunas, and virtually any other form you can imagine, are all available in Beppu. Many of the hot springs are said to have healing properties, and the University of Kyoto runs an institute there to study the therapeutic benefits of mineral baths. In contrast, the town itself is an unattractive place of souvenir shops, garish signs, pinball arcades, neon lights, and amusement parlors. The only way to enjoy Beppu is to enter into the unsophisticated spirit of it; the town may be gaudy, but its position on Beppu Bay, with the sea on one side and mountains behind it, is glorious.

Beppu is connected to Kumamoto by the JR Hohi line (three hours) and to Hakata station in Fukuoka by the Nichirin limited express train (2½ hours). Bus services also operate between Beppu and Kumamoto (via Aso on some journeys) along the Trans-Kyushu Highway (three hours, 55 minutes).

Mount Naka trail

YUFUIN SPA TOWN

Yufuin is a quiet, rural, and elegant spa town, one hour by bus from Beppu. It is situated on a highland plateau and contains delightful, traditional Japanese inns and *minshuku*, as well as a thatched-roof public bath house.

NAKADAKE TRAIL ROUTE

From the cable-car terminus on the rim of Nakadake there is a path up to the highest point of the mountain. From here, a trail leads to Mount Taka, then on to Sensui-kyo, a volcanic gorge, and finally to Miyaji JR station, one stop down the line from Aso station. The route takes from five to six hours and covers some rough ground. Few people follow it, but the views are exhilarating.

Coastal Beppu

SHOPPING IN FUKUOKA

Fukuoka's best-known local products are silk textiles (*Hakata-ori*), Hakata dolls, and kimono sashes (*Hakata-obi*). Hakata silk is not as smooth as most Japanese silk, and it is this slight roughness in texture for which it is valued. *Hakata-obi* are woven from local silk, and Hakata dolls are made from fired clay and then handpainted. Their trademarks are bright colors, characteristic expressions, and depiction of *geisha*, women, and young girls. The Iwataya department store, in the center of the Tenjin district, stocks a wide selection of local products.

A tented food cart dishes out the goods in Fukuoka

▶▶▶ Fukuoka-Hakata   186C4

The largest city on Kyushu Island, Fukuoka is also Kyushu's gateway to the rest of Japan. Fukuoka and the port of Hakata, now connected, were once separate cities, hence the confusion between the two names that sometimes arises in train timetables and maps.

This is a modern, commercial city, a good starting point and base for exploring the island. The people here (and in Kyushu generally) are said to be straightforward and warmhearted; they certainly retain a friendliness toward foreigners, perhaps lost in the more cosmopolitan cities of Tokyo and Osaka.

The bullet train terminates at Hakata (Fukuoka) station. Journey times from Tokyo and Osaka are six hours, 10 minutes and three hours, 20 minutes, respectively. By air to Fukuoka Airport, the only international airport in Kyushu, travel times are reduced to one hour, 40 minutes and one hour, five minutes, respectively. If you have the time, the train journey is an interesting way of seeing the area. All the main cities in Kyushu are connected to Fukuoka by train and bus.

There are two subway lines in the city. Line 1 links Hakata station to Tenjin, a major dining, shopping, and nightlife area, and to Ohori Park, the attractive city park surrounding Fukuoka Castle. Buses and tour buses leave from the Kotsu bus center opposite Hakata station and the Tenjin bus center near the subway stop. There is a tourist information office in Hakata station, where English is spoken and good maps of the city and surrounding area are provided.

Fukuoka is well known for its tented **food carts▶▶** that illuminate and line the sidewalks at night. Under canvas, customers squash onto a bench seat in front of a low counter, while the cook prepares local specialties on a mobile gas range and serves beer and *sake* (hot in the winter months). Shunko-bashi Street, at the southern end of Nakasu-kawa-bata (subway line 1) is the best-known location for outdoor eating carts.

Shofukuji Temple, the oldest Zen temple in Japan, once the monastic home of Sengai Gibon, the famous ink painter

SENGAI, SHOFUKUJI ABBOT

Sengai Gibon (1750–1837), one of Japan's most famous ink painters and calligraphers, was a Zen monk, having become a novice at the age of 11. His final formal position as a monk was as abbot of Shofukuji Temple in Fukuoka. Sengai retired in 1811, aged 61, and devoted the rest of his life to his work, which is renowned for its spontaneity and humor. A large collection of his art is on display in the Idemitsu Art Museum, Tokyo (see page 55).

Fukuoka Castle and Ohori Park►►, 20 minutes by subway from Hakata station, provide an oasis of greenery for city residents. Only a few gates and a simple turret remain of the castle, but it is situated on a high hill that commands a view of Fukuoka in every direction. The park was originally part of the castle's outer defenses, and some of it has been planted over the site of the old moat. In the center is a large pond surrounded by willow and azalea trees. Over 2,500 cherry trees grow here and in early April the park is a favorite place for raucous cherry blossom–viewing parties. Facing the lake to the southeast of the park is the Fukuoka City Art Museum (*open* 9:30–5:30; closed Mon), containing a collection of modern and Buddhist Japanese art and tea-ceremony utensils.

Shofukuji Temple►► is believed to be the oldest Zen temple in Japan. It was founded in 1195 by the priest Eisai, who went on to establish many other important Rinzai sect Zen temples in Kyoto and Kamakura. Eisai spent four years in China and returned not only with Zen Buddhism (known as Chan in China), but with the seeds of the country's first tea plants. The temple itself now seems rather neglected, although the bronze bell in the belfry is designated an important cultural property. However, to anyone interested in Zen it is an important shrine. Shofukuji is 15 minutes' walk from Hakata station and easy to find with a city map.

EXAMINATION SHRINE

Temmangu Shrine in Dazaifu, the ancient capital of Kyushu and within easy reach of Fukuoka, is dedicated to the god of scholarship. High-school students sitting the tough college entrance examinations come here in droves to pray for help, and local restaurants sell good-luck noodle dishes. The grounds of the shrine, planted with many cedar trees, are spacious and worthy of a long stroll. Dazaifu is 30 minutes by train from Nishitetsu Fukuoka station in Tenjin.

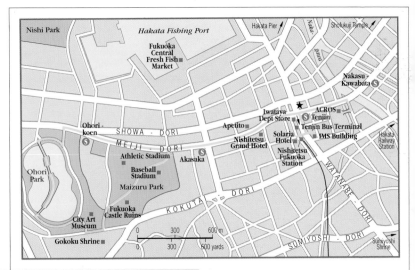

Fukuoka

Distance: 2 miles (3km); time: about 1½ hours.

This walk leads through Fukuoka's busy downtown shopping area, then follows the route of the old castle

moat to Ohori Park and the castle remains.

Start at the **Tenjin Iwataya department store►►**, located above the Tenjin subway station. There is an especially good food hall in the basement and there are occasionally cultural exhibitions on upper floors. From here, walk south past the bus terminal, with the **Solaria Hotel Building►** on your right, a recently constructed modern hotel built around a central well, with glass-walled elevators. There is a sports center and swimming pool open to nonresidents, as well as boutiques, restaurants, three movie theaters, an exhibition space, and an arena with fountains. On the opposite side of the street is the **Intermedia Station (IMS)►►**, a new, open-plan example of modern Japanese architecture. IMS contains many shops, restaurants, galleries, a car and motorcycle showroom with the latest models, a music store and, on the ninth floor (the Rainbow Plaza), a free library with newspapers, videos, and an information desk (at which English is spoken).

From Intermedia Station, walk north to **ACROS (Asian Crossroads Over The Sea)►►**, a vast building with four basement floors and 14 floors above ground devoted to all things Asian, including cultural events, conventions,

The Intermedia Station: outside ...

… and inside, with its dazzling galleries, stores, and showrooms

company offices, restaurants, and films. Walking west toward Fukuoka Castle, you will pass the **Nishitetsu Grand Hotel►** on your left, where there is a reasonably priced piano bar with views over the city, and the **Apetito►►**, a Western-style

bakery and restaurant, on your right.

Continue to Ohori Park, passing the moat of the old castle. Inside the park, there is a **coffee shop►►** with a terrace overlooking the lake and distant mountains. After a rest, visit the remains of **Fukuoka Castle** (see page 193 for information on the castle and park), which has good views over the city from its highest point.

POTTERY PRISON
Okawachi-yama village, a short bus or cab ride from Imari, was both home and prison for the many Korean potters brought here by the Nabeshima *daimyo*. A reconstruction of a porcelain factory here illustrates the conditions in which they worked out their lives. Okawachi-yama is still a functioning pottery village with 20 kilns in operation, and its narrow streets are crammed with shops and studios. Maps and information are available from the community showroom (*tenjikan*).

Hard at work in the Kyushu Ceramic Museum

Excursion

▶▶ The Saga pottery towns 186B4

Saga prefecture, in northwest Kyushu, is one of Japan's most important areas for the production of traditional porcelain and pottery. The two best-known kiln sites are Karatsu and Arita, each of which has given its name to a particular ceramic style. Imari, the port town from which all Saga ceramics have been shipped to the rest of Japan, has benefited by association, and Imari-yaki is also a famous name in Japanese porcelain.

Until the 17th century, the Japanese imported porcelain from China and Korea. Saga, which lies only 156 miles (250km) from the Korean Peninsula, was a base for Japanese invasions of Korea, and many potters from that country were brought back there as captives and obliged to teach their techniques to the Japanese. One of their number, Ri Sanpei, discovered kaolin, the raw material of porcelain production, near present-day Arita in 1616. The Nabeshima family, the local ruling clan, ensured that the Saga district retained a monopoly on porcelain by keeping their Korean artisans under close guard.

Nearby, Karatsu also benefited from Korean know-how, and the town's elegant stone pottery, much influenced by Korean Yi dynasty ware, is highly valued, especially by devotees of the tea ceremony.

The suggested itinerary for this excursion is Fukuoka–Karatsu–Imari–Arita–Fukuoka. To visit all three places in one day, you will need to use cabs to travel from Imari to Okawachi-yama (see panel), from there to Arita, and for travel around Arita itself. Each of the towns has a tourist office in or near the station.

Karatsu Depart from Hakata station, Fukuoka, initially by subway line 1 to Mei Hama, and then on the JR Chikuhi

Ranks of ceramics: the finished products on display

JAPANESE CERAMICS

The Japanese ceramic aesthetic is nothing, if not sublime. The earliest ceramics date back to the beginning of the 13th century with the introduction of Chinese techniques. The development of a true Japanese style, with its freedom, simplicity, and conscious, gentle irregularity of design and manufacture, was catalyzed 300 years later by the popularity of the tea ceremony.

197

line (one hour, 20 minutes in all). Karatsu, in northwest Saga, was for many centuries an important center of trade and commerce with China and Korea. It remains a relatively busy fishing port, but is best known as a summer beach resort. For pottery fans, two local kilns are particularly worth visiting. **Nakazato Taroemon kiln▶▶** (*open* 8:30–5:30), a 10-minute walk or a short cab ride from Karatsu station, has been with the same family for 13 generations. When the immediate past master, Nakazato Muan, was still alive he was designated a "Living National Treasure" for his artistry. There is a gallery exhibiting work for sale by the present master, Muan's son, and apprentices, and an area where visitors may watch potters at the wheel.

Ryuta-gama kiln▶▶ (*open* 8:30–5:30), a 15-minute cab ride from Karatsu station, is run by Nakazato Takashi, one of the younger sons of Nakazato Muan. The Ryuta-gama kiln incorporates a gallery, workshop, and potter's house. The work here demonstrates the best of traditional techniques as well as a freedom of spirit. Imari is one hour by JR Chikuhi line or by bus from Karatsu.

Arita Reached by train (20 minutes), or bus (40 minutes) from Imari, or by cab (20 minutes) from Okawachi-yama (see panel), Arita is the birthplace of Japanese porcelain. Over 150 kilns still operate in and around the town. The **Kyushu Ceramic Museum▶▶** (*open* 9–4:30; closed Mon), a short walk (10 minutes) from Arita station, gives a good, clear introduction to the development and various characteristics of particular Arita kilns, as well as to the ceramic art of Kyushu as a whole. The **Ceramic Art Museum▶**, 15 minutes' walk from Kami-Arita station (three minutes by train from Arita station), exhibits a collection of Arita porcelain dating from the 17th century to the present day. The nearby **Izumiyama Jisekiba▶▶**, the quarry discovered by Ri Sanpei, is still open, with a working kiln museum alongside.

ARITA PORCELAIN

The first porcelain products made in Arita were influenced by Korean, and later Chinese designs, but in the 1640s the Japanese potter Sakaida Kakiemon (1596–1666) introduced Japanese motifs and a technique of overglaze decoration. His own trademark color was persimmon red, but as his methods inspired his contemporaries, Arita ware came to be associated with colorful pieces decorated in patterns and influenced by Japanese textiles, especially those incorporating birds and flowers. The fine clay and translucent glazes that typify Arita ware came to the notice of the West and, following its acclaim at the Philadelphia Exhibition in 1876, became much valued by collectors.

TATSUDA SHIZEN PARK
This natural park (as opposed to a formal landscaped park, such as Suizenji Park) in Kumamoto contains the burial temple of the Hosokawa family, who took control of the district from the Kato clan, as well as the grave of Hosokawa Gracia (1563–1600), one of Japan's most famous female converts to Catholicism. Gracia was killed by order of her husband to ensure her freedom from capture by his enemies. Mariko, the heroine in James Clavell's book *Shogun*, was modeled on her. The park is a 15-minute cab ride from the city center.

Pruned trees, shaped bushes, and traditional stone bridge in Suizenji Park, a strolling garden constructed in the 17th century

▶ Kagoshima   186C2

This small, modern but relaxed city at the southern tip of Kyushu is a terminus for trains and national highways, and a main port for boats to Okinawa and other islands of the Ryukyu group. Mount Sakurajima, across the Kinko Bay from Kagoshima, is an active volcano that occasionally showers the city with black ash. Its last big eruption in 1914 generated enough lava flow to form the land bridge that now connects Sakurajima to the mainland. Kagoshima boasts no particular tourist attractions but it is off the beaten track and has a distinguished, cosmopolitan history. The three-hour train trip from Kumamoto passes through picturesque mountain and coastal terrain. JR Nishi Kagoshima station is a short walk from the city center; the local tourist office is next to it.

▶▶▶ Kumamoto   186C3

Kumamoto was badly damaged during World War II but the modern city, with its many tree-lined avenues and open spaces and a convenient cable car network, has developed its own character. This was once a nationally important political center and castle town, and retains the strong sense of identity and independence such power brings. The city's main attractions are the castle and the landscaped gardens of Suizenji Park, both dating from the early 17th century. During this time the city was chosen as the site of the southwestern headquarters of the Tokugawa shogunate. Despite its loss of national influence, Kumamoto remains at the geographical and administrative heart of Kyushu and provides a good alternative to Fukuoka as a touring base for the island. Kumamoto is one hour, 30 minutes from Hakata station, Fukuoka, on the JR Kagoshima line. Within the city, there are two cable car lines that connect all the main centers of interest. The tourist information office is in a booth in front of the JR station entrance.

Mount Sakurajima

Shrine offerings at Kumamoto Castle

Kumamoto Castle▶▶ (*open* 8:30–5:30, Oct–Mar until 4:30 PM), right in the heart of Kumamoto, was burned down in 1877 after a long siege, but the reconstruction (unlike other examples) has been well managed, and walking around the castle gives visitors a real sense of its former magnificence. The original fortress was built in 1607 by Kiyomasa Kato, feudal lord of the prefecture and a recognized master of castle architecture. It was originally constructed with 49 watchtowers (11 survive), 29 castle gates, and remarkable concave defensive walls (fitted with overhanging eaves and missile-dropping openings), which rendered conventional siege tactics almost useless. Nowadays, there are two main entrances to the castle, the most impressive being the southwest. From the top of the castle, there is a magnificent view of Kumamoto and Mount Nakadake smoldering in the distance. A museum within the walls exhibits relics of the castle's military past.

Suizenji Park▶▶ was constructed in 1632 as part of the villa grounds of the Hosokawa clan. It is designed as a miniature version of the old Tokaido highway, between Kyoto and Edo. Generations of gardeners have created a completely artificial landscape here from a natural habitat. Each pruned tree, hill, patch of water, or stone has been designed or chosen to represent a natural feature along the Tokaido. A tea house with *tatami* (straw floor mats) and fine views is located near the pond. To reach Suizenji Park, catch cable car 2 or 3 from outside the castle to Suizenji-koen-mae stop.

Much of the history of Japan is a history of warfare. Over the centuries powerful landowners, warriors, and clerics fought to control the rich rice-producing regions that would in turn give them political control of the country. The earliest types of castles (shiro) were built mainly from wood and earth, and during the Sengoku Jidai, the Age of the Country at War (1490–1600), large numbers of castles were built by daimyo to protect their domains from enemy attack.

THE WOODEN WARRIORS
During the 14th century, Kusunoki Masashige defended Chihaya Castle against large numbers of Hojo *samurai*. He put life-sized dummies dressed in armor behind shields near the castle walls. At dawn, the *samurai* attacked what they thought were the defenders trying to flee. As they drew close, hidden archers opened fire and dropped rocks from the walls, injuring or killing over 800 of the attackers.

Above: detail of Himeji Castle
Below: Kumamoto Castle

Early construction Building techniques were originally quite simple. Large wooden posts were driven into the earth at intervals of one *ken* (1¼ miles/2km). Between the large posts a framework of lighter bamboo poles was inserted, to which bundles of bamboos and reeds were tied. The walls were then coated with a mixture of red clay and stones to give them greater strength. Defensive towers and other buildings were made of wood. Walls built using this kind of wattle-and-daub technique were highly susceptible to weather damage, and a great deal of work was required to maintain the castles ready for battle.

As warfare increased both in intensity and duration during the Sengoku Jidai period, *daimyo* began to build more permanent and more powerful castles. Western techniques of fortification were introduced through the efforts of Portuguese Jesuit missionaries, and *hirajiro* ("castles on the plain") and *hirayamajiro* ("castles on the plateau") made their appearance. Whenever possible, natural features such as rivers, lakes, hills, and mountain crags or the sea were incorporated into the defenses, which in a typical castle would consist of a moat surrounding a number of concentric courts protected by massive stone walls. In the middle, stood a central compound (*honmaru*), within which a large central tower (*tenshu*) was built on a platform of pounded earth covered with huge stones.

Defense techniques Attackers faced a formidable number of defenses and obstacles. Openings (*hazama*) were left in the walls as loopholes through which archers and gunners could shoot down into the ranks of the enemy. Special chambers (*ishiotoshi*) were constructed over the walls with openings in the floors through which large stones or boiling water could be dropped onto the enemy. In some castles, the inner courtyards and buildings were constructed in such a way as to confuse any attackers who might breach the outer defenses: by abrupt changes of direction enemy troops were forced into killing grounds, where they could be attacked by archers and gunners firing from strongholds built into the defenses.

At the heart of the castle stood the main tower, consisting of a number of stories of decreasing size, with curving roofs and overhanging gables. The *tenshu* was the command post and watchtower from which any defense of the castle would be controlled. When Hideyoshi built his massive castle at Osaka in 1583 as both the seat of his government and as a symbol of his power, the *tenshu* was over 980 feet (80km) high, colored blue and gold.

Castle-smashing Hideyoshi, one of the greatest of castle builders, was also a castle destroyer—a reflection of his political savvy. As Hideyoshi increased his power, he sent out "castle-smashing commissioners" (*shiro wari bugyo*) to destroy the fortifications built by his defeated enemies. This policy was continued by the Tokugawa shogunate after they came to power. They decreed that each *daimyo* could only retain a single castle in his domains; all others had to be demolished. The surviving castles became centers of trade and industry, and *joku machi* (castle towns) grew up around the castles to supply the *daimyo* and his retainers.

Many surviving castles have been almost completely rebuilt, but some remain in their original state. Probably the most famous of all Japanese castles is Hideoshi's Shirasagi Castle (Castle of the White Crane), in Himeji (see page 162).

THE LAST SIEGE
In 1877, Satsuma *samurai* under the leadership of Saigo Takamori rose in rebellion against the imperial government of Emperor Meiji. Imperial troops held Kumamotojo Castle against a rebel force three times larger, who attacked the castle with both traditional and modern weapons. In an echo of the past, both attackers and defenders used troops equipped only with swords, who fought man to man on the battlements. Eventually the rebels were defeated and the castle retrieved.

Matsumoto Castle

DUTCH IN NAGASAKI

During the period of Japanese seclusion between 1639 and 1854, the only Westerners allowed by the Japanese to trade with Japan were the Dutch, who were restricted to a small, manmade island called Dejima in Nagasaki harbor. Only traders and prostitutes were allowed on and off Dejima, which has since been swallowed up in a land reclamation scheme and is marked only by a cable car stop. There is, however, a reconstruction of the island at the Dejima Historical Museum (cable car 7 to Dejima; *open* 9–5, closed Mon). Oranda-zaka, or Hollander Slope, a cobbled street behind the station, is lined with 19th-century Dutch residents' houses, and Nagasaki Holland Village, an hour by bus from Nagasaki station, is a complete reconstruction of a genuine Dutch village.

Glover Mansion

▶▶ Miyazaki 187D2

At Miyazaki, the administrative and economic center of Miyazaki prefecture in southern Kyushu, the climate is subtropical year round. The town's broad avenues are lined with palm trees, lush greenery abounds, and flowers are always in bloom. A seaside promenade and a beautiful coastline, designated as the Quasi-National Park, stretch to the south. Miyazaki was once a popular honeymoon destination, but nowadays Japanese couples prefer the more exotic shores of Australia and Hawaii, or the capital cities of Europe. Nevertheless, Miyazaki remains principally a Japanese tourist destination, and very few foreigners visit. Nearby Sengai resort is a popular spot, especially the nightly shows at the Ocean Dome.

There are direct trains from Hakata station, Fukuoka (six hours), Beppu (three hours, 45 minutes), and Kagoshima (three hours), and direct flights from Tokyo (one and a half hours). Tourist offices can be found at the JR station and at the airport.

▶▶ Nagasaki 186B3

Nagasaki, the target of the second atomic bomb dropped by the Allies on Japan in World War II is a city of many particular sights. Its history, coastal location, scenery, old city and foreign quarters, and the warm climate, tempered with sea breezes, make it a perfect place for relaxed exploration on foot or by cable car or rickshaw. The city is easy to navigate and many signs are in English.

Nagasaki is two hours by train from Hakata station on the JR Nagasaki line. The train station is connected to the city center by cable car, part of a system that links all the main sights. Most shopping, dining, and cultural activities are located in the south of the city. North of the city is the Peace Park and to the west Inasayama, a mountain-top park offering splendid views. A tourist information center is located outside Nagasaki station.

Glover Garden▶▶ (*open* Nov–Mar 8:30–5, Mar–Nov 8–6) is an open-air museum that displays Western-style

Nagasaki's Chinatown

NAGASAKI AND THE PORTUGUESE
Francis Xavier was the first missionary to set foot in Japan. He arrived in 1549 and left in 1551, leaving converts to continue his work. By 1579, Japanese Christians included six *daimyo* among their numbers. One of them, Omura Sumitada, ruled a remote area of northwest Kyushu, where the coastline was blessed with a good natural harbor. Here, with Portuguese help, Omura built the port of Nagasaki, which attracted the majority of Japan-bound Portuguese ships and quickly became a rich melting-pot of Eastern and Western cultures.

Detail, Kofukuji Temple

TOJIN YASHIKA ATO
In 1698, the shogunate ordered all Chinese in Nagasaki to live in a walled compound in the Tojin Hashika Ato quarter, in the southeast, an area evocative of an old Chinatown settlement. Nearby, Shinchi-machi is the present-day Chinatown, an excellent place for Chinese food.

houses built in the 19th-century Meiji period. The main attraction is the oldest Western-style building in Japan, Glover Mansion, built by Scotsman Thomas Glover in 1863, and still much as it was in his day. The park grounds that overlook the city are well maintained and peaceful, if somewhat spoiled by the hillside escalators leading to Glover Mansion. Take cable car 5 to Oura-Tenshudoshita stop to reach the gardens.

Situated in Teramachi, the Nagasaki temple district, **Kofukuji Temple▶▶▶** (*open* 8–5:30) was an important Obaku-Zen temple in the style of the Chinese Ming dynasty. Kofukuji is a 10-minute walk from the Kokaidonae cable-car stop. A 20-minute walk south through the Teramachi district leads to **Sofukuji Temple▶▶▶** (*open* 8–5), the first Obaku-Zen temple in Japan, founded in 1629 by a Chinese monk. Attractive, grassy gardens with tropical palms surround the temple, whose beautiful, red-painted main hall was constructed by Chinese carpenters.

The bomb that the Allies dropped on Nagasaki on August 9, 1945, was three times more powerful than the one that was dropped on Hiroshima, but it missed the main city and fell on a village on the outskirts of town. Even so, over three-quarters of the population of Nagasaki died (150,000 people). **Peace Park (Heiwa-koen)▶▶▶** was built on a hill near the site of the explosion. A bronze statue stands as a symbol of hope for peace, and several other sculptures have been given by foreign countries. In the International Culture Hall (*open* 9–6), there is a display of records and relics of the attack. Take cable car 1 or 3 to Matsuyama-cho stop.

BATTLE OF OKINAWA

The final land battle in World War II between Japan and the Allies took place on Okinawa. The American flag was raised on June 22, 1945, after 82 days of fierce fighting. The Japanese commander, General Ushijima, committed suicide, as did many soldiers and civilians. Over 250,000 Japanese died; 12,500 Allied soldiers were killed and 37,000 wounded. Despite such losses, the Japanese on the mainland did not surrender and the U.S. Command decided to drop atomic bombs on Hiroshima and Nagasaki.

204

OKINAWAN *SAKÉ*

Okinawan islanders make a variety of very potent *saké*. Two of the strongest are a *saké* matured in jars full of garlic cloves, and a concoction known as "snake juice," matured in a wide-necked jar containing the coiled body of a small, dead, poisonous snake. After 10 years' maturation the flesh is dissolved and only the bones remain.

Iriomote Island

▶▶▶ Okinawa   186A1

Okinawa is the largest island in the Ryukyu archipelago, which stretches south 812 miles (1,300km) from Kyushu through the Pacific and East China Sea, almost to the tip of Taiwan. Like the rest of the Ryukyu group, its culture has been influenced as much by China as by Japan.

Okinawa is a tropical island, warm in any season and scorchingly hot in July and August. The south of Okinawa, particularly around the capital, Naha, is heavily developed and ugly. However, in Naha itself the jumble of hotels, temples, McDonald's hamburger bars, ice-cream parlors, Shinto shrines, Japanese tourists, strip joints, karate *dojo* (gyms), old men and women in kimonos, and dense traffic, all fit comfortably together. The city is a great repository of Okinawan culture and the location of the best of Okinawa theater, dance, music, and cuisine.

Much of the north of the island is now also developed, but there are still a few small, traditional fishing and farming villages, surrounded by sugarcane and pineapple fields, and unspoiled beaches (nowadays often annexed by the fancy hotels). Coral-diving and tropical fishing are popular pursuits. Okinawa is also the birthplace of Japanese karate (see pages 206–207). To experience the unique Sino-Japanese lifestyle of this archipelago, you should travel to other islands in the Okinawan prefecture, such as Kumejima, Taketomi, and Iriomote. Okinawa is the center of ferry and air services to these islands.

Getting there There are direct flights and sea ferry services to Okinawa from Tokyo, Osaka, and Fukuoka. Flight times from mainland Japan are between 1 and 2½ hours; the ferry takes more than two days from Tokyo, and more than a day from Fukuoka. Ferries traveling from Okinawa link all the inhabited islands of the Ryukyu group. An air service links the larger islands. Tourist information is available at Naha airport (15 minutes by bus to Naha center) or Naha bus terminal.

Northern Okinawa The least spoiled part of the island, this is the most satisfying area to explore. Unfortunately, access to the north by public transportation is difficult and services are infrequent.

Hedo Misaki►► is the island's northernmost headland, where a clifftop road affords spectacular views of blue sea and outlying islands. The road circles the headland and passes through the tiny village of Oku, worth visiting for its traditional Okinawan houses. To reach Hedo Misaki take bus 20, 21, or 77 from Naha to Nago (two hours, 20 minutes), bus 67 Nago to Okuma Beach (two hours, 50 minutes), and bus 69 from Okuma to Hedo Misaki-iriguchi. From here, it is a 15-minute walk to the cliff.

Kijoka►►, a traditional village in northern Okinawa, is famous for *bashofu*, a textile similar to linen but made from banana fiber. Take bus 73 or 74 from Nago to Kijoka (one hour).

Southern Okinawa The island's principal craft, fashion shopping, and dining thoroughfare is Kokusai-dori, the long main street of **Naha**►►. Along its east side is Heiwa-dori, the central branch of a network of covered alleys and passageways that make up the market district. With stalls selling everything from obscure Okinawan vegetables to baseball caps, this area is the heart of the city.

Shuri, now a district of Naha, was the capital of the Ryukyu dynasty (1429–1879). The once royal city was used by Japanese high command as their headquarters and destroyed by American Forces during World War II in 1945 in the Battle of Okinawa. Parts of the castle—some exterior walls and two castle gates—have been restored. *Shurei-mon*, the Gate of Courtesy, a typical example of Okinawan architecture, was restored in 1958 and represents a symbol of the islanders' culture and independence.

Above and below: traditional costume in Shuri

FESTIVALS
Okinawa calendar of events: *Jiriuma* (January 20) a parade of women dressed in colorful *bingata* kimono; *Hari* (May 3 and 4) dragon-boat races; *Naha Otsunahiki* (October 10), two 820-foot- (250m-) long fat ropes, one "male," one "female," are intertwined, and a tug of war ensues between thousands of people.

Japanese martial arts are now practiced world-wide as methods of self-defense, self-discipline, and sport. While the classical systems of swords-manship and related methods attract a devoted following, the systems of judo, kendo, aikido, and especially karate are the most popular, and highly skilled non-Japanese teachers and practitioners can be found in countries throughout the world.

UECHI-RYU KARATE

One of Okinawa's most popular karate styles, Uechi-Ryu, was developed by Kanbun Uechi (1877–1945). He studied Chinese boxing at the Central Temple in Fukien province, China, where he was a student of Chou Tze-ho. After training with him for 13 years, Kanbun Uechi returned to Japan and became a farmer near Osaka. A young Okinawan persuaded him to start teaching and soon he opened a school. He taught there for 24 years before returning to Okinawa.

Weapons used in Okinawan karate

Okinawan karate origins Karate developed in Okinawa in the 19th century from a fusion of Chinese martial arts, brought by Okinawans from the Fukien province of mainland China, and an indigenous Okinawan system of empty-hand fighting called *te*. *Te* and simple weapon systems using farming and fishing implements were developed in response to a decree by the Chinese invaders of Okinawa, which forbade the use by the islanders of swords and other orthodox weapons.

In 1921, Crown Prince Hirohito visited Okinawa and for the first time saw a demonstration of karate by some school children. The demonstration was arranged by Funakoshi Gichin, then the chief instructor of a karate school on the island. It was a great success and Funakoshi went to Tokyo in 1922 to demonstrate his skills. This was the start of karate in Japan and around the world.

Modern karate Karate stresses kicking and punching, although some styles also teach throwing techniques, arm and wrist locks, and the use of traditional Okinawan weapons, such as the *bo* (staff), jointed *nunchaku* (flail), or *tekko* (brass knuckle).

Following the example set by the founders of judo, Funakoshi Gichin and other karate masters wanted karate to be seen as something more than simply a method of fighting. The development of a strong fighting spirit was important, but this had to be accompanied by an equally strong spiritual and moral element to avoid the misuse of the art.

Funakoshi Gichin wrote a code of 20 precepts, among which he said "Karate begins and ends with courtesy"; "There is no first attack in karate"; and "Karate is an auxiliary of justice." The teachings and practices of the arts of the sword were applied by him to the art of the empty hand; by so doing he hoped that karate would become a means of developing and preserving the *samurai* spirit.

In the West, karate is most commonly taught as a sport, but the older ideals of self-defense and self-discipline still have many followers.

Other martial arts Judo was described by its founder Kano Jigoro (1860–1938) as "The Way of Gentleness or of first giving way in order ultimately to gain the victory;"

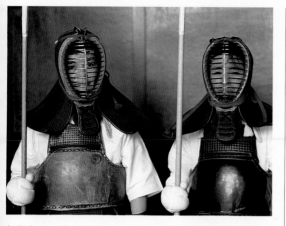

judo is practiced today as a competitive sport, in which the aim is to throw or lock an opponent according to strictly defined rules. The martial element has gradually declined because of this stress on judo as a sport, especially since judo became an Olympic event in 1964.

Aikido, "The Way of Harmony," was created by Ueshiba Morihei (1883–1969). As a young man, Ueshiba studied a number of ju-jitsu systems, as well as swordsmanship and spear-fighting. The techniques of aikido feature rapid turning movements, designed to blend with an attacker's movements so as to throw or unbalance him or her. Aikido masters are often compared with the eye of a hurricane: quiet in themselves, but difficult to approach because of the tremendous forces swirling around them.

Kendo, "The Way of the Sword," is very popular in Japan and has a growing number of followers in the West. Generally, kendo is taught as a sport *cum* combat, in which the practitioners wear protective armor and try to score points on designated targets with a bamboo sword (or *shinai*). The practice is derived from the older, classical systems of swordsmanship, and kendo practitioners generally regard the sports side of their art as the least important part of the discipline.

EVERYDAY KARATE

Karate on Okinawa is an everyday part of many people's lives. Training sessions do not have the obvious intensity and seriousness evident in Western and mainland Japanese schools. This sometimes disappoints Western visitors, who expect tough training schedules and strict discipline. Okinawan *karate-ka* train steadily, year in, year out, working on form, strength, body conditioning, and speed and developing a style that looks deceptively relaxed.

SAMURAI KENDO

It is common for kendo practitioners also to train in *ken-jutsu*, which features training with a real blade in techniques designed to dispatch an enemy as quickly and effectively as possible. The methods taught in the older *ken-jutsu* styles are the same techniques as taught to the *samurai*, and are based on the conditions and circumstances likely to be faced by a *samurai* on the field of battle.

A karate staff swinging into action

Wild mushrooms for sale

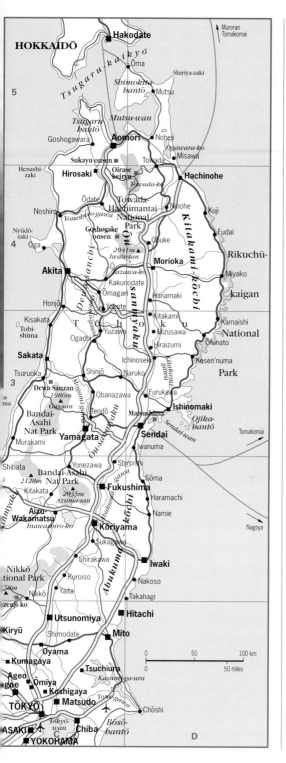

HOKKAIDŌ

Hakodate
Ōma
Tsugaru kaikyō
Shiriya-zaki
Shimokita-hantō
Mutsu
5
Tsugaru hantō
Mutsu-wan
Aomori
Noheji
Goshogawara
Ogawara-ko
Misawa
Sukayu onsen
Towada
Henashi-zaki
Hirosaki
Oirase keiryū
Hachinohe
Towada-ko
Ōdate
Ninohe
Kuji
Towada-Hachimantai
National Park
Noshiro
Yoneshiro-gawa
Ōu
Fudai
Nyūdō-zaki
Goshogake onsen
Ōfuke
4
Oga
2041m Iwate-san
Morioka
Rikuchū-
Akita
Tazawa-ko
Kitakami-kōchi
Miyako
Kakunodate
Hanamaki
kaigan
Honjō
Ōmagari
Yokote
Kitakami
Kisakata
T   c   h   o   Mizusawa
Kamaishi
Tobi-shima
Yuzawa
National
Ogachi
Hiraizumi
Ōfunato
Sakata
Ichinoseki
Kesen'numa
Park
Tsuruoka
Shinjō
Naruko
a-ma
Dewa Sanzan
1980m
Gas-san
Obanazawa
Furukawa
3
Tendō
Matsushima
Ishinomaki
Bandai-Asahi
Nat Park
Yamagata
Sendai
Ojika-hantō
Murakami
Iwanuma
Tomakomai
Shibata
Yonezawa
Shiroishi
Bandai-Asahi
2128m Nat Park
Sōma
Kitakata
2035m
Azuma-san
Fukushima
Haramachi
Aizu-Wakamatsu
Inawashiro-ko
Namie
Kōriyama
Nagoya
Sukagawa
Shirakawa
Iwaki
Nikkō
tional Park
Kuroiso
Nakoso
Yaita
Takahagi
Nikkō
zenji-ko
Hitachi
Kiryū
Utsunomiya
Shimodate
Mito
Ōyama
Kumagaya
Tsuchiura
0   50   100 km
Ageo
goe
Ōmiya
Kasumiga-ura
0   50 miles
Koshigaya
TŌKYŌ
Matsudo
Tone-gawa
ASAKI
Tōkyō-wan
Chōshi
Chiba
Bōsō-hantō
YOKOHAMA
D

Muroran
Tomakomai

The Japan Alps town of Takayama (see pages 214–215)

NORTHERN HONSHU The Tohoku region, in northern-most Honshu, has severe winters and a mountainous terrain, and remains one of the areas of Japan least affected by industrialization. The Hide, Kiso, and Akaishi ranges of mountains, known together as the Japan Alps, rise in a series of high, jagged snow-capped peaks strung across the middle of the southern end of northern Honshu, covering a vast area and providing a wide range of hiking, climbing, and skiing challenges. Nagano prefecture, within the Japan Alps, was selected to host the 1998 Winter Olympics.

TOHOKU Until the late 19th century, Tohoku was inhab-ited mostly by nomadic tribes of people known as Ainu. Gradually, Japanese settlers from the south drove the Ainu north to the island of Hokkaido, but the very cold, snowy winters and the distance from Tokyo continued to restrict Tohoku's settlement and commercial develop-ment. Even today, the area retains its long-standing traditions of farming and local crafts. It has a relatively rural, untouched air, marred only by some tourist facili-ties in the most popular national parks and historic towns.

Getting into Tohoku is quick and convenient on the Tohoku Shinkansen (bullet train), but once there and off the beaten track, local train journey times are slow and route-planning more complicated.

The main tourist season is the summer, which tends to be mild and dry; the first 10 days of August are particularly busy, with big festivals in Sendai, Akita, and Aomori.

SENDAI The largest city in Tohoku, Sendai was flattened in World War II and has since been rebuilt along the lines of most modern Japanese cities, with no exceptional features. It is, however, a reasonably good base from which to explore the rest of Tohoku and especially the

TOHOKU BACK-COUNTRY
Tohoku is the collective name given to the six prefectures of northern Honshu. It was once known by the Japanese as Michinoku, or "the end of the line." This image still sticks and, as a consequence, the area is avoided by conventional Japanese tourists, despite the many attractions of the region and the remarkable friendliness of the people.

neighboring Yamagata prefecture, a rural district where life is very much in traditional Tohoku style. Sendai is two hours by Tohoku Shinkansen from Tokyo's Ueno station.

JAPAN ALPS Mountains in Japan were once believed to be the sacred dwelling places of divine spirits. Some were climbed, consecrated, and made places of religious pilgrimage, but most mountain summits were avoided. However, in 1896 the Reverend Weston, a British missionary and mountaineer, set out to explore the area now known as the Japan Alps, and in the process popularized mountainclimbing in Japan (see panel, page 212). Matsumoto, an old castle town located on a high alpine plateau, is the gateway to the Japan Alps and a good base for exploring central Honshu, to the east. Takayama, in the heart of the Hida mountains, is another town worth visiting. Despite its popularity with Japanese visitors who know it as "little Kyoto," it is not as popular with foreign visitors.

KANAZAWA Although popular with the Japanese, Kanazawa is mistakenly neglected by foreigners. Partly an old Japanese castle town, with a thriving reputation as a center of traditional religions and arts and crafts (especially *noh* theater), and partly a very modern city with sophisticated shops and nightlife, Kanazawa is of manageable size and is best explored on foot. The city is five hours by train from Tokyo across the Japan Alps.

SADO Situated in the Sea of Japan, off the coast of Niigata prefecture, Sado Island was once a place of banishment for criminals and those out of political favor. It is a beautiful island with a slow pace of life, even between May and September, when there is usually a large influx of tourists.

ALPINE TOUR
Tateyama–Kurobe Alpine Route Tour takes a spectacular journey through the mountains using various modes of transportation. Tickets for the whole trip can be bought from Shinano-Omachi train station (one hour from Matsumoto on the JR Oito line), where the tour starts; it ends at Toyama, having proceeded en route by bus, cable car, train, and foot. The route is open from the end of April to the end of November, but is expensive and busy during holiday periods.

Vegetable handcart, Sado Island

FATHER OF THE MOUNTAINS
The Reverend Walter Weston popularized the term "Japan Alps" that fellow Englishman William Gowland had coined. Weston's 1896 book *Mountaineering and Exploration in the Japanese Alps* sparked much interest in Japan, and it earned him the title "Father of Mountaineering." Until that time the Japanese had seen their mountains as the sacred haunts of gods and spirits. In recognition of his exploration, he was awarded the Order of the Sacred Treasure (Fourth Class) by the emperor and a memorial was erected in his name in Kamikochi.

The Japan Alps

▶▶ Kamikochi   208B1

This village, really a collection of inns and lodges, shares its name with the high valley in which it stands. The area provides excellent hiking and climbing, and there are trails and mountain routes for every level of expertise.

Kamikochi is reached via Matsumoto by the private Matsumoto Dentetsu line to Shin Shimashima station (30 minutes) and then by bus (one hour, 20 minutes). The bus route takes a narrow and twisting mountain road and the scenery for the last 30 minutes of the journey is stunning. The road is closed by snow during the long winter months and opens only from the end of April to the beginning of November.

Since hotel development has been limited in Kamikochi, in summer accommodations are very scarce. Early spring and early October are the best times to visit. Camping and hiking equipment are available for rent and maps, route directions, and provisions may be had from local shops. Mountain huts with comfortable accommodations are found along the hiking trails.

▶▶ Matsumoto   208B1

Once an important castle town, Matsumoto is now a modern city in an alpine setting on a high plateau near many hot-spring resorts. As one of the gateways to the Alps, and the center of an excellent communications network, this is a particularly fine base for exploring both the Alps, to the west and north, and central Japan (Chubu district), to the east.

Matsumoto is two hours, 20 minutes by JR Chuo line limited express from Nagoya and two hours, 50 minutes on the same line, but from the opposite direction (Tokyo, Shinjuku station). There is a tourist office at Matsumoto station.

Matsumoto Castle▶▶▶ (*open* 8:30–5) is one of the oldest, best preserved, and most architecturally beautiful

The view from Matsumoto Castle

*Hiking country
at Kamikochi*

SACRED MOUNTAINS
The practice of leaving a monetary offering on mountain peaks is common throughout Japan. Many peaks have religious associations, and shrines and objects of veneration may be encountered (along with more worldly items such as vending machines) on some of the highest peaks. The first woman to climb Mount Fuji, in 1867, was Lady Parkes, the wife of the British ambassador, who ignored the taboo that prohibited women from sacred peaks (it was believed that the resident god abhorred "red pollution," or menstrual blood).

castles in Japan. Also known as Crow Castle (*Karasu-jo*), because the exterior walls are mainly black, it was begun in 1504, while the impressive six-storied *donjon* was completed in 1597. Climb the *donjon's* narrow, steep wooden staircase for panoramic views of the city. Matsumoto Castle was built for serious combat and its walls are peppered with battlements from which arrows and guns were fired and stones dropped on the attacking forces. To avoid crowds at the castle, go out of season or early in the day. The castle is a 20-minute walk through old Matsumoto, north and east of the train station; a map is available from the tourist office.

The **Matsumoto Folk Art Museum**►► (*open* 9–5; closed Mon), a 15-minute bus ride from the station to Shimoganai Mingeikan Guchi bus stop, exhibits domestic products of wood, bamboo, glass, and porcelain from Japan and other Asian countries.

► Nagano 208B1

Nagano prefecture was selected in 1991 to host the 1998 Winter Olympic Games. The resulting construction work includes a new Shinkansen (bullet-train) line from Tokyo to Nagano, as well as sporting facilities in surrounding alpine towns. Nagano's main attraction, 10 minutes by bus or cab from Nagano station, is the famous **Zenkoji Temple**►► (*open* 5:30–4:30), founded in the 7th century by Yoshimitsu Honda. One of the most important pilgrimage temples in Japan, it is attached to no particular Buddhist sect and is equally accessible to women and men. Millions flock to the Zenkoji Temple every year. The main hall is generally thick with the smoke of incense and the drone of Buddhist chanting. Unusually, in Japan's increasingly secular society, real religious fervor can be experienced here.

KEY TO PARADISE
The object for most pilgrims visiting Zenkoji Temple in Nagano is to touch "the key to paradise," and ensure their salvation. The key is a specific stone set in the wall of a tunnel that runs below the floor of the main hall. Devout pilgrims, most of whom are elderly, wend their way to the key along a pitch-black passageway.

Thatched farmhouse in Ogimachi

PRAYING ROOFS
The steep roofs of the thatched farmhouses in Shirakawago are designed to prevent a build-up of the snow that blankets the valley throughout the winter. They are described as *gassho-zukuri*—"hands held in prayer." (See pages 226–227.)

SAKE BREWERIES
The many traditional *sake* brewers in Takayama old town work from small home breweries, indicated by balls of woven cedar fronds hung from the roof eaves. The fronds are cut at the beginning of the brewing cycle, and by the time the *sake* is ready to drink have turned from green to brown. Brewers welcome visitors inside to look around, to taste and, if they wish, to buy their *sake*.

FESTIVAL CARTS
Takayama's famous festivals, the spring Sanno Matsuri (April 14–15) and fall Yahata Matsuri (October 9–10), feature elaborate and gorgeous floats (*yatai*), which are among the finest in Japan. Four floats designed in the early 19th century are on display at the Takayama Yatai Kaikan, up the street from Yoshijima House (*open* 8:30–5). The guardian shrine of Takayama, Sakurayama Hachiman-gu, celebrated in the fall festival, is housed next door.

▶▶▶ Ogimachi 208A1

This village is set in the Shokawa Valley, a two-hour bus ride from Takayama (see below). Surrounded by high mountains, the narrow valley is dotted with thatched *gassho-zukuri* farmhouses (see panel), terraced rice paddies, vegetable gardens, and flower beds. About 150 thatched dwellings have been built here, many serving as *minshuku*. The farmhouses were constructed to hold extended families: living space was on the first floor, while the upper floor was used for storage and craft work.

Ogimachi is well off the beaten track and a visit is best planned in conjunction with a trip to Takayama. To reach the village, take a bus from Takayama to Makido on the Nohi bus (one hour, 35 minutes) and a bus from Makido to Ogimachi (one hour). Buses are infrequent; plan your trip in advance. There is a tourist office in the village square.

▶▶▶ Takayama 208A1

Takayama is a highland city in the heart of the mountainous Hida district of west central Japan. The city has been modernized but retains a compactness and richness of traditional architecture and culture, earning its nickname "little Kyoto." The old town, centered around two narrow streets called Sannomachi and Ninomachi, contains many well-preserved old inns, tea houses, shops, and merchants houses with the latticed windows and over-hanging roofs characteristic of the Edo period.

There is much to see in Takayama, but one of the joys of being here is just to wander around on foot or rented bicycle. The city is laid out in a grid pattern and is easy to negotiate. English-language booklets and maps are available from the tourist office at the station, and there are several bike rental shops in the area. The Sannomachi district and most of the best sights are east of the station.

Takayama is two hours, 45 minutes by JR Takayama limited express from Nagoya. By bus from Kamikochi (May to October only) the journey is in two stages: first a bus to Hirayu Onsen (one hour, 15 minutes), then a bus to Takayama (one hour, 10 minutes).

The **Hida Minzoku Mura Folklore Village**▶▶▶ (*open* 8:30–5) is an open-air museum of old thatched Hida farmhouses that demonstrates how farmers and craft workers would once have lived and worked in this region, and gives a vivid account of rural life in medieval Japan. The village is within bus, biking, or walking distance, west of Takayama station.

One daily **Morning Market (Asa-ichi)**▶▶ (7 AM–noon) is held along the east bank of the Miyagawa River and in front of Takayama Jinya. Stands sell local produce, flowers, and crafts brought in from the surrounding countryside.

Sanmachi Suji▶▶▶ (*open* 9–5; closed Tue and Dec–Feb) was the merchant area during feudal times. Yoshijima House, at the north end of Shimo-Ninomachi Street, was built in 1905 as the fine but rustic home and factory of the well-to-do Yoshijima brewing family. Kusakabe merchant's house, next door, is less rustic and more imposing than its neighbor (same opening hours).

Once the residence of the *daimyo* of Hida, **Takayama Jinya**▶▶▶ (*open* Apr–Oct 8:45–5, Nov–Mar 8:45–4:30), a group of whitewashed buildings, is perhaps the best example of provincial Edo government offices in Japan. They were in use until 1969, and the audience chambers, the interrogation rooms (which contain instruments of torture), the gardens, and the rice stores, where the shogunate's rice tax was stockpiled, are now open to visitors.

Making rope sandals at the Hida Minzoku Mura Folklore Village

SHORENJI TEMPLE
The Zen Shorenji Temple was transported to Takayama in 1961 from the Shokawa Valley, part of which was flooded to make a reservoir. *Shojin-ryori* (Zen vegetarian food) is served at the temple (*open* Nov–Mar 8:30–5, Apr–Oct 8–6).

215

Takayama's Asa-ichi (morning market)

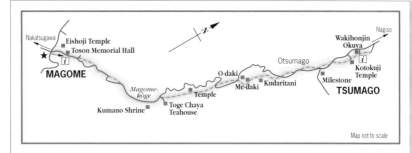

Walk

Kiso Valley

Distance: 6 miles (9.3km); time: 3 hours (wear hiking boots in winter). This gentle hike between two post towns in the Kiso Valley follows the Magome Pass, tracing the path of the old Nakasendo Highway, a major route between Edo (Tokyo) and Kyoto during the 18th and early 19th centuries.

To get to Magome, take the Chuo Honsen line from Nagoya to Nakatsugawa station (one hour, 15 minutes). From there, take the bus to Magome (35 minutes). From Tsumago, take a bus to Nagiso station on the Chuo Honsen line and then back to Nagoya or Matsumoto.

Leaving Magome, follow the main street away from the bus station past houses that appear ancient, but which are actually faithful copies of those destroyed by fire at the end of the 19th century. Once clear of the town, walk for 50 minutes along the paved road to the **Magome Pass (*Magome-koge*)▶▶▶**. Past the Toge Chaya Teahouse, take the path that drops away to the right from the main road. From here, the walk is downhill all the way to Tsumago.

The path leads past a small temple on the left, then, farther along, the site of a guardhouse that controlled the movement of timber from the Kiso Valley and meted out severe punishments to anyone smuggling timber.

After about 45 minutes, having twice crossed the paved road, the path comes to two waterfalls, the **O-daki** and **Me-daki▶▶**, one male, one female. Farther on from these is a milestone at a fork in the road, recording the distance in ri (79 *ri* or 200 miles/320km) from the capital, Edo (Tokyo). Take the right fork of the path, and walk for another 30 minutes to reach **Tsumago▶▶▶**.

The second post town from the south on the Nakasendo Highway, Tsumago retains the atmosphere of an Edo-era post town. Its main street,

which is lined with dark, wooden, shuttered houses, is particularly evocative. Although it is now enjoying new prosperity as a thriving tourist center, Tsumago was virtually deserted by the mid-1960s, due both to its position—far away from the main transportation routes—and to the massive migration to the big towns and cities during the postwar years. All of Tsumago's buildings are now under a strict preservation order.

Above and below: views of Tsumago, which still has the air of an old Edo-period town

REBELLION
Five hundred years ago, rebellious priests and peasants overthrew Kanazawa's feudal lord. They established an independent republic, which survived for 100 years until subdued by the warlord Oda Nobunaga, who awarded the city to his retainer, Maeda Toshiie.

Above and below: one of the geisha quarters

The Chubu Coast

▶▶▶ Kanazawa   208A1

This important provincial city, bordering the Sea of Japan in the Chubu region, is partly an old castle town and partly a modern city with busy department stores and a thriving nightlife. For those wishing to explore both modern and traditional Japanese cultures and architecture, it is an excellent place to visit. Off the main thoroughfare, which differs little from those of other Japanese cities, there are winding streets, dead-end alleyways, and moats designed to confuse would-be attackers of the central castle site, now marked only by its original eastern entrance, the Ishikawa-mon gate. Kanazawa is most easily reached by JR limited express from Kyoto (two hours, 30 minutes) or Nagoya (three hours). Alternatively, if you have visited Ogimachi and do not wish to return to Takayama, you can catch a direct bus to Kanazawa (three hours). There is an information office by the Kanazawa station exit.

The **Eastern Pleasure Quarter**▶▶ in the Higashiyama district was set aside in 1820 by the Maeda government as an entertainment area for high-ranking citizens. The most talented and beautiful of "free" *geisha* provided evenings of music, dancing, conversation, and perhaps other more intimate pleasures. The area is distinguished by a neat row of *geisha* tea houses, each with a slatted wooden façade and an oblong paper lampshade over its entrance. Rising costs and a demand for sleazier entertainment have reduced business, but some of the old atmosphere can still be experienced along Higashi main street. Shimake (*open* 9:30–5; closed Mon), the fifth house down the street on the left going east, is an elegant former *geisha* house open for viewing.

Situated beneath the castle mound is **Kenrokuen Garden**▶▶▶ (*open* 6:30 AM–6 PM; Oct 16–Mar 15, 8–4:30), Kanazawa's most famous attraction. Once the private

Kanazawa Market

garden of the Maeda lords, who ruled the city for three generations, Kenrokuen is officially categorized as one of Japan's three best gardens, and is said to combine perfectly the six qualities by which a park is judged: size, seclusion, running water, views, artificiality, and age. The best time to visit is early morning, before the arrival of parties of Japanese visitors. The moss-covered earth will still be moist with dew, and you can sit in solitude in the Moonflower Pavilion tea house and order bean-jam cakes and green whisked tea. Flowers bloom all year round.

The ordinary-looking **Myoryuji Temple▶▶** (*open* 9–4; *tours* last 30 minutes) is, in fact, a complex of secret chambers, trap doors, hidden tunnels and staircases, and a maze of corridors. It was constructed to confine and hold off invaders while the Maeda *daimyo* made his escape in the event of invasion of the city castle. Myoryuji, also called Temple of the Ninja (*Ninja-dera*), was connected to the castle by a tunnel. To get there, take a cab from the station or a bus to Nomachi Hirokoji stop and a further five-minute walk. Reservations are required (stop by the temple or telephone 41 2877), but generally a few last-minute walk-ins can be accommodated.

The old **Nagamachi *Samurai* District▶▶▶** is in the area that begins just behind the 109 Korinbo department store in central Kanazawa. Nowadays it consists mainly of one street, lined with traditional, privately owned *samurai* wooden houses, each hidden behind roof-topped mud walls. Fortunately, the Nomura Family House (*open* 8:30–5:30; *closed* first and third Wed of the month), once the home of a well-to-do *samurai* warrior, has been maintained in its original condition and is open to visitors. The design of the interior of the house is severe but extremely elegant, making extensive use of cypress, ebony, and persimmon wood.

EASTERN TEMPLE QUARTER
Rising behind the Eastern Pleasure Quarter, overlooking Kanazawa, is Utatsuyama mountain, scattered with 40 Buddhist and Shinto temples and shrines. Some are still in use; others are in decay. An exploration along the spiral roads and wooden paths reveals a history of changing architectural styles and old statues of Japanese heroes. On the flat summit is a park with trees, shrubs, and some grass on which sitting is allowed—a rare freedom in Japanese parks.

WESTERN PLEASURE QUARTER
This district was inhabited by enslaved, as opposed to "free" *geisha*, and was guarded by heavy gates. Its narrow streets and the temple quarters of the adjacent Teramachi district border the city on the western bank of the river.

Ryokan, traditional Japanese inns, are usually two- or three-story wooden buildings with the outward appearance of ordinary houses. They are, in fact, an expensive and exquisite way of experiencing Japanese culture and food.

JAPANESE INNS
These are cheap versions of *ryokan* and they are recommended if you are on a budget and wish to experience traditional Japanese customs and lifestyle. The rooms are *tatami* (straw-matted), divided by paper screens and sparsely but tastefully decorated. Meals are an optional extra.

NEW *RYOKAN*
In recent years, some Western-style hotels have begun to offer a *ryokan*-style experience for guests staying in *tatami* rooms. There are also a few private *ryokan* situated in modern apartment buildings. The ritual and the service are the same as in the traditional *ryokan* and often good value, but the ambience is usually less authentic.

A ryokan *interior ...*

Many *ryokan* are sited in naturally beautiful areas, but even those in cities have traditional inner gardens in which rocks, trees, and running water combine to create a feeling of natural scenic beauty. Service is flawless but restrained—as is the expected behavior of the guests. Room décor, the timetable of meals, and the general ritual tend to be the same in every inn.

Ryokan are generally costly and some of the more famous establishments in places such as Kyoto and Nara charge more than the best hotels, but they are worth at least one night's stay. The price includes a *kaiseki ryori* (dinner) (traditional and classic Japanese cooking) and breakfast in your room, and the services of a personal maid, who serves the 10- or 12-dish meal (of beautifully presented local specialties). After dinner, the maid converts the living room to a bedroom by pushing back the low, lacquered dining table and putting a futon and cotton-filled quilts on the *tatami* floor.

Furnishings in *ryokan* rooms are simple but elegant. In one corner is an alcove with a flower arrangement and a hanging scroll of a painting or poem. A lacquer dining table is surrounded with cushions and a television set is discreetly available. Most rooms have a veranda overlooking the garden, with chairs outside for periods of quiet contemplation.

Arrival and procedure On arrival, leave your shoes at the entrance; you will be handed a pair of slippers. On reaching your room, leave the slippers at the doorway and enter in your stockinged feet. The maid makes green tea for you and leaves. A perfectly ironed and starched *yukata* (kimono-style dressing gown) is available to wear after you have bathed in your private hot tub. It is perfectly acceptable and expected for you to wear a *yukata* for dinner or if you leave your room to explore your surroundings. In cold weather, a *tanzen* (padded kimono) is provided as well.

The maid arrives later with your dinner arranged on a very large tray of assorted lacquer dishes and pottery bowls. She places the tray just inside the door, bows, picks it up again and carries it to the table, then backs away, bows again, and leaves. If you do not want a Japanese breakfast—rice, fish, *miso* soup—the following morning, you are able to order coffee, toast, and orange juice instead.

Room rates *Ryokan* rooms are designed to accommodate one to four people, and charges depend on how many people are staying in the room. Unlike hotels, room rates vary greatly depending on the day and the time of the

... and courtyard

ear. Weekends, public holidays, and peak seasons are
the most expensive times. On an off-peak, mid-week day
you can book a *ryokan* for the price of a good hotel.
A service charge of 10 to 15 percent is added to the
room rate, and tipping is not necessary.

    Ryokan are divided into three categories: deluxe,
superior, and standard. The deluxe establishments do
not necessarily accept foreign guests. For further details
contact Japan Ryokan Association, 1–8–3 Marunouchi,
Chiyoda-ku, Tokyo, tel: (03) 231 5310.

Northern Honshu

EXILE

For the Japanese, exile was an appalling fate. Their identity was rooted in their place in society, and to be cut adrift from this relationship was akin to death. Depending upon the severity of the crime, banishment could be to a place between 700 and 3,000 miles (1,100 and 5,000km) away. The modern Japanese Penal Code, enacted in 1908, contains no provision for exile.

Taraibune, the washtub-style boats at Ogi

▶▶ Sado-Shima (Sado Island)   *208B2*

Exile was once a common Japanese punishment for criminals and politicians, religious leaders, or members of the imperial family who had fallen out of favor. Many such deposed statesmen, and even emperors, were banished to Sado Island, in the Sea of Japan off the coast of Niigata prefecture, western Honshu. When gold was discovered there during the Edo period, homeless people and prisoners were sent to Sado to work as forced labor in the gold mines. Its history has given the island a rather grim image and an air of melancholy; but Sado does have dramatic scenery, well-preserved villages, traditional farming landscapes, lovely beaches, and a culture all of its own.

Although relatively small, Sado is Japan's fifth-largest island in size. The population of less than 100,000 is increased tenfold by vacationers during the summer season. Two mountain chains run east to west along the north and south coasts divided by an extensive plain where the main towns and farmland areas are found. The old gold and silver mines, major tourist attractions, are located in the mountains, and the storm-battered coastline, with its sheer, plunging cliffs and tiny offshore islands, is also worth exploring.

Three main ferry crossings connect Sado Island with Niigata. Each offers a regular ferry and a hydrofoil. The hydrofoil crossings are approximately twice as expensive and take half the time. Niigata to Ryotsu (two hours, 20 minutes by ferry) is the most popular and frequent crossing; other alternatives are Niigata to Akadomare (three hours by ferry) or Joetsu (70 miles/110km southwest of Niigata) to Ogi (two hours, 40 minutes by ferry). Ogi is the most attractive port. Crossings are canceled during rough seas. Towns on the island are connected by regular bus services but the main sights are less accessible; the *Sado Teiki Kanko Josha-ken*, a two-day pass, allows unlimited

Fishing tackle at Ogi

DRUMS
Taiko are large, barrel-shaped Japanese drums. Village boundaries were determined by the farthest point at which a *taiko* could be heard. In recent times, village drumming rituals have become popular in Japan and many drumming troupes have been established. The most famous is the Kodo (the word means both "heartbeat" and "children of the drum") troupe, also known as the "Ondekoza Demon Drummers." When not on tour, the drummers live communally on Sado in spartan conditions.

use of all tour buses, the most convenient means of transportation. Comprehensive tours of the island depart from Ogi and Ryotsu (four to eight hours long). Alternatively, cars can be rented at each of the main ports.

The original center of the gold mining industry, **Aikawa▶▶**, one hour, 15 minutes by bus from Ryotsu, is one tenth the size that it was during the boom times. Visitors now come here to tour the Sado Kinzan Mine (*open* 8–5:30) and other related sights. Some of the extensive underground tunnels are open for viewing. Realistic mechanical figures and sound effects are used to re-create the original working conditions of mine laborers; many men died within a few years of their exile to Sado.

Senkaku Bay▶▶▶, to the north of Aikawa, boasts a stunning coastline with surreal rock formations. Excursion boats operate from Tassha, 15 minutes from Aikawa by bus; a clifftop path also starts from here. The west coast of the island, from Senkaku Bay to Cape Hajiki on the northern tip, is called Soto-Kaifu (Outer Coast); the east coast, southward from Cape Hajiki, is known as Uchi-kaifu (Inner Coast). The former has a dramatic, rugged beauty composed of strange rock formations, reefs, and cliffs, and is popular with tour buses. The latter is less exciting and quieter.

Ogi▶ is a working port, once best known for its strange, wooden *taraibune* (tublike boats), used by local women to collect seaweed and shellfish. You can rent one and paddle yourself around the harbor. The best reason to visit Ogi is to travel on to **Shukunegi▶▶▶**, 15 minutes to the west by bus. This is a delightful fishing village set in a cove with traditional houses and surrounded by trees and rice paddies.

A seashell mountain on Sado Island

The Sutra Library (Kyozo) at Chusonji. The inner chamber houses a Monju Bosatsu image, the Bhodisattva of wisdom and intellect

RIKUCHU-KAIGAN NATIONAL PARK
This stretch of rugged, rocky coastline is famous for its high cliffs, fantastic rock formations, small fishing villages, and marine life. It was, until very recently, an inaccessible area, but nowadays, with two private railroad lines, it is easier to explore. Buses go from Morioka to Kuji (about three hours) and from here you can take a train on the Kita Rias line to Shimano-koshi on the coast, where buses leave for the coastal zone of the park.

Detail, Chusonji Temple

Tohoku Central and East

▶▶ Hiraizumi   209D3

Today, Hiraizumi is a small country town, but during the 11th and 12th centuries the Fujiwara clan paid for the construction of many temples and palaces there with the proceeds of the gold they mined in the area, and Hiraizumi rivaled Kyoto. Few buildings remain from this great age, but the Golden Hall (Konjiki-do) of Chusonji Temple has survived and has recently been fully restored as one of Tohoku's major cultural attractions. The farmland areas around Hiraizumi are worth visiting for their wealth of traditional Japanese houses. Hiraizumi is 25 minutes from Ichinoseki, which is two hours, 25 minutes by Tohoku Shinkansen from Ueno station, Tokyo. Alternatively, Hiraizumi is two hours by local train from Sendai. There is a tourist office on the town's main street, to the right of the station.

Chusonji Temple▶▶▶ *(open 8–5)*, a short walk (20 minutes) or bus ride from the station, was founded in 850 and restored in the 12th century. Two halls, Konjiki-do and Kyozo, remain from this period: the other buildings in the temple complex date from the later Edo period. Konjiki-do, a small but impressive structure (now housed in a fireproof building) has black, lacquered exterior walls and gold-leaf and mother-of-pearl interior paneling. Kyozo, the original temple library, houses a magnificent Monju Bosatsu image riding a lion.

Once the most important temple complex in Tohoku, **Motsuji Temple▶▶** *(open 8–5)* is now marked only by the foundations of the 40 original main temples, but the beautiful Jodo-style paradise gardens (Heian period) have, remarkably, survived. The Hiraizumi Museum, housing relics of the Fujiwara clan, is in the garden domain.

▶▶ Morioka   209D4

Morioka is a castle town, founded by the feudal lord Nambu in the 16th century, and an old-established provincial university town. It is a charming place with many temples, an old merchant quarter, a vigorous cultural life, and a successful local craft industry. The Tohoku Shinkansen to Morioka from Ueno station in Tokyo takes three hours.

► Sendai   *209D3*

The largest city in Tohoku was flattened in World War II and has since been rebuilt along the lines of many other modern Japanese cities. It is a good base from which to explore the area of Tohoku, Matsushima (see panel), and the neighboring Yamagata prefecture, a rural district where life follows the traditional Tohoku style. Sendai is two hours by Tohoku Shinkansen (bullet train) from Tokyo's Ueno station.

►► Towada-Hachimantai National Park   *209D4*

Lying northwest of Morioka, this area is divided into southern and northern sections. Hachimantai, in the south, is a mountainous area of volcanic activity, better known for its *onsen* (hot springs) and thermal resorts than for scenic beauty.

Goshogake Onsen and Toshichi Onsen are two centers where people go to soothe away city stress and other ailments. Mixed bathing is the norm. The eastern entrance to the park is via Obuke, 40 minutes on the JR Hanawa line from Morioka (tour buses operate from here).

The Lake Towada area, which lies to the north, is a region of exceptional scenic beauty. The lake itself occupies a giant crater, and the gentle mountain ranges around the lake provide plenty of good hiking and skiing. There are many *onsen* nearby. Sukayu Onsen, to the north, which has a 1,000-person bath, is one of the best known. The pretty Oirase-keiryu (Oirase Valley) district, to the northeast, is also very popular with walkers, particularly in the fall, when the valley is especially beautiful. There is a frequent bus service from April to October, directly from Morioka to Lake Towada.

MATSUSHIMA BAY

Matsushima Kaigan station is 40 minutes by Senseki line from Sendai. This is the main stop for the famed Matsushima Bay (a very popular Japanese resort destination), which is dotted with small, pine-covered islands, some inhabited and others no more than tiny islets. The bay is regarded as one of Japan's "Three Famous Views" (the other two are Amano-hashidate, north of Kyoto, and Itsukushima, near Hiroshima), and as such has suffered from commercialism. The islands can be toured by cruiser from Matsushima Kaigan Pier.

225

A bright, airy, covered shopping arcade in modern Sendai

Filled with fresh air, easy to clean, and good to live in, traditional Japanese houses are healthy places, emphasizing simplicity, regularity, and refinement. Built of a small number of locally available materials, usually wood, bamboo, paper, woven straw, and stone tiles, they sit on stilts above the ground, allowing ventilation and giving protection to the structure from the effects of mildew and damp.

TATAMI ROOMS

Slippers are worn on wooden floors, but the inner *tatami*-matted rooms must be entered in bare or stockinged feet. The street, the genkan, the wooden corridors, and the *tatami*-matted rooms represent four levels of decreasing contamination between public and private places. The exclusion of dirt from the *tatami* rooms is important, as the floor is used both as an eating and as a sleeping surface—residents sleep on the floor.

A farmhouse lantern

Health and cleanliness The Japanese home contains several standard features for the maintenance of a clean and healthy house. The genkan is a paved area at the same level as the garden, with a raised wooden floor, where residents sit to remove their shoes before donning slippers to move into the house. The engawa, or veranda, is a well-protected porch that affords shelter from the sun in the summer without blocking low winter rays. The opening onto it allows plenty of air to circulate through the house, even during heavy rain. Like the genkan, the veranda has easily maintained floor surfaces, whose proximity to the garden facilitates cleaning. Symbolically, the engawa is the link between house and garden. It is associated with meditation in monasteries, where it is the platform from which nature is contemplated.

Tatami (straw floor mats) are located in all major rooms. Futons (Japanese mattresses) are simple, warm, easily cleaned, and unobtrusive. Made of canvas and stuffed with cotton batting or other firm material, with no springs inside, futons are easily folded twice and placed in cupboards designed to contain them. Aired frequently in the engawa, futons reflect by their number and pattern the age, status, and taste of their users.

Seasonal living Rooms are arranged and rearranged according to the way they are used. In the hot and humid summer, all room dividers made of sliding panels can be opened or removed, encouraging the flow of fresh air throughout the house. In winter, the rather loose association of open rooms with large openings to the outdoors can be converted to an arrangement of isolated rooms, which can be closed off from each other and the outside by sliding panels and outside shutters. In cold weather, families gather about the kotatsu, a table placed over a hibachi (a small brazier), which sits below the floor. This feature is equivalent to the western hearth, and is symbolic of the family unit.

To live well in the traditional Japanese house, considerable stress is placed on appropriate dress in summer and winter. The yukata is a lightweight, heavily starched, loose cotton garment worn in summer, which allows free circulation of air next to the skin. In winter, it is traditional to wear layers of heavier garments. Their full sleeves allow hand warming and, in a sitting position, the surface area is reduced and the body heat more efficiently retained. Clothing becomes a heavily insulated, personal tent.

Bathrooms In a traditional Japanese house, the lavatory and bathtub are never in the same room. They are regarded as separate and distinct, requiring their own space. The bath is frequently associated with the garden and contains enough room for several people to dress in an atmosphere of natural beauty and social ease. It is designed to give comfort and to allow bathers to be exposed and to relax. The lavatory is sometimes entered only upon leaving the house. It is situated carefully in order to reduce odors and social embarrassment. The lavatory compartment is always very well ventilated and may contain a flower arrangement.

GENKAN
Many visitors do not pass the *genkan*, thereby reducing the intrusion of dirt into private areas of the house. No animals are allowed past the *genkan*, although they may be allowed to sleep there. These customs ensure that most dirt is left in the *genkan*, where it can readily be removed to the street or garden.

Traditional houses at Ogimachi village

IDIOT LACQUER

Hirosaki's best known craft is the manufacture of Tsugaru-nuri, a type of lacquerware renowned for its durability, hence its nickname Baka-nuri or "idiot lacquer." It is made by putting 47 different colored layers of lacquer over the uneven wooden base of the object being treated. The surface is then polished smooth to produce a tough, multi-hued finish.

Tohoku West

▶▶ Hirosaki   209C4

Unlike nearby Aomori, this small, compact town escaped wartime bombing; it was postwar planners who destroyed much of the town's architectural heritage. Fortunately, the city retains some of its old winding alleys and has an appeal enhanced by the friendliness of the townspeople, the thriving local craft traditions, and some well-maintained sites of cultural interest. The tourist office by the station provides a map of the town and information in English.

Hirosaki is approximately four hours by train from Morioka, and 30 minutes by train from Aomori, the busy port town that usurped Hirosaki's position as the cultural and political center of Tohoku.

Lake Tazawa

▶▶ Kakunodate   209C4

The train journey to Kakunodate from Morioka (55 minutes, JR Tazawa line) passes fine mountain scenery on its way to this small and pretty town, which has one of the best-preserved collections of *samurai* houses in Japan. Found in the inner town (Uchimachi), the *samurai* neighborhood has about half a dozen original houses and gardens open to the public (9–5), of which Aoyagi, with its turf roof, is especially renowned. Kakunodate's founding lords were originally from Kyoto. They imported with them many weeping cherry trees and the town and its river banks are generously planted, so that, in season, cherry blossoms blow through the streets in clouds. The outer town (Tomachi), once the merchants' quarter, remains the commercial part of town. Kakunodate is well known for items made from cherry bark, a craft that was once the main source of livelihood for poorer *samurai*.

MELTING LOVE

Despite being extremely deep and situated in the north of Tohoku, Lake Tazawa never freezes over. According to local legend, a great beauty, transformed into a dragon, sleeps in the lake. To keep warm, she and her dragon husband make passionate love all winter long, and heat up the water.

▶▶ Tazawa-ko (Lake Tazawa)   209C4

This lovely crater lake, the deepest in Japan, has exceptionally clear water. The lake shore is being developed but still maintains a rustic atmosphere. Cruise boats operate from Tazawa-Kohan, where bicycles are also available for rent. In the surrounding countryside there are many isolated inns, with their own open-air hot-spring pools. Nyuto Onsen, connected by bus to Tazawa-ko, is the main resort and has smaller inns scattered around it. To get to Tazawa-ko, take the JR Tazawa line from Kakunodate (16 minutes) or Morioka (40 minutes). The tourist office is to the left of the station. From the station it is a 15-minute bus ride to Tazawa-Kohan on the lake edge.

Tamagawa Onsen▶▶ is an old spa town with a reputation for restorative and curative thermal springs. Many of its individual inns are of wooden construction and conditions are quite basic, but they provide a very interesting experience and a change from Japan's usual overcommercialization of natural resources. Reach the spa by bus from Tazawa-ko (1½ hours).

▶▶ Yamagata   209C3

Yamagata city is the capital of Yamagata prefecture, a largely unspoiled region in the heart of Tohoku. The Japanese are promoting the area as one which "remains largely undiscovered by the international tourist," and there is consequently much information available at the tourist office in Yamagata JR station, one hour, 15 minutes from Sendai by JR express train. Yamagata itself has few attractions and Dewa Sanzan and Mount Zao areas are mainly used by the Japanese as a base for summer hiking and winter skiing. Dewa Sanzan is composed of three peaks—Gassan, Yudono-san, and Haguro-san—each one an important sacred site, and the setting for Shinto shrines. Mount Zao is a very popular skiing destination in the winter months. Zao Onsen is the region's center of accommodation; a cable car operates from there to the mountain summit. Winter snowfall is generally heavy.

Yamadera▶▶ is a mountaintop monastery made famous by the *haiku* poet Matsuo Basho. The steep climb to the top is rewarded with wonderful views. The precincts are extensive and worth exploring.

BANDAI-ASAHI NATIONAL PARK
Occupying an area to the west and south of Fukushima and to the west of Yamagata, Bandai-Asahi includes some of the most beautiful, interesting, and accessible mountain and lake scenery in Japan. Azuma-san (the Azuma mountains), near Fukushima, offer moderate hiking. Access to Azuma-san is from Jododaira bus station on the Bandai-Asahi Skyline road. Fukushima is one hour, 40 minutes on the Tohoku Shinkansen line from Ueno station in Tokyo. Bandai-Kogen, at the center of Bandai Plateau, is 40 minutes from Fukushima on the Skyline road or three hours on the scenic Bandai-Asahi Lakeline road.

229

Yamadera, a place of mystery and stillness atop a steep, wooded mountainside

Hokkaido

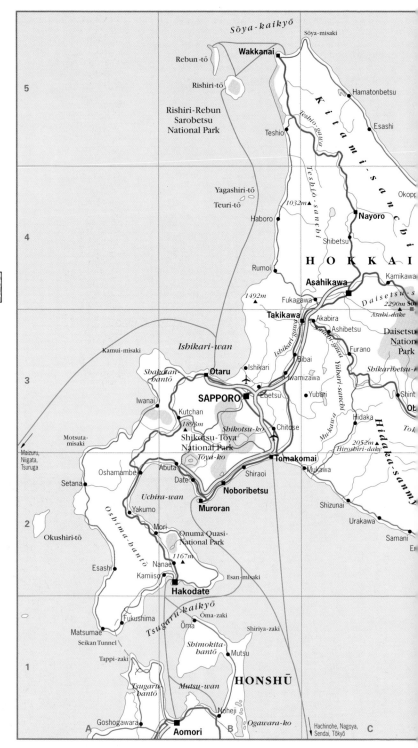

Sōya-kaikyō

Sōya-misaki

Wakkanai

Rebun-tō

Hamatonbetsu

Rishiri-tō

Esashi

Rishiri-Rebun
Sarobetsu
National Park

Teshio

Kitami-sanchi

Teshio-gawa

Yagashiri-tō

Teuri-tō

1032m▲

Okopp

Nayoro

Haboro

Shibetsu

H O K K A I

Teshio-sanchi

Rumoi

Kamikawa

Asahikawa

Daisetsu-s

1492m▲ Fukagawa

2290m Sō

Asahi-dake▲

Takikawa

Akabira

Ashibetsu

Daisetsu
Nation
Park

Kamui-misaki

Ishikari-wan

Ishikari-gawa

Furano

Shikaribetsu-

Sorachi-gawa

Shakotan-hantō

Otaru

Ishikari

Bibai

Yubari-sanchi

Shint

Iwanai

SAPPORO

Ebetsu

Iwamizawa

Yubari

Hidaka

Ob

Kutchan

1898m▲

Shikotsu-ko

Chitose

Mukawa

Tok

Shikotsu-Tōya
National Park

Tōya-ko

Tomakomai

2052m▲
Horoshiri-dake

Hidaka-sanmy

Motsuta-
misaki

Oshamambe

Abuta

Date

Shiraoi

Mukawa

Maizuru,
Niigata,
Tsuruga

Setana

Yakumo

Uchiura-wan

Noboribetsu

Shizunai

Urakawa

Oshima-hantō

Mori

Muroran

Okushiri-tō

Onuma Quasi-
National Park

Samani

E

Esashi

Nanae

1167m▲

Esan-misaki

Kamiiso

Hakodate

Fukushima

Ōma-zaki

Matsumae

Ōma

Shiriya-zaki

Seikan Tunnel

Shimokita-
hantō

Mutsu

Tappi-zaki

Tsugaru-kaikyō

1

Tsugaru-
hantō

Mutsu-wan

HONSHŪ

Goshogawara

Noheji

Ogawara-ko

Aomori

Hachinohe, Nagoya,
Sendai, Tōkyō

A   B   C

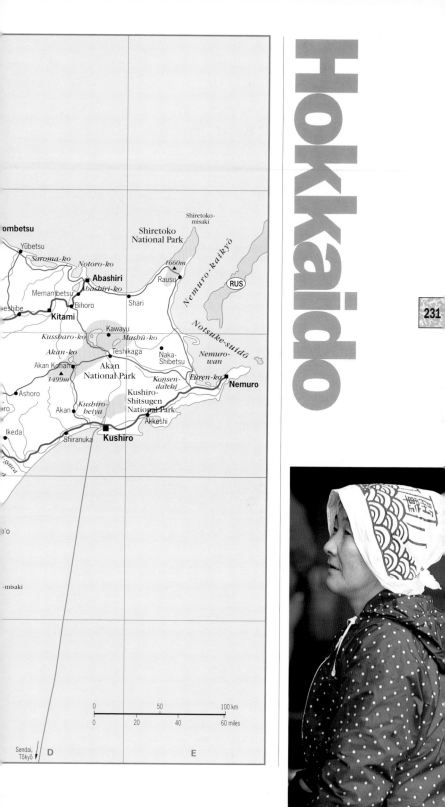

ombetsu

Yūbetsu

Saroma-ko

Notoro-ko

eshibe

Memambetsu

Abashiri

Abashiri-ko

Bihoro

Kitami

Shari

Shiretoko-misaki

Shiretoko
National Park

1660m

Rausu

Nemuro-kaikyō

RUS

Notsuke-suidō

Kawayu

Kussharo-ko

Mashū-ko

Akan-ko

Teshikaga

Naka-Shibetsu

Nemuro-wan

Akan Kohan

**Akan
National Park**

1499m

Füren-ko

Nemuro

Ashoro

Konsen-daichi

ro

Akan

Kushiro-heiya

**Kushiro-
Shitsugen
National Park**

Ikeda

Akkeshi

Shiranuka

Kushiro

'o

-misaki

gaua

a

0		50		100 km
0	20		40	60 miles

Sendai,
Tōkyō

D

E

The unspoiled serenity of Daisetsuzan National Park

SNOW FESTIVALS
Yuki Matsuri (snow festivals) are held throughout the winter in the parts of northern Japan that have heavy snowfalls. The most famous takes place in Sapporo for four days, from the first Wednesday in February. The festival began by chance when, in 1950, some high school students made six ice sculptures in Odori Park. Today, 2 million attend the festival each year. Over 200 elaborate ice carvings are displayed in the park, which is, in fact, a broad avenue, running east to west, bisecting the city center.

HOKKAIDO This northernmost and second largest of the four main Japanese islands is the least populous region of Japan. There are few cultural or historical reasons to visit Hokkaido, but if you love the outdoors it offers forests, mountain ranges, lakes, volcanoes, hot springs, open landscapes and the chance to hike, ski, and cycle. Hokkaido also has rich agricultural, fishing, and mineral resources.

Hokkaido is connected to Honshu by the 33-mile- (54-km-) long Seikan Tunnel, the world's longest, which runs under the Tsugaru Straits. The island is bordered by the Pacific Ocean to the south and north, by the Sea of Japan to the west, and by the Sea of Okhotsk to the northeast. Possession of four of the Kuril Islands, in the Sea of Okhotsk, is acrimoniously disputed by Japan and Russia.

JAPANESE COLONISTS Until the beginning of this century, wild and inhospitable Hokkaido was not considered habitable by the Japanese. They visited and settled only the island's coastal regions, to fish and collect seaweed. Some Ainu, one of Japan's original indigenous groups, lived in the interior, but there were no inland Japanese settlements or agriculture. Shortage of space on the other main islands, coupled with the return after 1945 of many Japanese colonists from abroad, led to the first real development of the island, and today over 5 million people live there.

SAPPORO The large, modern capital city, laid out on a grid system, has many parks, but is not a place to visit for great sights. It does, however, have an active and famous nightlife—the Susukino district is as lively as anything in Tokyo—and it provides a good base from which to explore the wilderness areas of Hokkaido. The tourist information office is at Sapporo station.

NATIONAL PARKS The national parks of Hokkaido are large, wild, and scenic and perhaps the main reason for visiting this remote region of Japan. Three of the major parks are listed here. **Daisetsuzan National Park** is the largest in Japan and one of the most unspoiled. A network of hiking paths gives access to most areas of the park and to many of the mountain peaks, none of which rises much above 6,996 feet (2,133m). Most of the accommodations available in the park include access to hot springs. **Akan National Park** is well known for its beauty and wildlife. It is dominated by volcanic peaks, but lakes and vast forests add variety. Akan lies in the east of Hokkaido and can be reached from Kushiro to the south. Kussharo-ko is the largest volcanic lake in Japan, and a focal point of the national park. **Shikotsu-Toya National Park** is in southwest Hokkaido, not far from Sapporo, and is known for its caldera lakes, volcanoes, hot springs, and forests. Lakes Toya and Shikotsu (the second deepest in Japan) give the park its name.

GETTING THERE Sapporo is 10½ hours by train from Tokyo. Chitose, 25 miles (40km) south of Sapporo, is Hokkaido's main airport. The approximate flight time from Tokyo is one hour and 20 minutes, and there are frequent train connections with Sapporo. Japan Air Lines (JAL) flights are scheduled to Chitose from Tokyo, Osaka, and Fukuoka. All Nippon Airways (ANA) and JAL also run services from many other Japanese cities.

There are ferry services from Tokyo to Tomakomai or Kushiro, and from many towns on the coast of Tohoku, such as Oma-Hakodate, Aomori-Muroran, and Noheji-Hakodate. There is a rail network on Hokkaido and internal flights between major cities.

FOOD

One of the unexpected surprises of visiting Hokkaido is the quality of the regional food. Restaurants tend to be reasonably priced and without pretension. Specialties include shellfish, salmon, herring, squid, sea urchin, corn on the cob, potatoes, and Chinese noodles (*ramen*). Genghis Khan, a Mongolian-inspired mutton or lamb barbecue cooked by the guest (or a chef) at the table, is another great favorite.

233

Japanese cranes

Abashiri

DUCKWEED
Lake Akan is famous for its rare spherical duckweed, called *marimo*, which is found in only a few lakes around the world. The green spheres absorb oxygen from the water and then float to the surface, where they exhale and sink. Examples of *marimo* may be seen in shops and information centers and in the *marimo* museum on a small island in the lake. A boat trip on the lake lasts one and a half hours and stops at the museum.

KUSHIRO GREAT MARSH
This is the home of the *tancho* (red-crested crane), brought back from the brink of extinction, and now forming a colony of around 400. They are shy birds who live deep in the marshes in summer. They come out of the deeper reaches in winter, and you can see them at the Red-Crested Crane Natural Park, south of Akan, where some are kept behind high mesh fences. A bus to the Crane Park from Akan Kohan bus terminal takes one hour, 15 minutes (get off at the Tsuru-koen bus stop).

▶▶ Abashiri 231D4

Although a small town, this is the main settlement on the Sea of Okhotsk. During the winter, the sea is ice-bound and the floes reach up to the beach. The inhabitants make their living from fishing in the summer months, when the local delicacies of shrimp and "hairy crab" are taken from the icy seas. Abashiri is the terminus of the JR Sekihoku line; the limited express takes five hours, 40 minutes from Sapporo. There is a tourist information office in the station. Flights from Sapporo's Chitose Airport to Memambetsu (near Abashiri) take 55 minutes by JAS.

The **Municipal Museum▶▶** (*open* 8:30–5) houses a collection of genuine Ainu artifacts and pre-Ainu material discovered in the Moyoro Shell Mound, site of an ancient Ainu dwelling place. One part of the Municipal Museum is the Abashiri Prison Museum (Abashiri Kangoku) which records the grim conditions suffered by the convicts who were used to develop the region.

Oroke Kinenkan▶ (*open* 8:30–5) is a museum dedicated to preserving the heritage of a small tribe of nomadic reindeer herders who live on Sakhalin island.

About 2 miles (3km) southwest of Abashiri, on route 39 is **Tento-zan▶▶** hill. From its observation tower, there are views of the Sea of Okhotsk and nearby mountain peaks.

▶▶ Akan National Park 231D3

Set in eastern Hokkaido, Akan National Park has three major caldera lakes, volcanic mountains, numerous hot springs, and extensive forests of primeval trees. Towns near the park are Bihoro (in the north) and Kushiro (in the south). Buses for the park leave from both towns (neither is of particular interest in its own right). Kushiro has an airport and there are flights there from Tokyo (one hour, 35 minutes) and Sapporo (40 minutes). Bihoro is five hours, 20 minutes from Sapporo by JR Sekihoku line limited express. Kushiro is 3½ hours on the same line from Bihoro. Within the park, the town of Akan Kohan is the most important resort area. There is a tourist information office near the town's bus terminal.

The easiest way to travel around the park is by sightseeing buses, although for more freedom you might prefer to rent a car for a few days. The tour buses are noisy and do not stop long at any of the sights; it is worth getting off at one, exploring on foot and then catching another tour bus later (this is allowed if you hold on to your ticket).

Ainu Kotan Village►, a 10-minute walk west of the bus terminal in Akan Kohan spa town, is a street of souvenir shops and a thatched-roofed center, where displays of Ainu dancing are held six times a day, from May to the end of October.

About 9 miles (14km) from Lake Mashu, **Kawayu Onsen**►► is a hot-spring resort near Io-san, an active volcano that vents steam from two ravines. Visitors often buy fresh eggs from the grocery store near the parking lot and boil them in the small pools of hot water.

Lake Akan►► lies in the western part of the park, surrounded by dense forests and two volcanoes: O-Akandake to the east (dormant) and Me-Akandake to the south (active). Both mountains can be climbed and are popular with hikers.

Lake Kussharo►► is the park's largest lake, and it attracts campers and watersports enthusiasts. The lake is at its most attractive in the fall, when the leaves of the surrounding trees change color.

Lake Mashu►►, a 20-minute drive from Teshikaga (one hour, 15 minutes by JR express from Kushiro), is almost 700 feet (213m) deep, and surrounded by high rock walls with little or no footholds. The best two viewing spots are on the western side.

Boiling mud at Akan National Park

The still waters of Lake Akan, set beneath two volcanoes and surrounded by forests

235

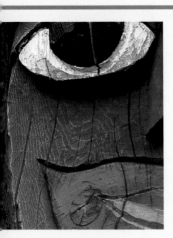

The ancestors of the Ainu were the original inhabitants of Japan. Organized into nomadic tribes who lived by hunting, fishing, and gathering, they roamed freely over the central and northern parts of Japan, but as waves of aggressive invaders and settlers moved in from the Asian mainland, they were pushed north-ward. The Ainu were formidable warriors, and constant fighting between them and the Japanese put a great strain on the resources of the emerging Japanese state. However, over the centuries the Ainu were pacified and controlled until, by the 19th century, they were restricted to their present settlements in Hokkaido.

236

PRAYER STICKS
Kotan-kara-kamui, the Spirit of the World, came from the skies to establish the land of the Ainu. On his return he forgot his chopsticks, and to prevent them rotting he turned them into willow trees. The Ainu still use willow to carve their *inau,* or prayer sticks.

Above: detail of an Ainu totem
Below: Ainu village

Genetically, the Ainu are related to the peoples of Siberia. Generally, they have lighter skin than the Japanese and the men exhibit a much greater growth of hair. According to custom, only "men strong in wisdom" were allowed to wear beards. Traditionally, young Ainu women were heavily tattooed on the mouth, on the arms, and on the backs of the hands before marriage.

Traditional houses Ainu now live in Japanese-style homes, but traditionally Ainu houses were rectangular wood-framed buildings, with dirt floors covered in reed mats, and thatched walls and roofs. Raised wooden platforms covered in mats or animal (often bear) skins were used for sleeping and an open-fire pit, placed in the center of the house, was used for cooking, heating, and religious purposes. Fire was sacred to the Ainu, and the hearth would often be decorated with *inau,* specially carved wooden prayer sticks, which are still found wherever the Ainu honor the spiritual beings they called *kamui* (similar to the Japanese *kami*).

Bear spirits Bears were held in high regard by the Ainu, and an important part of Ainu culture was the festival known as *iomante,* through which they paid their respects to the *kamui* of the bear. In times past, when the bears awoke from their winter hibernation, the men went into the woods and captured a cub, which would be taken to the village and cared for until it was about two years old. The animal was then sacrificed either by strangulation or by being shot with arrows. The head was removed and placed on a pole, and the flesh eaten at a feast that featured dancing by the men and gifts of *sake* to

the bear's head as gratitude for its sacrifice. By sending the spirit of the bear back
to its ancestors, the Ainu showed their
appreciation for its strength and courage,
attributes they hoped would become theirs,
as they believed the spirit of the bear would
be reborn as an Ainu.

Loss of culture Nowadays, almost all of the
25,000 Ainu living in Hokkaido are descendants of mixed Japanese and Ainu parent-
age. Sadly, very few either understand the
Ainu language or maintain their traditional
culture. This loss of language, customs,
and identity is partly due to past Japanese
government policy that forbids the use of
the Ainu language in schools. In the public
media, most Ainu customs were banned and in the
name of assimilation mixed marriages were actively
encouraged. Laws now protect the Ainu, but because of
discrimination they remain a poor minority group in Japan.
Also, inevitable intermarriage has led them toward even
greater assimilation into the mainstream of Japanese
society. Very recently, there has been some resurgence
of interest in Ainu traditions and language among the
younger Ainu.

The Ainu are often said to be the "Native Americans"
of Japan, and in the same way Ainu culture is now mainly
displayed in "Ainu villages," built specially for the tourist
trade. Sadly, most of them are grim, dispirited places. For
the tourist, perhaps the best exposition of genuine Ainu
traditions is to be found in the Ainu Culture Museum, in
Nibutani, near the town of Tomakomai, Hokkaido.

Top: Ainu festival
Above: an Ainu couple

**EXORCISM OF EVIL
SPIRITS**
According to Ainu belief,
sickness is caused by
evil spirits and healed
by driving them away. A
crippled man has his legs
and arms bound with
bulrush stems and cloth
and is gently beaten with
branches. The bindings
are then cut away and
thrown into a river, while
the Ainu shout at the
spirits to flee.

Hakodate by night

►►► Daisetsuzan National Park 230C3

Located in the center of Hokkaido, this is Japan's largest national park and a paradise for hikers. Its scenery is spectacular, with lakes, high mountains, deep gorges, waterfalls, forests, hiking trails, and the highest mountain in Hokkaido, Mount Asahidake (7,511 feet/2,290m). Sounkyo Onsen, at the edge of the spectacular Sounkyo Gorge, is one of the best places to stay (see also Asahidake Onsen, below) while exploring the park, as long as you can ignore the spa hotels, which seem to be designed to brazenly clash with the natural beauty of the surroundings. The only way to travel to Sounkyo Onsen is by bus. If you are traveling from Sapporo, leave the train at Kamikawa (2½ hours by JR Sekihoku line) and transfer to the local bus service (35 minutes to Sounkyo Onsen). A tourist information office, called the PC Center, is located near the bus station.

Asahidake Onsen►►► is a quiet, remote village, one hour, 40 minutes by bus from Asahikawa, which is on the JR Sekihoku line from Sapporo. Asahidake Onsen gives access to a two-hour ascent of Mount Asahidake and other mountain trails.

A cable car travels from Sounkyo Onsen to the terminal on **Kurodake Mountain►►**. Change here for a chair lift that travels up the mountain to the beginning of the hiking trails. An hour's steady walking will take you to the peak, where you will be rewarded by spectacular views of the surrounding mountains. Be sure to wear sturdy shoes or boots.

Lake Daisetsu►► was created by a rock and earth dam across the Ishikawa (river), which flows through the Sounkyo Gorge. An enjoyable way to visit the lake is to rent a bicycle from Sounkyo's bus terminal and pedal along the path that skirts the edge of the gorge. **Sounkyo Gorge►►** itself is 12 miles (20km) long and extends into the park from its northeast entrance. The valley is hemmed in by rocky cliffs almost 625 feet (190m) high. There are tremendous views at each turn of the road. Beyond Sounkyo Onsen, the gorge is renowned for its waterfalls; Ryusei-no-taki (Shooting Star) and Ginga-no-taki (Milky Way) are particularly attractive.

►► Hakodate 230B2

On a stumpy peninsula on the southwest coast of Hokkaido, Hakodate has been a fishing port since the 18th century. It was one of the first to be opened to trade with the West by the Treaty of Kanagawa in 1854.

A tourist information office is located to the right of JR Hakodate station. The Hokato Kotsu bus company runs a four-hour sightseeing tour of the city, which leaves from the railroad station.

A three-minute walk south of the JR station leads to **Asa Ichi►►**, a fish and vegetable market open 5 AM–noon, but at its peak at 8 AM. Over 400 shops sell a range of food, including *kegani* ("hairy crab"), generally considered to be one of the delicacies of Hokkaido.

Goryokaku►►, a Western-style fortress, was built in 1864 in the center of the city in the shape of a five-pointed star, allowing its defenders to concentrate a murderous crossfire on attackers. Seized by supporters of the Tokugawa family, it fell to troops loyal to Emperor Meiji in 1868. All that remain are the outer walls; the grounds have been turned into a park of 4,000 cherry trees. A small museum contains relics of the battle (*open* May–Oct 8–8, Nov–Apr 9–6).

The foreigners' **Motomachi District▶▶** features several Western-style buildings dating from the late 1800s and the early 1900s, including an Orthodox church founded in 1862. To get there, take a street car from the JR station to Jujigai stop (five minutes).

Mount Hakodate▶▶ is a small volcanic hill, 1,099 feet (335m) high, with famous views over the city and a restaurant on the summit. A bus leaves from the JR station for the 20-minute drive to the top.

See also pages 240–241.

IGLOO WEDDINGS

Lake Shikaribetsu is Daisetsuzan park's only natural lake. In the winter the lake freezes over and local people build a village of igloos on the ice, where they hold winter weddings. In March, the igloo village becomes the site of the local Shikaribetsu Kotan Festival.

Hakodate fishing boats

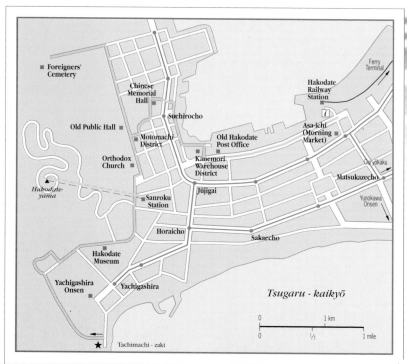

Walk

Hakodate

Distance: 3 miles (5km); time: 3 to 4 hours.

Hakodate occupies a strategic site on a fine harbor, backed by Mount Hakodate and overlooking the Tsugaru Straits. This walk starts at Cape Tachimachi on the Pacific Ocean, passes around the base of Mount Hakodate, through the old Western community of Motomachi, and ends at the Foreign Cemetery. There is also a possible detour to the Kanamori Warehouse district with its shops, cafés, and restaurants.

Start at Hakodate station (south of the station there is a large **produce market▶▶**, held Monday to Saturday 5 AM–noon, which is worth visiting). Take a cab to **Cape Tachimachi▶▶**, an Ainu word meaning "a place on the

rocks where you wait for fish and catch them with a spear," or take the trolley to the **Yachigashira Onsen▶** stop (20 minutes). There is a huge public spa here. Then it is a 15-minute walk south. To the east, in the distance, is Yunokawa Onsen, the oldest hot-spring resort in Hakodate.

Follow the route northwest and then northeast, passing the **Hakodate Museum▶▶**, which houses Ainu relics, before reaching Sanroku station. Here you can take a cable car to the top of **Hakodate Yama (Mount Hakodate)▶▶▶**. The night view from the top is rated superb, and few Japanese come to Hakodate without visiting the mountain at night to enjoy the spectacular view over the city. There is a café on the summit.

Continuing north, past the green onion domes of the **Orthodox Church▶** on your left, go through the old foreign community area of **Motomachi** (see page 239), a district of Western buildings that developed during Hakodate's period as a treaty port. **The Old Public Hall▶▶**,

completed in 1910, is representative of the Western-style architecture of the Meiji period, and has the feel of a British colonial structure.

Continue north along the road to the **Foreigners' Cemetery▶▶**, which is laid out on a hill overlooking the port and is filled with the graves of Russians, Chinese, English, French, and Americans. The oldest graves are those of two American sailors who fell ill and died during Admiral Perry's mission in 1854.

Take a cab back to Hakodate station or retrace your steps to the Old Public Hall. From here it is a 15-minute walk to the Suehirocho trolley stop, where you can catch a trolley. Alternatively, walk to the **Kanamori Warehouse District▶**, a waterfront development of shops and cafés. From here you can walk back along the waterfront to the train station.

Hakodate harbor, one of the first ports to be opened to foreign trading following the end of Japan's self-imposed period of isolation

Sapporo restaurants

OODLES OF NOODLES
Sapporo is famous for its *ramen* (noodles), which have Chinese origins. The most popular place to eat them is the Ramen Yokocho, an alleyway of 16 noodle shops situated one block east of the Susukino subway station.

SUMMER BEER FESTIVAL
Odori Park in Sapporo is the site of a renowned Summer Beer Festival. Between mid-July and mid-August, numerous Japanese breweries set up stalls in the gardens of the park, selling beer from 5PM onward in the evening. Noodle and corn-on-the-cob vendors and other snack food sellers set up shop, and there are usually a variety of live bands to add to the atmosphere.

►► Sapporo

230B3

The capital of Hokkaido has a population of 1.6 million and is the largest city on the island. Over a century ago it was no more than a collection of Ainu huts, but at the beginning of the Meiji Period the Japanese government decided to colonize the island. Following the advice of American experts, construction of the new city of Sapporo (from the Ainu meaning "big, dry river") was started in 1871. Streets were laid out in a 328-foot (100-m) grid system, with wide avenues and parks. There are few interesting buildings, but the grid design is easy to negotiate. The Sapporo transportation information office, in the underground concourse of Odori station, supplies information on the comprehensive and efficient city bus and subway networks (see page 232 for details of how to get to Sapporo and for snow festival).

Information in English about Sapporo and Hokkaido is available from the Sapporo City Tourism Department, Nishi-2-chome, Kita 2, Chuo-ku, tel: 011 211 2376 (*open* 9–5, Sat 9–1; *closed* Sun), or from the tourist office in Sapporo station (*closed* on the second and fourth Wed of every month). Sapporo International Communication Plaza, Kita 1, Nishi 3, Chuo-ku (*open* 9–9), has a reading room with newspapers and books in English.

The **Batchelor Memorial Museum►►** (*open* 9–4, Oct 1–Nov 3, 9–3; *closed* Mon and Nov 4–Apr 29) is in the grounds of the Botanical Gardens, which grow over 5,000 plant varieties. It houses the collection of an Englishman, John Batchelor, who was deeply interested in Ainu culture and people.

Sapporo's most famous landmark is its **Clock Tower►►** built in 1878 as part of Sapporo Agricultural College (now Hokkaido University), and now open to the public. Inside is a small museum illustrating the local history.

In 1876, Western influence established the first brewery in Japan; the **Sapporo Beer Garden and Museum►►** is built on the site of that original Sapporo Brewery. Free tours of the museum last about an hour, and run daily between 9 AM and 3:40 PM. The Beer Garden is open for the consumption of beer and food from 11:30 AM to 9 PM.

Nakajima Park▶▶ lies about 2 miles (3km) from Sapporo station and features a rose garden, boating lake, Nakajima Sports Center, and two buildings classified as national cultural treasures: the Hasso-an tea house and gardens, and the Hohei-kan, a Western-style building originally built as an imperial guesthouse.

▶▶▶ Shikotsu-Toya National Park   *230B3*

See map on page 246.

This 386-square-mile (1,000-sq-km) park near Sapporo features lakes, volcanoes, and the hot-spring spas of Toyako Onsen and Noboribetsu Onsen. Access is via the JR Sapporo–Hakodate line. For Lake Toya, leave the train at JR Toya station (two hours, 10 minutes) and take the bus to Toyako Onsen. For Noboribetsu Onsen, get off at Noboribetsu Station (one and a half hours) and take the bus from there (20 minutes).

Abuta Volcano Science Museum▶▶ (*open* 9–5), above the Toyako Onsen bus terminal, features photographs and lava displays of the huge eruption of Mount Usu in August, 1977, which covered 80 percent of Hokkaido with volcanic ash. The most interesting feature is the 350-seat "experience room," duplicating the effects of a volcano.

Jigokudani▶▶ ("Hell Valley"), at the northern edge of Noboribetsu Onsen, is a volcanic crater 1,476 feet(450m) in diameter, full of boiling water and mineral formations caused by the volcanic activity. A concrete path (Hell Valley Promenade) follows the left side of the crater, and leads to a lookout point over a large pond of boiling water called Ohyunuma. (*Continued on page 246.*)

INSTANT VOLCANO
Toyako Onsen, on the southwestern shore of Lake Toya, is a popular spa town, but it is also the place from which to visit Showa Shinzan, Japan's newest volcano. The volcano first emerged in 1943, appearing in a local farmer's wheat field (much to his surprise). Over the next two years it steadily grew to its present height of 1,312 feet (400m). Near by Showa Shinzan is the volcanic Science Museum (Abuta Kazan Kagakukan), which focuses on the development of this young volcano and other volcanic activity within the Shikotsu-Toya National Park.

243

Shikotsu-Toya National Park

Every large Japanese city has a "soapland"—an area of bars, massage parlors, night clubs, restaurants, and striptease joints. They used to be called "Turkoland," but the name was changed after complaints from the Turkish Embassy. The new name derives from the practice in Japanese massage parlors of soaping the customer all over while he lies on a rubber mattress.

PACHINKO

Bright, garish, noisy, and smoke-filled, *pachinko* pinball arcades are always found in soapland districts. There are over 10,000 of these establishments in Japan, and more than half the population admits to playing *pachinko* pinball machines on a regular basis. Players win tokens that they swap for prizes ranging from cigarettes to hi-fi equipment. Apparently *pachinko* was invented by a Korean in Nagoya who, after World War II, wanted to find a use for surplus ball bearings.

Amusement arcade

Outside, massage parlors are generally garishly illuminated with bright neon lighting, and tough-looking individuals stand by the entrances, trying to persuade passersby to go in.

Inside, soaping is for a basic fee. For an extra payment, the masseuse uses her hands and body to work the soap into a lather. The cost continues to rise depending on the customer's requirements.

A visit to soapland areas, which are quite safe for men and women to walk around can be instructive about Japanese sensibilities. For example, Japanese men—often company men, usually drunk, socializing after work—are not at all sheepish about their enjoyment of the district, and there is none of the furtiveness found in similar areas elsewhere in the world.

The Yakuza (the Japanese Mafia) are usually involved in the soapland business, and can sometimes be seen cruising through the streets in the large Cadillacs, favored by top Yakuza men. (Japanese import taxes have raised the prices of these cars, giving them extra status in their owners' eyes.)

The women who work in soapland districts often come from country areas or distant towns. They tend to earn as much money as they can for four or five years and then return home. Family or friends need not know what they have been doing, and there is no loss of face; many of the women go on to set up businesses, or find eligible husbands, and often do well. Japanese newspapers occasionally carry stories revealing that a well-known company boss or politician is married to a "soapland girl."

The Japanese government licenses particular soapland areas as part of a long tradition in Japanese society. In the 17th and 18th centuries, entertainment for townsmen and for visitors alike (and often the main reason for going to town) was the brothel and the theater. In large towns and at stage posts along main roads, such as the Tokaido, red-light districts were established and

Signs for soapland

licensed by the government. Women in brothels were graded and priced according to their class and background, and their skills in such arts as singing, dancing, the tea ceremony, music, and dress. Those of the highest rank were entitled to reject a customer they did not like. All, however, were controlled by pimps and were virtual slaves.

Nowadays, visiting a prostitute is not freely condoned in Japanese society, although there is still much less stigma attached than there is in the West. Technically, it is now against the law, but the practice thrives in soapland districts, especially in the so-called Pink Salons, the seedier cabaret clubs where the hostesses are available for extra services, and in the guise of "health" and "fashion" massages. Prostitution is often linked to organized crime.

For Japanese women, attitudes are gradually changing. It was recently reported in a respectable Japanese newspaper that some soapland districts now have Adonis bars staffed by handsome waiters and barmen available to their female customers to hire for sex. Apocryphal or not, such a story would certainly have failed to make it into print only a few years ago.

ALCOHOL

For the Japanese, there is no shame in getting drunk; in fact, in some circumstances, your hosts may expect you to drink too much. Beer and/or *saké* are the usual accompaniments to a meal. Guests do not pour their own drinks but allow their companions to do it, and are expected to pour theirs. An empty cup or glass is a signal that a fill-up is required.

Jigokudani (Hell Valley)

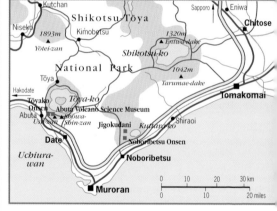

SILENT SPRINGS
Most people tend to stop over in Toyako Onsen and other hot-spring resorts in Shikotsu-Toya National Park only one night before moving on to explore another area. If you decide to stay another night or two, you will discover that you have the accommodations, and the hot baths to yourself daily, between check-out and check-in times.

(*Continued from page 243.*) **Noboribetsu Onsen▶▶** is a resort famous for its variety of hot-water springs. Eleven different types of mineral-saturated hot water, ranging in temperature from 113°F (45°C) to 197°F (91.5°C), and totaling over 10,000 tons a day, spring from the ground. Though not a sophisticated resort, this is the most popular spa town in Hokkaido, and is always crowded during holiday periods.

    Toyako Onsen▶▶, the main vacation center for the park, is a typical Japanese resort with many hotels, inns, and souvenir shops. Lake Toya is nearby, and boat trips across the lake are available. The hot-spring waters are famous for their curative qualities.

Travel Facts

Kansai International Airport

Arriving

By Air Narita, officially called New Tokyo International Airport, is the arrival and departure point for international flights to and from Tokyo. The best ways to get to and from the airport, which is 40 miles (64km) from the city center, are by bus or train. The airport limousine bus information and ticket office is in the arrivals lobby, just outside the exit from the customs hall. There are limousine bus services to Tokyo City Air Terminal (TCAT), Tokyo station, and major hotels (the bus goes from one hotel to the next in a circular route). Depending on traffic, the journey can take between 1½ and 2 hours. For travel back to the airport, take the bus at least three hours before departure time. If you leave from TCAT, you can check in for your flight and hand in your luggage, which is taken to the airport and put on your flight. (Some airlines do not provide this service.)

Japanese Railways (JR) offers two services from Narita to Tokyo station: the Narita Express (53 minutes) runs at least once every hour from 9:13 AM to 9:43 PM; Airport Narita (one hour, 24 minutes) runs every hour on the hour. Keisei Line Skyliner is a privately operated express train between Narita Airport and Keisei-Ueno station in Tokyo. It runs every 40 minutes between 6 AM and 8 PM, and takes exactly 61 minutes. From Ueno station you can take a taxi or subway (not recommended for your first visit) to your destination. There is a shuttle bus from the arrival hall at the airport to Keisei station, which is a short distance away. The Keisei information counter and ticket office is near the exit from the customs hall. You will have to pay airport tax on departure from Narita; buy a ticket at TCAT or at a tax counter at the airport (before entering the departure lounge).

The new **Kansai International Airport** is Japan's latest plunge into state-of-the-art construction work. In response to ever-growing demands for international and internal flight services, especially in the Kansai area (around Kyoto and Osaka), national government and private investors have spent 1.5 trillion *yen,* building the airport of the future. The airport is a huge man-made island, lying 3 miles (5km) off the Senshu Coast at the southern end of Osaka Bay, with air connections to 44 countries and 22 areas within Japan. It is joined to the land by a two-tiered access bridge, which carries rail and road services.

The airport is serviced by two rail lines, JR West and Nankai Electric RR. JR's Haruka Express runs directly to Kyoto through Shin-Osaka and Tennoji stations. Nankai runs two limited express trains from Namba. The first, the rapi:t α, runs non-stop between Namba and the airport (29 minutes). The second, rapi:t β, stops at Sakai (11 minutes) and other express points along the way. It is also possible to take non-express trains from other points to the airport.

High-speed sea services exploit the airport's marine location. The Jet Foil service to K-CAT on Port Island (Kobe) runs from 5 AM to 11:15 PM daily, taking only 30 minutes. The high-speed catamarans to Awaji and Tokushima take 34 and 90 minutes, respectively.

Limousine bus services is available to and from most areas in Kansai.

At present, Kansai Airport has two runways. Plans for the future include the construction of a third, auxiliary runway which will facilitate takeoffs and landings during difficult wind conditions. Kansai has taken the pressure off Osaka's old airport, Itami Airport, which now comfortably handles the majority of internal flights.

Customs regulations Clear passport control and collect your luggage before moving on to the "non-resident" customs counters. Drugs, pornography, and firearms are strictly prohibited. Nonresidents are allowed to bring in duty free: 400 cigarettes *or* 100 cigars *or* 500g tobacco; 3 bottles (760cc each) alcohol; 2 fl oz (50ml) perfume; other goods up to ¥200,000 in value. No allowance is given to people aged 19 or younger.

Travel insurance Standard travel insurance is advisable, including cover for medical care. Japanese hospitals have high standards but they are expensive, as are dental treatments. (English- and, to a lesser extent, German-speaking doctors and dentists are not uncommon.)

A public telephone: the color tells you the phone's function

Travel phones The travel phone is a service provided by JNTO to help tourists. If you get into difficulties or need information, you can use the travel phone anywhere in Japan and speak to somebody in English. Outside Tokyo and Kyoto, dial either of these numbers free: 0088 224 800 *or* 0120 444 800. In Tokyo or Kyoto, insert a ¥10 coin and dial 3201 3331 for Tokyo or 371 5649 for Kyoto. The Kyoto office is open every day of the year. The Tokyo office shuts Saturday and Sunday afternoons and on national holidays.

Visas, health matters Visitors from the U.S. need a visa only for visits of over 90 days; they are readily given and are free of charge. Apply to the Japanese Embassy for details (see page 264) and check requirements before you leave. Americans do not need any vaccination certificates to get into Japan. Once there, you do not need to take any special health precautions. It would be sensible for visiting males or females to take condoms with them.

249

Old and new walk side by side

Climate In general, the climate of Japan resembles the temperate climate of the east coast of the U.S., although the subtropical, southern island of Kyushu is warmer and the snowy, northern island of Hokkaido is colder. The best times to travel are in spring and fall. There are four distinct seasons. Spring begins in March (early April in northern Honshu and Hokkaido) and lasts until the beginning of June. April and May are warm and dry, good for traveling. From late March to mid-April, the *sakura* (cherry blossoms) ripen northward from Kyushu to Hokkaido. The summer and rainy seasons start in early June—a hot and humid time (except in Hokkaido). From mid-July to early September it remains hot, but not wet. Mountain areas are refreshing at this time of the year. Fall has clear skies and comfortable temperatures, although late September can be wet. Winter in the north and at high altitudes is cold, snowy, and beautiful. In other areas, temperatures rarely drop below freezing.

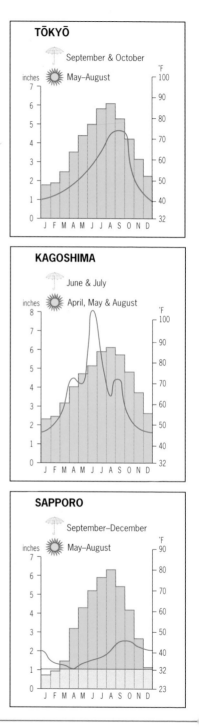

Money matters Credit cards are widely accepted in Japan, but cash is still the preferred way of paying bills in normal transactions, and the Japanese often carry huge wads of money around with them (a reflection of their safe society). Japanese currency is the yen and there are three types of bills and six different coins: 1,000, 5,000, and 10,000 yen bills; and 1, 5, 10, 50, 100, and 500 yen coins. Diners Club, MasterCard, Visa, and American Express are the major credit cards. Travelers' checks in yen or dollars are easily exchanged for cash at the banks, but are not readily accepted at small shops and restaurants. The rates of exchange at banks for cash and travelers' checks are invariably higher than in hotels. (If you intend to use a teller machine while in Japan, ask your bank at home if it has machines at your destination.)

Regions of Japan There are eight official regions in Japan, as follows: Hokkaido, Kyushu, and Shikoku, and the five regions of Honshu, the largest island: Tohoku, the mountainous rural northeastern region; Kanto, east central Honshu, Japan's most urban region (includes Tokyo); Chubu, the mountainous central region of Honshu, including the Japan Alps; Kinki, lying to the west and including Japan's second-largest industrialized area, centering on the cities of Osaka and Kobe, and the historical capitals of Kyoto and Nara; and finally, Chugoku on west Honshu, an agricultural and fishing region.

Time differences All of the islands of Japan are in the same time zone. London is nine hours behind (eight hours during British Summer Time), New York and Los Angeles 14 and 17 hours behind, respectively. Australia is one or two hours earlier; New Zealand is three hours earlier; Canada is 12½ to 18 hours later.

Tipping Tips are neither given nor expected. Large hotels and restaurants may, however, add a 10 to 15 percent service charge onto your bill. A government tax of 3 percent is added to food bills of ¥7,500 or less and 6 percent to bills over that sum; the same applies to combined food and accommodations bills of ¥15,000 or less and over ¥15,000.

251

When to go The Japanese all tend to take their vacations between similar dates and it is best to avoid these times. The three major vacation periods are: two or three days before and after New Year's Day; the week following Greenery Day (April 29), known as Golden Week; and the week that includes August 13–16, the Obon Festival, when many Japanese return to their hometowns.

The torii *(gate) at Itsukushima Shrine, Hiroshima. Founded in the 6th century, the shrine took its present form during the Heian period (795–1185). Since then it has been rebuilt seven times*

Trains Trains are the quickest way of exploring Japan. Japan Railways (JR) run 28,000 trains daily, and there are numerous private railroad lines. The fare system is complex and needs to be understood to avoid paying the highest prices. There is a basic fare for any train, calculated by the distance traveled. Added to this fare are various surcharges, mainly dependent on how fast the train is, but also on whether you reserve a seat or not, and on the class of travel.

There are four categories of train; the slower they are, the less you pay. The bullet trains (*Shinkansen*) are the fastest; limited stop express (Tokkyu or Cho-tokkyu) next to fastest; express (Kyuko) next to slowest; and local trains (Futsu) the slowest.

If you have limited time and no restrictions on your expenses, Shinkansen are the trains to use. On a budget (and in no great hurry), the best trains are a combination of the limited express for long journeys and the local trains for exploring a particular area.

If you wish to stop at places en route to your destination, purchase a ticket for the whole journey; you are allowed to make as many stops as you wish, as long as the date on your ticket remains valid for the whole journey. The period of validity is one day for 60 miles (100km), two days for 125 miles (200km), and then one day for each additional 125 miles (200km). Some restrictions may apply on Shinkansen routes; information on 03 3423 0111. You can get refunds on unused tickets and change routing once without any handling charge.

If you are not sure how much your fare is or where you are going, buy the cheapest ticket from a ticket machine or ticket office and pay any balance due at your destination; most stations have a fare adjustment counter.

Purchase reserved tickets at the "green windows," called *midori-no-madoguchi* in Japanese.)

If you intend to make a reasonable number of train journeys, it is worth buying a national or regional Japan Rail Pass. These are valid for one to three weeks and can save you quite a lot of money. You can purchase them

only outside Japan, and they allow you unlimited travel on all JR rail, bus, and boat services. Get a voucher from an authorized sales agent (lists available from JNTO) in your own country and exchange it for a rail pass at Tokyo or Osaka stations on your arrival, or better still from the JR counter at Narita Airport (*open* 7 AM–11 PM every day).

Do not carry a lot of luggage; busy trains usually have space for only one medium-sized suitcase.

Most trains have buffet cars and/or food and drink available from carts that are pushed up and down the aisles. They also sell *eki-ben* (box lunches), but those sold at stands at the station are usually cheaper and fresher.

All reasonably sized stations and all those on JR lines display station names in *kanji* and *Romaji* letters. The name of the station is in the middle of the nameboard with the preceding and following stations above and beneath it. Keep a careful watch for these nameboards when approaching a station. Sometimes there is only one, and it can flash past before you have seen it.

Try to avoid traveling during the peak rush hours (7–9 AM and 5–7 PM). All of the major stations are equipped with an information counter where you can get maps, accommodations advice, and assistance with your train travel from English-speaking assistants.

The following Japanese phrases may be useful for visitors who are traveling by train.

At what time does the train for Tokyo leave? *Tokyo yuki no densha wa nanji ni demasu ka?*
From which platform? *Nanban sen kara demasu ka?*
Where is platform 1? *Ichi ban sen wa doko desu ka?*
Does the train for Osaka leave from here? *Osaka yuki no densha wa koko kara demasu ka?*
I want to get off at Tokyo station. *Tokyo eki de oritai desu.*
Will you tell me when to get off? *Itsu oritara yoi ka oshiete kudasai?*
How many stations (before) I get off? *Koko kara nanbanme no eki de oriruno desu ka?*

Subways Many large Japanese cities have subway systems, most of them providing the quickest and cheapest way of moving about town. Subway maps are provided at station information counters or local tourist offices.

Buses Japan has an excellent network of local city and rural buses, and bus terminals are often adjacent to train stations, so it is easy to make use of both buses and trains. For long journeys, buses are slower and less comfortable than trains, but they are somewhat cheaper.

Japanese Railways provides a service of overnight long-distance buses on which the Japan Rail Pass (see pages 254–255) is valid.

Buses come into their own for local journeys. Unfortunately, many do not show their destination in *Romaji* (Japanese Roman script), so it is important to be sure of the number you wish to take, in which direction you want to take it, and where, if at all, you need to change buses. This information can be obtained from tourist offices.

Once you know your bus number and destination, write them on a piece of paper so that people can help you. Knowing how to pay once you are on board is much easier than catching the right bus.

As you enter the bus (at the back), take a ticket from the dispensing machine inside the door. It has a number on the back. A meter above the driver's head matches the cost of the fares against the numbers on the backs of the tickets. It rotates during the bus journey, increasing the fare against the ticket numbers accordingly.

As you get off, put your fare into the collecting machine by the driver's side. There is a box attached to the machine that will give change for coins and bills.

Taxis Taxis are quite expensive, but the fare shown on the meter is exactly what you pay: tipping is not the custom. It is a good idea to carry the address and telephone number of your destination in *Romaji* and to show the taxi driver.

After hailing a cab do not try to open the taxi door. The driver will open the curbside door by remote control. Similarly, do not try to close the door on leaving.

A red light on the dashboard indicates an available taxi; a green light means it is occupied.

The International Student Identity card, available in many countries from student organizations, entitles the holder to discounts at several art galleries, museums, theaters and so on, plus youth rail passes and reductions on some local transportation.

Car rental Cars can be reserved through Hertz-Japan (tel: 03 3356 8002) and other major companies including Nippon (tel: 03 3485 7196, English-speaking operator available) and Nissan Car Lease (tel: 03 5424 4123, English-speaking operator). An international driving license is required. Traffic drives on the *left*, the steering wheel is on the *right*, and speed limits vary, but generally the limit is 50 m.p.h. (80kph) on highways and 25 m.p.h. (40kph) in urban areas.

Renting a car locally to explore the immediate area can be a sensible proposition, but for traveling throughout the country, driving is not the best option. Train services are comprehensive, fast, and frequent; the roads, by contrast, are congested and not particularly well signposted and, off the major roads, signs are given in *kanji* (Chinese characters).

Ferries Frequent ferry services connect the main islands of Japan and local ferries connect all populated small islands to the nearest main ports as well as to other islands in the same group. Tokyo or Osaka to Kyushu or Shikoku or Hokkaido are popular main routes. Ferries are less expensive than air or rail, although obviously slower. Economy travelers occupy one large *tatami* (straw floor mat) room where they eat, sit, and sleep together. On longer routes, a small Japanese public bath is situated on the same deck. Private cabins also are available. Tickets and information can be obtained from travel agents based in Japan.

Travelers with disabilities In recent years, local authorities have invested a lot of time and money to make public buildings and means of transport accessible to the physically handicapped. Braille is in increasing evidence at ticket booths and along side place names on public maps, elevators, and government building floor plans, etc.

In addition, travelers to Japan will notice that many sidewalks in modern cities now have special markings so that the blind can "touch-feel"

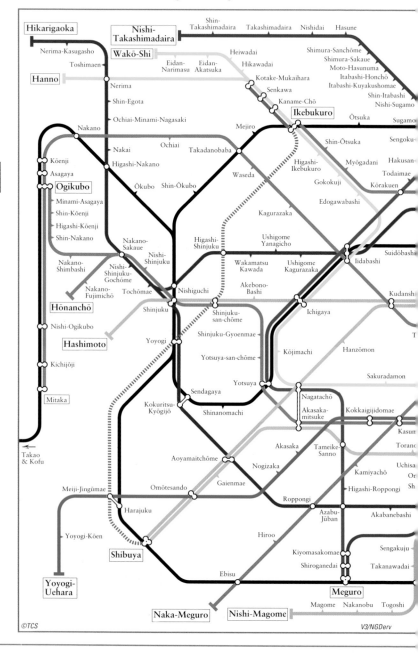

their way as they walk down streets. Loudspeakers have also been installed at road crossing points.

With advance warning, disabled travelers can receive assistance at Narita Airport and the limousine bus service is also accessible.

Written enquiries can be sent, well in advance of travel, to: Physically Handicapped Lifestyle Center, 1-44-2 Umegaoka, Setagaya-ku, Tokyo 154.

Lines under construction

*Uniformity is an early lesson
for Japanese school children*

Language The Japanese spend many
years at school learning English but
very few are confident of speaking it,
though it is probable that their
English is better than most visitors'
Japanese. The following Japanese
phrases are among those that are
likely to be most helpful. (In general,
end-of-word "u"s are not
pronounced.)

Mr. or Mrs. *san* after the surname (but
don't ever append it to your own
name)
Yes *hai*
Yes, I agree *hai, so des*
Thank you *(domo) arigato*
Yes, please *hai onegaishimasu*
No (rarely used) *iie*
No, I disagree *chigaimasu*
I am sorry *gomen-nasai*
Excuse me (also used to call waiter)
sumimasen...
Good morning *o-haiyo-gozaimasu*
Good afternoon *konnichi-wa*
Good evening *konban-wa*
Good night *oyasumi nasai*
Goodbye *sayonara*
Excuse me, do you speak English?
sumimasen, Eigo dekimasu-ka?
Yes, just a little *hai, sukoshi dake*
No, I can't *iie, dame desu*
(On starting a meal) *itadakimasu*
Cheers! *kampai!*
Thank you (for kindness) *domo arigato
gozaimash'ta*
Thank you (after a meal) *gochiso-sama
desh'ta*
What is your name? *o-namae wa?*
My name is "Smith" *watashi wa
"Smith" desu*

(I'm) ill *(watashi wa) byoki desu*
Help! *tasukete (kudasai)!*
hospital *byoin*
Police *Keisatsu*
How much is it? *ikura desu ka?*
for bed and breakfast *choshokutsuki*
for full board *sanshokutsuki*
excluding meals *sudomari desu*
does that include...? *wa tsuite imasu-
ka?*
meals *shokuji* or *go-han*
service *saabisu*
Have you anything cheaper? *Nanika
motto yasui no wa (arimasen ka?)*
Menu, please *menu o kudasai*
Check, please *go-kanjo onegaishimasu*
Do you accept credit cards? *credit
cardo tsukaemasu ka?*
coffee shop *kissaten*
restaurant *restoran*
beer *biru*
water *mizu*
milk *milku*
coffee *kohee*
Indian tea *kocha*
Japanese or Chinese tea *ocha*
sugar, please *satoh, kudasai*

For details of the Japanese writing
system, see pages 20–21.

The following are a few helpful
Japanese suffixes and terms:
-dera temple
-dori street or avenue
gai-jin foreigners
-gawa river
-ji temple
-jo castle
-ko lake
-koen park or gardens
-mon gate
onsen hot spring spas
ryokan traditional Japanese inns
sakura cherry blossoms
-san mount
sento public communal bath houses
shoji paper room-dividing screens
tatami closely woven straw floor mats
torii gate

Emergency telephone numbers
Police: 110; Ambulance/Fire: 119.
Press the red button on the telephone
and dial. No money is required. The
operator will answer in Japanese so
you will need the assistance of a
Japanese speaker. See page 249 for
details of English-speaking operators.

Health The Japanese have the highest life expectancy in the world. Japan is a clean, hygienic country and doctors are highly trained. Health insurance is recommended for travelers. Clinics with English-speaking doctors include: Hibiya Clinic, Hibiya Mitsui Building, 1-1-2 Yurakucho Chiyoda-ku, Tokyo (tel: 03 3502 2681) and Japan Baptist Hospital, 14 Yamanomotocho Kitashirakawa, Kyoto, Sakyo-ku (tel: 075 781 5191). English is spoken at the following hospitals: Ginza area: St. Luke's International Hospital (Sei Roka Byoin), 9-1 Akashi-cho, Chuo-ku (tel: (03) 3541 5151); Shinjuku area: International Catholic Hospital (Seibo Byoin), 2-5-1 Naka Ochai, Shinjuku-ku, (tel: 03 3951-1111).

Lost property If you forget something or leave it in a public place there is every chance it will still be there when you return. All public transportation systems, including taxi companies, have a lost and found service. In Tokyo:
Taxis (tel: 03 3648 0300)
JR (tel: 03 3231 1880)
Subway (tel: 03 3834 5577)
Buses (tel: 03 3815 7229)
The Tokyo Central Lost and Found Police Office is at 1-9-11, Koraku, Bunkyo-ku (tel: 03 3814 4151)

Archeologists excavating a site on Ishigaki Island

Pharmacies Japanese pharmacies sell the same range of goods as Western drug stores. Pharmacies are easily found in any town. In Tokyo, there is an English-speaking drug store at the American Pharmacy, Hibiya Park Building, 1-8-1, Yurakucho, Chiyoda-ku (tel: 03 3271-4034/5), open 9–7 Monday to Saturday, 11–7 Sunday and holidays.

Police Robbery is very rare in Japan and violent crime is even less likely. Japanese policemen and -women are helpful and approachable, but very few speak any English. Every Japanese district has its own "police box" (*koban*), usually near a busy intersection or station. The police on duty will help you find an address if you can show them a map of its location.

Media Japan has four daily English-language newspapers on sale in hotels or at major train stations. There are English editions of the *Asahi*, *Yomiuri*, and *Mainichi*, and the fourth is the independent *Japan Times*. The monthly English-language *Tokyo Journal* gives comprehensive reviews and lists of theater, film, art shows, and restaurants.

of the newspaper's editorial policy.

English-language television and radio programs are available at most large hotels.

Post offices The Japanese postal service is very efficient in delivering both domestic and foreign mail. Post offices are open 9–5 Monday–Friday, with cash deposits or withdrawal until 3 PM; Saturday 9–12:30 (main offices only); closed on Sunday and national holidays. The Central Post Office next to Tokyo station is open 24 hours a day. Small neighborhood post offices close on the second Saturday of each month. Mail boxes are red.

Takyubin (express delivery) service exists for sending heavy or bulky goods between hotels. This takes 24 hours, and those wishing to use the service should check that there will be someone at the other end to receive the goods.

Letters addressed in *Romaji*, sent to Japan or within Japan, should have the address printed in large, bold

Japanese newspapers differ from their Western counterparts in two main areas: a clear-cut stance in articles is avoided, and the publisher, rather than the reporter, assumes responsibility for the content of a story. A journalist is always expected to work closely within the framework

The distinctive red Japanese mail boxes are easy to spot

The urban architecture of Tokyo, ancient and modern

print to make it easier for the Japanese sorter to read. To mail a letter or postcard in Japan, take it to the post office and have it weighed. Post office clerks read *Romaji*. Large post offices may be used as *poste restante* addresses.

Telephones Public telephones are found virtually everywhere in Japan. Gray and green telephones accept both 10-yen and 100-yen coins and telephone cards. Red phones accept 10-yen coins only. Direct inter-city calls can all be made from these phones but international calls must be made from "International and Domestic Card/Coin Telephones"

located at international airports and hotels, and in some major office buildings.

To get the international information service dial 0057; for the international operator, dial 0051. Dial direct international calls as follows: 001 + the national number of the country being called + area code + local phone number. The national number of Australia is 61; Canada is 1; Ireland is 353; New Zealand is 64; the U.K. is 44 and the U.S. is 1. If the area code starts with a 0, omit it. To call Japan from Australia dial 0011 81; from Canada 011 81; from the U.K. and Ireland 00 81; New Zealand 0081 and the U.S. 011 81. Again, omit the area code's initial 0. Fax is widely used in Japan and most offices and hotels have their own fax machines.

Bottles of sake *ready to be enjoyed*

Camping and self-catering organizations There are some campsites in Japan, but they tend to be difficult to find and primitive. Camping is not a popular or common pastime. People on a tight budget who wish to cater for themselves would be better advised to stay in youth hostels. The Japan Youth Hostel Association is at Hoken Kaikan, 1-1 Ichigaya Sadohara-cho, Shinjuku-ku, Tokyo (tel: 03 3269 5831).

Children Young visitors are well catered for in Japan, and there are theme parks, aquariums, zoos, video display exhibitions, and other child-oriented events readily available throughout the country. There is also a Disneyland on the outskirts of Tokyo. Local tourist information centers have full details of their area's amenities.

Children in Japan are allowed to walk, cycle, and travel on public transportation on their own from a very early age, and family homes and schools are still found in city centers.

Japanese children really enjoy meeting foreign boys and girls and becoming pen pals with them. If you take children to Japan, they will have no difficulty in making friends, despite the language differences.

CONVERSION CHARTS

FROM	TO	MULTIPLY BY
Inches	Centimeters	2.54
Centimeters	Inches	0.3937
Feet	Meters	0.3048
Meters	Feet	3.2810
Yards	Meters	0.9144
Meters	Yards	1.0940
Miles	Kilometers	1.6090
Kilometers	Miles	0.6214
Acres	Hectares	0.4047
Hectares	Acres	2.4710
Gallons	Liters	4.5460
Liters	Gallons	0.2200
Ounces	Grams	28.35
Grams	Ounces	0.0353
Pounds	Grams	453.6
Grams	Pounds	0.0022
Pounds	Kilograms	0.4536
Kilograms	Pounds	2.205
Tons	Tonnes	1.0160
Tonnes	Tons	0.9842

MEN'S SUITS

U.K.	36	38	40	42	44	46	48
Rest of Europe	46	48	50	52	54	56	58
U.S.	36	38	40	42	44	46	48

DRESS SIZES

U.K.	8	10	12	14	16	18
France	36	38	40	42	44	46
Italy	38	40	42	44	46	48
Rest of Europe	34	36	38	40	42	44
U.S.	6	8	10	12	14	16

MEN'S SHIRTS

U.K.	14	14.5	15	15.5	16	16.5	17
Rest of Europe	36	37	38	39/40	41	42	43
U.S.	14	14.5	15	15.5	16	16.5	17

MEN'S SHOES

U.K.	7	7.5	8.5	9.5	10.5	11
Rest of Europe	41	42	43	44	45	46
U.S.	8	8.5	9.5	10.5	11.5	12

WOMEN'S SHOES

U.K.	4.5	5	5.5	6	6.5	7
Rest of Europe	38	38	39	39	40	41
U.S.	6	6.5	7	7.5	8	8.5

Electricity From Tokyo east to Hokkaido, the current is 100 volts at 50 cycles. Western Japan operates on 100 volts at 60 cycles. North Americans with electronic equipment that operates at 110/60 will have no problems. Europeans using devices designed to operate at 240/50 cycles will need to adjust them or, if they are not convertible, use a transformer. Some of the major hotels have 240/50 outputs.

Entrance fees Most Japanese museums, galleries, monuments, and nationally known temples and gardens charge entrance fees, which usually fall in the ¥300–¥800 range.

Opening times

Banks open Monday–Friday 9–3, Saturday 9–noon; closed Saturday afternoon, Sunday, and national holidays. **Museums** usually open April–October 9–5, November–March 9–4:30; closed Monday and December 29–January 3. Most museums stop letting people in half an hour before closing time. If a national holiday falls on a museum's weekly closing day, it closes on the following day instead.

    Shops open from around 10 AM. Some close around 6 PM; others stay open until much later. Many, but not all, in the central business district are open on Sundays and holidays.

    Department stores all open six days a week at 10 AM. Some stay open to 8 PM, although most close at 6 on Saturday and Sunday and holidays. Some are closed on Mondays, and others on Wednesdays and Thursdays.

Photography A huge array of cameras, processing facilities, and film of every sort is available in even the smallest Japanese town.

Places of worship The following places of worship in Tokyo hold services in English:
Anglican: St. Alban's, 3-6-25 Shibakoen, Minato-ku (tel: 03 3431-8534).
Baptist: Tokyo Baptist Church, 9-2 Hachiyama-cho, Shibuya-ku (tel: 03 3461 8425).
Catholic: St. Ignatius, 6-5 Kojimachi, Chiyoda-ku (tel: 03 3263-4584).
Jewish: Jewish Community of Japan, 3-8-8 Hiroo, Shibuya-ku (tel: 03 3400-2559).

Toilets Most of the modern restroom facilities in large towns provide Western-style toilets, but in rural areas Japanese squat-style toilets are still quite common. There are public lavatories in train stations and public parks (they do not provide paper); those in department stores and coffee shops are always cleaner.

Information on hand at the Grand Shrines of Ise

Customs and etiquette However Westernized modern Japan may appear, traditional etiquette continues to be very important. Most Japanese expect that, as a foreigner, you will not understand the complexities of their social behavior, and that you will behave according to Western rules. However, evidence of a basic understanding of Japanese values and a respect for them will certainly be appreciated, enjoyed, and acknowledged by the people you meet.

Status Japanese society is even today hierarchical, and spoken Japanese contains a battery of expressions that, used appropriately, set both the relative social positions and the gender of the speaker and the person spoken to. Both parties immediately know where they stand on the ladder of inferiority, equality, or superiority. Visitors, especially on business, are accorded a relatively high status, and may respond to this by being polite and effusive in expressing thanks even for minor favors. For receivers of hospitality—be it drinks, a meal, or a gift—it is customary to say *Arigato gozaimasu*, a polite "Thank you," at the time of receiving and at the next meeting. Saying "Thank you" several times symbolizes a long-term rather than a transitory relationship.

Groups versus individuals The Japanese have a tendency to think in terms of the social group they belong to, rather than as individuals. This leads to an intrinsic acknowledgement of the rights of the group over those of an individual member, and a close observance of family morals and taboos. Social harmony (*wa*) is highly valued in the workplace and at home. In business and politics, consensus opinion is vital before decisions or policies are made public, and an open display of conflict is viewed as deeply embarrassing.

Thinking ahead Forethought is another distinctive feature of Japanese behavior. It is always best to do things for others before being asked. For example, a host will try to anticipate what a guest might want or need. Tea or coffee and even a meal may be served without you asking for it. Room dividers (*fusuma* and *shoji*) in a traditional Japanese house do not have locks. If the *fusuma* is closed a person wishing to enter needs to choose correctly between knocking, calling out, or just going away.

Bowing The Japanese bow a lot to each other on meeting or departing. The depth and frequency of the bows depends on the status of the people involved. To be on the safe side, imitate any bows you receive. Hold both arms straight and bow with the

Bid for good luck at Motsuji Temple

262

upper body. Shaking hands is an alternative way of introducing yourself, and still a novelty to the Japanese. However, a strong handshake is not needed and would not be understood.

Conversation and smiling In conversation, it is common for the listener to nod and utter approving sounds. These do not, however, necessarily mean consent or agreement. In fact, in most cases they signal only that the listener is concentrating on what you are saying. Another possible source of misunderstanding is smiling. For a Japanese smiling may be a way of hiding embarrassment; don't take it to mean assent all the time. Smiling may even disguise inner sadness. Genuine happiness is indicated more accurately by creases in the corners of

A monk with a cold signs pilgrims' log books at Koya-san Temple

the eye. According to general Japanese thinking, disclosing such emotions would be to foist off one's problems onto another, to burden the listener and thereby show a lack of consideration.

Nose-blowing It is normal in Japan to clear your throat or sniff if you have a cold or a running nose (and even acceptable to spit discreetly in the street). However, it is considered rude to blow your nose in public. People you see wearing masks over their mouth and nose do so because they have a cold, not because of pollution. It is best to go to the bathroom, or some other private place, if you need to blow your nose.

Embassies and consulates in Tokyo
The U.S. embassy in Tokyo is at
1-10-5 Akasaka, Minato-ku
(tel: 03 3224 5000).

In the United States, you can contact
the **Japanese Embassy** at 2520
Massachusetts Avenue N.W.,
Washington D.C. 20008
(tel: 202/939–6800), or consulates in
the following cities:
Atlanta: 400 Colony Square Building
#1501, Peachtree Street, Atlanta, GA
30361 (tel: 404/892–2700)
Boston: Federal Reserve Plaza, 14th
Floor, 600 Atlantic Avenue, Boston,
MA 02210 (tel: 617/973–9772)
Chicago: 737 North Michigan
Avenue #1101, Chicago, IL 60611
(tel: 312/280–0400)
Los Angeles: 250 East 1st Street #1507,
Los Angeles, CA 90012
(tel: 213/624–8305).
New York: 299 Park Avenue, New
York, NY 10171 (tel: 212/371–8222)
San Francisco: 50 Fremont Street
#2300, San Francisco, CA 94105
(tel: 415/777–3533)

Tourist offices The Japanese National
Tourist Office (JNTO) operates three
main Tourist Information Centers
(TIC) in Japan. They give advice on
travel arrangements and accommodations and stock lots of useful free
literature. Most towns of any size
in Japan operate their own tourist
offices, normally within or near the
main train station.

Tokyo office: B.I.F., International
Forum, 3-5-1 Maruno-uchi, Chiyoda-
Ku, Tokyo 100 (tel: 03 3201 3331).
Open weekdays 9–5, Sat 9–noon;
closed Sun and national holidays.
Tokyo International Airport office:
Airport No. 2 Terminal Building,
Narita Airport, Chiba Prefecture
(tel: 0476 34 6251). Open 9–8.
Kyoto office: Kyoto Tower Building,
Higashi-Shiokojicho, Shimogyo-ku
(tel: 075 371 5649). Open weekdays
9–5, Saturday 9–noon; closed Sunday
and national holidays.

JNTO also operates a main office in
Tokyo and others abroad.
Japan (main office): Tokyo Kotsu
Kaikan Building, 2-10-1 Yurakucho,
Chiyoda-ku, Tokyo 100 (tel: 03 3216
2905). Worldwide JNTO web site
address: http://www.jnto.go.jp

In the United States, contact the
JNTO at:
Chicago: 401 North Michigan
Avenue, 770, Chicago, IL 60601
(tel: 312/222–0874)
Los Angeles: 624 South Grand
Avenue, Suite 1611, Los Angeles, CA
90017 (tel: 213/623–1952)
San Francisco: 360 Post Street,
Suite 601, San Francisco, CA 94108
(tel: 415/989–7140)
New York: 1 Rockefeller Plaza,
Suite 1250, New York, NY 10020
(tel: 212/757–5640)

Receiving a helping hand

Accommodations & Restaurants

ACCOMMODATIONS

There is no shortage of accommodations in Japan. In the cities there is a wide variety of options, while in rural areas there are usually *minshuku* (see pages 80–81), small inns and hotels, and some-times *ryokan* (see pages 220–221). The range of average prices for different categories of accommodations is as follows:

Hotel accommodations:
Expensive ($$$) ¥27,000–40,000
Moderate ($$) ¥17,000–26,000
Budget ($) ¥6,000–12,000

Other accommodations:
Ryokan ¥20,000–40,000 (includes breakfast and dinner)
Business hotels ¥8,000–12,000
Minshuku ¥6,000–8,000
Japanese inns ¥5,000–7,000
Youth hostels ¥1,000–3,000

266

Restaurants:
Lunch:
Expensive ($$$) ¥3,000 plus
Moderate ($$) ¥2,000–3,000
Budget ($) ¥1,000–2,000
Dinner:
Expensive ($$$) ¥4,500 plus
Moderate ($$) ¥3,000–4,500
Budget ($) ¥2,000–3,000

TOKYO

Akasaka Prince Hotel ($$$)
1-2 Kioi-cho, Chiyoda-ku tel: 03 3234 1111
First-class service, excellent views, quality postwar architecture, and tasteful modern room furnishings.

Akasaka Tokyu Hotel ($$/$)
2-14-3 Nagata-cho, Chiyoda-ku
tel: 03 3580 2311
Excellent central location, rooms not big but with all facilities, wide variety of restaurants. Popular: book well ahead.

ANA Hotel Tokyo ($$$)
1-12-33 Akasaka, Minato-ku
tel: 03 3505 1111
In the Ark Hills area, between Roppongi and Akasaka, a 37-story, 903-room block with a sober exterior and vast areas of marble inside. Facilities include a health club and pool, executive floor, and several restaurants.

Asakusa View Hotel ($$)
3-17-1 Nishi-Asakusa, Taito-ku
tel: 03 3842 2111
The only hotel with international facilities in this lively entertaining district. Nevertheless retains a very Japanese feel. Swimming pool, gymnasium, and Japanese garden.

Atamiso ($$)
4-14-3 Ginza, Chuo-ku
tel: 03 3541 3621
This small hotel (74 rooms) offers a friendly personal service. It is located close to central Ginza's nightlife and shopping.

Capitol Tokyu ($$$)
2-10-3 Nagatacho, Chiyoda-ku
tel: 03 3581 4511
Situated in the heart of Tokyo's governmental district. Meeting place for the city's power brokers. Quality service, fine cuisine, excellent Japanese garden and pond.

Edmont ($$)
3-10-8 Iidabashi, Chiyoda-ku tel: 03 3237 111
Unexpected back street location for a very modern hotel with a nevertheless warm inviting lobby and lounge. Double rooms are a very reasonable size and full equipped with all an executive traveler might need.

Elegant Inn Yasuda ($)
1-56-28 Matsubara, Setagaya-ku
tel: 03 3322 5546
Japanese inn offering Western- and Japanese-style rooms, air-conditioned. Good value.

Fairmont Hotel ($$/$)
2-1-17 Kudan Minami, Chiyoda-ku
tel: 03 3262 1151
For Tokyo this is an older style hotel (built in 1952). Small and quietly positioned near the Imperial Palace. Highly recommended during the cherry blossom season in spring.

Ginza Capitol ($$)
2-1-4 Tsukiji, Chuo-ku tel: 03 3543 8211
A basic business hotel with compact rooms, close to Tsukiji subway station, reasonably convenient for Ginza.

Ginza Ocean ($$)
7-18-15 Ginza, Chuo-ku tel: 03 3545 1221
A cut above the usual business hotel, with a friendly staff and a good Japanese restaurant.

Holiday Inn Tokyo ($$)
1-13-7 Hatchobori, Chuo-ku tel: 03 3553 616
Similar to any other Holiday Inn but with smaller rooms (relatively large for Tokyo, however). Western-style restaurant. Convenient for Tokyo station.

Hotel Ohgaiso ($)
3-3-21 Ikenohata, Taito-ku 110
tel: 03 3822 4611
Good location across from Ueno Park. Reasonably well-equipped rooms for the price. The windows can be opened (not common in Tokyo). Japanese- and Western-style food in restaurants. Doors close at 2 AM.

Hotel Okura ($$$)
2-10-4 Torano-mon, Minato-ku
tel: 03 3582 0111
Stately, formal, one of the first of the postwar grand hotels, with 883 rooms, many restaurants, an art gallery, and indoor and outdoor pools. Traditional atmosphere, spacious rooms, quietly sophisticated, popular with diplomats and businessmen.

Hotel Seiyo Ginza ($$$)
1-11-2 Ginza, Chuo-ku tel: 03 3535 1111
Very expensive, small, and luxurious hotel with highly personalized service. Staff-to-guest ratio is three to one! Reservations a must.

Ibis ($)
7-4-14, Roppong, Minato-ku tel: 033403 441
Straightforward business hotel. Basic no-frills accommodation but very convenient for Roppongi and its full-on nightlife.

Imperial ($$$)
1-1-1 Uchisaiwaicho, Chiyoda-ku
tel: 03 3504 1111
On the edge of Ginza, facing Hibiya Park, this is a city-within-a-city, with 1,059 rooms, over 20 restaurants, dozens of shops, a health club, and pool. Rooms are beautifully appointed, with superb views from the upper stories.

Keihin Hotel ($$)
4-10-20 Takanawa, Minato-ku
tel: 03 3449 5711
Slightly out of the way in Shinagawa district, but an excellent value, straightforward, modest hotel. There is usually somebody at the desk who can speak English.

Kikuya Ryokan ($)
2-18-9 Nishi-Asakusa, Taito-ku
tel: 03 3841 6404
Very small, with eight Japanese-style rooms, some with private bathroom. Just off Kappabashi-dori.

Kimi Ryokan ($)
2-36-8 Ikebukuro, Toshima-ku
tel: 03 3971 3766
A friendly little place with Japanese-style rooms, it is popular with Westerners and often full. Seven minutes' walk northwest of Ikebukuro station.

Mitsui Urban ($)
8-6-15 Ginza, Chuo-ku tel: 03 3572 4131
Efficient, clean economy hotel with some character. The façade is painted orange and this together with an accompanying sidewalk metal-tree sculpture has resulted in the hotel becoming a local landmark and meeting place. Handy for the Shimbashi business and bar district.

Miyako Hotel Tokyo ($$$)
1-1-50 Shirogano-dai, Minato-ku
tel: 03 3447 3111
A quiet comfortable hotel with a delightful Japanese garden. This sister hotel of the more famous Kyoto branch of the same name retains a restrained provincial air that offers a welcome rest from the hustle and bustle of Tokyo life.

New Otani Hotel ($$$)
4-1 Kioi-cho, Chiyoda-ku tel: 03 3265 1111
Huge hotel complex, largest in Japan, but offers restaurants and services to match. Attractive feature is its surprisingly large garden.

Palace ($$$)
1-1-1 Maruno-uchi, Chiyoda-ku
tel: 03 3211 5211
Overlooks the moats of the Imperial Palace. Elegant public areas and 394 beautifully appointed guest rooms. A subway stop from Ginza.

President Hotel ($$)
2-2-3 Minami Aoyama, Minato-ku
tel: 03 3497 0111
The only small, moderately priced hotel, located in the expensive Aoyama district. Rooms equipped to high standard and restaurants are recommended.

Roppongi Prince ($$$)
3-2-7 Roppongi, Minato-ku tel: 03 3587 1111
Compact 216-room hotel close to Roppongi's entertainments. The courtyard with a café and swimming pool is an asset.

Sakura Ryokan ($)
2-6-2 Iriya, Taito-ku tel: 03 3876 8118
Close to Ueno and Asakusa, with Western- and Japanese-style rooms.

Shiba Daimon ($$)
2-3-6 Shiba-Daimon, Minato-ku
tel: 03 3431 3716
This friendly hotel, which sees few Western guests, is located in the Tokyo Tower area. It has a good Chinese restaurant.

Shigetsu Ryokan ($)
1-31-11 Asakusa, Taito-ku tel: 03 3843 2345
Friendly, inexpensive Japanese inn, almost on the doorstep of Asakusa Kannon Temple.

Shinagawa Prince Hotel ($)
4-10-30 Takanawa, Minato-ku
tel: 03 3440 1111
Acceptable budget accommodations with reasonably sized rooms. Part of a sports complex; mainly young clients; 24-hour coffee bar.

Shinjuku Prince Hotel ($$)
1-30-1, Kabuki-cho, Shinjuku-ku 160
tel: 03 3205 1111
A business hotel with atmosphere. Central location on the edge of Kabuki-cho, Shinjuku's red-light district. Reasonably priced restaurants, 24-hour room service, small rooms, but good value for money.

Shinjuku Washington ($$)
3-2-9 Nishi-Shinjuku, Shinjuku-ku
tel: 03 3343 3111
A shiny modern business hotel near the Shinjuku skyscrapers, with 1,310 compact rooms and largely impersonal or automated services. Five minutes' walk from Shinjuku station.

Star ($$)
7-10-5 Nishi-Shinjuku, Shinjuku-ku
tel: 03 3361 1111
A small, functional but friendly hotel with 80 rooms, only a couple of minutes' walk from Shinjuku station and the entertainment district.

Tokiwa Hotel ($$)
7-27-9 Shinjuku, Shinjuku-ku
tel: 03 3202 4321
A good-value *ryokan*-style hotel with character. Western- and Japanese-style rooms. Good location in the heart of Shinjuku.

Tokyo Hilton International ($$$)
6-6-2 Nishi-Shinjuku, Shinjuku-ku
tel: 03 3344 5111
One of the high-rises of Shinjuku, with great views from the upper floors, 807 rooms, 5 restaurants, indoor and outdoor pools, and tennis courts.

Tokyo Kokusai International Youth Hostel ($)
Central Plaza 18F, 2-1-1 Kagurazaka, Shinjuku-ku tel: 03 3235 1107
Simple accommodations in a modern tower block. Reservations in advance are required. Send a letter with a self-addressed postcard for reply.

Tokyo Station Hotel ($$)
1-9-1 Maruno-uchi, Chiyoda-ku
tel: 03 3231 2511
Built in 1915, this hotel occupies much of the distinctive red-brick section of Tokyo station. Spacious, comfortable rooms with a rather faded elegance. Has a slightly eccentric air.

Westin Tokyo ($$$)
Ebisu Garden Place, 1-4-1 Mita, Meguro-ku
tel: 03 5423 7000
A stylish hotel with richly decorated public areas and 445 guest rooms, part of a new leisure development on the former Sapporo Brewery site.

Accommodations and Restaurants

Yaesu Fujiya ($$)
2-9-1 Yaesu, Chuo-ku tel: 03 3273 2111
Modern business hotel with central location behind Tokyo Station. The rooms are small but the restaurants are decent.

Yaesu-Ryumeikan ($$)
1-3-22 Yaesu, Chuo-ku tel: 03 3271 0971
Japanese inn offering Western- and Japanese-style rooms, air-conditioned. Good value.

YMCA Asia Youth Center ($)
2-5-5 Saragaku-cho, Chiyoda-ku
tel: 03 3233 0631
Men and women welcome. Rooms basic. Western and Japanese breakfasts served, indoor pool available. Doors close at midnight; 7–8 minutes' walk from Suidobashi or Jinbo-cho stations.

Nikko
You can see Nikko on a day trip from Tokyo. Most accommodations are in Japanese-style inns.

Nikko Kanaya Hotel ($$)
1300 Kami Hatsuishi-cho, Nikko
tel: 0288 54 0001
Very old, spacious, and busy. Helpful staff, excellent location.

Pension Turtle ($)
2-16 Takumi-cho tel: 0288 53 3168
Good location near Toshogu shrine. Comfortable rooms. Recommended.

CENTRAL HONSHU

Hakone
Fuji-Hakone Guest House ($)
912, Sengokuhara, Hakone-machi, Kanagawa 250-06 tel: 0460 4 6577
A simple but clean Japanese inn in quiet surroundings. The owners speak English. Worth a couple of nights' stay (two nights minimum) to explore the region.

Fujiya Hotel ($$/$)
359 Miyanoshita, Hakone-machi, Ashigarashimogun 250-04 tel: 0460 2 2211
Built in 1878—one of the oldest Western-style hotels in Japan. Charming character and traditional Japanese service. Fine gardens.

Naraya Ryokan ($$$)
162 Miyanoshita, Hakone-machi, Ashigarashimogun 250-04
tel: 0460 2 2411
Opposite the Fujiya Hotel. A *ryokan* that has been in the same family for many generations. Elegant, *tatami* rooms with mountain views. First-class Japanese cuisine and hot-spring baths.

Fuji Five Lakes
Hotel Ashiwada ($$)
395 Nagahama, Ashiwada-mura, Minami-Isuru-gun, Yamanashi 401-4 tel: 0555 82 2321
On the shore of Lake Kawaguchi, a new, functional Japanese-style hotel; good base for climbing Mount Fuji in season.

Kawaguchiko Youth Hostel ($)
Eight- minute walk from Kawaguchiko station
tel: 0555 72 1431
Busy during Fuji climbing season, otherwise quiet. Closed Nov–late Mar.

Ise-shima National Park
Asa ($$)
109 Nakano-cho, Ise-shi 516 tel: 0596 22 4101
A family-run wooden-built *ryokan* with twelve rooms located in a traditional neighborhood area. The room price includes two meals which usually include specialities. The *ryokan* has a good local reputation for its food. The rooms themselves contain delightful antique features and each room is different.

Hoshide Ryokan ($)
2-15-2 Kawasaki, Iseshi, Mie Prefecture 516
tel: 0596 28 2377
A simple, traditional *ryokan*. The owners serve macrobiotic food for breakfast and dinner. 7 minutes walk to Iseshi station.

Ise City Hotel ($$)
1-11-31 Fukiage, Iseshi, Mie Prefecture 516
tel: 0596 28 2111
Close to the Hoshide *roykan*, a conveniently located business hotel offering friendly service and quite small but comfortable rooms.

Izu Peninsula
Ginsuiso Hotel ($$$)
2977-1 Nishina, Nishi Izumachi, Kamo-gun, Shizuoka 410-35
tel: 0558 52 1211
Very expensive, classy resort; *ryokan*-style hotel with superb clifftop location. Book well in advance.

Haji Minshuku ($)
708 Sotoura-Kaigan, Shimoda City
tel: 05582 2 2597
A friendly *minshuku*. The owner speaks English. Close to the beach. Price includes two meals.

Kaikomaru Minshuku ($)
Nishi-Kamo-gun, Shizuoka 410-35
tel: 0558 52 1054
At the opposite end of the scale to Ginsuiso: a simple, family-run *minshuku*, with its own hot-spring bath. No English spoken.

New Fujiya Hotel ($$)
1-16 Ginza-cho, Atami, Shizuoka 413
tel: 0557 81 0111
A straightforward, efficiently run, resort hotel. Indoor and outdoor hot-spring baths. A functional base for exploring Izu Peninsula.

Shimoda Tokyu Hotel ($$/$)
5-12-1 Shimoda, Shimoda, Shizuoka 415
tel: 05582 2 2411
Located on a hill overlooking Shimoda Bay, with sea and mountain views. Outdoor swimming pool, hot-spring baths. Large and impersonal but very practical.

Kobe
Arcons Hotel ($$)
3-7-1 Kitano-cho, Chuo-ku tel: 078 231 1538
Small but well-run hotel on Kitano-cho Hill. Some rooms with sea views. Take a cab if you arrive at the main station.

Hana Hotel ($$)
4-2-7 Nunobiki-cho, Chuo-ku
tel: 078 221 1087
A smallish, well-run business hotel with more character than one usually expects from this style of establishment. Comfortable, if small, well-equipped rooms. Handy coffee shop serves snacks

Hotel Okura Kobe ($$$)
2-1 Hatoba-cho, Chuo-ku, Kobe 650
tel: 078 333 0111
Good location in Merikan Park and close to down-town shopping areas; 35-story hotel with elegantly furnished rooms and impeccable service.

Kobe Portopia Hotel ($$$)
6-10-1 Minatojima, Nakamachi, Chuo-ku
tel: 078 302 1111
A sleek, modern hotel with elegant rooms with large picture windows that look out over the city or the sea. To arrive in appropriate up-to-date style, take the Portline monorail from Sannomiya station or a 15-minute taxi ride from Shin-Kobe station.

Kobe Washington Hotel ($$)
2-11-5 Shimoyamate-dori, Chuo-ku, Kobe 650
tel: 078 331 6111
An efficiently run business hotel with an atmos-phere more pleasant than is usually found in such establishments. Convenient for a one-night stop.

Ryokan Takayama-so ($)
400-1, Arima-cho, Kita-ku, Kobe, Hyogo
Prefecture 651-14 tel: 078 904 0744
Set in one of the oldest spas in Japan. Manager speaks English. Good food, and a hot-spring spa on the premises.

Nagoya

Hotel Sunroute Nagoya ($$)
2-35-24 Meieki, Nakamura-ku, Nagoya 450
tel: 052 571 2221
An unexpectedly bright and cheerful business hotel. Public areas quite spacious, rooms small. Located very close to Nagoya station.

International Hotel Nagoya ($$/$)
3-23-3 Nishiki, Naka-ku, Nagoya 460
tel: 052 961 3111
High-quality, long established popular hotel with a European feel. Western and Japanese restaurants available.

Nagoya Miyako Hotel ($$)
4-9-10 Meieki, Nakamura-ku, Nagoya 450
tel: 052 571 3211
A medium-priced hotel offering good service and convenient central location.

Osaka

Holiday Inn Nankai ($$)
2-5-15 Shinsai-bashi-suji, Chuo-ku, Osaka 542
tel: 066 213 8281
Close to Namba station, shopping and nightlife areas. Spacious rooms; children under 12 stay free. Western and Japanese restaurants.

Hotel New Otani ($$$)
1-4-1 Shiromi, Chuo-ku, Osaka 540
tel: 066 941 1111
One of the best hotels in Osaka, set in a new, futuristic building that towers over Osaka Castle. Services are comprehensive, prices are steep. Excellent fitness club.

Hotel Granvia Osaka ($$)
3-1-1 Umeda, Kita-ku, Osaka 530
tel: 066 344 1235
Within the Osaka station complex—the lobby opens on to the station. Busy location but very convenient for a one-night stop. Fortunately, the hotel rooms are soundproofed. Some have fine views over the city.

Shin-Osaka Sen-1 City Hotel ($)
2-2-17 Nishi-Miyahara, Yodogawa-ku, Osaka
532 tel: 066 394 3331
A basic but adequate business hotel if you're on a budget. Some rooms have private baths; other-wise, there are public baths. Rooms reasonably well equipped. The hotel lobby is on the sixth floor of the building.

KYOTO

Higashiyama Youth Hostel ($)
112 Shirakawabashi-goken-cho, Sanjo-dori,
Higashiyama-ku tel: 075 761 8135
Well-situated for Kyoto station. Guests obliged to take dinner and breakfast. Book ahead in season.

Hiiragiya Ryokan ($$$)
Aneyakoji-agaru, Fuyacho, Nakagyo-ku
tel: 075 221 1136
Expensive; extremely distinguished guests.

Hiraiwa Ryokan ($)
314, Hayao-cho, Kaminoguchi-agaru,
Ninomiyacho-dori, Shimogyo-ku
tel: 075 351 6748
Popular, central Japanese inn. Showers and com-mon bath only.

Hotel Alpha ($$)
Kawaramachi, Sanjo-agaru, Nakagyo-ku
tel: 075 241 2000
Excellent location in central Kyoto. Comfortable, business-style hotel. Deluxe rooms brighter and bigger, worth the extra outlay. Restaurant serves classic Japanese cuisine.

Kyoto Century Hotel ($$)
680 Higashishiokoji-cho, Shiokoji-sagaru,
Higashinotoin-dori, Shimogyo-ku
tel: 075 351 0111
Near Kyoto station. Good-value Japanese-style rooms available.

Kyoto Holiday Inn ($$)
36 Nishihiraki-cho, Tekano, Sakyo-ku
tel: 075 721 3131
Far from city center, but provides good facilities and the best sports hotel complex (including an ice rink) in Kyoto. Shuttle bus to town center. Rooms for people with disabilities.

Kyoto Park Hotel ($$)
Sanjusangendo Side, Higashiyama-ku
tel: 075 525 3111
In eastern Kyoto opposite National Museum. Combines Western and Japanese features.

Kyoto Royal Hotel ($$)
Sanjo-agaru Kawaramachi, Nakagyo-ku
tel: 075 223 1234
Prime location on central Kawamachi-dori. Service is good and location convenient.

Kyoto Utano Youth Hostel ($)
29 Nakayama-cho, Uzumasa, Ukyo-ku
tel: 075 462 2288
Near Ryoanji Temple. Simple concrete structure offering basic accommodations. Bike rental and laundry facilities.

Matsuba-ya Ryokan ($)
Nishiiru Higashinotoin, Kamijuzuya-machi-dori,
Shimogyo-ku tel: 075 351 3727
Inexpensive Japanese inn close to Kyoto station and Sanjusangendo Temple. Homely atmosphere, shared bath.

Accommodations and Restaurants

Miyako Hotel ($$$)
Sanjo-Keage, Higashiyama-ku
tel: 075 771 7111
Well-established hotel with first-class reputation. Western- and Japanese-style rooms.

Nashinoki Inn ($)
Agaru Imadegawa, Nashinoki-dori, Kamigyo-ku
tel: 075 241 1543
North of Imperial Palace; a family-run *ryokan* in a quiet district.

New Miyako Hotel ($$)
Hachijo-guchi, Kyoto Station
tel: 075 661 7111
Sister hotel to the classier and more expensive Miyako Hotel. Across from Kyoto station. Rooms small but many restaurants and bars. Popular with younger Japanese travelers and tour groups.

Ohara Nenbutsuji Kaikan ($)
Raigoincho, Ohara, Sakyo-ku
tel: 075 744 2540
One hour by bus from Kyoto station. Take bus from stop 1 in front of Kyoto Central Post Office to Ohara.

Pension Higashiyama ($)
Sanjo-sagaru, Shirakawa-suji, Higashiyama-ku
tel: 075 882 1181
Located in eastern Kyoto, by the Shirakawa canal. Clean, small hotel, constructed in 1985. Western- and Japanese-style rooms available. Doors close at 11:30 PM.

Takaragaike Prince Hotel ($$$)
Takaragaike, Sakyo-ku
tel: 075 712 1111
Located in the north of the city. Large rooms, views of mountains and forests.

Tani House ($)
8 Daitokuji-cho, Murasakino, Kita-ku
tel: 075 492 5489
Japanese-style inn run by friendly Japanese couple. Popular with foreign visitors on a tight budget. Near Koto-in temple.

Tawaraya Ryokan ($$$)
Fuyacho, Aneyakoji-Kita, Nakagyo-ku
tel: 075 211 5566
Very expensive, traditional *ryokan*, generally acknowledged as one of the finest in Japan. Booked months in advance.

Three Sisters Inn Annex ($$)
Heian Jingu, Higashi Kita Kado, Sakyo-ku
tel: 075 761 6333
A traditional Kyoto *ryokan*-style inn accustomed to foreigners. Quiet and comfortable accommodations.

Temple Accommodations

The following temples accept foreign guests; book in advance by letter. Vegetarian breakfast usually included in the price. Dormitory-style accommodations are the norm.

Hiden-in Temple ($)
35 Sennyuji Sandai-cho, Higashiyama-ku
tel: 075 561 8781
From Kyoto station take bus 208 to Sennyuji-michi stop.

Myokenji Temple ($)
Teranouchi Horikawa, Kamigyo-ku
tel: 075 414 0808
From Kyoto station take bus 9 to Horikawa Teranouchi stop.

Myorenji Temple ($)
Teranouchi Omiya higashi, Kamigyo-ku
tel: 075 451 3527
Same as for Myokenji Temple.

WESTERN HONSHU

Hagi

Hokumon Yashiki Ryokan ($$/$)
210 Horiuchi, Hagi-shi, Yamaguchi Prefecture 758 tel: 08382 2 7521
Ryokan inn, with spacious rooms and traditional service, in old *samurai* neighborhood near castle grounds.

Tomoe Ryokan ($$)
608 Hijiwara, Hagi-shi, Koboji Yamaguchi Prefecture 758 tel: 08382 2 0150
An elegant old inn with lovely gardens. Food excellent. Bath and toilets shared.

Himeji

Himeji Castle Hotel ($$)
210 Hojyo, Himeji 670 tel: 0792 84 3311
Near the station and the castle. Outdoor swimming pool and Western-style restaurant.

Hiroshima

ANA Hotel Hiroshima ($$/$)
7-20 Nakamachi, Naka-ku, Hiroshima
tel: 082 241 1111
One of Hiroshima's best hotels, five minutes' walk from the Peace Park and business district. Rooms spacious and well equipped.

Hiroshima City Hotel ($$)
1-4 Kyobashi-cho, Minami-ku, Hiroshima
tel: 082 263 5111
Regular business hotel right across from the station. Convenient for a one-night stop.

Ikedaya Minshuku ($)
6-36 Dobashi, Naka-ku, Hiroshima
tel: 082 231 3329
Good accommodations near Peace Park. Dinner and breakfast included in the price.

Mitakiso ($$$)
1-7 Mitaki-cho, Nishi-ku
tel: 082 237 1402
A highly recommended traditional *ryokan*. The better rooms look inward toward a delightful Japanese garden. The public baths are an absolute treat and the cuisine, served in your rooms, first class. Room rates include dinner and breakfast. Worth a night's stay if you can afford a room overlooking the garden.

Kurashiki

Ryokan Kurashiki ($$/$)
4-1 Honmachi, Kurashiki 710
tel: 0864 22 0730
Splendid *ryokan* in the heart of old Kurashiki. Constructed from an old merchant's house and connecting rice and sugar warehouses. Excellent restaurant attached that serves classic *Kaiseki* Japanese food.

Matsue

Horaiso Ryokan ($$)
Tonomachi, Matsue 690 tel: 0852 21 4337
Pleasing *ryokan* in private location near the castle.

Tokyu Inn ($$)
590 Asahimachi, Matsue 690
tel: 0852 27 0109
Handy location across the street from Matsue station. Part of a business hotel chain. Reasonably sized rooms and most facilities that you might require.

Miyajima
Jyukeiso Ryokan ($$)
Miyajima, Saeki-gun 739-05
tel: 0829 44 0300
A family run *ryokan*, on a small hill east of the pier. English spoken; Western breakfast available on request.

Okayama
Culture Hotel ($$)
1-3-2 Gakunan-cho, Okayama City 700
tel: 0862 55 1122
Imaginatively designed hotel with cheerful rooms and a friendly staff. Western-style restaurant.

Tsuwano
Meigetsu Ryokan ($$)
Tsuwano-cho, Kanoashi-gun 699-56
tel: 08567 2 0685
Excellent traditional *ryokan* located in the middle of town.

Wakasagi no Yado Minshuku ($)
Tsuwano-cho, Kanoashi-gun 699-56, Shimane-ken *tel: 08567 2 1146*
Small, family-run *minshuku*. Japanese and Western breakfast. Japanese dinner.

SHIKOKU

Kochi
Hotel Takasago ($)
2-1 Ekimae-cho, Kochi-shi, Kochi 780
tel: 0888 22 1288
Slightly scruffy *ryokan*, but food is fine, and price reasonable.

Washington Hotel ($)
1-8-25 Otesuji, Kochi-shi, Kochi 780
tel: 0888 23 6111
Within easy reach of the castle. Fairly large rooms, friendly staff.

Matsuyama
ANA Hotel Matsuyama ($$$)
3-2-1 Ichiban-cho, Matsuyama 790
tel: 0899 335511
Matsuyama's best hotel, in the city center. Near the cable car for Matsuyama Castle and streetcar stop for Dogo Onsen. Variety of bars and restaurants.

Shinsen-en Youth Hostel ($)
22-3 Dogohimezaka Otsu, Matsuyama 790
tel: 0899 336366
Near Dogo Onsen, busy in season. Laundry and bike rental facilities.

Taikei Business Hotel ($$)
3-1-15 Heiwa Dori, Matsuyama 790
tel: 0899 43 3560
Cheerful, pleasant business hotel with more character than most of its kind. Public baths and saunas on the premises.

Shodo island
There are numerous *minshuku* on the island. Book when you arrive in Tonosho, or at the tourist office in Takamatsu before you leave (see pages 182–183).

Takamatsu
Hotel Kawaroku ($$)
1-2 Hyakken-machi, Takamatsu 760
tel: 0878 21 5666
A combination of *ryokan* and ordinary hotel. Western- and Japanese-style rooms, Japanese food served in your room or Western food in the hotel restaurant. In the heart of the city.

Takamatsu Grand Hotel ($$)
1-5-10 Kotobuki-cho, Takamatsu 760
tel: 0878 51 5757
Near the station, shopping arcades, and the pier. Lobby on third floor with views over Tamamo Park.

KYUSHU

Aso National Park
Pension Flower Garden ($)
3096-4 Takamori, Takamori-machi, Kumamoto-ken *tel: 09676 2 3012*
Western-style pension in pretty setting. Good food. Cab ride from Takamori station, or call and the hotel will arrange to pick you up.

Yamaguchi Ryokan ($$)
Tarutama Onsen, Choyo-son, Kyushu
tel: 09676 7 0006
Mountain *onsen* set in delightful countryside. Cab ride from Aso-Shimoda station.

Beppu
Sakaeya Minshuku ($)
Ida, Kannawa, Beppu 874 *tel: 0977 66 6234*
Well-established *minshuku* with its own hot-spring baths. House is old and has character. Food basic but well cooked. Book ahead.

Suginoi Hotel ($$$)
Kankaiji, Beppu 874 *tel: 0977 24 1141*
Beppu's best known, largest, and most opulent hotel, more like a mini resort. Gigantic baths. Not the ideal place if you are seeking peace and quiet.

Tamanoyu ($$$)
Yufin-cho, Oita-ken *tel: 0977 84 2158*
Yufin hot-spring resort is one hour by bus from Beppu and an elegant, fashionable, and sophisticated alternative to it. The Tamanoyu is expensive but an exceptionally refined and charming traditional inn. Despite this, the atmosphere is relaxed, making a stay here even more worth the premium.

Fukuoka/Hakata
Chisan Hotel Hakata ($$)
2-8-11 Hakata-eki-mae, Hakata-ku
tel: 092 411 3211
A friendly, well-run business hotel, five minutes' walk from the Guchi exit of Hakata Station. Higher-priced rooms are larger with sea views. The Japanese and Western breakfast are good value.

Clio Court Hotel ($$)
5-3 Hakataeki-Chuogai, Hakata-ku 812
tel: 092 472 1111
Modern, chic hotel designed by Rei Kurokawa. Rooms are decorated in a variety of styles; you can

271

choose when you book. Western and Japanese restaurants and cheaper food bars. No single rooms.

Dazaifu Youth Hostel ($)
1-18-1 Sanjo, Dazaifu 818-01
tel: 092 922 8740
Open to visitors with or without a YH card, this is clean, budget accommodation with self-catering facilities. The rooms are *tatami* floored and sleeping is on futons.

Hotel New Otani ($$$)
1-1-2 Watanabe-dori, Chuo-ku, Fukuoka 810
tel: 092 714 1111
First-class hotel with services to match. Rooms large and very tastefully decorated.

Mitsui Urban Hotel ($$)
2-8-15 Hakata-ekimoe, Hakata-ku
tel: 092 451 5111
A straightforward business hotel. The rooms have good facilities and, despite being small, feel airy because of their relatively large windows. A 10-minute walk from the Guchi exit of Hakata station.

Toyo Hotel ($$)
1-9-36 Hakata-eki, Higashi, Hakata-ku 812
tel: 092 474 1121
Business hotel conveniently located by Hakata station. Functional but comfortable enough. Rooms on top floors have more light.

Kagoshima
Kagoshima Hayashida Hotel ($$)
12-22 Higashisengoku-cho, Kagoshima 892
tel: 099 224 4111
In the center of town. Rather eccentric, space-age theme in the décor.

Shigetomiso Ryokan ($$$)
31-7 Shimizu-cho, Kagoshima 890
tel: 099 247 3155
Very expensive *ryokan* that is set in a former villa once belonging to the Shimizu ruling clan.

Kumamoto
Kumamoto Shiritsu Youth Hostel ($)
5-15-55, Shimazaki-machi, Kumamoto 860
tel: 096 352 2441
Efficiently run youth hostel, open to both men and women. Proprietor can speak English.

Maruko Hotel ($$)
11-10 Kamitori-cho, Kumamoto 860
tel: 096 353 1241
Japanese inn-style hotel with mainly *tatami* rooms, which are comfortable and air-conditioned. Western and Japanese meals are available.

New Sky Hotel ($$)
2 Higashiamidaji-cho, Kumamoto 860
tel: 096 354 2111
Modern, large, and attractive hotel that offers excellent amenities at a reasonable price. Enjoys a convenient location—near Kumamoto Castle and Suizenji Park.

Miyazaki
Seaside Hotel Phoenix ($$)
3083 Hamayama Shioji, Miyazaki 880-01
tel: 0985 39 1111
Mix of Japanese- and Western-style rooms. Relaxing and cheerful. Facilities of the more expensive sister Sun Hotel Phoenix are available.

Nagasaki
Nagasaki Grand Hotel ($$$)
5-3 Manzai-machi, Nagasaki 850
tel: 095 823 1234
Well-established, small and discreet hotel, which has a beer garden. Laid out in a tropical setting and open in spring and summer.

Nagasaki Youth Hostel ($)
2 Tateyama-cho, Nagasaki 850
tel: 095 823 5032
Located near Nagasaki station. Open to nonmembers. Accommodations are basic, but laundry facilities are provided for residents.

Nagasaki Washington Hotel ($$)
9-1 Shinchi-machi, Nagasaki 850
tel: 095 828 1211
Part of a dependable chain of business hotels. Convenient for sightseeing. Located in the Hamano-machi shopping district and close to Chinatown.

Sakamoto-ya Ryokan ($$$)
2-13 Kanaya-machi, Nagasaki 850
tel: 095 826 8211
An elegant wooden *ryokan* that provides a personalized service to its guests. *Shippoku* (a Nagasaki meal of various dishes) served on request.

Tanpopo Minshuku ($)
21-7 Hoeicho, Nagasaki 852 tel: 095 861 6230
Basic *tatami* rooms at budget prices. The concrete building is ugly but within walking distance of Peace Park. The nearest station is Urakami; call from there and the hotel will arrange to pick you up.

OKINAWA

Central Okinawa
Okinawa Hotel ($$/$)
1478 Kishaba, Kitagusuku-son, Nakagami-gun, Okinawa tel: 098 935 4321
On a hill in central Okinawa; fine views and comprehensive service. Outdoor swimming pool is surrounded by tropical plants.

Naha
Okinawa Harbor View Hotel ($$$)
2-46 Izumizaki, Naha-shi, Okinawa
tel: 098 853 2111
Set on the island, providing a combination of the best city and resort hotel.

Pacific Hotel Okinawa ($$)
3-6-1 Nishi, Naha-shi, Okinawa
tel: 098 868 5162
Good, comfortable, and slightly less expensive than the Harbor View.

NORTHERN HONSHU

Kakunodate
Hyakusuien Minshuku ($)
31 Shimonaka-machi, Kakunodate, Senboku-gun tel: 0187 55 5715
Central *minshuku* in a converted 19th-century warehouse. Old-fashioned *irori* hearth and mini-museum included on the premises.

Ishikawa Ryokan ($/$)
32 Iwase-machi, Kakunodate, Senboku-gun
tel: 0187 54 2030
Modern but quite unpretentious and welcoming

Japanese inn, run by friendly family who serve good food.

Kamikochi

Kamikochi Imperial Hotel ($$$)
Kamikochi, Azumi-mura, Nagano-ken
tel: 0263 95 2001
Modern, high-class lounge hotel run by the Imperial Hotel of Tokyo.

Nishi-Itoya Sanso Inn ($$)
Kamikochi, Azumi-mura, Nagano-ken
tel: 0263 95 2206
Traditional wooden inn. Accommodations with meals. Near Kappabashi bridge.

Kanazawa

Garden Hotel ($$)
2-16-16 Honcho, Kanazawa 920
tel: 076 263 3333
A rather welcoming business hotel located close to the station. Rooms are small, but beds are a comfortable size and windows open. Practical for a short stay.

Kanazawa Tokyu Hotel ($$/$)
2-1-1 Kohrinbo, Kanazawa 920
tel: 076 231 2411
New hotel in the center. Public areas spacious. Guest rooms are small but rooms on the higher floors have good views.

Miyabo Ryokan ($$$)
3 Shimo-Kakinokibatake, Kanazawa 920
tel: 076 231 4228
Traditional and very expensive inn surrounded by the oldest private garden in the city. The best rooms open on to the garden.

Murataya Ryokan ($)
1-5-2 Katamachi, Kanazawa 920
tel: 076 263 0455
Relaxed Japanese inn in the middle of town. No private baths, but *tatami* rooms comfortable.

Matsumoto

Hotel New Station ($$/$)
1-1-11 Chuo, Matsumoto 390
tel: 0263 35 3850
Convenient location near train station. Friendly business hotel offering good value. In-house food delicious.

Matsumoto Tokyu Inn ($$)
1-3-21 Fukashi, Matsumoto 390
tel: 0263 36 0109
Better class of business hotel, close to the train station. Cheaper rooms are small, bigger rooms rather expensive, but a pleasant place to stay if you are using it as a base for exploring the area.

Morioka

Hotel Metropolitan Morioka ($$/$)
1-44 Morioka, Ekimae-dori, Morioka, Iwate 020
tel: 0196 25 1211
Within the station complex. The rooms are designed for sleeping rather than lingering, but there is a good Chinese restaurant on the premises.

Ogimachi

Accommodations in Ogimachi are restricted to thatched farmhouses, *minshuku* bed, break- fast, and dinner accommodations. Book at the village tourist office (tel: 0576 96 1751).

Sado Island

Sado Seaside Hotel ($)
80 Sumiyoshi, Ryotsu-shi, Sado Island
tel: 0259 27 7211
Cheerful, inexpensive hotel. A short cab ride away from the Ryotsu ferry port. Japanese-style rooms with private bath.

San Kei Kan Minshuku ($)
Negai 260, Ryotsu-shi, Sado Island
tel: 0259 26 2440
Friendly, family-run *minshuku* by the beach. No English spoken.

Sendai

Dochuan Youth Hostel ($)
31 Kitayashiki, Ohnoda, Taihaku-ku, Sendai, Miyagi 98 *tel: 022 247 0511*
Thirty minutes by bus or cab from the station, this is the best youth hostel in the region. A converted thatched-roofed farmhouse set on the edge of the countryside.

Sendai Hotel ($$)
1-10-25 Chuo, Sendai, Miyagi 980
tel: 022 225 5171
Modern, but well-established, reputable hotel, located close to the station.

273

Takayama

Hishuya Ryokan ($$/$)
1-464 Kami Okamotocho, Takayama 506
tel: 0577 33 4001
Good traditional inn near Hida-no-sato village outside Takayama. Quiet and refined atmosphere.

Kinnikan Ryokan ($$/$)
48 Asahimachi, Takayama 506
tel: 0577 32 3131
First-class traditional Japanese inn in the heart of old Takayama. Small and popular; best to book ahead.

Yamakyu Minshuku ($)
58 Tenshoji, Takayama 506
tel: 0577 32 3756
A cross between a *minshuku* and a *ryokan*. Reputations for good food and a delightful public bath.

Yamagata

Goto Matabei Ryokan ($$)
2-2-30 Hatago-machi, Yamagata 990
tel: 0236 22 0357
Old, fairly comfortable Japanese inn. Plenty of character and simple but well-prepared food.

Washington Hotel ($$)
1-4-31 Nanoka-machi, Yamagata 990
tel: 0236 24 1515
Straightforward, functional business hotel, part of a chain that generally provides good service.

HOKKAIDO

Abashiri

Sakura-so Minshuku ($)
27-41 Omagari, Abashiri-shi, Hokkaido
tel: 0152 44 2337
Straightforward with pleasant atmosphere. Helpful, friendly owners.

Accommodations and Restaurants

Akan kohan

Akan Angel Youth Hostel ($)
*5-1 Shuri Komanbetsu–Akan-Kohan, Akan 085,
Hokkaido tel: 0154 67 2309*
Well-run youth hostel. Busy in season.

Nibushi no Sato Minshuku ($)
*Kussharo-Kohan, Teshikaga-cho, Kawakami-
gun, Hokkaido tel: 0154 83 2294*
A cab ride out of Akan-Kohan village. Has its own
hot-spring baths. No English spoken.

Yamaura Hotel ($$)
*Akan-Kohan, Akan 085, Hokkaido
tel: 0154 67 2311*
Small hotel on the lakeside at the southern end of
Akan-Kohan village. Mainly Japanese-style *tatami*
rooms. Western-style rooms tend to look away
from the lake.

Hakodate

Hotel Hakodate Royal ($$)
*16-9 Omori-cho, Hakodate 040
tel: 0138 26 8181*
Western-style hotel. Efficient, cheerful staff. Cab
ride from the station.

Niceday Inn ($)
*9–11 Otimachi, Hakodate 040
tel: 0138 22 5919*
The Proprietors speak no English but give foreign
guests a warm welcome. No food, but many
restaurants nearby.

Noboribetsu Onsen

Akiyoshi Hotel ($$/$)
*Noboribetsu Onsen, Noboribetsu 059,
Hokkaido tel: 01438 4 2261*
Ryokan-style hotel, friendly, efficient service.
Central location. One of the best places to stay in
the area.

Kiyomizu Ryokan ($)
*60 Noboribetsu, Onsen-cho, Noboribetsu 059,
Hokkaido tel: 01438 4 2145*
Japanese inn a short walk from the bus terminal
serving good *tempura*.

Suzuki Ryokan ($$)
*Karurusu Onsen, Noboribetsu-shi, Hokkaido
tel: 01438 4 2285*
A 30-minute cab ride out of Noboribetsu Onsen in
a quiet mountain location. Large old inn equipped
with a traditional hot-spring bath.

Sapporo

Fujiya Santus Hotel ($$)
*Nishi 7, Kita 3, Chuo-ku, Sapporo 060
tel: 011 271 3344*
Small hotel offering a warm welcome and very
good value for money. Located near JR Sapporo
station and shopping district.

Hotel Alpha Sapporo ($$/$)
*Nishi 5, Minami 1, Chuo-ku, Sapporo 060
tel: 011 221 2333*
Classy city hotel near shopping district and the
Susukino nightlife area. Good service, friendly
staff.

Nakamuraya Ryokan ($)
*Nishi 7, Kita 3, Chuo-ku, Sapporo 060
tel: 011 241 2111*
Japanese inn with modern facilities and local food.
Near station and city center.

Sapporo Washington Hotel II ($$)
*Nishi 6, Kita 5, Chuo-ku, Sapporo 060
tel: 011 222 3311*
Better class of business hotel. Part of a reputable
chain.

Sounkyo Onsen

Daisetsu zan Shirakaba-so Youth Hostel ($)
*1418 Higashikawa-machi, Kamikawa-gun,
Hokkaido tel: 0166 97 2246*
Accessible by bus from Asahikawa or Sounkyo
Onsen. Scenically located hostel with its own hot-
spring baths and good food.

Kumoi Ryokan ($$)
*Sounkyo, Kamikawa-gun, Hokkaido
tel: 01658 5 3553*
New Japanese inn with its own hot-spring bath and
some rooms with private bath. Western breakfast
is provided on request.

Sounkaku Grand Hotel ($$)
*Sounkyo, Kamikawa-gun, Hokkaido
tel: 01658 5 3111*
A *ryokan*-style hotel. One of the better and more
reasonably priced of the many resort establish-
ments in the area. Always busy in summer.

Toyako Onsen

Okoiso Minshuku ($)
*83 Sobetsu-cho, Sobetsu-Onsen, Hokkaido
tel: 01427 5 2522*
In a small *onsen* district 1 mile (2km) west of
Toyaku Onsen. Good, clean establishment serving
fine food.

Showa Shinzan Youth Hostel ($)
*103 Sobetsu-cho, Sobetsu-Onsen, Hokkaido
tel: 01427 5 2283*
The hostel is slightly shabby but has a good hot-
spring bath.

Toya Park Hotel ($$)
Toyako Onsen, Hokkaido tel: 01427 5 2445
Small hotel offering attractive views of the lake.
Excellent service provided. The manager speaks
English.

RESTAURANTS

Almost all large Japanese towns and cities
have an abundance of restaurants to suit every
imaginable taste and budget. At home, space
is usually too limited for socializing—and eating and drinking out is very much a part of the
Japanese way of life.

Whether you are buying street food or dining in
an expensive restaurant, service and hygiene
standards are first class. With such a large
choice available, the Japanese tend to dine out
in their own neighborhoods and to travel only to
establishments with a particular reputation or a
special style of food.

Keep in mind the strategic problem of finding a
restaurant in a strange district. The Japanese
address system is complex and even cab
drivers often have to stop and phone a place
on the way there.

If you see a likely establishment during the
day, ask for a business card: they usually have
a map on the back, which can be shown to the
cab driver.

Cash is preferred to credit cards, especially in smaller establishments.
Price categories per person, without drinks:
Expensive ($$$) over ¥8,500
Moderate ($$) ¥2,500– 8,500
Budget ($) under ¥2,500

TOKYO

Ajanta ($)
3-11 Nibancho, Chiyoda-ku
tel: 03 3264 6955 Subway: Kojimachi
This Indian restaurant is an old favorite, with the simplest of settings but one of the most comprehensive menus in Tokyo. The vegetarian and non-vegetarian, south and north Indian dishes are as authentic as you will find.

Antonio's ($$)
Dai 22, Daikyo Building, First Floor, 7-3-6
Minami Aoyama, Minato-ku tel: 03 3797 0388
Subway: Omotesando
Excellent Italian food at a reasonable price. Traditional service in classic restaurant surroundings (e.g. starched white tablecloths). Location alongside busy expressway not the best, but once inside the noise and bustle can be forgotten.

Bengawan Solo ($$)
7-18-13 Roppongi, Minato-ku
tel: 03 3408 5698 Subway: Roppongi
Indonesian restaurant serving good *rijsttafel* (a variety of dishes served on one tray) at a fairly reasonable price.

Benjarong ($$)
Miyata Building 2F, 1-4-12 Kabukicho,
Shinjuku-ku tel: 03 3209 7064
Subway: Shinjuku
An elegant Thai restaurant with cuisine to match, beautifully prepared by the former chef of a top Bangkok hotel. The menu is fully explained in English. Lunch prices are much lower than those at dinner.

Bentenyama Miyako ($$)
2-1-16, Asakusa, Taito-ku tel: 03 3844 0034
Subway: Asakusa
Famous *sushi* and *sashimi* restaurant founded in 1866. The atmospheric interior seems to have been changed little since then. Popular with the *sushi* cognoscenti. To taste a range of *sushi*, order the set 12-piece menu.

Bougainvillea ($$)
Romanee Building 2F, 2-25-9 Dogenzaka,
Shibuya-ku tel: 03 3496 5537
Subway: Shibuya
Vietnamese food may yet challenge Thai for the "ethnic" crown. This popular place has a wide choice of authentic dishes: noodle soups, crab with coriander, spring rolls, sweet-and-sour pork or chicken, meatballs, crisp salads.

Chez Pierre ($$$)
1-23-10 Minami Aoyama, Minato-ku
tel: 03 3475 1400 Subway: Nogizaku
Classic French cooking that has been maintained at a consistently high standard over a period of many years. They have an excellent range of pastries and gateaux, so make sure you leave room for a dessert. Comfortable, very French interior. Bar with stools where you can eat alone and not feel out of place.

Edo-Gin ($$)
4-5-1 Tsukiji, Chuo-ku tel: 03 3543 4401
Subway: Tsukiji
Well-established and popular, serving *sashimi* and *sushi* made from the freshest fish from the nearby market. You can see some swimming in a tank.

Flo ($$)
4-3-3 Jingu-mae, Harajuku
tel: 03 5474 0611 Subway: Omotesando
Authentic French food in French bistro surroundings. Good value, especially the all-you-can-eat buffet upstairs.

Fukusushi ($$)
5-7-8 Roppongi, Minato-ku tel: 03 3402 4116
Subway: Roppongi
Authentic, traditional Japanese *sushi* served in sleek, fashionable surroundings. English-language menus available. Cocktail bar for pre-dinner drinks.

Futaba ($)
2-8-11 Ueno, Taito-ku tel: 03 3831 6483
Subway: Ueno
Ueno is well known for *tonkatsu* (fried pork cutlet), eaten with rice, soup, and pickled vegetables; this is one of the oldest restaurants serving the dish.

Goemon ($$)
1-1-26 Hon-Komagome, Bunkyo-ku
tel: 03 3811 2015 Subway: Hakusan
An excellent restaurant specializing in tofu dishes. Delightful, tiny Japanese garden. Outdoor eating in warm weather.

Gold Leaf ($$$)
Taisei Koki Building B1F, 5-4-12 Hiroo, Shibuya-ku tel: 03 3447 1212 Subway: Hiro-o
In Tokyo, Thai food is booming. This is one of the most attractive places in the city to eat it, with a décor of teak wood and black lacquer complementing the colorful dishes. Bangkok-trained chefs prepare subtly spiced salads, soups laced with the quintessential Thai ingredients of lemongrass, coriander, chili, and coconut milk, and delicious curries. Service is polished and the menu explains it all in English.

Han ($$)
4-3-20 Torano-mon, Minato-ku
tel: 03 3578 8293 Subway: Kamiya-cho
One of a chain, with real Japanese atmosphere and traditional cooking. An eager young man kneels to take your order, tapping it into his hand-held terminal. Lots of small dishes give you a chance to try new experiences or old favorites.

Hard Rock Café ($$)
5-4-20 Roppongi, Minato-ku
tel: 03 3408 7018 Subway: Roppongi
Hamburgers, salads, and snacks, ice creams and pie, to the sound of loud music. Long lines form at weekends.

Hassan ($$)
BIF Denki Building 6-1-20 Roppongi, Minato-ku
tel: 03 3403 8333 Subway: Roppongi
A busy traditional restaurant with a choice of *tatami* (straw mats) or chairs. The set menus of *tempura*, *sukiyaki*, and *shabu-shabu* include all-you-can-eat options, at a higher price, for the very hungry.

Hayashi ($$/$)
4th Floor, Sanno Kaikan Building, 2-14-1
Akasaka tel: 3582 4078
Serves the dishes of Hida, a mountainous region

275

Accommodations and Restaurants

in central Honshu. Old farmhouse atmosphere. Specializes in food grilled over *hibachi* at your table.

Heichinrou ($$)
Shibuya Hillside building, Second Floor, 1-19-3 Jinnan, Shibuya-ku tel: 03 3464 7888
Subway: Shibuya
The Heichinrou opened its doors many years ago and has been busy ever since serving classic Chinese food of consistently high quality. Popular with Japanese and Chinese customers alike. Lunch time set meals and afternoon dim sum good value.

Heirokunzushi ($)
5-8-5 Jingumae, Shibuya-ku
tel: 03 3498 3968 Subway: Meiji Jingu-mae
An economical way to eat *sushi*: little dishes, each containing a pair of pieces, circle past you on a conveyor belt and you pick the dishes that take your fancy. The chefs work to replace the *sushi* while they chat with customers.

Higono-ya ($$)
AG Building 1F, 3-18-17 Minami-Aoyama, Minato-ku tel: 03 3423 4462
Subway: Omotesando
Tasty combinations of fish and shellfish, vegetables and meats grilled on bamboo skewers. Traditional décor of black wood and white screens.

Honke Ponta ($$)
3-23-3, Ueno, Taito-ku tel: 03 3831 2351
Subway: Ueno-hirokoji
Opened before World War II and still run by the same family, this *tonkatsu* restaurant has a deserved reputation for serving the best pork in town. Seafood also available. Worth a visit just for the interior décor, which has remained pretty much unchanged in the last 50 years.

Inakaya ($$$)
3-12-7 Akasaka, Minato-ku tel: 3586 3054
Subway: Akasaka
Lots of noise and atmosphere. Heaps of various types of food; select whatever you wish and the chef, on a raised platform behind the counter, will cook it to order.

Jinya ($$)
My City Building 7F, Shinjuku Station, 3-38-1 Shinjuku-ku tel: 03 3352 0018
Subway: Shinjuku
Family-style Japanese cooking, beautifully presented. There is a choice of *tatami* or conventional table and chairs.

Johnny Rockets ($)
Coco Roppongi Building 2F, 3-11-10 Roppongi, Minato-ku tel: 03 3423 1955
Subway: Roppongi
Good, freshly made hamburgers, french fries, and salads, and other fast food staples.

Kisoji ($)
Ginza Jujiya Building 5F, 3-5-4 Ginza, Chuo-ku tel: 03 3567 0406
Subway: Ginza
A convenient Ginza spot for budget set-menu lunches of soup and rice with fish or chicken.

Komagata Dojo ($$)
1-7-12 Komagata, Taito-ku tel: 3842 4001
Subway: Asakusa
Dojo are small river fish, and this establishment has been serving them in a variety of dishes for nearly 200 years. *Tatami* (mat) seating.

Konomi ($$$)
1-7-2 Nishi-Asakusa, Taito-ku
tel: 03 3843 7773 Subway: Tawaramachi
A small restaurant in the Kappabashi district, specializing in the cuisine of Kyoto. *Kyobento*, a double-decker lacquered box lunch of two dozen little seasonal dishes, is an aesthetic treat.

Kusa No 1 ($$)
4-6-7 Azabu Juban, Minato-ku
tel: 03 3455 8356 Subway: Roppongi
Authentic Korean food served in no-frills manner in simple surroundings. Nevertheless, popular with Koreans from the local Korean Embassy and Japanese daring enough to sample the strong flavors and smells of this under-recognized cuisine.

Kyubei ($$$)
8-7-6 Ginza, Chuo-ku tel: 03 3571 6523
Subway: Higashi-Ginza
Founded many years ago, and still going strong, this restaurant has some of the most expertly made *sushi* to be found anywhere in Japan.

La Tour d'Argent ($$$)
New Otami Hotel, 4-1 Kioi-cho, Chiyoda-ku
tel: 03 3239 3111 Subway: Akasakamitsuke
The first branch outside Paris of the famous La Tour d'Argent. Absolutely the finest French and Japanese-inspired dishes in opulent surroundings. Very expensive.

Lintaro ($$)
BIF Seigetsudo Building, 5-9-15 Ginza, Chuo-ku tel: 03 3571 2037 Subway: Ginza
Lintaro Mizuhama is the friendly owner of the restaurant that bears his name, and he is often to be found chatting to the diners or directing the service. He's a Ginza native and expert: his family has been here for centuries. The deep basement room is a surprise, with its high ceiling and Italian Renaissance pictures. The food is Italian but with Japanese flair. Superbly fresh salads and vegetables come from the restaurant's gardens.

Mai-Thai ($$)
1-18-16 Ebisu, Shibuya-ku
tel: 03 3280 1155 JR: Ebisu
This small, cheerful, and popular spot in a side street, serves a typical Thai menu at reasonable prices. One of a growing choice of eating places in the fast-developing Ebisu area.

Mominoki House ($$$)
2-18-5 Jingu-mae, Harajuku tel: 3405 9144
Subway: Harajuku.
Excellent natural foods restaurant serving idiosyncratic menu inspired by macrobiotic/ French/ Japanese foods and cooking styles. Good-value fixed-lunch.

Nakase ($$$)
1-39-13 Asakusa, Taito-ku
tel: 03 3841 4015 Subway: Asakusa
A famous and long-established *tempura* restaurant near Nakamise-dori. Follow your nose to the delicious smells, but be prepared to wait. Often the line forms outside the door well before opening time. Lunch is the best—for economy, and because the area closes down early.

Nanbantei ($$)
4-5-6 Roppongi, Minato-ku
tel: 03 3402 0606 Subway: Roppongi
A popular *yakitori* (grilled food) restaurant with very friendly atmosphere.

Rice Terrace ($$)
2-7-9 Nishi-Azabu, Minato-ku
tel: 03 3498 6271 Subway: Nogizaka
A relaxed setting for some of the best Thai food in Tokyo. The service is friendly but polished. Try to get a table downstairs; the upper level is cramped.

Robata ($$/$)
1-3-8 Yuraku-cho, Chiyoda-ku
tel: 03 3591 1905 Subway: Yuraku-cho
Set in a replica of an old Japanese farmhouse with an authentic rustic interior. Good regional cuisine.

Rock 'n' Roll Diner ($)
Big Ben Building B1F, 2-5-2 Kitazawa,
Setagaya-ku tel: 03 3411 6565
Subway: Yoyogi-uehara
American-style salads, hamburgers, and sandwiches in a big, busy 1960s environment.

Roppongi Sumida ($$$)
Aoba Roppongi Building B1F, 3-16-33
Roppongi, Minato-ku tel: 03 5570 5777
Subway: Roppongi
Teppanyaki grilled delicacies expertly prepared from fresh crab, abalone, prawns and other seafoods, and steak.

Ryu Sushi ($)
5-2-1 Tsukiji, Chuo-ku tel: 03 3541 9517
Subway: Tsukiji
It is hard to get any nearer to the source of supply than this little *sushi* bar next to the market halls. Unusual for the Tsukiji location, the owner is not the senior chef but another sort of artist, the painter Ryutaro Shiina. He is normally in attendance from an early hour, greeting the customers who mostly work in the market. It's a great place to satisfy your hunger, after a predawn visit there.

Sakafuji ($)
1-6-1 Asakusa, Taito-ku tel: 03 3843 1122
Subway: Asakusa
A bright and friendly modern restaurant on three floors, next to Hotel TOP. *Yakitori, kushiage, tempura,* and *teppanyaki* are among the many choices.

Samovar ($$)
2-22-5 Dogenzaka, Shibuya-ku
tel: 03 3462 0648 Subway: Shibuya
Authentic Russian stews and soups, kebabs, rye bread, beers, and vodkas.

Samrat ($)
Shojikiya Building 2F, 4-10-10 Roppongi,
Minato-ku tel: 03 3478 5877
Subway: Roppongi
One of the first of the Indian wave and still popular, serving *tandoori* dishes and curries on the milder side. The all-day buffet is a bargain. Branches include: Koyas One Building 6F, 13-7 Udagawa-cho, Shibuya-ku.)

Sanjugo Danya ($)
B1F, Shibuya City Hotel, 1-1 Maruyama-cho,
Shibuya-ku tel: 03 3770 9835
Subway: Shibuya
The "35 Steps" is a Japanese-style bistro, with East-West country cooking to suit local and European tastes. Take your shoes off and choose a seat at the counter or one of the low tables. The staff don't speak much English, but a few words go a long way.

Sasanoyuki Restaurant ($$)
2-15-10, Negishi, Taito-ku tel: 03 3873 1145
Near JR station Uguisudani

Specializes in *tofu* dishes. A good selection of vegetarian fare available.

Shabu Zen ($$)
5-17-16 Roppongi, Minato-ku
tel: 03 3585 5600 Subway: Roppongi
A big restaurant specializing in *shabu-shabu*, including "all-you-can-eat" deals. The American beef is less costly than the local.

Shigeyoshi ($$$)
Olympia Co-op Olympia B1F, 6-35-3 Jingu-mae,
Shibuya-ku tel: 03 3400 4044
Subway: Meiji Jingu-mae
A small counter and a few tables, with the chefs in full view. The cooking is utterly traditional, from the Nagoya area. Lunch prices are reasonable. .

The Siam ($)
World Town Building 8F, 5-8-17 Ginza, Chuo-ku
tel: 03 3572 4101 Subway: Higashi-Ginza
This one has been around for years, and it is still serving tasty Thai standards at prices that are economical, for Ginza, especially at lunchtime.

Takeno ($$$)
6-21-2 Tsukiji, Chuo-ku tel: 03 3541 8698
Subway: Tsukiji
Fine *sashimi* and *sushi*; fish fresh from the market. Most of the lunch customers are market professionals: the evening crowd comes from far and wide, drawn by the Takeno's reputation. At the *sushi* counter, the chefs keep their jewel-like creations coming until you reluctantly call a halt.

277

Tamazushi ($)
B2F Ginza Core Building, 5-8-20 Ginza, Chuo-ku
tel: 03 3573 0057 Subway: Higashi-Ginza
Quick service of good *sushi*, with economical set menus and *à la carte*, depending on what is in season. At lunchtime, you may have to wait for the business crowd to clear.

Ten-Ichi ($$)
6-6-5 Ginza, Chuo-ku tel: 03 3571 1949
Subway: Ginza
Well-known *tempura* establishment founded in 1930 by Isao Yabuki, who raised the standard of *tempura*-making to an art.

Tokai-en ($)
1-6-3 Kabukicho, Shinjuku-ku
tel: 03 3200 2934 Subway: Shinjuku
An enormous Korean operation, with all-you-can-eat bargain lunches. Spicy seafood, stews, and bulgogi barbecues are specialties. Boisterous in late evening.

Tokyo Kaisen Restaurant ($$)
36-1 Kabukicho, 2-chome, Shinjuku-ku
tel: 03 5273 8301
Above a 24-hour fish market. Choose from a huge variety of fish downstairs, take it upstairs and the staff will prepare it for you.

Torigin ($)
4-12-6 Roppongi, Roppongi tel: 03 3403 5829
Subway: Roppongi
A simple *yakitori* also serving rice casseroles in their own pots. Popular with local office workers, but there is an English menu. Good for a quick, flavorsome, meal and drink. .

Tsukiji ($$)
Miyuki Building B1F, 5-6-12 Ginza, Chuo-ku
tel: 03 3571 0071
Subway: Higashi-Ginza
A bright and busy all-day restaurant in the heart of

Accommodations and Restaurants

Ginza. The set menus at lunchtime are attractive and reasonably priced.

Tsunahachi ($)
3-31-8 Shinjuku tel: 3352 1012
Subway: Shinjuku (east exit)
This is the largest of a chain of inexpensive *tempura* restaurants. Helpful and popular with young people. Set meals represent the best value.

Yabu Soba ($)
2-10 Awajicho, Kanda tel: 3251 0287
Subway: Awajicho
Established in 1880, this is one of the most famous *soba* noodle shops in Tokyo. English menu available.

Zakuro ($$)
basement TSB Kaikan Building, 5-3-3 Akasaka
tel: 3582 6841 Subway: Akasaka
Popular *shabu-shabu* restaurant, which also offers inexpensive *sukiyaki* and *obento* (box lunches). English menu.

CENTRAL HONSHU

Hakone

Fujiya Hotel Dining Room ($$)
Fujiya Hotel, 359 Miyanoshita, Hakone machi
tel: 0460 2 2211
In the graceful old dining room of a classic period hotel in Miyanoshita on the Hakone Tozen railroad. Good service.

Kobe

Gaylord ($$)
Basement, Meiji Seimei Building,
8-3-7 Isogami-dori, Kobe tel: 078 251 4359
Good Indian food, especially Tandoori dishes, in up-market Indian restaurant surroundings. Lunchtime specials are excellent value. Popular with foreign residents.

Marrakech ($$)
Maison de Yamate basement, 1-20-15
Nakayamata-dori tel: 078 241 3440
Authentic North African food prepared by the friendly (English-speaking) Moroccan owner and chef. Atmospheric interior. Popular establishment, so book in advance to be sure of a table.

Masaya Honten ($)
1-8-21 Nakayamate-dori, Kobe
tel: 078 331 2890
A very popular noodle restaurant that is fast, cheap, and good.

Misono ($$$)
1-7-6 Kitanagasa-dori, Kobe tel: 078 331 2890
One of Kobe's oldest steakhouses. The beef comes from local cattle reared in traditional style and is cooked at your table.

Nagoya

Kishimen-tei ($)
3-20-4 Nishiki, Naka-ku, Nagoya
tel: 052 951 3481
Tiny place with a reputation for serving the best *kishimen* noodles (a Nagoya specialty) in town.

Yaegaki Tempura Restaurant ($$)
4-2-10 Nishiki, Naka-ku, Nagoya
tel: 052 263 1818
Long-established restaurant serving fresh fish and vegetable *tempura*. English menu available.

Osaka

Capricciosa ($)
2-8-110, 105 Nambanaka tel: 066 631 5155
Pizza and pasta Italian establishment serving large portions at low prices. Relaxed atmosphere.

Fuguhisa ($)
3-14-24 Higashi-ohashi, Higashinari-ku, Osaka
tel: 066 972 5029
Specializes in *fugu ryori* (blowfish cuisine). Good, unpretentious cooking at a price difficult to beat.

Hankyu Grand Building Restaurants $/$$
32 Bangai, Osaka.
The top four floors of this building near Osaka station have a wide range of eating establishments serving Japanese and Western food.

Kuidaore ($$)
1-8-25 Dotonbori, Osaka tel: 066 211 5300
A popular restaurant serving a variety of Japanese food. Four floors—prices rise as you go up. Watch out for the mechanical clown outside the entrance.

Le Rendevous ($$$)
The Plaza, 2-2-49 Oyodo-Minami
tel: 066 453 1111
Osaka's most famous French restaurant. Seasonally based cooking of the highest standard Small intimate establishment. Service formal and discreet. Men are asked to wear jackets and ties.

Mimiu ($$)
6-18 Hiranomachi 4 chome, Chuo-ku, Osaka
tel: 066 231 5770
Old tea house-style establishment, the home of *udon-suki*, noodles simmered at your table in a pot with seasonal ingredients.

The Seasons ($$$)
Hilton International, Osaka, 8-8 Umeda
1-chome, Kita-ku tel: 066 347 7111
Elegant European food in plush, but friendly surroundings. Very close to Osaka station.

KYOTO

Agatha ($$)
2nd floor, Yurika Building, Kiyamachi-dori,
Sanjo-agaru, Nakagyo-ku tel: 223 2379
Robatayaki (charcoal grill) restaurant. Creative cooking, fun atmosphere, and popular, especially with the fashion crowd.

Ajiro ($$)
Myoshinji Minami-mon-mae, Hanazono, Sakyo-ku tel: 463 0221
Shojin ryori temple cooking in a restaurant setting. Meals served in private rooms. Near south gate of Myoshinji temple. Open to 6 PM only.

Ashiya Steak House ($$/$)
172–13 Kiyomizu 4-chome, Higashiyama-ku
tel: 541 7961
Friendly establishment in a charming traditional house, serving excellent Kobe beef.

Hirano-ya ($$)
Maruyama Koen, Chion-in, Minami-mon-mae,
Higashiyama-ku tel: 525 0026
Attractive tea house specializing in traditional 300 year-old Kyoto dish, made from simmered yams or potatoes and dried cod.

Hyotei ($$$)
Kusakawa-cho 35, Nanzenji tel: 771 4116
One of the best *kaiseki* restaurants in Kyoto. Beautifully presented meals served in a small but

handsome house opening onto a lovely garden. *Tatami* mat seating in private rooms.

Izeki ($$)
Pontocho Shijo Agaru, Nakagyo-ku
tel: 221 2080
Beautifully arranged *kaiseki*-style set menus in tasteful restaurant at moderate prices.

Izusen ($)
Daijiin-nai, Daitokuji-cho, Murasakino, Kita-ku
tel: 491 6665
Fast service, inexpensive temple food in a sub-temple of Daitokuji. Open to 5 PM only.

Kaihaji ($$)
Masamune 20, Momoyama-cho, Fushimi-ku
tel: 611 1672
Unusual Chinese-style *shojin ryori* food from Zen temple of the Obaku sect. Shared dishes. Open to 5 PM only.

Mankamero ($$$)
Inokuma-dori, Demizu-agaru, Kamigyo-ku
tel: 441 5020
Very expensive, traditional, old establishment (1716) serving food of the Yusoku-ryori style, once the cuisine of the imperial court. If you can afford it, it is a very special night out. To try the food at a more reasonable price, eat here for lunch and order the fixed-price *take-kago-bento*.

Minokichi ($$/$)
Sanjo-agaru, Dobutsuen-mae dori, Sakyo-ku
tel: 771 4185
Established in 1735, one of Kyoto's best-known restaurants. Variety of menus served in a complex of buildings. Delightful garden. The restaurant's specialty is *Kyo-kaiseki*, with eight dishes.

Misoka-ankawamichiya ($)
Fuyacho-dori, Sanjo-agaru
tel: 221 2525
Perhaps the most famous *soba* noodle shop in Kyoto. Small, with tiny rooms, opens out onto a central courtyard. Located at this premises, in old Kyoto, for the past 300 years.

Nishiki ($$)
Nakano-shima, Koen-uchi, Arashiyama, Ukyo-ku
tel: 075 871 8888
Set on an island right in the middle of the Oi River. The tea house serves excellent *Kyo-ryori*.

Oiwa ($)
Nijo-sagaru, Kiyamachi-dori, Nakagyo-ku
tel: 231 7667
A variety of deep-fried kebabs served in a renovated treasure house.

Okutan ($$)
36-30 Fukuchi-cho, Nanzenji
tel: 771 8709
Founded over 300 years ago as a vegetarian restaurant; one of the oldest and best *tofu* places in Kyoto. Beautiful garden.

Rokusei ($$)
71 Nishitenno-cho, Okazaki, Sakyo-ku
tel: 751 6171
Good Kyoto cuisine in a tasteful modern restaurant overlooking tree-lined canal.

Takasebune ($)
Nishikana, Chiyamachisagaru, Shijo-nishi, Shimogyo-ku
tel: 351 4032
Excellent *tempura* and *sashimi* dishes served at very reasonable prices.

WESTERN HONSHU AND SHIKOKU

Hagi
Fujita Soba-ten ($)
59 Kumagai-cho, Hagi
tel: 08382 2 1086
Friendly handmade *soba* restaurant. Also sells *tempura*. Closes 7 PM and second and fourth Wednesday of each month.

Hiroshima
Okononi-mura ($)
5-21 Shin-tenchi, Hiroshima tel: 082 241 8758
Two floors of stalls each selling their own versions of *okonomi-yaki*, a Japanese-style pancake with a variety of fillings.

Suishin ($$)
6-7 Tatemachi, Naka-ku, Hiroshima
tel: 082 247 4411
Specializes in *kamameshi*, a rice casserole cooked with fresh fish and other ingredients. Very busy, in the middle of town. Five floors of dining rooms.

Kurashiki
Kamoi-zushi ($)
1-3-17 Chuo, Kurashiki tel: 0864 22 0606
Very reasonably priced *sushi* in a grand old rice granary. *Nuku-sushi*, a steamed rice and fish dish, is the house specialty.

Matsue
Minami-kan ($$/$)
14 Suetsugu Honmachi Matsue
tel: 0852 21 5131
Excellent *kaiseki* cuisine and local seasonal specialties in modern surroundings.

Matsuyama
Shin-Hamasaku ($$)
Sanban-cho-4-chome, Matsuyama
tel: 0899 33 3030
Spacious restaurant in the middle of town. Serves fresh Inland Sea fish dishes, local dishes, and a variety of other Japanese fare.

Unkai ($$/$)
6th floor, ANA Hotel, 3-2-1 Ichiban-cho, Matsuyama tel: 0899 33 5511
Near the city center and castle. Excellent service, sophisticated surroundings.

Takamatsu
Maimai-tei ($$)
18–5 Higashita-machi Takamatsu
tel: 0878 33 3360
Extremely good *sanuki-udon* (thick, white, wheat-flour noodle) dishes. Small, unpretentious restaurant. The owner/chef makes some of his own utensils.

Takamatsu Grand Hotel ($$)
1-5-10 Kotobuki-cho, Takamatsu
tel: 0878 51 5757
Near the station and port. Two Japanese restaurants on its third floor.

Tenkatsu ($$)
Hyogomachi, Takamatsu tel: 0878 21 5380
Popular *tempura* and *sushi* restaurant in the Hyogomachi shopping mall near the station. The *sashimi* is prepared from fish that swim around,

279

oblivious, in a tank in the restaurant. Seating is on *tatami* (mats), or on stools at the counter.

KYUSHU AND OKINAWA

Beppu
Amamijaya ($)
1-4 Jissoji, Beppu tel: 0977 67 6024
Specializes in handmade flat noodle dishes. Wall display of local crafts.
Fugumatsu ($$)
3-6-14 Kitahama, Beppu tel: 0977 21 1717
Blowfish (*fugu*) restaurant. Simple, straightforward Japanese-style restaurant. *Fugu* and other fresh fish dishes are of good quality.

Fukuoka
Gourmet City ($)
Basement, Hotel Centraza, 4-23 Hakataeki-Chuogai, Fukuoka tel: 092 461 0111
Collection of about 10 restaurants offering variety, economy, and convenience (near bullet-train exit of Hakata station).
Hemmingway's ($)
2718 Maizuru, Tenjin tel: 092 714 0986
Friendly relaxed bar/pizza house. Open late, good value.
Ichiki ($)
1-2-10 Maizara, Chuo-ku tel: 092 751 5591
A friendly, relaxed bar/restaurant. Try the skewered fish or meat dishes.
Tsukushino ($$$)
15th Floor, ANA Hotel, 3-3-3 Hakata-Eki-mae, Fukuoka tel: 092 471 7111
The best classic Japanese food. Impressive views over the city. English menu available.

Kagoshima
Ajimori ($$)
13-21 Sennichicho tel: 0992 24-7634
Shabu-shabu establishment specializing in *satsuma kuroshabu*, a Kagoshima favorite made from the meat of a small black pig reared locally. The flesh, lighter and more tender than regular pork, is cooked by you at your table by dipping into a boiling broth. Delicious, generous portions and good value.
Noboraya ($)
2-15 Horie-cho tel: 0992 26 6697
Popular *ramen* restaurant in the middle of town. Large portions at low prices. Watch the kitchen staff at work while you eat. Good place to relax and enjoy the local atmosphere.
Satsuma ($)
27-30 Chuo-cho, Kagoshima tel: 099 252 2661
Local cuisine; try the *satsuma-age*, deep-fried fish sausage and sweet yams.

Kumamoto
Mutsugoro ($$)
Basement, Kumamoto Green Hotel, 12-11 Hanabata-cho, Kumamoto tel: 096 325 2222
Small restaurant serving local dishes (mainly horse meat) and various seafood.
Senri ($$)
Suizenji Koen Park, Kumamoto tel: 096 384 1824
Within Suizenji Park. Dishes, including horse meat, eel, and river fish. Western and *tatami* seating.

Miyazaki
Kuretake ($)
Basement, Nikko Building, 3-2-10 Nishi, Tachibana-Dori, Miyazaki tel: 0985 24 2818
Local specialties. Try *hiyajiru*, a cold fish soup served over hot rice.

Nagasaki
Fukiro ($$$)
146 Kami Nishiyama-machi, Nagasaki tel: 095 822 0253
Old wooden building with *shoji* screens and *tatami* mats, set on a clifftop stone staircase near Suwa Shrine. Specializes in *shippoku* meals, a Nagasaki specialty in which a variety of small dishes are served all together. Four or more diners are usually required for a *shippoku* feast.
Hamakatsu ($$)
1-14 Kajiya-machi, Nagasaki tel: 095 823 2316
Modern restaurant serving reasonably priced *shippoku* (minimum two people) and a variety of set menus that feature local dishes. This is a good place to try the local cuisine.
Shikai-ro ($)
4-5 Matsugae-machi, Nagasaki tel: 095 8822 1296
Five floors seating over 1,500 people. Popular restaurant that was responsible for inventing *champon* two centuries ago—a Chinese-inspired, thick noodle dish. English menu available.

Naha
Heiwa Dori Shopping Arcade ($)
Heiwa Dori, Naha, Okinawa.
Food stands in the arcade sell a very wide variety of Japanese dishes. You can eat your meal there without ceremony or get it to go.
Ryotei Naha ($$/$)
2-2-11 Tsuji, Naha, Okinawa tel: 098 868 2548
Good local cuisine combined with a floor show of authentic Okinawa folk dance.
Sam's by the Sea ($)
10th floor, Naha Shopping Center, 2-14-17 Nishi, Naha, Okinawa tel: 098 862 6660
The Sam's chain is run by an American ex-military family and their restaurants combine Western and Japanese cooking. Large portions, good service. Lighting may be a little dim for some tastes.

NORTHERN HONSHU

Kanazawa
Kaga Tobi ($)
Kohrinbo 109, 2-1 Kohrinbo, Kanazawa tel: 076 262 0535
Set on a back street just behind the Kohrinbo 109 department store, the Kaga Tobi serves a wide variety of good Japanese dishes.
Kanko Bussankan ($)
2-20 Kenrokumachi, Kanazawa tel: 076 222 7788
In the Ishikawa Prefectural Products Center, near the Kenrokuen Garden main entrance. Open during the daytime only (10–6), serving *sashimi*, noodles and the local cuisine, *kaga-ryori*, which uses mountain vegetables, shellfish (particularly tiny sweet shrimp), and river fish.

Miyoshian ($$)
.-11 Kenrokumachi, Kanazawa
el: 076 221 0127
n the Kenrokuen garden; established for over a
entury. *Tatami* mats and views over the pond.
Kaga-ryori considered to be the best in Japan.

Matsumoto

Kura ($$)
2-2-15 Chuo, Matsumoto tel: 0263 33 6444
Sushi and *tempura* restaurant in a mud-walled,
moated old house in the heart of town.

Raja ($)
-3-20 Ote, Matsumoto tel: 0263 36 9096
Vegetarian establishment with English menu avail-
ble. Food well prepared.

Raiman ($$/$)
4-2-4 Ote, Matsumoto tel: 0263 32 0882
Deservedly well-known French restaurant serving
excellent food in rustic Japanese setting.
urnished with Matsumoto *mingei* furniture. Close
o the castle.

Sendai

Aji Tasuke ($)
4-4-13 Ichiban-cho, Sendai tel: 022 225 7672
Small, popular place serving simple, but delicious
are at inexpensive prices. Their specialty is grilled
beef tongue, which is served at lunch and dinner
with oxtail soup and rice mixed with barley. Perfect
or a cold northern Honshu day. Closed Tuesdays.

Kintanabe Bekkan ($$)
2-9-34 Kokubun-cho, Sendai
el: 022 227 3478
busy fish restaurant serving everything from
ashimi to a whole baked fish. Informal light meals
erved at the counter, more complete meals
erved in rooms at the back.

Kawashiya ($$/$)
4-5-42 Ichiban-cho, Sendai tel: 022 222 6645
Probably the best seafood restaurant in town.
atami seating.

Kakitoku ($$)
4-9-1 Ichiban-cho, Sendai tel: 022 222 0785
very long-established, locally famous oyster bar.
lot to be missed if you enjoy eating oysters.
teak and non-shellfish dishes are also available
n the menu.

Santarom ($$$)
-20 Tachi-machi, Sendai tel: 022 224 1671
n elegant restaurant serving traditional dishes
uch as *tempura*, *shabu-shabu*, *fugu*, and *suriyaki*.
ervice and food are excellent. Weekday set
unches offer the best value.

Takayama

Sakusho ($$/$)
2-98 Baba-cho, Takayama tel: 0577 32 0174
ituated in an old mansion house in the eastern
art of town near Shorenji temple. A nationally
nown restaurant with a reputation for top-class
hojin-ryori, the vegetarian fare served at Buddhist
emples.

Kofune ($)
Vanasato-cho 6-6, Takayama
el: 0577 32 2106
noodle shop close to the station. Convenient
nd inexpensive fare. An English-language menu

is available—which is quite unusual in such an
establishment.

Suzuya ($$)
24 Hanakawa-cho, Takayama
tel: 0577 32 2484
Small restaurant, decorated in rustic Takayama
style, serving local specialties. Try the *sansai-ryori*,
mountain vegetables, and *ayu*, a river fish grilled
with soy sauce or salt.

HOKKAIDO

Hakodate

Bay Restaurant ($$)
11-5 Toyokawa-cho, Hakodate
tel: 0138 22 1300
Housed in a waterfront warehouse. Seafood dishes in unusual combinations, such as tuna fish in
coconut milk.

Matsumae ($$)
Hakodate Kokusai Hotel, 8th Floor, 5–10
Otemachi, Hakodate 040
tel: 0138 23 5151
Seafood restaurant. Hokkaido specialties. Good
harbor views.

Sapporo

Hyosetsu-no-Mon ($$)
S5W2 tel: 011 521 3046
Popular restaurant in the Susukino district. If
you like crab, this is the place to visit because
the menu is entirely composed of king crab
dishes. It's a noisy, lively place. They have a
menu written in English with accompanying
photos of the dishes.

Ramen Yokocho ($)
A small alley in Susukino (one block south and
running vertical to Susukino Avenue) packed with
shops selling Sapporo *ramen* (Chinese-style noodles, the local specialty). For the current favorite,
join the longest line.

Round Midnight ($$)
Hotel Arthur, SIOW6, Sapporo
tel: 011 561 1000
This refined but relaxed well-run establishment
offers good value set lunches and dinners, which
include a bargain "all you can eat" option. Mixed
Japanese, Chinese, and Western. Very highly
recommended.

Sapporo Biru-en ($$)
N6, E9 Sapporo tel: 011 742 1531
Sapporo's original brewery, now a German-style
beer garden. The house specialty is a cook-it-your-
self lamb and vegetable barbecue called Genghis
Khan, washed down with lots of beer.

Silo ($$)
Minami 5, Nishi 3, Chou-ku, Susukino,
Sapporo tel: 011 531 5837
Hokkaido specialties including smoked deer meat,
sliced frozen salmon, bear meat, potatoes, and
corn in a rustic old building.

21 Club ($$$)
Hotel Arthur, SIOW6, Sapporo
tel: 011 561 1000
An elegant restaurant with an art deco theme. It
is the highest dining room in the city and the
views are breathtaking. Good quality Western and
Japanese food, excellent service.

Index

282

Index

283

Index

Index

Picture Credits and Contributors

Picture credits

The Automobile Association would like to thank the following photographers, libraries, and associations for their assistance in the preparation of this book.

BRITISH MUSEUM 40a Battle of Yaskina, 41b Courtesans; **BRUCE COLEMAN COLLECTION** 233 Japanese cranes; **MARY EVANS PICTURE LIBRARY** 33a Courtesan, 34b Amaterasu (sun goddess), 42b Commodore Perry, 42c Perry's expedition, 45a Emperor Meiji, 104/5a Daimo & Suite, 110a Yokohama earthquake 1923, 110b Earthquake cartoon; **M. GOSTELOW** 51a Tokyo Asakusa, 61 Sengakuji, 64b Market Tsukiji, 65 Marking tuna (Tsukiji), 66 Yasakuni Shrine war memorial museum, 248b Tokyo Ikebukuro; **ROBERT HARDING PICTURE LIBRARY** 24b Preparing for *sumo* wrestling, 237a Ainu 'Marimo' festival Hokkaido; **MICHAEL HOLFORD** 38b Akita armor; **HULTON DEUTSCH COLLECTION LTD** 46b US Marines, Okinawa, 47 Pearl Harbor; **JAPAN NATIONAL TOURIST ORGANIZATION** 16 & 17a Kansai International Airport, 32b Okutsu Onsen, 80b Minshuku, 99 L Yamanaka, 220a Ryokan; **KOBE CITY MUSEUM** 112 Painted screen; **KYOTO NATIONAL MUSEUM** 36b Clay farmer; **MAGNUM PHOTOS** cover silhouette; **THE MANSELL COLLECTION** 39 *Samurai* warrior, 40b Iyeyasu, 41a Hideyoshi, 43 Emperor Meiji & Empress, 237b Ainu man & wife; **OTA MEMORIAL MUSEUM OF ART** 60b Kataoka Nizaemon VII in role of Ki-no-Natora; **PICTURES COLOUR LIBRARY LTD** 4a Tokyo, 265a Tokyo snack stall; **POPPERFOTO** 111a & 111b Kobe earthquake; **REX FEATURES LTD** 44b Emperor Hirohito; **D. SCOTT** 104 Kanbara stage sixteen of the Tokaido, 104/5 Shono stage forty-six of the Tokaido, 105 Fukuroi stage twenty-eight of the Tokaido; **SPECTRUM COLOUR LIBRARY** 5c Cherry blossom (Ueno Park), 9a Sanja festival, 12a Robots, 13b Assembly line, 16b Bullet train, 18a Yushima shrine, 24a *Sumo* wrestlers, 25 *Sumo* wrestling, 31 Karatsu festival, 36a Kasuga shrine Nara, 93 Shinkansen bullet train, 94/5 Mt. Fuji, 98 Mt. Fuji & Kawaguchi Lake, 101b Mt. Fuji & Hakone Komagatake ropeway, 103 Hakone Mt. Fuji & L. Ashi, 124 Zen Garden Daitokuji Temple, 135a Daisen-in-Zen Garden, 16? Himeji Castle, 175a Wakayama Mt. Koya Ryn Onsen, 207a Naginata Martial Art, 220b Tsumago interior of Waki Hojin, 225 Miyagi Sendai shopping center, 247a Tokyo Shibuya; **TOKYO NATIONAL MUSEUM** 34a Clay human mask; **VICTORIA & ALBERT MUSEUM** 76a & 76/7 Swords; **ZEFA PICTURES LTD** 10b Ibukushima shrine, 11 Mt. Fuji, 20a Calligraphy, 26a Sign, 27 Shinjuku, 44a "Kansei Three Beauties," 45b Kuntsada Cherry blossom viewing, 46a Hiroshima ruins, 51b, 58a, 58b & 59 "Kabuki Theater," 89a Portrait face.

All remaining pictures are held in the Association's own library (AA PHOTO LIBRARY) and were taken by JIM HOLMES with the exception of pages 2, 18b, 19a, 20b, 28a, 29b, 30b, 50, 52a, 55, 56, 62a, 63, 64a, 68/9, 73a, 78/9, 84b, 88a, 91a, 92a, 117, 131a, 137, 142a, 143, 158, 159a, 159b, 167b, 201, 219, 249, 251, 255, 256a, 264 which were taken by D. Corrence and page 62 which was taken by R T Alford.

The Automobile Association would also like to thank Nicolas Soames of Naxos Audiobooks and the Japan National Tourist Organization (JNTO) in London for their help during the preparation of this book.

Acknowledgments

The author would particularly like to thank Harry Cook and Simon Halewood for their assistance with the research for some sections of this book, Helen Morgan for her expert typing of the manuscript, and David Hodgson for his considerable and valuable help in updating this most recen: edition of *Exploring Japan*. The author would also like to thank Terry Randsley, Philip Quirk, and Glen Walford.

Contributors

Original copy editor: Nia Williams

Revision verifier: David Scott   Revision copy editor: Sally Harding